The Human Tradition in America

CHARLES W. CALHOUN
Series Editor
Department of History, East Carolina University

The nineteenth-century English author Thomas Carlyle once remarked that "the history of the world is but the biography of great men." This approach to the study of the human past had existed for centuries before Carlyle wrote, and it continued to hold sway among many scholars well into the twentieth century. In more recent times, however, historians have recognized and examined the impact of large, seemingly impersonal forces in the evolution of human history—social and economic developments such as industrialization and urbanization as well as political movements such as nationalism, militarism, and socialism. Yet even as modern scholars seek to explain these wider currents, they have come more and more to realize that such phenomena represent the composite result of countless actions and decisions by untold numbers of individual actors. On another occasion, Carlyle said that "history is the essence of innumerable biographies." In this conception of the past, Carlyle came closer to modern notions that see the lives of all kinds of people, high and low, powerful and weak, known and unknown, as part of the mosaic of human history, each contributing in a large or small way to the unfolding of the human tradition.

This latter idea forms the foundation for this series of books on the human tradition in America. Each volume is devoted to a particular period or topic in American history and each consists of minibiographies of persons whose lives shed light on that period or topic. Well-known figures are not altogether absent, but more often the chapters explore a variety of individuals who may be less conspicuous but whose stories, nonetheless, offer us a window on some aspect of the nation's past.

By bringing the study of history down to the level of the individual, these sketches reveal not only the diversity of the American people and the complexity of their interaction but also some of the commonalities of sentiment and experience that Americans have shared in the evolution of their culture. Our hope is that these explorations of the lives of "real people" will give readers a deeper understanding of the human tradition in America.

Volumes in the Human Tradition in America series:

Ian K. Steele and Nancy L. Rhoden, eds., *The Human Tradition in Colonial America* (1999). Cloth ISBN 0-8420-2697-5 Paper ISBN 0-8420-2700-9

Nancy L. Rhoden and Ian K. Steele, eds., *The Human Tradition in the American Revolution* (2000). Cloth ISBN 0-8420-2747-5 Paper ISBN 0-8420-2748-3

Ballard C. Campbell, ed., *The Human Tradition in the Gilded Age and Progressive Era* (2000). Cloth ISBN 0-8420-2734-3 Paper ISBN 0-8420-2735-1

Steven E. Woodworth, ed., *The Human Tradition in the Civil War and Reconstruction* (2000). Cloth ISBN 0-8420-2726-2 Paper ISBN 0-8420-2727-0

David L. Anderson, ed., *The Human Tradition in the Vietnam Era* (2000). Cloth ISBN 0-8420-2762-9 Paper ISBN 0-8420-2763-7

Kriste Lindenmeyer, ed., *Ordinary Women, Extraordinary Lives: Women in American History* (2000). Cloth ISBN 0-8420-2752-1 Paper ISBN 0-8420-2754-8

Michael A. Morrison, ed., *The Human Tradition in Antebellum America* (2000). Cloth ISBN 0-8420-2834-X Paper ISBN 0-8420-2835-8

Malcolm Muir Jr., ed., *The Human Tradition in the World War II Era* (2001). Cloth ISBN 0-8420-2785-8 Paper ISBN 0-8420-2786-6

Ty Cashion and Jesús F. de la Teja, eds., *The Human Tradition in Texas* (2001). Cloth ISBN 0-8420-2905-2 Paper ISBN 0-8420-2906-0

Benson Tong and Regan A. Lutz, eds., *The Human Tradition in the American West* (2002). Cloth ISBN 0-8420-2860-9 Paper ISBN 0-8420-2861-7

Charles W. Calhoun, ed., *The Human Tradition in America from the Colonial Era through Reconstruction* (2002). Cloth ISBN 0-8420-5030-2 Paper ISBN 0-8420-5031-0

Donald W. Whisenhunt, ed., *The Human Tradition in America between the Wars, 1920–1945* (2002). Cloth ISBN 0-8420-5011-6 Paper ISBN 0-8420-5012-4

Roger Biles, ed., *The Human Tradition in Urban America* (2002). Cloth ISBN 0-8420-2992-3 Paper ISBN 0-8420-2993-1

Clark Davis and David Igler, eds., *The Human Tradition in California* (2002). Cloth ISBN 0-8420-5026-4 Paper ISBN 0-8420-5027-2

James C. Klotter, ed., *The Human Tradition in the American South* (2003). Cloth ISBN 0-8420-2977-X Paper ISBN 0-8420-2978-8

The Human Tradition in AMERICA from the COLONIAL ERA through RECONSTRUCTION

THE HUMAN TRADITION IN
AMERICA FROM THE
COLONIAL ERA
THROUGH
RECONSTRUCTION

No. 11
Human Tradition in America

Edited by
Charles W. Calhoun

A Scholarly Resources Inc. Imprint
Wilmington, Delaware

© 2002 by Scholarly Resources Inc.
First published 2002
Second printing 2002
Printed and bound in the United States of America

Scholarly Resources Inc.
104 Greenhill Avenue
Wilmington, DE 19805-1897
www.scholarly.com

Library of Congress Cataloging-in-Publication Data

The human tradition in America from the colonial era through
Reconstruction / edited by Charles W. Calhoun.
    p. cm.—(Human tradition in America ; no. 11)
  Includes bibliographical references and index.
  ISBN 0-8420-5030-2 (alk. paper)—ISBN 0-8420-5031-0 (pbk : alk.
paper)
    1. United States—History—Colonial period, ca. 1600–1775—
Biography. 2. United States—History—Revolution, 1775–1783—
Biography. 3. United States—History—1783–1865—Biography. 4.
Reconstruction—Biography. I. Calhoun, Charles W. (Charles William),
1948– II. Series.

E176 .H936 2002
973—dc21   2001049152

For

Elizabeth Banks Calhoun,

whose unfolding biography

I delight to witness

About the Editor

CHARLES W. CALHOUN received his B.A. from Yale University and his Ph.D. in history from Columbia University. He is a professor of history at East Carolina University, Greenville, North Carolina, and a past president of the Society for Historians of the Gilded Age and Progressive Era. The recipient of several research grants, including a National Endowment for the Humanities fellowship, he is a specialist in the politics of the Gilded Age. His publications include *The Gilded Age: Essays on the Origins of Modern America* (1996) and *Gilded Age Cato: The Life of Walter Q. Gresham* (1988). He currently serves on the Editorial Board of the *Journal of the Gilded Age and Progressive Era*.

Contents

Introduction

Charles W. Calhoun

The distinct character of each human being is the distillation of a unique set of experiences: biological inheritance, placement and movement in particular surroundings, interaction with other humans, successes enjoyed, disappointments borne, accidents endured, plans fulfilled, dreams thwarted. Each of us is the sum of what we have gone through.

The same is true of nations, aggregates of individuals. Certainly, the physical setting—geography, topography, and climate—has much to do with the course of a nation's history, but it is humans' interaction with that physical circumstance and with one another that truly marks out a country's destiny. Some individuals—a George Washington, an Eleanor Roosevelt, a Martin Luther King—have loomed large in the forging of American destiny. But it is the premise of this volume that other lesser-known Americans have played a vital role as well—not indispensable as individuals perhaps but taken altogether fully essential in the definition of the nation.

Traditionally, when historians have ranged beyond the examination of well-known and influential historical actors, they have explored the impact of large, seemingly impersonal forces and developments such as demographic change, industrialization, urbanization, and secularization. In the past fifty years of historical inquiry, statistical analysis has provided a powerful tool for depicting the contours of these forces. Yet, more and more, scholars have come to recognize that each of these large movements represents countless small deeds and decisions by individual Americans, sometimes acting in concert, sometimes acting alone. The purpose of this book is to telescope the lens from the wide-angle group portrait down to the focused individual close-up.

In the eighteen brief biographies presented here the emphasis is less on representativeness than on variety. These stories illustrate how truly diverse the American experience has been. Yet the very centrality and pervasiveness of this diversity point to two other themes that have dominated American history and that implicitly connect these essays.

First, the diversity is not simply a matter of idiosyncratic individuals; it is also found in the tremendous heterogeneity of the groups that have constituted the American population. From the initial contact between indigenous peoples and migrant Europeans, a central fact of American life and civilization has been the encounter of distinct groups of people of widely varying origins and culture. Many of the life stories presented here illustrate the diverse ways in which Americans have negotiated and contested the boundaries between racial and ethnic groups.

Second, at the heart of the American story is the persistent tension between liberty and community. Americans have placed a high premium on dynamic individuality, on the right of each person to chart his or her own destiny. Yet Americans have never adopted liberty as license or the right to flout the legitimate requisites of the community. They have embraced the pursuit of happiness as a basic tenet, but they have also conceived that pursuit as limited by the rights of other individuals and the larger community, where ideally the rights and interests of all are mediated for the common good. Again, many of the lives portrayed in this volume illuminate the multiplicity of ways Americans have coped with these paradoxical impulses. Of course, the tragically egregious exception in the story of American liberty, the enslavement of Africans and their descendants, demanded coping skills of a wholly different sort.

The interplay of disparate groups is amply illustrated in the essay on Squanto. Even before Europeans arrived, what became New England had long been the scene of rivalry among native nations. The arrival of Europeans exacerbated those rivalries, as different Indians sought to use relations with Europeans against their native enemies. Initially, the non-threatening fur-trading lifestyle of the French inured to their benefit in striking positive relations with natives, but by sheer force of numbers the English quickly began to have a greater impact on the indigenous peoples. Squanto not only helped the English at Plymouth survive the rigors of the Massachusetts wilderness. He also played an indispensable diplomatic role not only in mediating relations between the English and the natives but also in helping to establish the tributary trade of the Indians with the English. Thus he served as a skilled cultural, political, and economic broker.

Anne Hutchinson's troubles in Massachusetts Bay exemplify the tension between liberty and community. The Puritanism that both she and her accusers espoused underscored the highly individualistic relationship between a person and God, with only a marginal role for organized ritual.

Yet in Hutchinson's eyes the colony's ministers had placed too great a stress on conformity with their rules as the key to salvation. When she vented her objections, John Winthrop and the magistrates saw her strictures as an assault on the community, especially as embodied in their authority over it. Her greatest religious offense was taking the Puritan notion of individual relations with God too far—claiming divine revelation—and the magistrates, assuming to speak for the community, expelled her.

For Caspar Wistar, as for countless other Americans over the centuries, American liberty signified the possibility to rise economically. Born in the German Palatinate, where economic status was an inheritance one could rarely transcend except through the influence of patrons, Wistar journeyed to Pennsylvania in the early eighteenth century. There he cultivated the aid of Quaker patrons, even converting to their church, as he began a rapid climb to wealth and influence. He became a wealthy merchant and successful land speculator. In the latter role he helped the colony's English proprietors profitably transfer land to thousands of German immigrants, thereby functioning as a cultural and economic broker between Pennsylvania's two most important European groups. He aided German immigrants in other ways as well, including extending credit to them and paying their passage in return for indentures. Wistar achieved substantial influence among his countrymen in Pennsylvania and emerged as an important political counselor to them in their relations with the colonial government. He thus played crucial roles in mediating between Pennsylvania's ethnic groups and in securing order to the wider community.

In the 1740s, while Wistar enjoyed the height of his influence in easing German immigrants into the free society of Pennsylvania, Olaudah Equiano was a boy in Africa, soon to be kidnapped by slave traders and transported into slavery in America. His initial sojourn in America was relatively brief, however, for a British sea captain purchased and carried the diminutive lad with him when he entered naval service during the Seven Years' War. Equiano learned to read and write and converted to Christianity and thought his war service warranted his freedom, but instead his owner sold him to a slave-trading merchant in the West Indies. His new owner prized his skills and permitted him to engage in petty trade. In this way, Equiano gleaned enough money to purchase his liberty. He made his way to England, where he led a reasonably good life until his failure to save a friend from recapture as a slave precipitated a personal psychological crisis that sparked Equiano's spiritual rebirth as a Christian. Although he had briefly participated in plantation management and slave trading, he became an active abolitionist and an advocate for Africans in England. Near the end of his life he published his autobiography, which amounted to a searing indictment of slavery and the slave trade. Although he spent relatively little time in America, Equiano's experiences offer an unusual perspective on the permeability of the boundaries between liberty and slavery and between blacks and whites in the eighteenth century.

The life of Equiano's contemporary, Eliza Lucas Pinckney, strikingly illustrates how in colonial America the slavery of some constructed and sustained the liberty of others. As a young wealthy plantation mistress surrounded by laboring slaves, Eliza enjoyed the liberating leisure to indulge in a host of intellectual pursuits. She read widely, maintained a far-flung correspondence, engaged in a number of handicrafts, and, most important, conducted agricultural experiments that yielded not only intellectual gratification but also financial profit. As a young woman she skillfully managed the plantations of her absent soldier-father. Although she narrowed the range of her activities somewhat during her fourteen-year marriage, her widowhood witnessed a revival of the independence she had formerly known. For Eliza Pinckney, independence was the key to liberty, and she never tired of sharing that lesson with her brothers, sons, and grandchildren. So doing and as the mother of sons who were renowned Revolutionary patriots, she presented a superb example of republican motherhood.

While Eliza Pinckney's sons won fame at the head of troops during the Revolution, American independence could not have been won without the efforts of the thousands of men who followed in the ranks, men such as Benjamin Gilbert and Jacob Nagle. A Massachusetts farm boy, Gilbert entered the fray in the wake of Lexington and Concord and quickly moved on to New York, where he saw most of his fighting. Pennsylvanian Nagle entered the service with his father at age fourteen and soon saw heavy fighting at Brandywine Creek. Both these men left vivid accounts of their experiences that show that the struggle for the exalted cause of American liberty was, on the ground, often an arduous, confused, filthy, frightening, debilitating, and miserable business. Gilbert remained in the fight for the duration of the war, though spending much of it on relatively placid garrison duty that afforded him ample free time for libertine diversions. Nagle left the army after Brandywine and, after a hiatus, went to sea on an American privateer, was briefly a prisoner of war, and wound up serving on a British man-of-war. After the war, Gilbert married, settled on a farm in New York, and became a solid citizen and middling Federalist politician. Nagle served in the Royal Navy and later in the merchant marine, essentially becoming a rootless vagabond. Eventually he retired from the sea in America and spent the last years of his life in itinerant poverty. Both these men shouldered arms for American independence, but afterward the unfathomable interplay of chance and character led them to choose vastly different paths to pursue their personal independence.

If the success of the Revolution confirmed the liberty to choose for white Americans such as Gilbert and Nagle, it opened no new array of options for most African Americans still trapped in agricultural slavery in the South. Even so, the Revolution's rhetoric of liberty did induce states north of the Mason-Dixon line to enact immediate or gradual abolition, and in the South a momentary surge of abolitionist feeling led masters to liberate thousands of slaves. By 1800 more than 6,000 of these freed blacks had settled in Philadelphia, the new Republic's temporary capital. Although the city had a reputation for abolition and reform sentiment, its white population turned out to be less than welcoming to the African Americans, and they quickly recognized that they must look to themselves, not whites, to construct the new meaning and practice of liberty. One of their most influential leaders was Absalom Jones, principal founder of the African Church of Philadelphia, which was designed as a haven for black Christian worship, education, and mutual assistance, free of white domination. Soon affiliated with the Episcopal denomination as St. Thomas's African Episcopal, Jones's church formed the platform from which he led his parishioners in defending against white racism, building schools, and founding mutual benefit and literary societies. Thus, Jones proved himself skillful not only at guiding his followers spiritually but also in nurturing their sense of independence and self-assertion among themselves and in the larger community.

If race acted as a prime determinant of one's status and role in the community in early America, so also did one's gender. Although the "cult of true womanhood" with its emphasis on purity, piety, domesticity, and submission, would not reach full flower until the mid-1800s, a century and more of European civilization in North America had wrought clear expectations as to what role a woman ought to play. Marriage and motherhood lay at the heart of her purpose and function. Yet demographic change and other circumstances dictated that some women would not follow that path. Indeed, the first half of the nineteenth century witnessed a minor counterpoint in a "cult of single blessedness." The never-married Rebecca Dickinson of western Massachusetts was an early exemplar of this latter proclivity. The keeper of a remarkable diary, Dickinson frequently lamented her lonesomeness, but she passed up opportunities to marry and tended to dread rather than welcome extended visits from family members. Whether she ever fully admitted it, she seems to have embraced her independence, which rested on two foundations. First, she was able to make do economically thanks to her skill as a gownmaker and a grant of land from her father. And second, she endured, if she did not quite relish, her singlehood through a deep sense of communion with her God. Thus grounded, Dickinson was able to set the terms by which she related to her community, and despite her own frequently expressed sense of despair, she won the admiration and affection of most of the people among whom she led her detached existence.

We know about Rebecca Dickinson's introspective ruminations largely because of the remarkable diary she left. Sacagawea, a much more widely known woman, left not a single record of her own. Her deeds have come down to us in the journals of the various members of the Lewis and Clark expedition, and her later life has been conveyed less reliably in Indian oral tradition. As historian Laura McCall suggests, Sacagewea remains something of a historical enigma. On one level, the journals tend to treat her almost tangentially, as if she were some vague and inessential adjunct to the expedition. But a careful reading of those same journals shows that at critical moments she proved indispensable in feeding the group, charting its path, and translating and negotiating with her fellow natives. In after years, her actions became encrusted with myth, as she became a symbol of strong and effective womanhood for Susan B. Anthony and other women eager to construct a usable past. More recently, new western historians have begun to rethink the benefits of her agency in the opening of the West to "conquest." In this view, her service as a broker between two cultures led inevitably to the clash of those cultures that marked the subsequent decades of native-white interaction in the West. Other historians, however, are reluctant to espouse this collaborationist interpretation, and Sacagawea remains a figure of controversy.

The confrontation of cultures was one of intense immediacy for Peter P. Pitchlynn, whose mother was a member of the Choctaw Nation and whose father was a Euro-American. As an adult, Pitchlynn was able to operate in both the Native American and the white world, but to some degree he was suspect in each. The grounds of the suspicion differed, however. Some Choctaws distrusted him because of his education and other marks of identification with white culture, but those Euro-Americans who rejected him did so on the basis of blood. For the most part, however, Pitchlynn sought to adapt the skills he acquired in the white world to leadership of the Choctaws. He unsuccessfully opposed the removal treaty of 1831 and then led a party of his people from Mississippi to their new land in present-day Oklahoma. He applied his literary skills in the drafting of a consti-

tution for the Choctaw Nation, and in the 1850s he became a semiperma-
nent representative of the Nation's interests in Washington. But while
Pitchlynn prospered economically through the operations of his plantation
in the territory, the Nation itself suffered from interracial strife with unsavory whites who took refuge in its domain. Pitchlynn returned to the
Nation during the Civil War and helped shield it from the impact of the
fighting that devastated large portions of the Indian Territory. In the postwar years he returned to his broker's role in Washington, particularly trying to get federal compensation for lands taken in 1831, a resolution that
did not come until after his death. At the heart of Pitchlynn's story was a
life-long effort to liberate his people from the evil effects of racism endem-
ic in the surrounding Euro-American community.

Liberty and equality for his people were the life-long quests of Hosea
Easton, a free African American who took active part in the abolition
movement in the 1830s. Born of highly assertive free parents in Massachusetts, Easton was destined at an early age to labor for liberty. In one of
his earliest speeches he decried slavery and racial discrimination as not only
evil but also egregiously destructive of human potential. Nor was the iniq-
uity limited to the South. Easton's own church in Hartford, Connecticut,
was the target of white mobs in the 1830s. Increasingly, he came to realize
that self-improvement by northern blacks could accomplish little until
whites were persuaded to rise above their racist notions. He stressed in his
speeches and writings the need not only to rid the land of slavery but also
to find ways to reverse the devastating impact of the institution and of
racial discrimination generally. Easton's emphasis on the totally dehumanizing force of slavery, however, increasingly ran counter to the abolitionist
tactic of putting articulate and clearly capable escaped or freed slaves such
as Frederick Douglass in the forefront of the crusade's effort. While Easton
presented graphic portrayals of slaves' victimhood, other black and white
abolitionists sought to emphasize their persistent humanity and their ability to act for themselves if set free. Lost, then, was Easton's message that
true liberty for blacks would require not merely abolition but a white
repentance for racism that would open the way for true equality.

True equality for women was also a long way distant in the nineteenth
century, as is clear from the experiences of Laura Wirt Randall. In some
ways the wealthy Virginian Randall was less free to chart her own course
than the working-class craftswoman Rebecca Dickinson of rural
Massachusetts. The first-born of doting parents, Randall received every
opportunity and encouragement to develop her fine intelligence. Her parents gave her a thorough classical education, and she thought of devoting

her life to intellectual pursuits, perhaps as a teacher. But as she neared the time when most young women turned to marriage, her parents began to stress the importance of her education not for the independence it might provide her but for how it might equip her to be a good wife and mother. She resisted the push toward marriage, however, rejecting three suitors in the space of two years. Finally, after a long and agonizing courtship during which Laura remained resistant to marriage, she gave in to pressure and accepted a proposal. But as she had suspected would be the case, her married life was miserable; her husband's affections waned, and she rapidly deteriorated under the burden of household and maternal duties compounded by ill health. Thus trapped, she died at the birth of her fourth child, two months after her thirtieth birthday.

In part, Caroline Healey Dall pursued the life of which Laura Wirt Randall only dreamed. Born to wealth like Randall, Dall was pushed to excel intellectually by her father. She, too, received a thorough education, which, like Randall's was cut off in her midteens. But living in the intellectually saturated atmosphere of Boston, Dall was able to continue her education informally by attending lectures, exhibitions, and the like. Moreover, she came under the tutelage of accomplished mentors from the city's Transcendentalist community. In what was perhaps a moment of weakness, she married an impecunious minister, but after ten years she found herself effectively abandoned when he left for missionary work in India. Still married but left largely to fend for herself and her two children, Dall turned to teaching, lecturing, and writing. Necessity thus presented her with a kind of liberty Laura Wirt Randall never achieved. From the platform of her own unconventional life, Dall used her lectures and writings to advocate women's rights. Citing scientific evidence as well as sentimental reasons, she argued that a woman should be as free as a man to develop her own nature, and she particularly stressed equality of economic opportunity. Yet Dall had a prickly personality that excluded her from the inner circle of women's rights organizers. Her role, therefore, was not to marshall forces but to forge ideas in the nineteenth-century battle for women's liberation.

George Washington Harris, a Pennsylvanian by birth who spent nearly all his life in east Tennessee, was worlds apart from Dall, but he, too, used his writing in quest of a liberation of sorts. Harris ran through a number of jobs, from skilled metalworker to steamboat captain to farmer to railroad conductor to small-bore politician. Although he harbored aspirations to enter the planter class, he never achieved that goal, but he did attain a solid, if debt-burdened, respectability that embraced clean living, hard work, a wife and family, and Presbyterian orthodoxy. Yet lurking within Harris was another self that scorned and mocked all the propriety and reputation he held and pursued. This other self Harris set free through a series of humorous short stories that ridiculed the overwrought mores of Southern society. His main character was the anarchic ne'er-do-well Sut Lovingood, whose adventures partook largely of practical jokes, sexual escapades, and assaults on authority in every guise. While Harris moved from occupation to occupation and lived a modestly middle-class life, he found release from the humdrum cares of that existence through the anti-social antics of his free-spirited literary creation. But even though Harris could mock the pretensions that typified Southern life, he resented Northern attacks against the South and a social structure resting on slavery. When the sectional crisis reached its head, Harris, unlike many of his east Tennessee neighbors, furiously beat the secessionist drum.

The war that Southern secession sparked upended the settled life of George Washington Harris and virtually all other Americans. The Civil War also put American liberty to its severest test and in the end secured its greatest triumph through the eradication of slavery. Among those caught up in the fighting on the front line was Irish American Peter Welsh. A personal crisis touched off by a drinking binge, rather than the trumpet call of liberty, prompted Welsh's impulsive enlistment, and within days he found himself in the thick of the fight at Antietam. Like most of his Irish-American countrymen, Welsh had little love for blacks and he opposed abolition. Nonetheless, the searing force of battle soon fired his belief that the Union cause did represent a transcendent purpose—nothing less than a critical test of whether free government itself could endure. As a naturalized citizen whose own roots lay in the monarchical Old World, Welsh found the consequences of the fierce trial of republicanism both immediate and profound. Hence, he accepted the freeing of the slaves if that was required to ensure the survival of the American Republic as a beacon of liberty to the rest of oppressed mankind. Although historians argue about what motivated Civil War soldiers to fight, Welsh stands as an exemplar of those who came to embrace the noble goals articulated by Lincoln and other national leaders. In the end, succumbing to a wound in the spring of 1864, Peter Welsh, like Lincoln a year later, became a martyr to that higher cause.

When Sgt. Peter Welsh received his fatal wound at Spottsylvania, one of the generals commanding the Union troops that day was Winfield Scott Hancock. Although he never exercised a major independent command, Hancock earned a reputation as a "superb" officer who excelled at translating the broad conceptions of commanders into actual operations by the

men in the field. A graduate of West Point and a veteran of the Mexican
War, Hancock was a career soldier who was well equipped to command
troops. He took part in many of the war's most important engagements
and earned lasting fame for his handling of Union troops during the desperate fighting at Gettysburg. But his substantial contributions to final
Union victory notwithstanding, Hancock, a states-rights Democrat, never
approved the war aims of the more radical wing of the Republican party
leaders in Washington. In Reconstruction political struggles he sided with
President Andrew Johnson, and during a three-month stint at New
Orleans in 1867–1868 he labored to undo the accomplishments of his
more radical predecessor, Gen. Philip Sheridan. Fresh from this operation,
Hancock attracted both Southern and Northern support for the
Democratic presidential nomination in 1868 but was not chosen. A conservative at heart, Hancock remained in the army, and during the 1877
nationwide railroad strike he led federal troops against the laborers.
Hancock finally won the Democratic presidential nomination in 1880, but
he lost a close race to James A. Garfield. Although Hancock skillfully mastered the new methods of warfare, he resisted the new ideas of liberty and
equality that the Union cause came to represent and ended as a champion
of the rearguard notions of the postwar Democratic party.

Hancock's reputation rests in some measure on a biography by his
wife published a year after his death. The quest for reputation in the postwar years sometimes appeared to rage as hotly as during the war itself, and
in no case was this more apparent than that of George E. Pickett, one of
Hancock's best-known Confederate adversaries at Gettysburg. As with
Hancock, the fight for Pickett's historical standing was waged not by
Pickett himself but by his wife, LaSalle Corbell Pickett. However, there the
comparisons end. Although Almira Hancock no doubt embellished her
husband's exploits, her interpretation was not inconsistent with other
accounts. LaSalle Pickett, in contrast, seems to have fabricated much of the
story she told and even to have invented supposed correspondence from
her husband. Nor were her many publications entirely consistent. While
she dutifully praised her husband as brave and chivalrous, she also sometimes portrayed him as pacifistic compared to her own purported strength
and boldness. In reality, the war seemed to have unhinged both the
Picketts. George never got over his monumental failure at Gettysburg and
increasingly lost control over himself, to the point of sanctioning an
unwarranted mass execution of Union prisoners in North Carolina that
almost earned him prosecution as a war criminal after the war. LaSalle saw
some of the war's destruction firsthand, and she must have watched with

profound horror the psychological desolation of her husband as well as the annihilation of her society. She spent much of the postwar years constructing an idealized, if not totally fictional, portrait of her husband and a revanchist interpretation of the war's origins and meaning. Her work buttressed the burgeoning Lost Cause myth of the benign Old South, which as the nineteenth century drew to a close did much, in the name of sectional reconciliation, to undermine the liberty of the freed slaves and their descendants.

Securing that new liberty was the all-consuming passion of Willis Augustus Hodges in the Reconstruction years. Hodges was an African American born in 1815 into a free, prosperous farming family in southeastern Virginia. The assertiveness of Hodges's family, especially his outspoken preacher brother, spurred harassment by local whites, which escalated in the wake of the Nat Turner revolt. Bridling under this abuse, Hodges moved to New York City in 1836 and soon joined the growing abolition movement. During the Civil War, he served as a Union scout in Virginia and also as an advocate for African Americans in his home region in their dealings with federal occupation forces. At the war's end, he moved immediately to organize blacks politically and stepped up this activity with the advent of congressional Reconstruction and black suffrage. With a solid vote from African Americans he won election to Virginia's 1867 constitutional convention, where he played a leading role. Hodges saw the convention as an opportunity to reorder Virginia society and the relations between blacks and whites. He labored to remove every trace of racial distinctions from the Virginia constitution and fought (unsuccessfully) for integrated public schools. In the end, the document Hodges and his black and white Republican colleagues produced was designed to secure the liberty and equality promised by the outcome of the war. On paper they succeeded, and Hodges had a minor career in local government for a few years. Ultimately, however, the racism of the white conservatives prevailed in Virginia and elsewhere, and the reforms of Reconstruction were undone. Northern whites essentially acquiesced in this reversal, and the triumph of true equality and liberty would have to wait another hundred years.

In the two and a half centuries that separated Squanto from Willis Hodges, America had undergone profound changes: huge growth and diversification of the population; independence from Great Britain; economic change and the incipient development of a national market; challenges to the subjugation of women; Civil War and Emancipation; and the brief and sadly premature experiment of Reconstruction. As this period drew to a close, even more dramatic change lay ahead, for the next decades witnessed the transformation of the country from a largely localized, agricultural, and traditional society to one that was national, industrial, and modern. In those succeeding years the two fundamental themes traced in this volume would continue. With a vastly expanded immigration, the American populace became even more diverse, and the conundrum of mediating among the multiplicity of peoples became even more acute. The career of liberty went forward, sometimes haltingly, but over the long haul toward a wider range for freedom and opportunity, although their full scope for all Americans is yet to be achieved. In the modern era, as in the earlier centuries, the nation's evolution represented the summation of countless acts and choices by individuals, each forming a part of the human tradition in America.

The essays included here appeared in earlier volumes in the Human Tradition in America series. Chapters 1 through 4 are taken from *The Human Tradition in Colonial America* (edited by Ian K. Steele and Nancy L. Rhoden); Chapters 5 through 7 appeared in *The Human Tradition in the American Revolution* (edited by Nancy L. Rhoden and Ian K. Steele); Chapters 8, 9, and 13 are from *Ordinary Women, Extraordinary Lives: Women in American History* (edited by Kriste Lindenmeyer); Chapters 10, 11, 12, and 14 appeared in *The Human Tradition in Antebellum America* (edited by Michael A. Morrison); and Chapters 15 through 18 are drawn from *The Human Tradition in the Civil War and Reconstruction* (edited by Steven E. Woodworth).

I am grateful to the individual chapter authors and to the volume editors—Kriste Lindenmeyer, Michael A. Morrison, Nancy L. Rhoden, Ian K. Steele, and Steven E. Woodworth.

1

Squanto
Last of the Patuxet

Neal Salisbury

Squanto (d. 1622) is one Native American of the early colonial period whose name is familiar; he is known primarily because the Pilgrims and their historians have found him useful. A Native American who spoke English and taught newly arrived colonists to plant corn was not only providential, but he also easily became part of an idealized Thanksgiving tableau of Native Americans inviting and justifying the Pilgrim presence in Patuxet. As we learn more of Squanto's story, he emerges as a clever and adaptable captive and refugee who finds a momentary role in Pilgrim settlement and Wampanoag survival. It may have been because he was a captive elsewhere that Squanto survived the spread of a disease that destroyed his village of Patuxet. That epidemic made the Wampanoag particularly interested in the Pilgrims' survival, and made Squanto valuable to both communities. The treaty that he helped arrange lasted nearly half a century, in part because it was the sole legitimacy for Pilgrim landownership; the Pilgrims never had a charter. Tempted to extract more than was thought appropriate from his position as broker between these societies, Squanto effectively destroyed his own position.

Neal Salisbury is a leading expert on relations between Native Americans and Europeans in colonial New England, the author of *Manitou and Providence: Indians, Europeans, and the Making of New England, 1500–1643* (1982), and coeditor, with Philip J. Deloria, of *A Companion to American Indian History* (2002). He teaches colonial and American Indian history at Smith College, Northampton, Massachusetts.

An enduring American legend tells of a lone Indian named Squanto, who rescued the Pilgrims from the wilderness by teaching them how to plant corn and introducing them to friendly Native Americans. In so doing, the legend implies, he symbolically brought about the union of the English colonizers and the American land. Although recent events and

An earlier version of this essay appeared in David Sweet and Gary B. Nash, eds., *Survival and Struggle in Colonial America* (Berkeley, CA: University of California Press, 1981), 228-46. Copyright © 1981 by The Regents of the University of California. This modified version is published by permission of the University of California Press.

scholarship have undermined such self-serving representations of early Indian-white relations, Squanto's story retains significance. For when placed in its historic and cultural contexts, it reveals the range of qualities called forth among Native Americans during the early colonization of New England.

As befits a mythic hero, the time and circumstances of Squanto's birth are unknown. His birth date can only be inferred from what the sources say and do not say. The firsthand descriptions of him, written between 1618 and his death in 1622, do not suggest that he was strikingly young or old at that time. All we can safely conclude is that he was probably in his twenties or thirties when he was forcibly taken to Europe in 1614.

Although Squanto's early years are obscured by a lack of direct evidence, we know something of the cultural milieu that prepared him for his unexpected and remarkable career. Squanto, or Tisquantum, was a Wampanoag Indian from the village of Patuxet. Patuxet maintained close ties with the other Wampanoags around Plymouth Bay, on Cape Cod, on the islands of Martha's Vineyard, and westward to the principal Wampanoag community on Narragansett Bay. The Wampanoag spoke Massachusett, a language they shared with the Massachusett and Pawtucket Indians to the north. The differences between Massachusett and other languages spoken by Native Americans in what is now southern New England were minimal, so that the Wampanoag could communicate with Indians throughout this region. Like other coastal villages south of the Saco River, Patuxet was positioned to allow its inhabitants to grow crops, exploit marine resources, and have easy access to wild plants and animals. In accordance with the sexual division of labor maintained by virtually all eastern North American Indians, Squanto's major activities would have been hunting game and certain kinds of fishing. The women at Patuxet, on the other hand, were in charge of farming, the gathering of wild plants and shellfish, and the preparation of all foods. Squanto would also have fashioned a wide variety of tools and other items and participated in the intensely ritualized world of trade, diplomacy, religious ceremonies, recreation, warfare, and political decision making that constituted public life in Patuxet.

The training of young men in precontact southern New England was designed to prepare them for that world. Among the Wampanoag, Plymouth leader Edward Winslow wrote: "A man is not accounted a man till he do some notable act or show forth such courage and resolution as becometh his place."[1] A Dutch official from New Netherland noted that young Wampanoag men were left alone in the forest for an entire winter. On returning to his people in the spring, a candidate was expected to imbibe and vomit bitter poisonous herbs for several days. At the conclusion of his ordeal, he was brought before the entire community, "and if he has been able to stand it all well, and if he is fat and sleek, a wife is given to him."[2]

As a result of such testing, young Wampanoags learned not only how to survive but also how to develop the capacities to withstand the most severe physical and psychological trials. The result was a personality type that Europeans came to characterize as stoic, the supreme manifestation of which was the absolute expressionlessness of prisoners under torture. Although the specific content of such training did little to prepare Squanto for his later experiences in Málaga, London, or Newfoundland, it imparted a sense of psychological independence and prepared him for adapting to the most demanding environments and situations.

Wampanoag men such as Squanto also exercised their independence in making political judgments and decisions. As elsewhere in southern New England, a Wampanoag political leader, or sachem, was drawn from one of a select group of families. The sachems distributed garden plots to families and exercised certain judicial prerogatives. They also represented their community on diplomatic and ceremonial occasions. But a sachem's power was derived directly from the members of the community. To secure economic and political support he needed leadership ability as well as a family name. Community members could oblige a faltering sachem to share the office with a relative or to step down altogether. Moreover, major political decisions were reached through a consensus in meetings attended by all adult males. Squanto came from a world, then, where politics was a constant and integral component of a man's life.

Squanto was even better prepared for his unusual career if, as seems probable, he was a *pniese* (elite warrior and sachem's counselor) in his community. In preparation for this position, young men were chosen in childhood and underwent unusually rigorous diets and training. The purpose of this preparation was not simply to fortify them and develop their courage but also to enable them to call upon and visualize Hobbamock, a deity capable of inflicting great harm and even death on those whom he did not favor. Hobbamock appeared in many forms to "the chiefest and most judicious amongst them," in Winslow's words, "though all of them strive to attain to that hellish height of honor."[3] It is clear that those who succeeded in the vision quest had developed the mental self-discipline demanded of all Indians to an extraordinary degree. By calling on Hobbamock, the *pnieses* protected themselves and those near them in battle and frightened their opponents. They were universally respected not only for their access to Hobbamock and for their courage and judgment but also for their moral uprightness. Because of his psychological fortitude, his particularly astute grasp of Indian politics and protocol, and his continued sense of duty to his community even after its demise, it is quite likely that Squanto was a *pniese*.

The few recorded observations of Patuxet during Squanto's early years show that it was a very different place from the "wilderness" that the Plymouth colonists later described. Both Samuel de Champlain in 1605 and 1606 and John Smith in 1614 noted that most of the coast between Massachusetts and Plymouth Bays was under cultivation. The colonists were told, probably by Squanto himself, that in Plymouth Bay "in former time hath lived about 2,000 Indians."[4] The total Wampanoag population in 1615 was probably about twenty thousand, most of whom were concentrated in village communities ranging in size from five hundred to fifteen hundred individuals. Squanto's homeland, then, was far more densely settled before the English arrived than afterward.

Although no one could have known it at the time, Squanto was born at a turning point in the history of his people and his region. For a century, Europeans had been trading and skirmishing with, and sometimes kidnapping, Native Americans along the coast. At the time of Squanto's birth, however, these activities had not been extended south of Canada on a regular basis. Occasional visits from European explorers and traders and the Native Americans' own well-established exchange routes brought some iron tools and glass beads to Patuxet. But these visits were too infrequent to have induced any lasting economic or cultural changes. Unlike some fur-trading Indians to the north, the Wampanoag had not become dependent on European trade items for their survival.

The turn of the century marked an intensification of French and English interest in New England's resources. The differing economic goals of the colonizers from the two countries gave rise to differing attitudes and policies toward the region's Native Americans. The French were concerned primarily with furs. Following Champlain's explorations of the New England coast in 1605 and 1606, French traders using his descriptions and maps began to visit annually and to cultivate an extensive trade as far south as Cape Cod. Their goals encouraged the maintenance of friendly relations with coastal Indian communities and even the development of broad regional ties among the native peoples.

For the English, however, furs were at best a useful by-product of more pressing interests. Beginning with Bartholomew Gosnold's expedition in 1602, they showed a preference for extracting resources such as fish and sassafras that did not require the cooperation of native communities. Moreover, they thought in long-range terms of making Indian land available to English farmers, a goal that virtually guaranteed eventual conflict with Native Americans. The English cultivated Indian allies only to gain their assistance in establishing colonies, and English methods were generally more coercive than those of the French. Nearly every English expedition from Gosnold's to that of the *Mayflower* generated hostility with Native Americans. By 1610, taking captured Indians to England had become commonplace. Would-be colonizers such as Sir Ferdinando Gorges hoped to impress their captives with the superiority of English culture, to learn as much as they could about the lay of the land, and to use them as mediators with local Indians. They also displayed their captives prominently in order to attract financial and public support in England for their projected colonies.

John Smith, the former Virginia leader, witnessed the results of the competition between the two colonial strategies when he explored the coast from the Penobscot River to Cape Cod in 1614. Smith found that he had arrived at the end of an active trading season. Aside from one Englishman's cozy monopoly at the mouth of the Pemaquid River, all of the ships were French. The better-endowed region north of the Pemaquid had yielded 25,000 skins that year, and Smith judged the south capable of producing as many as 6,000 to 7,000 annually. He himself had retrieved 1,300 pelts, mostly beaver, in the wake of the French departure. He also found that all the Indians in the area he visited were friendly with one another through three loose regional alliances. Ostensibly formed to resist incursions from the Micmac in eastern Canada, the friendship chain had an economic function as well, for Smith noted that some primarily horticultural Indians in southern New England traded corn to Abenaki hunting groups farther north. In return, the horticulturalists obtained some of the Abenaki's supply of European trade goods. Though only minimally developed by 1614, this trade was already fostering a specialized division of labor among France's clients in New England.

The extent of Wampanoag participation in the corn trade is unknown, but Squanto and his people were producing substantial surpluses of furs by the time of Smith's visit in 1614 and had gained at least some acquaintance with the Europeans. From the visits of Champlain, Smith, and the traders, Squanto had learned something of European approaches to trade, diplomacy, and military conflict and had witnessed some of their technological accomplishments. But the regularized trade was less than a decade old. The ease with which groups of Patuxet men were manipulated by Smith and his officer, Thomas Hunt, in 1614 suggests that they had not developed the wariness toward Europeans, particularly the English, of the more experienced Indians to the north.

Squanto's life reached a sudden and dramatic turning point with Hunt's visit. Smith had returned to England, leaving Hunt in charge of his fishing crew to complete the catch and carry it to Málaga, Spain. Before departing, Hunt stopped at Patuxet. Using his association with Smith, who had left on friendly terms, he lured aboard his ship about twenty natives, including Squanto. Quickly rounding Cape Cod, he drew off seven more Indians from Nauset and then turned east for Málaga. Hunt's action marked the English as an enemy of all the Wampanoags. Referring to southeastern New England, Gorges said that Hunt's action had resulted in "a warre now new begunne betweene the inhabitants of those parts and us," while Smith condemned Hunt for moving the Indians to "hate against our Nation, as well as to cause my proceedings to be more difficult."[5]

Native outrage at Hunt's action was reinforced by the near-simultaneous return of an earlier Wampanoag captive, Epenow, a sachem of Capawack, on Martha's Vineyard. Epenow had been seized three years earlier and taken to Gorges's house in England. On constant public display, he learned English well and impressed Gorges and others as "a goodly man of brave aspect, stout and sober in his demeanour."[6] Thus his fabricated tales of gold on Martha's Vineyard were eagerly seized upon; and in 1614, Gorges commissioned a voyage under Nicholas Hobson, accompanied by Epenow as a guide. Epenow had apparently planned his escape all along, but the news of Hunt's deed hardened his desire for revenge. As the ship drew near his island, Epenow escaped under a cover of arrows from the shore. A fierce battle ensued with heavy casualties on both sides. Among the injured was Hobson himself, who returned to England empty-handed. Epenow thereafter constituted one source of the anti-English sentiment that the Plymouth colonists would encounter six years later.

Meanwhile, Squanto and his fellow captives reached Málaga, where Hunt tried to sell them as slaves. A few had already been sold when, according to Gorges, "the Friers of those parts took the rest from them and kept them to be instructed in the Christian faith."[7] What happened to Squanto over the next three years is not clear. Particularly intriguing are questions about the extent and influence of his Catholic instruction and the means by which, in William Bradford's words, "he got away for England."[8] We know only that by 1617 he was residing in the London home of John Slany, treasurer of the Newfoundland Company, where he learned, or at least improved, his English and his understanding of colonial goals. In the following year, he went to Newfoundland itself, presumably at Slany's instigation. Here for the second time he met Thomas Dermer, an officer with Smith in 1614 who now worked for Gorges. Dermer was so impressed with Squanto's tales of Patuxet that he took him back to England to meet Gorges. Although the strategy of employing captive Indians as guides had backfired several times, Gorges was ready to try again. He saw in Squanto the key to countering French domination of the New England fur trade and to reestablishing England's reputation among the Indians. For his part, Squanto knew, as had earlier captives, how to tell Gorges what he wanted to hear in order to be returned home. In March 1619 he and Dermer were bound for New England.

Moving in the circles he did, Squanto undoubtedly knew something of the epidemic that had ravaged New England, including Patuxet, during his absence. A Gorges expedition under Richard Vines had witnessed what Vines called simply "the plague" at Sagadahoc in 1616 in reporting on its effects. Most notable was the immunity of the English; while most of the Indians were dying, Vines and his party "lay in the Cabbins with those people, [and] not one of them ever felt their heads to ake."[9] This immunity and the 75-to-90 percent depopulation among the Indians make it clear that a virgin-soil epidemic of European origin had been planted in New England's isolated disease environment. Although the specific instigator cannot be identified because of the frequency with which Europeans were visiting New England, it is noteworthy that the stricken zone, as reported by Dermer in 1619, was the coast from the Penobscot to Cape Cod—precisely the area encompassing the loose coalition of Indian groups engaged in trade with the French and one another. At its southern extremity the epidemic spread among the Wampanoags, including those at Pokanoket, located at the head of Narragansett Bay. But the sickness did not affect the Wampanoags' Narragansett rivals on the western side of the bay who traded with the Dutch in New Netherland. This pattern suggests that the epidemic was of French origin.

Squanto found his hometown of Patuxet completely vacated. Most of its inhabitants had died, and the survivors had fled inland to other villages. He surely noticed, as did others, the undergrowth that had overtaken the formerly cultivated fields and the vast numbers of unburied dead whose "bones and skulls," in one Englishman's words, "made such a spectacle ... it seemed to me a new found Golgotha."[10] The depopulation was so great that the Narragansetts were able to force the weakened Wampanoags at Pokanoket to abandon their position at the head of Narragansett Bay and to retain only the eastern shore.

The Narragansetts' avoidance of the epidemic gave them a greater advantage than that derived from numbers alone. In the view of their stricken neighbors, the Narragansetts' good health reflected their faithful sacrifices to the deity, Cautantowwit. The ritual worlds and belief systems of the Wampanoags who survived, however, had been badly shaken by the epidemic. The usual practice of gathering with the powwow (medicine man) in a sick person's wigwam could only have helped spread the disease more rapidly. With even their powwows succumbing, the Wampanoags could only conclude that their deities had aligned against them. Being unable to observe the proper burial rituals, the survivors also had to fear the retribution of the dead. Their momentary fear that they had lost touch with sources of spiritual power to which others had access would be a critical factor in facilitating Squanto's later political success.

As Dermer's expedition traveled overland from Patuxet in the summer of 1619, Squanto's presence and diplomatic skill enabled the English to break through the antagonism toward them and to make friendly contacts at Nemasket (near Middleboro) and Pokanoket (near Bristol, Rhode Island). For once an Indian captive had performed as Gorges had hoped. But as Dermer returned to his ship and prepared to sail around Cape Cod, Squanto took his leave to search for surviving Patuxet Wampanoags. On his own, Dermer was unable to persuade the Indians at Monomoy (now Pleasant Harbor) of his good intentions. He was captured and barely succeeded in escaping. After a seemingly cordial meeting on Martha's Vineyard with Epenow, the former Gorges captive, Dermer was attacked off Long Island and again managed to escape. Returning to New England in the summer of 1620, he was captured by his newly made friends at Pokanoket and Nemasket, and released only after Squanto interceded on his behalf. Dermer, with Squanto, then proceeded to Martha's Vineyard, where they were attacked by Epenow and his followers. Most of the crew was killed this time, while the luckless captain escaped with fourteen wounds and died later in Virginia. Squanto was again made a captive, this time of his fellow Wampanoags.

In a letter written after his release at Nemasket, Dermer attributed his reception there to the Wampanoags' renewed desire for revenge. He noted that another English crew had just visited the area, invited some Indians on board their ship, and then shot them down without provocation. The incident could only have revived the Indians' suspicions of the English that had prevailed before Squanto's return. These suspicions were now focused on Squanto himself, as Dermer's accomplice, and led to his being turned over to Massasoit, or Ousamequin, the leading Wampanoag sachem, based at Pokanoket. Here, Squanto remained until he was ransomed by the Plymouth colonists in March 1621.

In the autumn of 1620, the Wampanoag homeland was vastly different from a decade earlier when French traders had begun to frequent it regularly. Fewer than 10 percent of its 20,000 former inhabitants were still living, and they were now consolidated into a few tiny communities. The region was vulnerable, as never before, to exploitation by outsiders. Pokanoket and its sachem, Massasoit, had been subjected to a humiliating tributary relationship with the Narragansett, who were emerging as the most important political force in New England because of their size and their control of Indian-European trade links east of Long Island. Moreover, the decimated Indians could no longer count on the fur trade as a means of compensating for other weaknesses. Always limited in both the quality and quantity of its fur resources, the region's loss of most of its hunters now made it an unprofitable stop for traders.

Although he was their captive, Squanto was able to capitalize on Pokanoket's despair. "He told Massasoit what wonders he had seen in England," according to a future settler, "and that if he could make [the] English his friends then Enemies that were too strong for him would be constrained to bow to him."[11] He did not have to wait long to be proved right. In December 1620, less than six months after Dermer's departure, word reached Pokanoket that a shipload of English colonists had established a permanent settlement at Patuxet.

Like the other Puritans who later settled New England, the group at Plymouth (for so they renamed Patuxet) were motivated by a combination of religious and economic motives that shaped their attitudes toward Native Americans. Their persecution by the Church of England and their self-imposed exile to the Netherlands had only sharpened their desire to practice their exclusionary, intolerant separatism without external interference. While seeking literally to distance themselves from English ecclesiastical authorities, the settlers were endeavoring to reinforce their English identities. They had abandoned their Dutch haven for fear that their children would become assimilated there. Finally, though ostensibly migrating to fish and trade for furs, the colonists actually sought land to improve themselves materially and, they supposed, spiritually. Neither very rich nor very poor, most were small farmers and artisans who sought to escape the shortage of land and inflated prices that threatened their tenuous economic independence. Although Plymouth lacked the sense of divine mission of the later nonseparatist Puritan colonies, its goals of religious and ethnic exclusivity and its desire for land had clear implications for its relations with the Wampanoag and other native peoples.

These implications were apparent in Plymouth's early policies and attitudes toward the Indians. In a major promotional pamphlet published in 1622, Robert Cushman restated what had already become a familiar justification for dispossessing Native Americans of their lands: "Their land is spacious and void, and there are few and do but run over the grass, as do also the foxes and wild beasts. They are not industrious, neither have art, science, skill, or faculty to use either the land or the commodities of it, but all spoils or rots, and is marred for want of manuring, gathering, ordering, etc. As the ancient patriarchs therefore removed from straiter places into more roomy . . . so is it lawful now to take a land which none useth, and make use of it."[12] Cushman's statement was consistent with the emerging European doctrine of *vacuum domicilium*, by which "civil" states were entitled to the uncultivated lands of those in a "natural" state. Although Plymouth's own "civility" was formalized by the hastily contrived Mayflower Compact, its financial backers had anticipated its need for more than an abstract principle to press its claim—among its own people as well as among any natives whom they might encounter. Accordingly, they had hired Miles Standish, a soldier of fortune fresh from the Dutch wars, to organize the colony militarily. It was Standish who would shape Plymouth's Indian policy during its first generation.

Standish began to execute this policy even before the *Mayflower* arrived at Patuxet. Landing first at Cape Cod, the settlers aroused hostilities by ransacking Indian graves, houses, and grain stores. At Patuxet they also stirred suspicions during the first four months of their stay. But their own situation grew desperate during their first New England winter. They lost half their numbers to starvation and disease and were ill prepared for the approaching planting season. In this condition, they could no longer expect to alleviate their shortages through pilferage with impunity. The impasse was broken one day in March 1621 by the appearance of Samoset, an Abenaki sachem from the Pemaquid River community that had been trading with the English for more than a decade. Samoset learned of the needs and intentions of the colony and returned a few days later with Squanto.

The Wampanoags had been watching the Plymouth group throughout the winter. With Samoset and the newly useful Squanto offering advice and experience, they concluded that the time was ripe to befriend the settlers instead of maintaining a hostile distance. Such an alliance would enable them to break the grip of the Narragansetts, whose haughty demeanor stung even more than that of the English. Nevertheless, the decision was not to be taken lightly. William Bradford wrote that the Indians did first "curse and execrate them with their conjurations" before approaching the settlers.[13] But this description betrays his fear of witchcraft as it was understood by Europeans, rather than his comprehension of Indian rituals. More likely, the Wampanoags were ritually purging themselves of their hostilities toward the English.

Samoset and Squanto arranged the meeting between the Wampanoags and Plymouth colonists that resulted in their historic treaty, in which each side agreed to aid the other in the event of attack by a third party, to disarm during their meetings with each other, and to return any tools stolen from the other side. In addition to these reciprocal agreements, however, several others were weighted against the natives. Massasoit, the sachem at Pokanoket, was to see that his tributaries observed the terms; the Indians were to turn over for punishment any of their people suspected of assaulting any English persons (but no English settlers could be tried by Indians); and, the treaty concluded, "King James would esteem of him [Massasoit] as his friend and ally."[14] The colonists' understanding of this last honor was made explicit by Plymouth's Nathaniel Morton, who wrote that Massasoit, by the treaty, "acknowledged himself content to become the subject of our sovereign lord the King aforesaid, his heirs and successors, and gave unto them all the lands adjacent to them and theirs forever."[15] Morton made clear that among themselves the English did not regard the treaty as one of alliance and friendship between equals, but rather as one of submission by one party to the domination of the other, according to the assumptions of *vacuum domicilium*.

For the Wampanoags, however, the meaning of a political relationship was conveyed in the ritual exchange of speeches and gifts, not in written clauses or unwritten understandings based on concepts such as sovereignty that were alien to them. From their standpoint, the English were preferable to the Narragansett because they demanded less tribute and homage while offering more gifts and autonomy and better protection.

The treaty also brought a change in status for Squanto. In return for his services, the Wampanoags now freed him to become guide, interpreter, and diplomat for the colony. Thus, he finally returned to his home at Patuxet, a move that had, as we shall see, more than sentimental significance. Among his first services was the securing of corn seed and instruction in its planting, including the use of fish as fertilizer.

Squanto also enabled Plymouth to strengthen its political position in the surrounding area. He helped secure peace with some Wampanoag communities on Cape Cod and guided an expedition to Massachusetts Bay. His kidnapping by anti-English Wampanoags at Nemasket and subsequent rescue by a heavily armed Plymouth force speaks compellingly of his importance to the colony. Moreover, this incident led to a new treaty, engineered in part by Squanto, with all the Indian groups of Massachusetts Bay to the tip of Cape Cod, including even Epenow and his community. By establishing a tributary system with the surrounding Indian bands, Plymouth was filling the political vacuum left by the epidemic and creating a dependable network of corn suppliers and buffers against overland attack. In so doing, however, Plymouth incurred the resentment of the Narragansett by depriving them of tributaries just when Dutch traders were expanding their activities in the bay. In January 1622 the Narragansett conveyed their displeasure by sending colony leaders a snakeskin filled with arrows. On Squanto's advice, Plymouth's leaders returned the skin filled with powder and shot. The Narragansett sachem, Canonicus, refused to accept this counterchallenge, in effect thus acknowledging the colony's presence and political importance.

However effective it appeared, Plymouth's system of Indian diplomacy was fraught with tensions that nearly destroyed it. A Pokanoket *pniese*, Hobbamock (named for the powerful spirit), became a second adviser to Plymouth in the summer of 1621. Whether the English thought that Hobbamock would merely assist Squanto or would serve to check him is unclear. In any event, Squanto was no longer the only link between the colony and the Indians; indeed, being from Pokanoket, Hobbamock had certain advantages over him. As one whose very life depended on the colony's need for him, Squanto had to act decisively to check this threat to his position. His most potent weapon was the mutual distrust and fear still lingering between English and Indians; his most pressing need was for a power base so that he could extricate himself from his position of colonial dependency. Accordingly, he began maneuvering on his own.

Squanto had been acting independently for several months before being discovered by the English in March 1622. As reconstructed by Edward Winslow: "His course was to persuade the Indians [that] he could lead us to peace or war at his pleasure, and would oft threaten the Indians, sending them word in a private manner we were intended shortly to kill them, that thereby he might get gifts to himself, to work their peace; so that whereas divers [people] were wont to rely on Massasoit for protection, and resort to his abode, now they began to leave him and seek after Tisquantum [Squanto]."[16] In short, he sought to establish himself as an independent native political leader. At the same time, he endeavored to weaken Pokanoket's influence on Plymouth by provoking armed conflict between the two allies. He circulated a rumor that Massasoit was conspiring with the Narragansett and Massachusett Indians to wipe out the colony. The English quickly verified the continued loyalty of Pokanoket but, though angry at Squanto, were afraid to dispense with him. Instead, they protected him from Massasoit's revenge, which brought tensions into the Pokanoket-Plymouth relationship that were finally assuaged only when Squanto died later in the year.

In seeking to establish his independence of Plymouth, Squanto was struggling for more than his survival. As Winslow put it, he sought "honor, which he loved as his life and preferred before his peace."[17] What did honor mean to Squanto? For one thing, of course, it meant revenge against Pokanoket, not only for threatening his position at Plymouth but also for his earlier captivity. But it meant more than that. Squanto appears, in a short period of time, to have gained substantial influence among Wampanoags loyal to Massasoit. Winslow indicated, unknowingly and in passing, the probable key to this success. The news of Massasoit's alleged treachery against Plymouth was brought, he said, by "an Indian of Tisquantum's family."[18] Contrary to the Plymouth sources (all of which were concerned with establishing the colony's unblemished title to the land around Plymouth Bay), there were certainly a few dozen Patuxet survivors of the epidemic at Pokanoket, Nemasket, and elsewhere. Although Squanto undoubtedly sought the loyalty and tribute of others, it was to these relatives and friends that he would primarily have appealed. The honor that he sought was a reconstituted Patuxet community placed under his own leadership and located near its traditional home.

Squanto's hopes were shattered when his plot collapsed. With Massasoit seeking his life, he had, in Bradford's words, "to stick close to the English, and never durst go from them till he dies."[19] Squanto's isolation from other Indians and his dependence on the colonists help to explain their willingness to protect him. In July, Squanto again engineered an important breakthrough for Plymouth by accompanying an expedition to Monomoy, where suspicion of all Europeans persisted. The Wampanoags here had attacked Champlain's party in 1606 and Dermer's in 1619. Standish's men had taken some of their corn during a stop at Cape Cod in November 1620. Now, as Winslow phrased it, "by Tisquantum's means better persuaded, they left their jealousy, and traded with them."[20] Monomoy's leaders agreed to turn over eight hogsheads of corn and beans to the English. But as the expedition prepared to depart, Squanto "fell sick of an Indian fever, bleeding much at the nose (which the

Indians take for a symptom of [impending] death) and within a few days died there."[21]

By the time of Squanto's death, the Plymouth colony had gained the foothold it had sought for two and one-half years. The expedition to Monomoy marked the establishment of firm relations with the last Wampanoag community to withhold loyalty. Although the colony was now feeding itself, the collection of corn remained a symbolic means of affirming the tributary relationships that bound Wampanoag communities to the English. These accomplishments would have been infinitely more difficult, if not impossible, without Squanto's aid. But it is questionable whether his contributions after the summer of 1622 would have been as critical. Thereafter, the colony's principal dealings were with the hostile Massachusett and Narragansett Indians beyond Patuxet's immediate environs. Moreover, the world in which Squanto had flourished was vanishing. A rationalized wampum trade had begun to transform Indian-European relations in southern New England. And the end of the decade would bring a mighty upsurge in English colonization that would surround and dwarf Plymouth. Within the restrictions imposed by his dependence on Plymouth's protection, Squanto would have adapted to these changes, but his knowledge and skills would no longer have been unique nor his services indispensable.

Notes

1. Edward Winslow, "Good Newes from New England," in *Chronicles of the Pilgrim Fathers*, ed. Alexander Young (Boston, 1841), 363.

2. Isaack de Rasieres to Samuel Bloomaert, c. 1628, in Sydney V. James Jr., ed., *Three Visitors to Early Plymouth* (Plymouth, MA, 1963), 79.

3. Winslow, "Good Newes," 357.

4. Emmanuel Altham to Sir Edward Altham, September [?] 1623, in James, *Three Visitors*, 29.

5. James Phinney Baxter, ed., *Sir Ferdinando Gorges and His Province of Maine*, 3 vols. (Boston, 1890), 2:211; Edward Arber, ed., *Travels and Works of Captain John Smith*, 2 vols., 2d ed. (Edinburgh, 1910), 1:219.

6. Baxter, *Gorges*, 2:20–21.

7. Ibid., 1:210.

8. William Bradford, *Of Plymouth Plantation*, ed. Samuel Eliot Morison (New York, 1967), 81.

9. Baxter, *Gorges*, 2:19.

10. Thomas Morton, *New English Canaan*, ed. Charles Francis Adams Jr. (Boston, 1883), 132–33.

11. Phineas Pratt, "A Declaration of the Affairs of the English People that First Inhabited New England," *Massachusetts Historical Society Collections*, 4th ser., 4 (1858): 485.

12. Dwight B. Heath, ed., *A Journal of the Pilgrims at Plymouth*, orig. title *Mourt's Relation* [1622] (New York, 1963), 91–92.

13. Bradford, *Of Plymouth Plantation*, 84.

14. Heath, *Journal*, 57.

15. Nathaniel Morton, *New Englands Memoriall* [1669], ed. Howard J. Hall (New York, 1937), 24.

16. Winslow, "Good Newes," 289.

17. Ibid., 289–90.

18. Ibid., 287.

19. Bradford, *Of Plymouth Plantation*, 99.

20. Winslow, "Good Newes," 301.

21. Bradford, *Of Plymouth Plantation*, 114.

Suggested Readings

I have treated fully the context within which Squanto lived and acted in *Manitou and Providence: Indians, Europeans, and the Making of New England, 1500–1643* (New York, 1982). For additional information on native peoples and cultures in southern New England and surrounding regions, see Bruce G. Trigger, ed., *Northeast*, vol. 15 of *Handbook of North American Indians*, general ed. William C. Sturtevant (Washington, DC, 1978). For perspectives on the larger history of Native Americans in the colonial era, see Bruce G. Trigger and William R. Swagerty, "Entertaining Strangers: North America in the Sixteenth Century," and Neal Salisbury, "Native People and European Settlers in Eastern North America, 1600–1783," both in *The Cambridge History of the Native Peoples of the Americas*, vol. 1, *North America*, ed. Bruce G. Trigger and Wilcomb E. Washburn (Cambridge, England, 1996), pt. 1, 325–98, 399–460; Francis Jennings, *The Invasion of America: Indians, Colonialism, and the Cant of Conquest* (Chapel Hill, NC, 1975); and Ian K. Steele, *Warpaths: Invasions of North America* (New York, 1994). On epidemic disease and depopulation among Native Americans, see Alfred W. Crosby, *The Columbian Exchange: Biological and Cultural Consequences of 1492* (Westport, CT, 1972); and Russell Thornton, *American Indian Holocaust and Survival: A Population History since 1492* (Norman, OK, 1987).

2

Anne Hutchinson, the Puritan Patriarchs, and the Power of the Spirit

Marilyn Westerkamp

Anne Hutchinson's life (1591–1643) reveals the possibilities and limitations of a woman's spiritual leadership in Puritan New England. Anne's family allowed her to gain a private religious education, and her husband had the resources and temperament to allow her to follow a religious quest to Massachusetts. Patriarchal authority—in home, parish, or court—did not initially try to prevent Anne's powerful service to her religious community; she was a full member of the church, and her talents were useful in strengthening that community. Puritanism had only recently changed from a religion protesting Anglican authority in England to a church trying to maintain authority in New England. Was Puritanism clear on the role of earthly authority in salvation, or did the banishment of Roger Williams and Anne Hutchinson represent the banishment of alternative views equally characteristic of Puritanism? In God's name, Puritans already had a long history of defying magistrates and ministers. Charismatic Anne Hutchinson attracted the support of powerful Puritans of both genders who challenged the religious and political leadership of the young colony. She even inspired civil disobedience. Did the magistrates' actions reflect Puritan attitudes concerning the proper role of women in society, or was the appeal to patriarchy a sign of the weakness of the case that John Winthrop was trying to make? With the emigration, banishment, or recantation of Hutchinsonians, would Puritanism, as practiced, be narrower and more patriarchal after 1637 than it had been before?

Marilyn Westerkamp has published authoritatively on colonial American religious history, including *Triumph of the Laity: Scots-Irish Piety and the Great Awakening, 1625–1760* (1987). She teaches American colonial, religious, and women's history at the University of California, Santa Cruz.

In November 1637, Anne Hutchinson was banished from the colony of Massachusetts Bay. The sentence concluded her two-day trial before the General Court and resolved the most serious crisis that had threatened the colony during its first decade. The importance of the trial was reflected in the number and rank of people involved, including most of the colony's officials: the governor, deputy governor, magistrates, and local representatives from the towns. Additionally, many of the clergy attended and demonstrated, through their testimony, a vested interest in the outcome. This trial has long fascinated historians, for it seems less an equitable trial of justice than a ritual performance acted out so that Massachusetts leaders could do what they had already decided to do: namely, rid themselves of Hutchinson. In other words, the government brought her to trial to justify and ensure her forced departure. The magistrates had many grievances. She socialized with persons who had challenged the government, and she had assumed a leadership role not proper to women. These were relatively minor complaints that she easily discounted in court. Of a more serious nature, however, she was charged with sedition against the colony's ministers, a charge more difficult to prove because the evidence was initially so controversial. More serious still was the suggestion of blasphemy involving false claims about her relationship with God, but this question remained unresolved. The final exchange of the trial said it all. When Hutchinson asked, "I desire to know wherefore I am banished?" she was silenced. "Say no more, the court knows wherefore and is satisfied."[1]

The hostility surrounding Hutchinson at that moment starkly contrasted with the vast popularity she had enjoyed as a religious leader only eighteen months before. Intellectually gifted and personally charismatic, she had welcomed many to her home for private prayer and study. Her guests included men as well as women; many were among the highest leaders in the colony. Between sixty and eighty persons came weekly to hear her expound upon the week's sermons and advise them in their spiritual journeys, and she had, according to leading minister John Cotton, greatly helped many women of the town. "I doubt not but some of you [women] have also received much good from the Conference of this our Sister and by your Converse with her: and from her it may be you have received help in your spiritual Estates."[2] Yet by November, she seemed almost friendless and powerless as she fought for her freedom, her own beliefs, and her status as a spiritual leader called by God. Who was this woman who attracted so many disciples? And why did government officials of this colony less than eight years old, a colony in the wilderness, find it necessary to throw her out?

Anne Marbury Hutchinson lived during an era of rising Puritan power, a time when the Puritan movement was growing in both numerical size and political strength. Puritans can best be described as religious reformers who hoped to "purify" the Protestant Church of England of all vestiges of Roman Catholicism. About fifteen years after Martin Luther had ignited the Protestant Reformation on the European continent, the

English church had declared itself separate from Rome. For twenty-five years, religious insecurity, even chaos, ensued under the disjointed reigns of the barely Protestant Henry VIII, the devoted reformer child-king Edward VI, and the equally resolute Roman Catholic Mary. Upon Mary's death in 1558, the church, under the guidance of Queen Elizabeth, began to follow a middle road between closeted Roman Catholics and the somewhat more open Puritans who struggled to further the work of reformation. Puritans wanted to eliminate all formal church rituals, judging such practices man-made and therefore artificial. These included prayers read from books, patterns of gestures and signs, and any aspect of community worship whose words and actions were explicitly fixed by the institution. Puritans also rejected extraneous unscriptural elements such as graven images (statues, pictures, stained glass), candles, vestments, and holy day celebrations. Additionally, Puritans rejected the hierarchy of the Anglican Church as unbiblical. They denied that bishops had any scriptural right to authority over congregations or ministers, finding instead that the early church communities of the New Testament deferred to the congregation as the primary seat of authority. They complained that the Anglican clergy frequently lacked erudition, or even moral respectability. Puritans called for a return to clerical accountability, to godly conduct, and to the plain preaching and plain worship outlined in the Scriptures. By the end of the sixteenth century, Puritan reformers had united themselves in a formidable religious and political coalition driven by a spiritual authority lodged in Puritans' intense relationship with God.

Like most Reformed Protestants of this era, Puritans were followers of John Calvin's theology. They believed in the total depravity of humanity, the inability of people to save themselves, and the gracious mercy of God in lifting a few chosen, or the elect, out of their evil pathways and bringing them to salvation. The atonement of Christ, through his Crucifixion, was a miracle, and the elect were able to accept Christ's love in faith through the intervention of divine grace, a grace that was irresistible. In other words, God empowered those few elect to have faith; the rest were left to the terrifying punishment they so justly deserved. Puritans believed that, from the beginning of time, all individuals had been predestined to either salvation or damnation. They knew that their destiny had been decided by God's arbitrary will, and no amount of virtuous acts or evildoing could change a believer's ultimate fate. Oddly enough, this lesson did not destroy hope or create anarchic pleasure-seeking. Instead, most Puritans, who were generally convinced of the real potential for their own salvation, struggled to convince themselves and others that they were indeed among the elect. At some points, they were afflicted with great anxiety; at others, they were filled with the supreme joy of divine assurance in a salvation that no person could destroy, because it was, in fact, effected by God.

Dissatisfied with the spiritual "emptiness" of Anglican services led by uninspired pastors, many felt justified in turning to private religious meetings to satisfy their spiritual cravings. Laypersons gathered weekly, sometimes more frequently, to pray, study, and preach. They discovered among themselves the piety, inspiration, and even knowledge absent on Sundays. They followed personal moral regimens of labor, rest, and carefully prescribed pleasures. They also recommended to each other reliable, reformed ministers known for their learning, personal piety, and spiritual guidance. All persons were required to educate themselves, pray, study, and follow Christ; and while they might enjoy the assistance of sympathetic clerics and one another, the spiritual quest was a lonely one, traveled by the individual in direct relationship with God. Then God offered grace, the soul was transformed, and salvation was realized.

Anne Marbury was born in 1591, the second of thirteen children. Her childhood was spent in the Puritan stronghold of Lincolnshire, East Anglia. Her parents, Bridget Dryden and Francis Marbury, were among the lesser gentry in England. As a girl, Anne Marbury would not have been formally educated, but from what is known about her parents, it might safely be supposed that she was well educated by them. Bridget Dryden was connected to a well-placed family network that would produce the poet laureate John Dryden in 1631. Francis Marbury seems to have been an obstreperous clergyman and a published theological writer who was deeply committed to the value of education. Ordained a deacon in 1578, Francis Marbury was, within a year, summoned before the London Consistory Court. There he publicly accused the bishops of ordaining unfit men and was therefore imprisoned. Seven years later, he was curate and schoolmaster in the town of Alford. Although he complained in 1590 that he had been silenced and deprived of his living, within four years he was preaching again, and silenced again. The primary charges centered on his outspoken criticism of the clergy, especially his call for better-educated ministers. In 1605 about three hundred pastors were removed from their congregations in an effort to stop the rising Puritan tide. Since Marbury had confined his comments to clerical standards of learning and avoided other criticisms of the Church of England's structure, theology, and practice, his infractions were deemed comparatively minor, and he was advanced in this period of a scarcity of clergy. He moved his family to

London in 1605, and held a series of respectable pulpits and livings there until his death in 1611.

At twenty-one, Anne Marbury married William Hutchinson, a successful merchant living in her hometown—Alford, England. There the Hutchinsons prospered for twenty-two years, and during those years Anne bore fourteen children, all but two of whom survived into adulthood. Very little is known about the Hutchinsons during this central period of their lives. Alford seems to have been a good choice for business as William's trade increased with his family, and his reputation and status rose accordingly. But it was also a good choice for a clergyman's daughter who was deeply interested in the affairs of the soul and who embraced the cultural critique and spiritual intensity of the Lincolnshire Puritan community. Some twenty miles south, in the larger city of Boston, St. Botolph's Church was pastored by the renowned John Cotton. Although the Hutchinsons could travel there only occasionally, Anne found his preaching so inspiring that she attended his services whenever the long journey could be made. It is difficult to ascertain whether this was Anne's or William's desire. If the Hutchinsons' New England years fairly reflected their marriage, William pursued his economic and political callings while Anne attended to the spiritual side. Although a believer himself—William would become a member of the congregation after he had arrived in Massachusetts—he left religious leadership to his wife. In any case, Cotton so impressed Anne with his theological understanding and his experience of grace that she and her family followed him to New England and joined his congregation there.

After King Charles I ascended the throne in 1625, the Church of England became more committed to its bishops and its formalistic rituals, and the troubles of Puritans increased. More and more laypersons were fined or imprisoned for refusing to attend church services or to pay their tithes to support the ministers. Clergymen sympathetic to Puritanism were defrocked, deprived of their livings, and imprisoned because they refused to perform the sacraments or read prayers from the church's official prayer book, challenged the authority of bishops, or openly criticized the Anglican magisterium. In response to Charles's heightened efforts to control, if not eradicate, the Puritan influence, a group of merchants and investors looked toward colonization as the best way to escape the intensified persecutions. Others judged that the increased decadence within the Church of England warned of the impending Apocalypse foretold in Revelation. Seeing themselves as the saved remnant of the New Israel, many Puritans followed an impulse to escape divine vengeance upon England and build a godly commonwealth according to scriptural precepts.

On April 7, 1630, under the sponsorship, though beyond the control, of King Charles, some seven hundred settlers embarked for New England. During the next six years, the region would absorb hundreds, often thousands, of immigrants annually. These were not adventurers seeking great fortunes, but husbands and wives with their children, relatives, and servants planning to build a permanent colony. For most of the 1630s and 1640s, Massachusetts Bay would be led by John Winthrop, a man of affluence and influence in East Anglia, a man with the knowledge and mental strength to serve as the founding governor of the colony. He moved the primary settlement from the exposed Salem to the relatively sheltered seaport that they would call Boston. He divided the original settlers into seven different companies, or towns, assigned them land, and then organized colonists to build shelters and gather food while he negotiated with the native peoples for land and food supplies. He ordered, at his own expense, additional (and necessary) food stores for the winter. Within a year, owing largely to the dedication of the people and the guidance of Winthrop, the colony of Massachusetts was economically self-sufficient.

It would be difficult to overestimate the importance of religion in the New England world, not only in the lives and hearts of individuals but also in the very construction of the government. The colony's magistrates and ministers agreed with Winthrop's description of the experimental settlement as a "City on a Hill," a shining example to the rest of the world, a godly colony privileged by God and therefore strictly obligated to operate according to divine law. They envisioned their society as the New Israel and structured their churches and their government according to biblical guidelines. While their legal system conformed to the English common law, their criminal code was based upon Leviticus, the third book of the Old Testament. This religious worldview was not merely evident in legal codes, but it had also been internalized by every committed Puritan believer.

The Hutchinson crisis cannot possibly be understood apart from the deeply religious nature of the colony and its English inhabitants. Every town organized its own church and called its own pastor, and there were literally dozens of ministers available. Some of the best and the brightest clerical stars made their way to New England. People met for religious services on Sunday mornings and evenings, and, in response to popular requests, weekday lectures were delivered. Although individuals had to apply to become members of the church, demonstrating their election by means of godly behavior and personal testimony, almost all of the colonists joined their congregations. Some congregants took notes during sermons; many kept personal journals to track their own spiritual progress. Additionally, laypersons continued to hold private prayer meetings where they pored over sermons, clarified difficult points, studied theological texts, and shared with others the experiences of their souls and their hopes for salvation. That Anne Hutchinson held private meetings in her home was not in any way odd or disruptive, particularly since she originally invited only women to share a space in which they could speak freely, ask questions, and reveal the work of the Spirit in their lives. One of the more revealing omissions in the original Hutchinson record is the absence of any official concern about, or even acknowledgment of, these early gatherings. Historians have not even determined precisely when the meetings began. Magistrates and ministers became concerned about her work only after the weekly attendance had reached sixty to eighty persons, and only after her disciples' criticism of the Bay Colony's ministers became public.

Hutchinson's influence over more than sixty persons, in a town of perhaps six hundred, threatened the social and cultural foundations of this society. Puritan leaders envisioned themselves as patriarchs in the biblical sense. Old Testament patriarchs and kings became role models, and their recorded wisdom, reinforced by the Apostle Paul's pronouncements in the Epistles, guided Puritans toward an orderly society. While some few were called to exercise power as magistrates and ministers, and many more as husbands and fathers, most men, and certainly all women, were called to subject themselves to the rule of others. In the Bible, Puritans found a clearly ordered family system that arranged all persons into hierarchical pairs: master over servant, parent over child, husband over wife. Of course, religion did not serve alone; secular authorities, including English tradition and the common law, also reinforced patriarchal structures. In most ways, Anne Hutchinson's life mirrored that of her peers. Her years in England had been spent as the daughter of a minister, wife of a small merchant, and mother of fourteen children. Her labors were domestic; her status was defined by the legal construct of coverture, which placed a wife under the "cover" of her husband and denied her any civil standing.

Apart from explicit legal restrictions, women were as active as men in defining the traditions that constructed their lives, sometimes accepting customs and at other times transforming practices within their own sphere. The housewife, by virtue of her skills and experience, controlled the domestic economy. Moreover, women produced not only food and clothing but also children; and in the birthing chamber, women controlled a women-only space. The politics of reproduction and midwifery reflected the power located and contested within the household, and it is not surprising to find that Anne Hutchinson had gained a reputation as a skilled midwife. When describing Hutchinson's early success among Boston women, Winthrop looked toward her proficiency in the birthing chamber: "Being a woman very helpful in the times of child-birth, and other occasions of bodily infirmities, and well furnished with means for those purposes, she easily insinuated herself into the affections of many."[3] In the early seventeenth century, Puritan men were generally content to allow women such domestic authority. But when an Anne Hutchinson grew too strong, or actually confronted the male leadership, governors could (and did) retreat with security into the customs, laws, and biblical texts that established absolute male control and female subservience. With haphazard logic but consistent politics, ministers and magistrates found extensive justification for the patriarchy that served their own interests so well.

In 1634, Anne Hutchinson had landed in Boston, one year after John Cotton was established as the teacher of the Boston congregation. There she found a colony scarcely four years old and a town that was little more than a village with great ambitions. As Boston had only five hundred inhabitants, the Hutchinsons significantly increased the population. Their entourage numbered twenty-five persons: the couple, their eleven children, a daughter-in-law, two spinster cousins, a sister, a brother, a sister-in-law, and at least six servants. Additionally, William's wealth and substance earned him immediate recognition. At a time when social and geographic place mattered deeply, the Hutchinsons were assigned a house lot directly across from Governor Winthrop, and William was allotted six hundred acres, a clear acknowledgment of his rank, since he was a merchant, not a farmer. He represented Boston at the General Court and served in town and church leadership roles as the head of a family that added twenty-five people to the town and fourteen members to the congregation. As the wife of a prominent merchant, Anne would have found a respectable position among Boston's matrons. Beyond this, her healing gifts established some early authority, but her biblical knowledge and theological sophistication also were soon greatly admired. Such skills and abilities increased her reputation independently of William, but her rise to prominence, and ultimate downfall, inexorably tied her husband's stature to her own.

For a while there were no problems. In the same month that the Hutchinsons joined the church, John Wilson sailed for England to try, for a third and final time, to persuade his wife to come to Massachusetts. People had been quite clear about this matter. It was a scandal that Wilson was here without his family; and if his wife still refused to sail, he should remain in England. In Wilson's absence, Cotton served as the sole pastor, and Hutchinson probably instituted her private religious meetings. Her superior intellect and charisma made her a natural leader, and she quickly moved beyond explicating his sermons to preaching her own. At some point, women began to bring their husbands, and soon Hutchinson was holding two weekly meetings, one for women only and one for both women and men. Her enemies estimated a general attendance of sixty to eighty persons, an estimate that is supported by the large number of men who would be disciplined by the government for their subversive activities as Hutchinsonians. In 1635, Wilson, with his wife, returned to Massachusetts and the pulpit at the Boston Church; so, too, did the hot-tempered minister John Wheelwright, Hutchinson's brother-in-law, arrive. These two rigid, uncompromising personalities would become key performers as the controversy took hold, and the presence and activities of each one would stir his rival to greater exertions in the cause of truth.

Trouble when it first arose concerned neither of those men but Cotton's dissatisfaction with the theology of his colleagues, including Wilson. Anne Hutchinson and her followers agreed with Cotton's opinion and promoted his views, but the early (and private) dispute occupied Cotton and a few ministers. One theological issue involved the relationship between human effort and salvation. The Calvinist principles of predestination and election placed salvation completely in the hands of God. Believers could have no responsibility for their salvation because they had no ability to effect it. Grace extended to the elect transformed their thoughts and actions, and such saints became recognizable through their sanctified, or godly, behavior.

Cotton and the Hutchinsonians emphasized God's free, unconditional offer of divine grace and thus stressed the futility of human action and the value of an absolute, passive dependence upon an all-powerful God. While most New England ministers did not deny the twin truths of predestination and election, they thought that undue emphasis upon these two principles might lead to irreligion and anarchy. They understood the anxiety of believers desperate for some sign of their salvation and emphasized the hope that lay in the evidence of sanctification. Moreover, many promoted an idea that the potential saint could prepare for grace. Although acknowledging that human effort had no impact upon God, ministers encouraged people to study Scripture, attend services, watch their conduct, and pray so that they would be ready to receive divine grace. Such efforts may have kept believers from feeling desperate and lost, but

Cotton found in this "preparationism" disturbing hints of salvation through works—earning your way into Heaven. Because Cotton enjoyed a gentle, conciliatory personality, he might well have been able to resolve quietly his differences with those colleagues had not Hutchinson and her followers become involved. In her meetings she had apparently condemned those who preached sanctification and preparationism, which challenged most ministers, and her disciples expressed those misgivings publicly and aggressively.

A second dispute involved the question of the union of the Holy Spirit with the saint. While most theologians rejected outright any idea of a persistent divine presence within the soul, Cotton embraced a belief in the indwelling of the Spirit, although he did not mean that any divine properties were communicated or granted to the believer. This question was not merely academic. Here was lodged the center of Hutchinson's charisma. She spoke and preached out of an authority that came not from a university education or a congregation's call (of course, women could not be called to ordination), but from the authority of the Spirit within. One disciple described her as "a Woman that Preaches better Gospel than any of your black-coats that have been at the Ninniversity, a Woman of another kind of spirit, who hath had many Revelations of things to come, and . . . I had rather hear such a one that speaks from the mere motion of the spirit, without any study at all, than any of your learned Scholars, although they may be fuller of Scripture."[4]

In 1636, in response to the continuing strife, Puritan authorities held conferences, one in October and a second in December. Ostensibly, the clergy met to discuss their disagreements with Cotton, Wheelwright, and Hutchinson. How extraordinary that Hutchinson, a layperson and a woman, would attend such a conference! This reveals much about the situation in Massachusetts. The problem was not with Cotton questioning the preaching of other clergy, but with Hutchinson doing so. It might be argued that by bringing her to what was essentially a clerical conference, the clergy acknowledged her leadership. While they certainly denied her any legitimate claim to such a role, their actions unconsciously confirmed the strength of her spiritual authority. Any person suspected of heretical views, particularly a laywoman, could have been dealt with privately, but Hutchinson had so many followers that she had become a public figure. However, they could not afford to deal with her publicly because they might lose. At this point she was quite powerful; she had the support of Cotton, three magistrates, several deputies to the General Court, the majority of the congregation of the Boston Church, including the two lay elders, and the current governor of the colony, Henry Vane. Even if they did succeed in bringing her to trial and banishment, an open confrontation risked the immediate emigration of those leaders, including Cotton. Winthrop hoped to retain as many leaders as possible. Eventually, Hutchinson would be brought to public trial twice, before the state and before the church. But at this time the clergy seemed more interested in buttressing their own position, perhaps by persuading her to accept their arguments and their authority. Consequently, they chose a peculiar public-private meeting: a private conversation that could be reported publicly. John Cotton remembered the first conference as fairly successful at achieving a common theological understanding, but the events of that autumn and the following year demonstrated that a final confrontation had merely been delayed.

A series of public confrontations began in the last months of 1636. Since these were the actions of men, Hutchinson was not directly involved. However, both the clergy and magistrates would later work on the assumption that Hutchinson was privately directing the charge. Boston's Hutchinsonians challenged the authority of Wilson by calling John Wheelwright as a third minister to the Boston Church; the effort was derailed by a small minority led by Winthrop, who invoked a technical rule that a pastoral call must be unanimous. Wilson then delivered a sermon on the sadly divided condition of the churches, pointing to the rise of new, dangerous opinions and further irritating his congregation. The General Court called for a "Day of Fasting" to pray for reconciliation, and Cotton invited Wheelwright to preach. He delivered an outrageous sermon that revived the theological controversy, attacked the concept of the fast itself, and argued that any who strove to do God's work were hypocrites pretending to salvation through their own merits. Encouraged by Wheelwright's sermon, the Hutchinsonians took their struggle into the outlying towns, heckling preachers, irritating their congregations, and refusing to serve in the militia organized to fight the Pequot, a local Indian nation, because the militia's chaplain was John Wilson.

The Hutchinsonians may have dominated Boston, but their influence ended there. When the General Court met in March, a strong anti-Hutchinson coalition was evident. They approved Wilson's sermon, charged Wheelwright with sedition, and refused to consider petitions filed by Wheelwright's supporters. At Winthrop's recommendation, they moved the June elections to Newtown, effectively disenfranchising most Bostonians because they could not travel so far. At the June session, before petitions for Wheelwright could be read, Winthrop's faction called for elections, and the new majority elected Winthrop as governor and threw the two Boston magistrates and Henry Vane out of office. Boston in turn elected Vane and Hutchinsonian William Coddington as its two deputies. The honor guard refused to escort Winthrop into Boston, but this was merely a last show of defiance. The tide had turned, and Winthrop spent the rest of the summer dismantling the coalition and preparing for Anne Hutchinson's trial.

Concerned about the possible arrival of new Hutchinson recruits, the General Court enacted a law ordering that no strangers could stay in Massachusetts more than three weeks without the explicit permission of the magistrates. They also passed a resolution that condemned lay efforts to dispute doctrine with the preacher. Of greatest importance, the court forbade Hutchinson's meetings: "That though women might meet (some few together) to pray and edify one another; yet such a set assembly (as was then in practice at Boston), where sixty or more did meet every week, and one woman (in a prophetical way, by resolving questions of doctrine, and expounding Scripture) took upon her the whole exercise, was agreed to be disorderly, and without rule."[5] The magistrates and clergy then called yet another conference, without Hutchinson, to address Cotton's opinions and create a theological consensus. They identified eighty-two errors and nine unsavory phrases, many involving the connections between human effort and divine grace. Some errors, however, concerned the nature of faith and revelation, hinting in official documents, for the first time, of a hidden but primary issue at the heart of the crisis.

Once an intellectual compromise had been reached, Winthrop dealt with the Hutchinsonians. Henry Vane had already left the colony disillusioned, as had several leading merchants and their families. Wheelwright was summoned, convicted of sedition, and banished, and leading Hutchinsonian men were questioned and, depending on their answers, were forgiven, disarmed, disfranchised, fined, and/or banished. Only then, on November 7, could Mistress Hutchinson, "the head of all this faction . . . the breeder and nourisher of all these distempers . . . a woman of haughty and fierce carriage, of a nimble wit and active spirit," be brought safely to trial.[6] And even with all his pretrial maneuvers, Winthrop further shored up his strength by holding the meeting of the General Court in Newtown, that is, outside Boston.

Because Hutchinson's trial could end in her banishment, she could only be tried by the General Court. It was neither a criminal court moderated by a justice nor a supreme court with a panel of justices but rather the entire colonial government of governor, magistrates, and town representatives. While usually functioning as a legislature, the General Court did serve as the highest judiciary in the colony. In this incredible confrontation with the amassed political authority of the colony, Hutchinson revealed her formidable intellectual prowess. For one and one-half days she ran circles around her opponents. They quoted Scripture; she quoted back. They interpreted a verse against her; she responded with an alternative text. Winthrop began with a lengthy, condemnatory, rather frightening speech accusing her of disturbances, errors, and discord; he then demanded a response. She replied that she could not answer charges until she knew precisely what they were. She put Winthrop immediately on the defensive, for he had very few specific charges, and those he did have were supported only by hearsay.

He first said that she broke the Fifth Commandment—Honor thy father and thy mother—because she countenanced those who had signed the Wheelwright petitions and challenged the authority of the General Court, that is, their parents. She responded that she might entertain persons as children of God without approving their transgression. After a quick verbal thrust and parry, a frustrated Winthrop asserted that she did adhere to the petitioners' cause, she did endeavor to promote their faction, and thus she dishonored the magistrates, who stood as her parents, breaking the Fifth Commandment. Further, the Court did "not mean to discourse with those of your sex."[7] Undoubtedly, Winthrop hoped to silence her, and perhaps calm the uneasiness of the General Court, by dismissing the right and ability of a woman to hold, maintain, and debate a dissenting opinion. However, such flourishes did not change the fact that debates with this woman continued.

Winthrop moved on to her private meetings. The Scriptures clearly forbade women to teach publicly, but, answered Hutchinson, her home was not public, and the Bible taught the duty of elder women to instruct younger ones. When questioned about men attending these meetings, she insisted that at mixed ones only the men spoke, and Winthrop had no evidence to countermand her assertion. When Winthrop refused to acknowledge that her biblical citations provided a rule for her leadership, she asked whether she must "shew my name written therein?" In a second outburst of frustrated authority, Winthrop announced that the meetings must end because he said so. "We are your judges, and not you ours and we must compel you to it."[8] She agreed to accept the court's order.

However, her acquiescence did not satisfy the magistrates. They wanted her gone, for, as Deputy Governor Thomas Dudley complained during the trial, three years before the colony had been at peace, but from the moment that Hutchinson arrived, she had ignited great disturbances. Knowing that she was the primary problem, they sought weightier charges in order to banish her, and so they turned to her criticism of the clergy. If she had argued that the clergy were not preaching the true pathway to salvation, she implied that the colony's spiritual guides were beneath the regard of an ordinary congregant. The clergy believed, and the magistrates agreed, that such a view had to be curtailed and condemned, but Winthrop had to prove that Hutchinson had delivered such derogatory opinions. Initially, the magistrates' complaints sounded like hearsay and rumor. Magistrates had certainly heard the uncomplimentary opinions held by some Hutchinsonians about certain clergymen, but the magistrates had apparently never heard Hutchinson herself utter any such statements. Nor could they expect her followers to testify against her. Instead, Dudley and Winthrop opened a third fruitless dialogue, accusing Hutchinson of making statements that she then denied. Finally, cleric Hugh Peters, who hoped that he and other ministers "may not be thought to come as informers against the gentlewoman," proceeded to inform against her.[9] At the December conference, Peters reported, Hutchinson had discounted their abilities and spirituality. She had said that they preached a Covenant of Works, that is, salvation through human endeavor, and so argued that they were not true ministers of the Gospel. Several clerics testified to their own memory of her statements, providing corroboration for each other's accounts. Hutchinson challenged her clerical accusers, at one point asking John Wilson for the notes that he took at the conference. The day ended with yet another standoff.

On the following morning, Hutchinson brilliantly redirected and enlivened the proceedings by demanding that those clergymen testifying against her swear an oath. In this request, she invoked standard legal procedure. She had read Wilson's notes and she asserted that she remembered the conversations differently. This obvious affront to the clergymen's veracity ignited a self-righteous defense of the reliability and sincerity of the ministers, but doubt had been raised, and the clergy proved reluctant to swear, lending credence to Hutchinson's challenges. She then asked that three witnesses be called. Although supporter John Coggeshall was frightened into silence, and church elder Thomas Leverett proved able to utter only three sentences before he was rebuffed by Winthrop, a third witness delivered his troubling testimony in full. John Cotton had not wanted to testify, but his own memory of the conference agreed with Hutchinson's account. He regretted that he and his colleagues should be compared, but he did recall mild disagreements, and the difference was not then "so ill taken as it is [now] and our brethren did say also that they would not so easily believe reports as they had done and withall mentioned that they would speak no more of it, some of them did; and afterwards some of them did say they were less satisfied than before." He also asserted that he "did not find her saying they were under a covenant of works, nor that she said they did preach a covenant of works."[10]

By this point, the trial was proving a disaster for Winthrop. Hutchinson had responded to the initial charges with skill and finesse. She outmaneuvered her opponents in scriptural argument and then graciously agreed to their demands. The later, more serious charge of sedition against the ministry held great promise, but it had to be substantiated with ministers' reports of a private conference held a year before. Just as the momentum seemed strongest, Hutchinson derailed the prosecution with the reasonable demand for sworn testimony, underlining the weakness of the prosecution's evidence. In the midst of the procedural discussion, three witnesses challenged the clerical version of the conference; and, while two were easily silenced, Cotton's personal authority and prestige demanded the court's attention. Winthrop was running out of arguments. Hoping to invoke the law to legitimate proceeding against Hutchinson, Winthrop found that she could use the trial to expose him and his government.

Hutchinson chose this moment to proclaim her vision. Turning to her own spiritual conversion, she told the court of her early religious experiences: her doubts, her ultimate dependence upon God, and God's response to her pleas. She granted that she had become "more choice" in selecting a minister, for God had led her to distinguish the voices of truth.

> *Mr. Nowell:* How do you know that that was the spirit?
> *Mrs. H.:* How did Abraham know that it was God that bid him offer his son, being a breach of the sixth commandment?
> *Dep. Gov.:* By an immediate voice.
> *Mrs. H.:* So to me by an immediate revelation.
> *Dep. Gov.:* How! an immediate revelation.
> *Mrs. H.:* By the voice of his own spirit to my soul.[11]

Pouncing upon her testimony, Winthrop and other accusers pursued this question of revelation. They believed that any claim to a miraculous revelation was blasphemy, for the age of miracles had long passed. By the end of the proceedings, the overwhelming majority of the court would agree with Winthrop's disingenuous conclusion: "Pass by all that hath been said formerly and her own speeches have been ground enough for us to proceed upon."[12]

Had she really condemned herself? The examination continued long after her extraordinary claim, and new witnesses testified to previous prophetic declarations. Still, this testimony produced not an immediate censure but a prolonged debate upon the nature of revelation itself. In the Puritan mind, claiming revelation was not necessarily blasphemy. When asked to denounce her, Cotton refused, and instead began a protracted, abstract discourse upon the two types of revelation: the miraculous and the providential. A miraculous, direct revelation would represent a delusion; however, any believer might recognize and interpret a special Providence, or symbolic revelation communicated through the workings of nature. He could not judge her without further clarification, and while Hutchinson expressed her conviction in a special Providence, her opponents accused her of prophesying the miraculous. Another stalemate threatened. At this point, the court returned to earlier charges, and three ministers did testify under oath. This testimony satisfied those members of the court who believed that she was dangerous, but hesitated to pass judgment without following proper legal procedures. With satisfied consciences, the General Court avoided the labyrinth of proving blasphemy and, resting comfortably with sedition, banished Anne Hutchinson.

Many historians have judged Hutchinson weak in proclaiming her revelations. Surely a woman who displayed such intelligence during her trial knew better than to open this door. However, the moment might also be seen as one of exceptional strength. She began by warning, "Now if you do condemn me for speaking what in my conscience I know to be truth I must commit myself unto the Lord."[13] She seemed to revel in her prophetic moment, as the court remained riveted upon her words. The leadership wanted, indeed needed, these revelations discounted, and several witnesses tried, without much success. More than providing evidence against her, Hutchinson's claims of direct revelation seem to have frightened Winthrop. He revealed this anxiety in his own analysis:

> Mistress *Hutchinson* having thus freely and fully discovered herself, the Court and all the rest of the Assembly . . . did observe a special providence of God, that . . . her own mouth should deliver her into the power of the Court, as guilty of that which all suspected her for, but were not furnished with proof sufficient to proceed against her, for here she hath manifested, that her opinions and practise have been the cause of all our disturbances, & that she walked by such a rule as cannot stand with the peace of any State; for such bottomless revelations . . . if they be allowed in one thing, must be admitted a rule in all things; for they being above reason and Scripture, they are not subject to control.[14]

Long suspected of charisma grounded in her prophetic revelations, Hutchinson undermined the authority of secular and sacred leaders with her own spiritual power. At last she had openly claimed her own spiritual authority, for which her opponents were profoundly grateful, but they remained unable to convince many people, including Cotton, that her pronouncements were blasphemous. Winthrop and the clergy returned to charges of sedition and procedural rules of evidence, winning her banishment with the agreement of all but three participants. Winthrop must indeed have been satisfied.

Following this trial, the Hutchinsonian community divided. Some acknowledged their fault and remained in Massachusetts; some followed Wheelwright to a new colony in what would become New Hampshire; others, including the Hutchinson family, settled in Rhode Island. Because she was sentenced at the beginning of winter, the court extended a questionable mercy, permitting Hutchinson to remain in the colony until the spring but demanding that she live in the home of an unsympathetic clergyman. While many of her followers, including her husband and her young children, moved on to Rhode Island, Hutchinson became the unhappy focus of extensive clerical counsel. Supposedly in the interest of her conviction, repentance, and ultimate salvation, ministers engaged in an intellectual barrage that explored esoteric questions and doctrines that had been raised in neither of the 1636 conferences nor in her examination before the General Court. All of this material would be brought forward to her final examinations before the church.

A congregation had authority solely over its members, and the only sentences that a congregation could pass against a member were admonition, suspension from membership, or excommunication. A church trial such as this one usually represented the last efforts of a community to bring one of its errant members back into the fold; all of those penalties, including excommunication, were meant to sound an alarm and recall the lost saint to godliness. In moving to such examinations at this point, the community was working completely backwards. Generally, a church member might be dealt with by her church, but if she proved unrepentant to the point of excommunication, and her sins were egregious, she might then be charged before the government. To be fair, ministers may not have wanted to risk a church trial until this point. Hutchinson might well have survived unscathed, since the majority of the Boston Church members were her followers. Bringing her to a church trial after her banishment had been ordered would be quite after the fact. Was this merely a vindictive clergy seeking further revenge? What did the clergy hope to accomplish?

Of course, the Boston Church, in March 1638, had been chastised and transformed. Many Hutchinsonians were simply no longer in Boston, while others had acquiesced to the government's demands. Thus, a new Boston Church considered charges against Hutchinson. The examination explored her beliefs concerning the soul's immortality, the body's resurrection, and the union of the individual spirit to Christ—questions that she only began to explore at the insistence of the clergy that winter. As Hutchinson repeatedly noted, none of these questions had been asked before. However, by pushing her to assert opinions on complex questions that she had not much considered, the clergy might evoke heretical statements that no knowledgeable theologian would uphold. As predicted, her accusers were dissatisfied with her responses, and the congregation ordered John Cotton to deliver the sentence of admonition, because she respected him so highly. Unsaid, but of great importance to the other clergy, was the fact that delivering this admonition would fix Cotton's alignment with the majority position. A week later, Hutchinson again appeared before the church, acknowledging errors of extravagant expressions. She also tried to accept responsibility for her errors and to confess that she had slighted the ministers, but her sincerity was challenged. She was repenting only those errors discovered after November and left untouched the questions raised at her November trial. Her failure to address those issues was a mutual one; her examiners did not want to revisit a primary focus of continued disagreement. The theological issues were murky, her continued adherence to her revelations troubling, but, fortunately for her accusers, her "insincerity" made her a liar. Because she had troubled the church with errors, upheld her revelations, and had "made a Lye," she was excommunicated. She left the congregation for the last time accompanied by one person, her longtime follower Mary Dyer.

Anne Hutchinson then joined her family in Rhode Island. William served in the leadership of the new community, and the two grew frustrated at the bickering among the residents. After William died in 1642, Hutchinson and her seven younger children moved to Long Island where, in August 1643, she and six of the seven children were killed by Indians. In this violent end, some New Englanders found the divine vindication of Winthrop's work and judgment. "I never heard that the Indians in those parts did ever before this, commit the like outrage upon any one family, or families, and therefore God's hand is the more apparently seen herein, to pick out this woeful woman, to make her and those belonging to her, an unheard of heavy example of their cruelty above all others."[15]

Looking back over those three years during the first decade's settlement, the Hutchinsonians represented many threats to the governing elite. Personally, Winthrop had lost support among Boston's leadership and his premier position, sitting as deputy under twenty-two-year-old Governor Vane. The Hutchinsonian crisis also involved competition between Boston and the outlying towns that would support Winthrop against his own community. The theological differences were problematic, though initially resolvable, since both sides agreed that divine grace was freely granted, human effort had no impact upon salvation, and sanctified behavior was evidence of election. The involvement of the laity in the debates, and its criticism of the standing clergy, exacerbated the situation as people on each side, both clerical and lay, began to oversimplify issues and stereotype their opponents.

Still, the Hutchinsonian crisis involved more than politics, social conflict, and theological disputes. Under both of the trials and all of the accounts ran a current of male fury at the audacity of a woman to challenge the patriarchal magisterium. At her November trial, magistrates grieved that in leading these private meetings she was stepping outside her prescribed role. Winthrop would later say that she was more husband than wife, and he described William as "a man of very mild temper and weak parts, and wholly guided by his wife."[16] Additionally, extremely vindictive, misogynist comments followed the childbirth tragedies experienced by Mary Dyer and Anne Hutchinson. Dyer's deformed child was stillborn in October 1637, while Hutchinson was reported to have given birth to some thirty monsters in Rhode Island. "And see how the wisdom of God fitted this judgement to her sin every way, for look as [Hutchinson] had vented misshapen opinions, so she must bring forth deformed monsters." Both Dyer's and Hutchinson's deformed infants were seen as judgments: clear, harsh expressions of divine displeasure. Thomas Weld asserted that "God himself was pleased to step in . . . as clearly as if he had pointed with his finger, in causing the two fomenting women in the time of the height of the Opinions to produce out of their wombs, as before they had out of their brains, such monstrous births as no Chronicle (I think) hardly ever recorded."[17] These were punishments tied to, or perhaps growing out of, their corrupt femaleness. Weld seemed to say that she was a disgusting woman, an unwomanly woman. She could not even give birth.

Overall, it really is not surprising that the Puritan ministers and magistrates, committed as they were to their own patriarchal authority, would do everything possible to destroy her. She was a powerful woman who had attracted a significant community of female followers, and her example as a religious leader could have brought women to question their own acceptance of a subordinate domestic role. Her punishment certainly served as a deterrent to any other woman who might step outside the household.

What is astonishing, however, is the trouble that she caused. If this truly had been an unbending patriarchal society, if Puritans truly felt that women had no authority and no power, they would not have worried about her. Rather than simply ignore her, or quietly censure her in church, the leadership brought her into clerical conferences and banished her from the colony, but not before further destroying her credibility through excommunication. Obviously, women could have power in this society in one of the colony's most important arenas—religion. Anne Hutchinson heard the voice of the Holy Spirit and said so. That is, she believed that God spoke through her, and so did many Bostonians. To women and men of influence, she spoke as a prophet.

Seventeenth-century Massachusetts was a paradoxical society that embraced an intense, personal spirituality and yet valued an ordered hierarchy as outlined in the Bible. People embraced the voice of the Holy Spirit, for it offered personal assurance of salvation and privileged community efforts to establish an exemplary biblical commonwealth. Still, Puritan leaders knew that God did not respect earthly inequalities of wealth, class, education, and gender. They knew that the ignorant, the poor, and women could be touched by the Spirit, and they did not want to share their civil or spiritual power with any women. The charismatic Hutchinson, whose experience of the Holy Spirit was revealed in prophetic speeches, undermined the established secular and sacred authority. An intellectually powerful woman who criticized clergymen represented a threat to order at many levels. During the state trial, Anne Hutchinson successfully countered biblical arguments and acceded to all demands that she cease public activity, yet she was still dangerous to the leaders. Even in silence, a woman claiming an authority from God that was recognized by the majority of her community represented a threat to the standing order. A woman who received revelations from God was under no civil or clerical control. In the end, although the ostensible cause for her banishment was sedition, the primary factors that drove her accusers were her leadership of women and men, her claims to prophetic revelations, and the challenge that these threats represented to their own magistracy and patriarchal power.

Notes

1. "Examination of Mrs. Hutchinson at the Court at Newtown," 1637, in David D. Hall, ed., *The Antinomian Controversy, 1636–1638: A Documentary History* (Middletown, CT, 1968), 348. The spelling in all quotations has been modernized.

2. "A Report of the Trial of Mrs. Anne Hutchinson before the Church in Boston," 1638, in Hall, ed., *Antinomian Controversy*, 370.

3. John Winthrop, *A Short Story of the Rise, reign, and ruine of the Antinomians, Familists & Libertines* (1644), in Hall, ed., *Antinomian Controversy*, 263.

4. Edward Johnson, *Wonder Working Providence of Sions Saviour in New England, 1628–1651* (1659; facsimile reprint, New York, 1974), 96.

5. John Winthrop, *Winthrop's Journal "History of New England," 1630–1649*, ed. James Kendall Hosmer (New York, 1908), 1:234.

6. Winthrop, *Short Story*, 262–63.

7. "Examination of Mrs. Hutchinson," 314.

8. Winthrop, *Short Story*, 269; "Examination of Mrs. Hutchinson," 316.

9. "Examination of Mrs. Hutchinson," 319.

10. Ibid., 332–37

11. Ibid., 336–37. This exchange is also summarized in Winthrop, *Short Story*, 273–74.

12. "Examination of Mrs. Hutchinson," 345.

13. Ibid., 337.

14. Winthrop, *Short Story*, 274.

15. Thomas Weld, "Preface" to Winthrop, *Short Story*, 218.

16. Winthrop, *Journal*, 1:299.

17. Weld, "Preface" to Winthrop, *Short Story*, 214. From the extraordinarily graphic descriptions provided by Winthrop, medical historians believe that Dyer's child was afflicted with severe spina bifida, while Hutchinson, possibly in menopause, expelled a hydatidiform mole.

Suggested Readings

Barker-Benfield, Ben. "Anne Hutchinson and the Puritan Attitude toward Women," *Feminist Studies* 1 (1972): 65–96. An outstanding interpretive essay analyzing the nature of Puritan religious culture in conflict with the society's commitment to patriarchal order.

Battis, Emery. *Saints and Sectaries: Anne Hutchinson and the Antinomian Controversy in the Massachusetts Bay Colony.* Chapel Hill, NC, 1962. Battis's psychological portrait of Hutchinson is grounded more on speculation than evidence, and the psychoanalytic theory he applies does not fit well with the evidence that does exist. However, his reconstruction of Hutchinson's male supporters is quite detailed and helpful.

Erikson, Kai T. *Wayward Puritans: A Study in the Sociology of Deviance,* 33–107. New York, 1966. An exploration of the nature of deviance through a historical study of three incidents in the early history of Massachusetts: the persecution of Quakers, 1656–1665; the Salem witch trials, 1692–1693; and the Hutchinsonian controversy.

Gura, Philip F. *A Glimpse of Sion's Glory: Puritan Radicalism in New England,* 237–75. Middletown, CT, 1984. A detailed discussion of Puritan dissent in New England that includes a rewarding chapter on Hutchinson.

Hall, David D., ed. *The Antinomian Controversy, 1636–1638: A Documentary*

History. Middletown, CT, 1968. Contains most of the key historical documents, including two independent accounts of the examination before the General Court. The first can be found in John Winthrop's *Short Story of the Rise, reign, and ruine of the Antinomians, Familists & Libertines.* The second account, "Examination of Mrs. Anne Hutchinson at the Court at Newtown," is an anonymous and less hostile transcription. The original document is now lost, but it was once appended by Thomas Hutchinson, Hutchinson's great-great-grandson, to his *History of the Colony and Province of Massachusetts Bay* (Boston, 1767).

Johnson, Edward. *Wonder Working Providence of Sions Saviour in New England, 1628–1651.* 1659; facsimile reprint, New York, 1974. A history of Massachusetts during its founding decades.

Koehler, Lyle. "The Case of the American Jezebels: Anne Hutchinson and Female Agitation during the Years of the Antinomian Turmoil, 1636–1640." *William and Mary Quarterly* 31 (1974): 55–78. An engaging essay examining Hutchinson and her female followers as forerunners to feminism.

Lang, Amy Shrager. *Prophetic Woman: Anne Hutchinson and the Problem of Dissent in the Literature of New England.* Berkeley, CA, 1987. A literary study looking at the history of Hutchinson's experience and its impact on nineteenth-century American literature.

Morgan, Edmund S. *The Puritan Dilemma: The Story of John Winthrop,* 134–54. Boston, 1958. A readable biography of Winthrop with a good, descriptive chapter on the Hutchinsonian crisis.

Norton, Mary Beth. *Founding Mothers and Fathers: Gendered Power and the Forming of American Society.* New York, 1996. A detailed analysis of gender politics in New England during its first fifty years that includes a chapter devoted to Hutchinson called "Husband, Preacher, Magistrate," 359–99.

Rutman, Darrett B. *Winthrop's Boston: Portrait of a Puritan, 1630–1649,* 135–63. New York, 1965. An excellent monograph on the first two decades of Boston's history, incorporating a fine chapter on the Hutchinsonian crisis and its relation to city and colony politics.

Westerkamp, Marilyn J. "Anne Hutchinson, Sectarian Mysticism, and the Puritan Order." *Church History* 59 (1990): 482–96. Places Hutchinson within the context of English Puritanism and argues for the importance of gender in understanding the conflict.

Williams, Selma R. *Divine Rebel: The Life of Anne Marbury Hutchinson.* New York, 1981. An extremely readable biography, studying Hutchinson in the context of English Puritan culture.

Winthrop, John. *Winthrop's Journal "History of New England," 1630–1649,* ed. James Kendall Hosmer. 2 vols. New York, 1908.

3

Caspar Wistar
German-American Entrepreneur and Cultural Broker

Rosalind J. Beiler

The life of Caspar Wistar (1696–1752) is a success story that seems stereotypical. Changing conditions in his native Palatinate encouraged him to leave home, and his savings allowed him to pay his own passage and thereby avoid indentured servitude in Pennsylvania. By his own account, he arrived in Philadelphia without any money and with a fellow immigrant as his only friend. Through good fortune or careful planning, Wistar quickly gained access to cash and credit. Within seven years of his arrival, he was an established button maker, a Quaker convert, a naturalized British subject, a property holder, and a merchant. Two years later he married into a prominent pioneering German Quaker family, and Wistar's political and business associations thereafter seem prudent, yet profitable. His role as adviser, employer, master, and landlord to a large number of new German immigrants may well have been mutually beneficial, although he was certainly in a position to exploit these people. As a new migrant of good family, Wistar was able to attract other German migrants and to broker legal business between arrivals and their homeland. Wistar's own prosperity was impressive; his ability to establish his seven children as substantial property holders was remarkable.

Rosalind J. Beiler's most recent monograph is entitled *Becoming American: The Transatlantic World of Caspar Wistar, 1650–1752*. She teaches early American history at the University of Central Florida.

On September 16, 1717, Caspar Wistar, a twenty-one-year-old German-speaking immigrant, stepped onto the dock in Philadelphia. According to his own account, he had spent all but nine pence of his life savings on the voyage, and had borrowed three *pistolines* from Abraham Riehm, his only friend on the ship. When his shipmates went in search of something to eat and drink, the young man was forced to wander the

The research for this essay has been supported by the Fulbright Commission, The Philadelphia Center for Early American Studies, The Pennsylvania Historical and Museum Commission, Harrisburg, and The Henry Francis du Pont Library at Winterthur, Wilmington, Delaware.

streets because he could not afford the taverns' prices. Like his contemporary, Benjamin Franklin, Wistar purchased a loaf of bread and then set out to explore the city. He soon met a cider maker, who offered to pay him in apples in return for his help. His poverty and his first American meal of apples and bread made a lasting impression on the young immigrant.

Wistar may have been nearly penniless when he first arrived in Pennsylvania, but by the time he died in 1752, he was a prominent, wealthy leader among the German-speaking community in this British colony. The story of his position among fellow immigrants is intricately woven together with his meteoric rise from rags to riches. Wistar does not fit the traditional definition of a cultural broker; he never acted as an official interpreter or a treaty negotiator between European and Amerindian peoples, nor did he consciously set out to become a leader among his fellow immigrants. Instead, Wistar sought economic security and the social status that had eluded his family in Europe. A combination of the particular circumstances in Pennsylvania and his creative use of those conditions propelled him into his mediating role.

What were the strategies that Wistar used to secure his position in British America? How did his pursuit of wealth contribute to his rise as a leader? Wistar's role as a cultural broker evolved as he struggled for survival in the new and very different environment of eighteenth-century Pennsylvania. First, he set out to develop professional connections through religious institutions and family networks. Second, he shrewdly used his reputation, creativity, and credit to provide services to the Pennsylvania Proprietors. Finally, Wistar tapped into a common cultural identity to help other immigrants like himself begin their lives in America. By pursuing profits and simultaneously offering aid to immigrants, Wistar helped to bridge the gap between Anglo-American and German-speaking cultural groups in colonial Pennsylvania. In the process, he gained the economic stability that he had set out to achieve.

The young man's story begins, however, on the other side of the Atlantic in Waldhilsbach, a small village southeast of Heidelberg. Wistar was born and baptized there in 1696 as Hans Caspar Wüster.[1] The firstborn son of a forester or hunter, he and his family belonged to the growing government bureaucracy of the Elector of the Palatinate, a small principality in what is today Germany. That membership influenced almost every aspect of the Wüsters' daily lives: it determined their occupations and economic status, it affected their relationships with their neighbors, and it influenced their decisions about religious affiliation.

As foresters and hunters, Wistar's grandfather and father were responsible for protecting the state's natural resources and for helping to gain revenue from them. They also aided the Elector in his elaborately staged hunts designed to impress the aristocracy and heads of other states. At a time when burgeoning government bureaucracies symbolized the wealth and power of the state, official positions promised appealing social status and economic security.

Performing the tasks of a forester, however, required a fine balancing act. By the early eighteenth century, land and resources were shrinking as the Palatinate recovered from a century of wars and as the population once again began to expand. While the government sought to increase its revenues from the forests, villagers struggled to hold on to land and usage rights that they had claimed for centuries. Foresters were caught in the middle of this tug-of-war. If, in the line of duty, a forester denied his neighbors access to firewood or meadows too severely, villagers could make his life miserable—as Wistar's father discovered. His neighbors filed a lengthy suit against him when they believed he had abused his power as a forester, and they made it difficult for him to purchase village property. On the other hand, if he did not properly protect the state's resources from his neighbors, a forester could easily be replaced by someone whose patronage connections in the Elector's court were stronger. Wistar grew up in this world, where negotiating between various interests was interwoven with every aspect of his daily life and where opportunity was increasingly limited.

According to his own account, Wistar received little formal education as a child. Instead, he worked for his father, hunting and fowling, until he was a teenager. When he was seventeen, he went to the Elector's hunting lodge at Bruchhausen, where he served the chief huntsman, Georg Michael Förster, as an apprentice. The prestige associated with his position in the Elector's entourage is evident in the substantial salary he supposedly received: 69 *Gulden*, 20 *Kreuzer* (£7.5 sterling), a clothing allowance, and a per diem allowance while performing government duties. In comparison, his father received an annual salary of 64 *Gulden* (£7 sterling), 16 *Malter* of wheat, and free firewood for his tasks as a forester. (A Pennsylvania laborer's family of four needed £32 sterling to cover the costs of food, clothing, heat, and shelter for one year in 1762.) While Wistar was at Bruchhausen, however, a series of changes occurred in the government that created difficulties for foresters and hunters. The new Elector, who came to power in 1716, ordered a series of reforms and salary freezes in the forestry administration. For the next three years, foresters and hunters received little of their pay as their superiors worked to trim costs and positions from the bureaucracy.

In the midst of these freezes and at a time when prospects for newly trained hunters looked particularly grim, "the Lord of all Lords inspired" Wistar to travel to Pennsylvania.[2] Family traditions maintain that his father offered to give Wistar his forester's position, which the young man would have inherited as the oldest son, if he remained at home. But his own account notes that his heart was so taken with the "new land" that he refused to stay, despite the emotional trauma of leaving home against his parents' wishes. Instead, he said a tearful good-bye to family and friends, collected the money he had managed to save, and boarded a ship for Philadelphia.

When Wistar arrived in the city in 1717, the conditions he found in Philadelphia forced him to the bottom of colonial society. In contrast to the Palatinate, Pennsylvania had no forestry administration; William Penn and his descendants did not command a corps of hunters. The difference between the two worlds meant that Wistar could not do the job for which he had trained in Europe. Consequently, he was reduced to hauling ashes for a soap maker named John Bearde, a job well below the social status of a Palatine hunter and forester. To complicate matters, Wistar could not communicate well in English. As a result, he suffered from misunderstandings with his master's wife and feared that he was not working hard enough.

Although his station as a wage laborer made a lasting impression on the immigrant, Wistar did not remain in his humble position for long. Within a year and a half, he began an apprenticeship as a brass button maker, an occupation he continued to pursue throughout his life. Long after he became a wealthy merchant and land speculator, the immigrant still identified himself as a brass button maker. For Wistar, promotion from a wage laborer to an artisan was the first step in securing his place in his new home.

While he was working to obtain some job security, Wistar also set out to raise his social status. An apprenticeship as a button maker was one step above hauling ashes, but it carried little of the prestige that he associated with being a government official in the Palatinate. The young man had watched his father's status among his neighbors vacillate as changes at court shifted his patronage connections. He assumed that in America, as in Europe, his place in society depended on establishing relationships with the right people.

One of the ways that Wistar improved his position was by seeking out

Quaker patrons. Shortly after his arrival, he realized the importance of Quaker merchants in Penn's colony. Wealthy Friends controlled much of Philadelphia's economy and dominated provincial politics. Like his grandfather and father, who sought patrons in the Elector's governmental bureaucracy to elevate their social position, Wistar understood the importance of finding Quaker sponsors.

Perhaps the most obvious group of Quaker patrons whom Wistar sought were the German-speaking Friends at Germantown who had preceded him to the colony. Common language and culture created an instant bond between him and the settlers there. A group of Quaker families from Krefeld, a town in the Rhine River Valley not far from the Palatinate, had settled Germantown in 1683. In the following twenty-five years, additional families from villages close to Wistar's home joined the earliest settlers of the town. When the young man arrived in 1717, many of his shipmates had family and friends who had already settled in Germantown. Although he claimed to have only one friend in the colony, the people at Germantown understood the world that Wistar had left behind, and he knew their leaders were well connected to Pennsylvania's government.

The immigrant's first step toward acquiring Quaker patrons was to change his religious affiliation. Wistar was the son of a Lutheran father and a Reformed mother. He and a sister were baptized in the Reformed Church, while their seven siblings were baptized according to Lutheran rituals. Furthermore, a brother and two sisters converted to the Catholic Church upon becoming adults. The ecumenical nature of Wistar's family resulted from the peculiar circumstances of the Palatinate during the period. Traditionally, the ruling Elector determined the official church. Consequently, Lutheran and Catholic subjects were baptized, married, and buried in the Reformed Church throughout the second half of the seventeenth century, while continuing to think of themselves as Lutheran or Catholic. Between 1680 and 1705, however, frequent changes in power led the government to recognize publicly the legitimacy of all three churches. Thereafter, Wüster family members chose the religious affiliation most likely to promote their positions as officials or within their communities.

Changes in public affiliation, however, did not diminish the importance of their religious beliefs. Family members shared personal assumptions about their spiritual lives that remained distinct from their stated affiliation with a particular church. The spiritual language that Wistar used in his American letters to his widowed mother and siblings in Europe indicates a common set of beliefs even though they all belonged to different churches. For the Wüsters, therefore, joining the church of one's patrons was not a sign of insincerity or a lack of religious conviction. It was simply the continuation of a long-standing division in the Palatinate between public religious affiliation and private belief.

Like his father and siblings in Europe, Wistar realized the importance of religious connections for establishing his reputation in Pennsylvania. As early as 1721, the immigrant indicated his Quaker sympathies by signing a declaration of allegiance to the King of England rather than swearing an oath. The declaration was a legal tool designed to permit Quakers, who had scruples against taking oaths, to promise loyalty to Great Britain. By 1726, Wistar had become a member of the Philadelphia Monthly Meeting of Friends and thereby gained entrance into the dominant network of merchants and political leaders in the province.

At the same time he was seeking Quaker patrons, Wistar joined the ranks of American property holders. In 1721 he purchased a prime city lot on High Street in Philadelphia. Precisely how he raised £210 "American Money" (£153 sterling) in less than four years to acquire the property remains a mystery. Wistar entered Philadelphia during a period when opportunities for artisans to invest in real estate were greater than in Boston or New York. While it seems unlikely that he saved the entire amount from his apprenticeship wages, he may have supplemented his savings with an informal loan from a Germantown or Philadelphia Quaker.

Wistar soon took further measures to secure his property. According to British law, the children of non-British immigrants could not inherit land unless their parents had become naturalized citizens. While provincial governments tried to guarantee such rights for their settlers, Parliament and the courts in the mother country did not always approve their attempts. News of the legal difficulties that Pennsylvania Germans faced in leaving legacies of land spread back to Europe. Several months after Wistar arrived, Pennsylvania's Commissioners of Property warned some of his shipmates that the government could not guarantee their rights to pass on land to their heirs. The newcomers replied that they were already aware of the colony's laws and responded favorably to the recommendation that they become naturalized British subjects.

Wistar, like his fellow immigrants, clearly understood the potential danger of losing his investment. While most of his shipmates did not become citizens until later, he submitted a petition to the legislature requesting naturalization in 1724. Within several months, the assembly passed an act that gave Wistar, fellow German John Cratho, and French immigrant Nicholas Gateau the right to "have and enjoy all lands and tenements . . . by way of purchase or gift of any person or persons whatsoever . . . as if they had been born natural subjects of this province."[3]

Wistar's naturalization act went beyond property concerns, however. It included an additional clause granting the petitioners the privilege of participating in international trade. The act stated that they were "free and fully able and capable to trade, traffic, load, freight and transport all and all manner of goods, wares and merchandises not by law prohibited to be imported or exported, as if they had been of the natural liege people and subjects of the King of Great Britain born in this province."[4] Wistar's bill was the third private naturalization act to be passed in the colony, and none of the previous ones had included trading privileges.

The success of Wistar's petition indicates that he had established his reputation among the "better sort" of Pennsylvanians. At the same time that his bill was under consideration, the assembly debated another naturalization petition from a group of nearly four hundred German-speaking settlers. Isaac Norris, a member of the Provincial Council, noted that the petitioners were "mostly unknown to the Assembly or the better sort of the Inhabitants."[5] The legislators echoed Norris's sentiment when they determined that local officials should inquire into the petitioners' "Characters, Belief and Behavior" before issuing certificates qualifying them for naturalization.[6] Interestingly enough, the assembly required no character references for Wistar; two days after its debate, it approved his bill. The fact that he was acquainted with at least one influential Quaker legislator, Anthony Morris, undoubtedly worked in his favor. Just three years earlier, Wistar had signed the will of his father, Anthony Morris Sr., as a witness.

Wistar's naturalization also signaled the beginning of his diverse American career. By 1724 he very likely had completed his apprenticeship as a button maker and set up his own business. Wistar had been in the colony long enough to be familiar with the career trajectories of Philadelphia's "better sort." Like many of them, he intended to add mercantile activities to his artisan profession. In 1725 he joined eight partners in establishing the Abbington Iron Furnace in New Castle County (in present-day Delaware). At least one of the partners, Thomas Rutter, was a Germantown resident of Quaker background. Many of the other investors were Philadelphia merchants; several served in the legislature. At the same time, Wistar began to import hardware and other merchandise from continental Europe. By 1726 the thirty-year-old immigrant was listed in the *Weekly Mercury* as one of the "principal" merchants of Philadelphia.

Having established himself as a merchant and investor, Wistar turned his efforts toward beginning a family. Early in 1726 he had applied to the Philadelphia Monthly Meeting for permission to marry, as was customary for Quakers in good standing. One of the men appointed to verify his status as an upstanding Friend was Evan Owen, Wistar's partner in the Abbington Iron Furnace. In May his request was approved, and he married Catharine Jansen, the American-born daughter of Dirk and Margaret Milan Jansen. Catharine's parents were well-established Germantown Quakers who had lived in the colony for more than twenty-five years. By the time of Wistar's marriage, Dirk Jansen owned a considerable amount of land and was a justice of the peace for Philadelphia County.

In marrying Catharine Jansen, Wistar chose a wife from a background similar to his own family's class of officials in the Palatinate. A justice of the peace was the closest position in Pennsylvania's local government structure to Waldhilsbach's village magistrate. Just as his father had attempted to secure his position in the village by marrying the daughter of the magistrate and Reformed elder, so Wistar chose the daughter of a Quaker justice of the peace as his wife. An alliance with the Jansen family anchored his position in Pennsylvania society and signaled his acceptance among the German Quaker community.

By 1726, Wistar had succeeded in creating a place for himself in the British colonies. He had trained in a new occupation, built patronage relationships within religious and family networks, and entered the career path of prominent Philadelphia merchants. Wistar's success resulted from his creative adaptation of his European experience to his Pennsylvania context. Conditions in the colony, however, allowed him to move well beyond the world he had known as a child.

Having established his presence and reputation among Philadelphia and Germantown Quakers, Wistar turned his energies toward ensuring economic security for his children. The couple's first son, Richard, was born in 1727; and over the next thirteen years, there were six more children. To obtain the land and wealth necessary to ensure the future of his growing family, Wistar courted the favor of Pennsylvania's Proprietary family and their agents. Two specific sets of circumstances—the chaotic state of Pennsylvania's Proprietary affairs and the simultaneous influx of German-speaking immigrants—aided Wistar's entrepreneurial pursuits. He astutely recognized the governing family's needs and shrewdly set out to furnish a solution that would enhance his position and his income.

Wistar had entered the colony at a time when Pennsylvania's political affairs were in a state of confusion. One year after his arrival, Proprietor

William Penn had died in England. In his will, Penn left most of his American holdings to his three sons: John, Thomas, and Richard. When Penn's children by his first wife contested the will, a lengthy legal battle for control of the colony ensued. While the suit wound its way through the British court system, the trustees assigned to oversee Penn's affairs in America hesitated to sell land to anyone. Since it was not clear who held the Proprietary rights to the colony, the appropriate authority for offering clear land titles also remained in doubt.

Penn's estate was finally settled in 1727, in the same year that Richard Wistar was born and Wistar's brother John arrived in the colony. By that time, the elder Wistar recognized the value of investing in Pennsylvania land. New settlers were arriving in large numbers, and anyone who owned property could make a nice profit. Since Penn's sons inherited a substantial mortgage with the colony, they were interested in generating as much revenue as possible from land sales. Consequently, anyone with access to capital could profit from buying land.

Wistar bought his first large tract in 1728 when the Commissioners of Property agreed to sell him two thousand acres in the colony's back-country in return for £153 sterling in bills of exchange and £128 in Pennsylvania money. Not only was Wistar willing to pay the going rate of 50 percent on his bills of exchange, but he also paid cash for additional land. Having befriended James Steel, the Penns' land agent, Wistar persuaded the Proprietors to sell him twenty-five hundred additional acres the following year. Between 1729 and Thomas Penn's arrival in the colony in 1732, the immigrant was one of Pennsylvania's few sources of income for its debt-ridden Proprietors.

In addition to supplying revenue, Wistar also was willing to invest his capital in risky real estate ventures. Two tracts of land in his original 1728 purchase were in a territory that the Penns had not yet bought from the Delaware Indians. More than one-third of the immigrant's second major land transaction, which Steel had negotiated on his behalf, was in tribal territory. Although the Commissioners of Property discouraged the Penns from selling land before buying it from the Indians, the Proprietors were more concerned with raising money than with the legality of their land titles.

Wistar not only purchased land without clear title, but he also participated in some of the Penns' more controversial strategies to raise revenue. The immigrant was among the "eight close Proprietary associates" who received land in a private lottery after the Penns' public lottery scheme of 1735 failed. The Proprietors had hoped to net £15,000 by selling tickets for unsettled land. When they discovered that the plan was illegal because the colony had a law against lotteries, they held a secret drawing instead in which Wistar received over five thousand acres.

Once again, he purchased property that the Penns had no right to sell; efforts to clear the title to some of the lottery land resulted in the famous Walking Purchase of 1737, a legally questionable transaction. To justify the purchase, William Penn's sons produced an old document that Penn had negotiated with the Delaware Indians in 1686. According to the document, the boundaries of the purchase were to be measured by the distance a man could walk in a day and a half. Penn's sons claimed that although their father had paid the price for the land, the walk had never occurred. After careful planning, walkers marked off a region that was much larger than the Indians had intended and that included the land sold two years earlier through the private lottery. By investing in the lottery land, Wistar proved willing to take part in risky transactions while providing a solid source of revenue for the Proprietors.

A second set of circumstances that aided Wistar in his land speculation and in courting the favor of the Proprietors was the influx of immigrants into the colony. In the decade following Wistar's arrival, several shiploads of settlers had docked at Philadelphia's port and numerous German-speaking colonists from New York had migrated to Pennsylvania at the invitation of Governor William Keith. Issues of immigration quickly became intertwined with land-settlement policies and political maneuvering in the colony.

James Logan, one of the Trustees listed in Penn's will and the family's Pennsylvania agent, noted constantly the problems created by immigrants while the legal battle over Penn's legacy raged in England. He reported to Penn's widow in 1726 that the family's interests were suffering: "Your lands to the Northw[ar]d are overrun by a number of those unruly Palatines . . . invited hither in 1722 by Sr. William [Keith] . . . and the southern parts are in the same manner possessed by as disorderly persons who have lately floc'd in . . . from Ireland."[7] Because the Trustees could not grant clear titles to new settlers, immigrants simply squatted on land that appeared uninhabited and claimed they would pay for it when Penn's estate was settled. By 1726, Logan believed that nearly one hundred thousand acres were "possessed by persons, who resolutely sitt down and improve, without any manner of Right or Pretense to it."[8] While he may have been exaggerating the amount of land claimed by the squatters, new colonists were posing a very real problem for officials trying to settle the colony in an orderly fashion.

Nor did immigration problems subside. In 1727, Logan reported that instead of the three ships of German-speaking settlers that were expected, a total of six with more than twelve hundred foreigners had arrived. In addition, eight or nine ships had landed at New Castle from the north of Ireland. The Palatine and Irish newcomers all predicted large numbers of fellow countrymen planning to make the journey the following year. "Both these sorts sitt frequently down on any spott of vacant Land they can find without asking questions," Logan reported.[9] He believed that few of those who were settling the land had the means to purchase it. Consequently, Logan proposed that the Penns grant the land to others who could pay cash and extend credit to the new settlers. The only other option was for the Penns to rent to the squatters. Rents, however, had proven impossible to collect in the Lower Counties (Delaware), where a boundary dispute with Lord Baltimore of Maryland threatened the settlers' titles. Logan believed that the new squatters would use a similar rationale for refusing to pay rents until the family's legal affairs were clarified.

Isaac Norris, another Trustee, was pessimistic about how to obtain money from the German "free Booters or those voluntary or unlicensed settlers on your lands." Norris believed that the "large number, the insolence of some, & the povertie of most" would make the situation difficult to handle. He suggested that it would "require some person or Persons of great care & discretion to be the active agents in agreeing with those settlers."[10]

Although he was not officially appointed as such an agent, Wistar proved to be precisely the kind of person whom Norris was looking for. Wistar had established his reputation as a Philadelphia Quaker merchant and investor who was a partner with several political figures in the Abbington Iron Furnace. He was a solid source of credit and cash at a time when specie and bills of exchange were difficult to find in the colony. Wistar was also a German-speaking immigrant who could communicate with the new arrivals. Through his land purchases, Wistar allowed the Proprietors and their agents to settle German immigrants in a more orderly fashion.

At the most basic level, Wistar helped to sort out the trustworthy Germans from the "lower sorts." He gave advice on the reputations of his fellow countrymen who wanted to purchase land. The Commissioners of Property, for example, noted next to Thomas Hean's request for a warrant that Wistar had verified his honest character and promised that Hean would pay for his land. Throughout the next decade, Wistar and his father-in-law vouched for the credibility of German immigrants and submitted payments to the commissioners on their behalf.

As a land speculator, Wistar also provided a solution to the problems of German-speaking squatters. Between 1729 and his death in 1752, he received patents for more than twenty thousand acres of unimproved land in Philadelphia, Bucks, and Lancaster Counties. Most of that land he resold to German immigrants and their descendants; indeed, most of the purchasers of Wistar's land recorded in Philadelphia County deeds prior to 1777 had German names. Similarly, a majority of the people who bought his land in Berks, Bucks, Lancaster, Montgomery, and Northampton Counties were of German descent. In many cases, Wistar's purchasers—the squatters about whom Logan and Norris had complained—were already living on the property he had sold them. By acquiring large tracts and reselling them to German immigrants, Wistar furnished the Proprietors with the means for clearing up titles in the colony's backcountry.

Thus Wistar, in pursuing financial security, surveyed the opportunities around him. He recognized that the Proprietors' agents controlled land, the primary form of wealth in Pennsylvania. By building on his reputation, his access to capital, and his cultural background, Wistar made his services indispensable to the Penns. In purchasing backcountry land, he provided them with much needed revenue and a solution to the problems of settling new immigrants.

The Penns were not the only ones to benefit from Wistar's land speculation, however. The newcomers needed someone to help them get a start in the New World in the same way that the Germantown Quakers had helped Wistar. By giving them advice, selling them land, lending them money, and purchasing the contracts of indentured servants, he aided German-speaking immigrants in adjusting to their new life. Wistar's attempts to help his fellow immigrants had begun even before their departure from Europe. In 1732, after conditions aboard the ships arriving in Philadelphia began to deteriorate, he wrote a letter to potential settlers in Europe that was published throughout the Rhine Valley. In it, Wistar described a ship in which a large number of the passengers had died as a result of the deplorable conditions on board. The survivors were "nearly all sick, weak, and worst of all, poor and without means, in consequence of which they are a heavy burden on the residents here, where money is very scarce."[11] Wistar recommended, therefore, that individuals make their decision to emigrate carefully, and he gave practical advice to those who determined to make the journey.

In addition to the conditions on the voyage, Wistar prepared potential settlers for what they might expect in Pennsylvania. He noted that the colony was "for some years past a very good country, and like all other new colonies, little inhabited." As a result, early immigrants such as he had been able to purchase large tracts for small amounts of money: "Because the wild land called for much labor . . . we were glad when ships arrived here bringing Germans, for these were at once redeemed, and by their labor earned so much that they too soon were able to purchase land." In the meantime, however, so many German, Irish, and English people had settled in Pennsylvania "that now he who wishes to obtain land must seek it far in the wilderness, and pay dear for it besides."[12]

While at first glance his letter seems to contradict the interests of a speculator who wanted purchasers for the forty-five hundred acres he had acquired, Wistar's advice actually worked to his advantage. Not only did the widespread circulation of his letter offer name recognition to potential immigrants, but it also portrayed him as a benefactor. Wistar became identified as someone who would help immigrants in need. Consequently, those who decided that they had the resources to travel to Pennsylvania often turned to him for help. At the same time, his letter forewarned settlers of the high prices that Wistar was charging for his properties. When families did not have sufficient cash to buy land, he provided them with mortgages.

Wistar also aided fellow Germans by extending them credit. As early as 1733 he was attempting to retrieve money from the family members of Heinrich Hiestand at Ibersheimer Hoff in the Palatinate. He had lent Hiestand, who lived in Pennsylvania, 130 *Gulden*, 2 *Kopfstück* (£14 sterling). It took Wistar nine years to retrieve the sum from Hiestand's creditors in the Palatinate, and the process involved numerous people and connections in America and the Rhine and Neckar Valleys. In addition to other debts he retrieved from Europe, Wistar's inventory listed bonds, mortgages, and book debts valued at £23,209 Pennsylvania currency due his estate at his death. The overwhelming majority of the names listed on the bonds were German.

As the immigrant population shifted in the 1740s from family groups with some resources to young single men with little money, Wistar found additional ways to offer aid. He purchased indentures for those who arrived without the means to pay for their passage. To fulfill their contracts, they worked as brass button makers, laborers at his new glass manufactory, or servants in his home or shop. In 1746, German immigrant John Peter Lambert, with the consent of his mother, indentured himself as an apprentice to Wistar for thirteen years. As part of this contract, Wistar promised to teach the young man to read and write English. In that same year, Wistar paid for the passage of Abraham Zimmerman, Melchior Zimmerman, and Ursula Dichter in exchange for indentures of five, six, and seven years, respectively. By the 1750s most of the sixty people who earned their living at Wistar's New Jersey glassworks were indentured servants. In the inventory of his estate taken in 1752, four "Servant Lads" with German names were listed along with Wistar's button-making tools, and three servant girls were listed with his shop goods. In offering contracts to immigrants, Wistar helped them learn a trade and become familiar with Anglo-American culture. Because he shared their heritage but also understood Pennsylvania's institutions, the entrepreneur acted as a cultural broker to the Germans migrating to the colony in the 1730s and 1740s.

While Wistar provided services to both the Proprietors and to other immigrants, his motives were not purely altruistic; he benefited tremendously from his position in the middle. His profits from land speculation were astounding. Of the 2,000 acres that he bought in 1729, Wistar sold 698 acres in parcels to Jacob Huddlestone, Henry Shate, Peter Andrews, and Jacob Stauffer. From the tracts sold, Wistar netted a profit of almost 200 percent. The remaining plantation, with 1,300 acres and all of the cattle belonging to it, he willed to his daughter Margaret. The profits from his 1729 purchase were typical of his speculation. In another series of transactions for land that he purchased in 1732, Wistar paid about £12 Pennsylvania currency for 100 acres and resold it at a rate of £50 for 100 acres.

Wistar's land speculation supplied him with extensive amounts of capital, but it also allowed him to furnish his children with impressive legacies. In his will, written less than one month before his death, he left his wife and children cash disbursements totaling £4,450, eleven city lots, and over five thousand acres of Pennsylvania land. Each of his children received at least one city lot in Philadelphia and land in the outlying counties. His only surviving sons, Richard and Caspar, and his oldest daughter, Margaret, each received a plantation with household goods and cattle. His three younger daughters, Catherine, Rebecca, and Sarah, inherited undeveloped land in Bucks and Philadelphia Counties. Although many of Philadelphia's leading Quakers sought to leave legacies of land to all of their children, Wistar's bequests were unusual in their size and value.

In addition to his wealth, Wistar's mediating role also gave him an international reputation as a leader among American Germans. The letter that he wrote in 1732, warning immigrants of deplorable ship conditions and giving them advice about Pennsylvania, was published throughout continental Europe. Moreover, he corresponded regularly with business associates in the Rhine and Neckar Valleys. These men purchased goods for Wistar and distributed and collected money and letters on his behalf.

Wistar's international reputation and business networks led to his involvement in retrieving numerous European legacies on behalf of friends and acquaintances in America. Georg Friedrich Hölzer, his business associate in the Palatinate, sought to obtain money in Europe that Wistar's siblings in America had inherited. Before long, other immigrants also were using his connections to retrieve legacies. By 1742, Hölzer was reporting his progress on five different inheritance cases that he was working on for Wistar.

Name recognition and a dependable transatlantic network helped to turn Wistar's house and shop into a communication center for Pennsylvania Germans. In 1737, Durst Thommen, a Swiss immigrant who settled with his family near Wistar's backcountry land, wrote to his European friends that they should send their letters addressed to him at Wistar's house in Philadelphia. Wistar, whose acquaintance he had made when he first arrived, would be sure to forward messages or letters. Wistar and his brother John, who was also a Philadelphia shopkeeper and shared the same business connections, provided an informal postal service for the immigrant community.

Wistar's success in using his transatlantic networks for communication and financial transactions, in turn, increased his reputation among American Germans. In one case, John Theobald Endt, a merchant in Germantown, recommended to a European friend that he send his American niece's legacy to Pennsylvania to invest because the interest rate was so much higher than in Krefeld. Endt suggested that his friend appoint three trustees for the money, among whom were Wistar's brother John and his cousin, David Deschler. Previously, Endt had suggested Wistar as one of the trustees, but he had died in the meantime. Wistar's reputation for handling money responsibly and for helping other Germans begin their new lives in America allowed him to become a patron to the Pennsylvania settlers and their European families.

His position of prominence among the immigrant community became well known among Anglo-American colonists as well. In 1738, John Bartram, a naturalist with whom Wistar had become friends, mentioned him in a letter to William Byrd II, a wealthy planter in Virginia. Byrd was advertising for people to settle his land at Roanoke. Bartram reported that he had presented Byrd's scheme in a favorable manner to

Wistar, "to whome many of ye Palatines resorts both for advice & assistance."[13] In his reply, Byrd offered Wistar or any of his countrymen as much of his Roanoke land as they wanted to buy.

By the late 1730s, Wistar's position as a leader among German immigrants was well established, and his wealth and social status made him less dependent on the Proprietors. Between 1738 and 1742 a series of events occurred that led the Penns and their supporters, who had once relied on Wistar's help for settling their colony, to recognize the influence he had gained. Throughout the 1730s, the period during which Wistar purchased most of his land, the relationship between the Proprietors and the assembly was relatively cooperative. Thomas Penn's presence in the colony and his land purchases from the Indians partially resolved the tensions of the previous decade. In addition, an ongoing boundary dispute between Lord Baltimore of Maryland and the Penns created an outside threat that encouraged compromise within the province's government. In order to strengthen his claim to the disputed territory, Thomas Penn allowed immigrants to settle on the land without paying the full purchase price.

Toward the end of the decade, however, the political climate began to change. In 1738, Lord Baltimore and Penn reached a compromise on the border dispute between Maryland and Pennsylvania. Penn immediately set out to reform his land policies. He issued a mandate requiring settlers who had not paid for their land in full to remit their remaining balances within a short period or face legal proceedings. At the same time, Penn replaced several well-known, trusted Proprietary officials with outsiders less sympathetic to the colonists' interests. Finally, in early 1739, news reached Pennsylvania that King George's War had broken out.

For the next several years, tensions between the Quaker-dominated assembly and the Proprietors' supporters, led by prominent Anglicans, increased. Preparing the colony for defense was central to the conflicts. The Quaker assemblymen, who had religious scruples against going to war, refused to allocate money to support a militia. To raise the necessary funds, Proprietary officials tried to unseat the Quaker majority in the assembly. As a result, the elections of the early 1740s became hotly contested, tumultuous affairs.

It was during the election for assembly representatives in 1742 that the extent of Wistar's influence among the German population became apparent. In past elections, most Pennsylvania German voters had supported Quaker legislators, for many of the early immigrants belonged to religious groups that shared the Quakers' pacifist positions. However, the majority of the more recent arrivals belonged to the Reformed and Lutheran churches and had no scruples against going to war. This was the constituency whose vote the Proprietary faction worked hard to win.

When mobs of Germans from the backcountry arrived in Philadelphia for the 1742 election, however, they sided with the Quakers. According to Richard Peters, an Anglican and a staunch supporter of the Penns, Wistar, his brother John, and Christopher Sauer had ruined the tenuous coalition of support that the Proprietary party had constructed among the Germans. Whenever backcountry settlers had come to Philadelphia, the Wistars had told them the real purpose for raising a militia was to eject colonists who had not paid for their land. As proof, the Wistars cited the Proprietors' arrest of settlers who refused to pay back rents and fines in the Lower Counties (Delaware), where the assembly had passed a militia act. The Wistars implied a connection between the two events. Peters noted that "these storys were greedily swallowed by those ignorant People & being improved by Sower [Christopher Sauer], who took care to see his Countrymen as they returned thro' Germantown, they were fix'd beyond a possibility of stirring them."14

Wistar, who had used his capital and credit to help the Proprietors solve the immigrant problem in the previous decade, became a patron who now protected the interests of his own constituency. He and his brother had convinced their fellow countrymen that the prospect of Proprietary supporters gaining a majority in the assembly was a greater threat to the immigrants' property than the impending war. By doing so, Wistar demonstrated his ability to turn his role as a broker into a position of political power.

Nor did Wistar's influence over the Pennsylvania Germans diminish. In 1750, Governor James Hamilton wrote a letter to Thomas Penn in which he used Wistar as an example of the dangers in conferring the rights of Englishmen on German immigrants "before they know how to use them." Hamilton noted that Wistar, "whom I remember wheeling ashes about this Town," was now worth £60,000, an estate that placed him among the wealthiest men in the colony. The governor believed that German-speaking immigrants such as Wistar would soon have "the wealth & power of the province in their hands," and that they would "either make a bad use of it themselves, or devolve it on some Demagogue, who may thereby be able to give the Government perpetual uneasiness." Hamilton acknowledged "the benefits that accrue to this province from the Industry of these people," but viewed them as a threat to the provincial government. The immigrants, he argued, did not understand Pennsylvania's laws or language, and "yet they are become the most busy at all Elections, which they govern at pleasure."[15]

Hamilton's paranoia captures beautifully the results of Wistar's activities as a cultural broker. By 1750 he had used his mediating role between the Proprietors and the other German-speaking immigrants to amass a fortune. The wealth and power that he had accumulated in the process now posed a threat to Proprietary supporters trying to secure their own political control. Hamilton feared that Wistar, his brother, and the small group of business-men who had arrived early in the flow of German-speaking settlers might gain control over the growing crowds of immigrants. If they did so, neither the Proprietary supporters nor the Quakers would be able to manipulate their support, and Pennsylvania's politics would dissolve into chaos.

Wistar did not, however, become the "demagogue" feared by Hamilton. Within two years, the successful immigrant died, leaving his widow and sons to carry on his various business enterprises. His six surviving children married Anglo-American Quakers and became fully integrated into Phila-delphia's elite society. If the legacies he left to his children are any indication, Wistar successfully achieved economic security for his family.

In part, timing and good fortune influenced Wistar's accomplish-ments; he arrived in Philadelphia at a period when the city's economy and social structure were particularly fluid. Wistar's success was also shaped by the way that he maneuvered within the colony's relationships of power. He began by learning a profession and establishing a religious identification to help him solicit patronage and build new family networks. Like his father, who constantly negotiated between conflicting interests, Wistar then took a position in the middle, between Pennsylvania's Proprietors and the newly arriving immigrants. As a land speculator, he offered solutions and his services to the Penns. The success of those services, however, depended on a steady stream of German-speaking settlers. At the same time, his role as a cultural broker would have failed without the resources of his business enterprises. Wistar's climb from hauling ashes to his position as a wealthy merchant was determined by his ability to combine entrepreneurial pur-suits with mediating Anglo-American culture for his fellow immigrants. That combination, in turn, allowed him to become a powerful patron within Philadelphia's German community.

Notes

1. "Wistar" was the English phonetic spelling of his name, which he began to use in

legal documents after 1721. German-language documents in America and Europe continued to use the original spelling, "Wüster."

2. "Ein Kortzer Bericht von Caspar Wistar," Morris Family Papers, Historical Society of Pennsylvania, Philadelphia (hereafter cited as HSP).

3. James T. Mitchell and Henry Flanders, eds., *The Statutes at Large of Pennsylvania from 1682–1801* (Harrisburg, 1895), 3:424–26.

4. Ibid.

5. Isaac Norris Sr. to S. Clements, April 30, 1725, Norris Papers, Isaac Norris Sr. Letterbook, 1716–1730, 422, HSP.

6. Gertrude MacKinney and Charles F. Hoban, eds., *Pennsylvania Archives*, 8th ser., 8 vols., *Votes and Proceedings of the House of Representatives of the Province of Pennsylvania, 1682–1776* (Harrisburg, 1931–1935), 2:1569.

7. James Logan to Hannah Penn, February 9, 1726, Penn Papers, Official Correspondence, HSP, 2:181, 313 (hereafter cited as PPOC).

8. James Logan to Hannah Penn, March 11, 1726, PPOC, 1:185.

9. James Logan to the Penns, November 25, 1727, Logan Papers, James Logan Letterbook, 4:153–54, 160, HSP.

10. Isaac Norris to John Penn, April 30, 1729, Isaac Norris Letterbook, 1716–1730, 522–25, HSP.

11. "Caspar Wistar's Letter of December 4, 1732," in Henry S. Dotterer, ed., *The Perkiomen Region, Past and Present*, 3 vols. (Philadelphia, 1899–1900) 2, no. 8:120. Another translation of this letter is in *Pennsylvania German Society Proceedings and Addresses* 8 (1897): 141–44. A partial copy of the original is in Morris Family Papers, HSP.

12. Ibid., Morris Family Papers, HSP.

13. Edmund Berkeley and Dorothy Smith Berkeley, eds., *The Correspondence of John Bartram, 1734–1777* (Gainesville, FL, 1992), 98–99.

14. Richard Peters Letterbook, 1741–43, 28, Peters Papers, HSP.

15. Governor James Hamilton to Thomas Penn, September 24, 1750, PPOC, 5:55.

Suggested Readings

The sources for information on Wistar's life are extensive on both sides of the Atlantic but of varying nature. The history of his family in the Palatinate is drawn from court records and government administrative documents in Abteilung #77 (*Pfalz Generalia*) in the Badisches Generallandesarchiv in Karlsruhe, Germany. The family's genealogy and references to its members' religious affiliation are based on church records at the Evangelisches Oberkirchenrat, Karlsruhe. A draft of Wistar's autobiography and a series of letters between him and a business correspondent in the Palatinate form the core of primary sources about his life in Pennsylvania. These documents are in the Morris Family Papers and the Wistar/Wister Family Papers at the Historical Society of Pennsylvania, Philadelphia. Information from wills, land records, Quaker Meeting minutes, and letters in the Logan, Peters, Norris, and Penn Papers, all available at the Pennsylvania State Archives, Harrisburg, or the Historical Society, supplemented the data drawn from private manuscripts. For general reading on German immigrants or Pennsylvania during this period, see Aaron S. Fogleman, *Hopeful Journeys: German Immigration, Settlement, and Political Culture in Colonial America, 1717–1775* (Philadelphia, 1996); Gary Nash, *Urban Crucible: Social Change, Political Consciousness, and the Origins of the American Revolution* (Cambridge, MA, 1978); Sally Schwartz, *"A Mixed Multitude": The Struggle for Toleration in Colonial Pennsylvania* (New York, 1987); and Alan Tully, *William Penn's Legacy: Politics and Social Structure in Provincial Pennsylvania, 1726–1755* (Baltimore, 1977).

4

Olaudah Equiano
An African in Slavery and Freedom

Robert J. Allison

Olaudah Equiano (1745–1797) was the quintessential captive. Although he spent little time in colonial America, his boyhood and kidnapping were well-remembered experiences common to thousands of Africans who ended their days in plantation slavery. Captives often cope with their trauma by identifying with their captors, which may help to explain something about Squanto as well as Equiano. Yet his exceptional life came to include achieving personal freedom, publishing his autobiography, and generally defying all the usual bounds of slave life. Equiano's unusual slavery meant that he grew up among the English, became a sailor, made friends among the English, and married an Englishwoman, eventually becoming an activist prominent in the British abolition movement. How important was race to Equiano? He organized the Sons of Africa and fervently promoted the abolition of the slave trade, but he recounted that fellow Africans were the ones who initially captured and sold him. He assisted in slave trading and plantation management for a time after he bought his freedom, and he advocated interracial marriage. His *Interesting Narrative* was consciously a part of the abolition movement; how would that purpose affect his version of his own story?

Robert J. Allison is the editor of Equiano's *The Interesting Narrative of the Life of Olaudah Equiano, or Gustavus Vassa, the African* (1995) and the author of *The Crescent Obscured: The United States and the Muslim World, 1776–1815* (1995). He is an associate professsor of history at Suffolk University in Boston.

Olaudah Equiano (pronounced o-lah-OO-day ek-wee-AH-no) was born in the Ibo village of Isseke (in present-day Nigeria) in 1745. At the age of eleven he was kidnapped by slave traders; he spent ten years as a slave in the West Indies, in America, and in the British navy before buying his freedom in 1766. As a free man, Equiano traveled throughout the Western world, from the Arctic to Nicaragua and the West Indies, from Cádiz to Genoa, Philadelphia, and New York. Living in London in the 1780s, when the slave trade reached its peak, Equiano contributed to the international movement against it. With other Africans in London, he formed the Sons of Africa to promote the interests of Africans in England

and its colonies. As part of this lobbying effort, Equiano wrote newspaper articles, petitioned Parliament and the Queen to end the slave trade, and in 1789 published his autobiography, *The Interesting Narrative of the Life of Olaudah Equiano, or Gustavus Vassa, the African*. One of the first abolitionist books by a former slave, Equiano's story is unique because he recorded virtually every part of the slave's experience: childhood in Africa, capture and sale to other Africans and to Europeans, the Middle Passage from Africa to the Americas; plantation labor in the West Indies and America; and the American slave trade from the Caribbean to the mainland. He also wrote about life after slavery, his twenty years as a freeman of color in England and America.

Equiano was the youngest son of seven children, six boys and one girl. His name connoted good luck: the word *ola* means ring, a sign for luck, and *ude* means a pleasant sound. His father was one of the village leaders, and his mother was active in the marketplace. He thought of his childhood as happy and prosperous, as the farming village produced plenty to feed the people. Equiano remembered the abundant corn, poultry, goats, tobacco, pineapples, yams, and cotton, and the women weaving and dyeing colorful calico cloth to wear and trade. The market drew buyers and sellers from distant areas, trading for the cloth and produce of Isseke. From the south, African traders brought European goods: guns, woolen cloth, and hats. These African traders also dealt in slaves.

Slavery in traditional African societies was a form of punishment for crimes such as adultery or robbery, or it could be a penalty for prisoners of war. Slaves were exiled from their own communities and forced to join another. While they were denied certain privileges in their new homes—in some cases, they were not allowed to eat with their masters—in other respects, slaves in African society did not live differently from free people. Equiano's father owned slaves, and some slaves even had slaves of their own, who could one day become free members of their new society. The European demand for slaves had changed the nature of this African trade. European slave merchants typically did not leave the coast of Africa but found willing African partners to kidnap slaves in the interior. The Aros, another Ibo clan living between Isseke and the coast, profited from the European demand. Equiano remembered that the Aro traders "carried great sacks with them" in which to confine unwilling captives.

Equiano recalled in his autobiography that when the adults were at work in the fields, a lookout was posted in the village to watch for slave catchers. He remembered once raising the alarm; but on another day, when "only I and my dear sister were left to mind the house, two men and a woman got over our walls, and in a moment seized us both, and, without giving us time to cry out, or make resistance, they stopped our mouths, and ran off with us into the nearest wood."[1] They were forced into the sacks and carried from the village. When they were some distance away, they were released from the sacks and marched off. Ultimately, they were separated. Equiano was sold in a distant village to an African goldsmith; after some months he was sold again, in another village, to serve as companion to a boy his own age.

Over several months as a slave in what is now southern Nigeria, Equiano wrote that he

> continued to travel, sometimes by land, sometimes by water, through different countries and various nations, till, at the end of six or seven months after I had been kidnapped, I arrived at the sea coast. . . . The first object which saluted my eyes when I arrived at the coast, was the sea, and a slave ship, which was then riding at anchor, and waiting for its cargo. These filled me with astonishment, which was soon converted to terror, when I was carried on board. I was immediately handled, and tossed up to see if I were sound, by some of the crew; and I was now persuaded that I had gotten into a world of bad spirits, and that they were going to kill me. Their complexions, too, differing so much from ours, their long hair, and the language they spoke (which was very different from any I had ever heard), united to confirm me in this belief. . . . When I looked round the ship too, and saw a large furnace of copper boiling, and a multitude of black people of every description chained together, every one of their countenances expressing dejection and sorrow, I no longer doubted of my fate. . . . [He fainted, but some of the traders revived him.] I asked them if we were not to be eaten by those white men with horrible looks, red faces, and long hair.[2]

The African merchants who had brought Equiano on board assured him that the white men would not eat him. The merchants collected their pay and left him. He never saw his home or family again.

Equiano and the other slaves loaded at this port were "soon put down under the decks, and there I received such a salutation in my nostrils as I had never experienced in my life: so that, with the loathesomeness of the stench, and crying together, I became so sick and low that I was not able to eat, nor had I the least desire to taste anything."[3] A slave ship usually carried up to four hundred captives, chained together in the hold for the two-month voyage across the Atlantic. With little ventilation, the crowded hold was hot, dark, and filthy. European traders spent months on the African coast visiting different ports to collect captives from as many different nations as possible so that the slaves would not be able to communicate with one another and rebel as a group. Despair among the captives was so great that many did rebel, or take the opportunity, when on deck for a brief gasp of fresh air, to throw themselves into the ocean to drown.

The Europeans saw Equiano's refusal to eat as rebellious, and he was beaten. Among the other captives he found some Ibos who gave him to understand that "we were to be carried to these white people's country to work for them. I then was a little revived, and thought, if it were not worse than working, my situation was not so desperate."[4] After all, he had worked at home and during his months of slavery in other African villages. He had questions: Did these white people live "in this hollow place (the ship)"? He did not see any European women: Were there only men in their country? And what made the ship go? No one could answer this question, since the slaves were packed below where they could not witness the art of navigation. Were the whites spirits who controlled the ship through magic? He began to fear them, he wrote later, because they "looked and acted, as I thought, in so savage a manner; for I had never seen among any people such instances of brutal cruelty; and this not only shown towards us blacks, but also to some of the whites themselves." One white sailor was "flogged so unmercifully with a large rope near the foremast, that he died in consequence of it; and they tossed him over the side as they would have done a brute."[5]

Equiano was one of fifty thousand Africans carried to the New World in the 1750s. The Portuguese had brought the first African slaves to Europe in 1441, and in the 1490s the practice had extended to the Americas. By 1756 it was well organized and brutally efficient. Of the estimated eleven million Africans brought to the Americas between 1518 and 1850, more than half came after 1750. Nearly half were taken to the sugar plantations of Brazil, about 40 percent to the Caribbean. The rest, or about 7 percent, were taken to mainland North America, principally to work on rice, tobacco, or (in the nineteenth century) cotton plantations, although slaves also worked on small farms, as urban servants, and as skilled craftsmen and sailors. The ship carrying Equiano landed first at Barbados, whose sugar plantations made it one of British America's wealthiest colonies. Equiano was astonished here to see two-story brick houses and men riding on horses. He had never seen a horse and thought that "these people were full of nothing but magical arts."[6]

More memorable than the horses, however, was the slave market. The arrival of a ship from Africa was an important event in Barbados, and planters and their agents would assemble at the marketplace early, hoping to have the first choice of the new laborers. Equiano wrote that on the beat of a drum, "the buyers rush at once into the yard where the slaves are confined, and make choice of that parcel they like best. The noise and the clamor with which this is attended, and the eagerness visible in the countenances of the buyers, serve not a little to increase the apprehension of terrified Africans, who may well be supposed to consider them as the ministers of that destruction to which they think themselves devoted. In this manner, without scruple, are relations and friends separated, most of them never to see each other again."[7]

No one bought Equiano. He was young and small, apparently not suited to the hard labor of sugarcane cultivation. He was taken on board a sloop and sent to Virginia, where he stayed briefly on a tobacco plantation. Years later he remembered a few details of his weeks in Virginia. The cook, a black woman, wore an iron muzzle. A wall clock and a portrait both seemed to watch Equiano, who was put to work brushing flies away from the dozing planter. From this plantation, where he was called "Jacob," Equiano was bought by a British sea captain, Michael Pascal, who planned to bring the young slave to England as a gift for a friend. Equiano was taken on horseback to Pascal's ship, the *Industrious Bee*. Pascal renamed the boy after the sixteenth-century Swedish king and hero of a popular English play, "Gustavus Vasa, the Deliverer of His Country." Equiano at first resisted the new name, a resistance that "gained me many a cuff" before he submitted to being Gustavus Vassa.[8]

Also sailing on the *Industrious Bee* was Richard Baker, a Virginian just a year or two older than Equiano. Baker explained the ways of white people to the young African, becoming his companion and interpreter. Equiano had often noticed his master and Dick reading and "had great curiosity to talk to the books as I thought they did, and so to learn how all things had a beginning. For that purpose I have often taken up a book, and have talked to it, and then put my ears to it, when alone, in hopes it would answer me; and I have been very much concerned when I found it remained silent."[9] Although the books kept silent, Equiano soon learned how to read them, an unusual achievement for a slave. He spent the spring of 1757 on the Channel island of Guernsey, with the family of Captain Pascal's mate. The mate's wife, who was teaching her own daughter to read and write, gave Equiano the same lessons.

This interlude on Guernsey did not last. As Equiano had sailed from Virginia, England and France had gone to war. Captain Pascal was called into the King's service on the warship *Roebuck*, and Equiano would serve his master and the Empire in Canada, the Atlantic, and the Mediterranean. The ability to read and to write down his experiences during these years of war marked a transition in Equiano's thinking. When he had first encountered Europeans on the coast of Africa, he had thought them spirits who moved their ships by magic. Now, just a few years later, he "was so far from being afraid of anything new" that he longed to get into battle, and his grief at losing his home and family faded in the excitement of war and the company of other boys on the ship. He began to box in shipboard matches arranged by the captain and other officers.[10]

After a long cruise north of England, which to his regret did not involve any battles, Equiano returned to London, ill with chilblains, a painful swelling of the feet and hands caused by prolonged exposure to cold. He remained in the hospital for months, visited by two cousins of Captain Pascal, the Guerin sisters. Dick Baker having died in the war, the Guerins became Equiano's newest European friends, and the three remained close for the rest of their lives. They began to tell him of the Christian faith, and the Bible stories of the ancient Hebrews reminded him of his own Ibo childhood. Equiano began his conversion to Christianity, a faith that would deepen throughout his life. He recovered from his illness and crossed the Atlantic to participate in the siege of Louisbourg, a French fortress at the mouth of the St. Lawrence River. He remembered years later seeing a British officer shot in the open mouth by a French musketball, holding in his hand an Indian's scalp. After the British victory, he returned to England in February 1759 to be baptized in the Anglican Church at St. Margaret's, in Westminster.

Equiano began to feel more at home in this new world. In 1760, then a swaggering fifteen-year-old veteran of the British navy, he had a furlough on the Isle of Wight. Just four years after his kidnapping, he relates, "I was one day in a field belonging to a gentleman who had a black boy about my own size; this boy having observed me from his master's house, was transported at the sight of one of his own countrymen, and ran to meet me with the utmost haste. I not knowing what he was about, turned a little out of his way at first, but to no purpose: he soon came close to me, and caught hold of me in his arms, as if I had been his brother, though we had never seen each other before."[11] Equiano did not immediately perceive a kinship with this black boy on the Isle of Wight. Now calling himself Gustavus, he said that he felt more English than African.

Nevertheless, his status was still ambiguous. He may have felt English, but not all English people would treat him as an Englishman. The next years would bring many painful reminders of his status. Having served both his master and the Empire, Equiano, when the war ended, expected and was told by other sailors that he deserved freedom as well as a share in his ship's prize money. Instead, Captain Pascal sold him. Equiano was forced onto a ship for the West Indies, where he was sold on the island of Montserrat. His new owner was a Philadelphia Quaker named Robert

King, a slave trader even though Quakers had condemned slavery in 1727, and Philadelphia's Quakers would bar slaveholders from their meetings in 1774. Perhaps his involvement in the slave trade led to his move from Philadelphia to Montserrat, where he shipped sugar and slaves from the West Indies to Georgia and South Carolina and bargained there for rice and beef to feed the Caribbean workforce. King recognized Equiano's value as a skilled sailor able to read, write, and calculate. Pascal had even sent a character reference noting Equiano's honesty. He became part of the trade network holding together the British colonial system in America.

Equiano had been part of the community of sailors in the British navy; his growing Christian faith also made him part of a larger world. But in the West Indies he was cut off from these ties of community; he was constantly cheated in his business transactions, as the word of a black man counted for nothing in the courts of the British West Indies. He was always in danger of being kidnapped to work on the sugar plantations, of which he had heard incredible but true tales of horror: of free men kidnapped into slavery; of slaves branded, tortured, and beaten to death; and of owners and overseers raping women and young girls, then selling the children of their lust. Equiano recorded all of these stories as well as his own experiences to convince people in England of slavery's brutal nature. West Indian slavery was considered to be its most savage form.

Working for King made Equiano part of the slave system. One option to improve his lot was to become a merchant. He started with three pence and "trusted to the Lord to be with me." On a voyage to St. Eustatius, a Dutch island that served as a general trading post in the West Indies, Equiano used his three pence to buy a glass tumbler. On his return to Montserrat he sold the tumbler for six pence, which he used on his next trip to St. Eustatius to buy two more tumblers. Through several trips between the two islands, Equiano continued to double his capital, until after a month he had more than a dollar and "blessed the Lord that I was so rich."[12] Equiano continued this slow but steady accumulation of capital, combining his trust in divine Providence with his own business skill, investing not only in glasses but in gin, oranges, and chickens. After three years he had accumulated more than £40, enough to invest in his largest purchase. On July 10, 1766, he bought himself. Ten years after he had been kidnapped, Equiano became free.

For his first two years as a freeman, Equiano continued to work for King, trading slaves from the Caribbean into Georgia and South Carolina. On one trip the captain died, and Equiano, who had learned some sailing and navigation, steered the ship safely into port. But skilled as he was,

Equiano was not given the job of captain. King hired an inexperienced white man to command the next trading voyage, and against Equiano's judgment the young captain sailed too close to the Bahama reefs. The ship foundered. The captain ordered Equiano to nail down the wooden planks over the hold so the cargo of slaves could not escape. The ship was in danger of sinking, and the white crew raided its rum supply and drank themselves into a stupor. Equiano disobeyed the order and released the slaves. With their help and that of one Dutch sailor, he repaired the ship's longboat and made for a nearby island. The captain warned them not to leave the ship, as he thought he saw cannibals walking on the beach. Equiano ignored his warning, and as he rowed nearer to shore, he watched the captain's cannibals one by one take to the air. They were flamingos.

Equiano now acted as captain, forcing the drunken sailors into the longboat to row them to safety. Although saved through his own efforts, Equiano attributed the miracle to God, and he vowed that if he survived to leave the West Indies, he would return to London and pursue his religious faith. He considered the shipwreck a warning; and when he published his *Interesting Narrative* twenty years later, he included an appropriate verse from the Book of Job about men who do not listen to the voice of God.[13]

Equiano did listen, and he took the shipwreck as a sign to leave the West Indies and the sinful world of American slavery. His work on the slave ships was a reminder of his own failings. Trips to Savannah were especially difficult. In Savannah, black people, either slave or free, were kept under tight control. Equiano himself was arrested there for having a light on after 9 P.M., when all blacks had to put their lights out. He was beaten almost to death by a drunken doctor and, another time, nearly kidnapped and sold as a slave. He was astonished then, in this place of brutal immorality, to pass a church packed with white and black Georgians. Full churches, he had noted, were rare in the West Indies. He was even more intrigued to learn that George Whitefield, the great evangelist, was preaching inside. Equiano pushed through the door to see him "sweating as ever I did on Montserrat beach," as he exhorted the Georgians to lead Christian lives.[14] Equiano did not know that Whitefield had long been a friend of Georgia, nor did he know that Whitefield and the colony's founder, James Oglethorpe, had envisioned it as a utopia. It became a utopia based on slavery, however, and by 1765 even Whitefield's Georgia orphanage was supported by slave labor.

Hoping to free himself from the sinfulness of the New World, Equiano returned to England and looked up his friends, the Guerin sisters. He told them of his adventures "at which they expressed great wonder, and freely acknowledged it did their cousin, Captain Pascal, no honor."[15] A few days later, Equiano encountered Pascal in a Greenwich park: "When he saw me he appeared a good deal surprised, and asked me how I came back? I answered, 'In a ship.' To which he replied dryly, 'I suppose you did not walk back to London on the water.' As I saw, by his manner, that he did not seem to be sorry for his behavior to me, and that I had not much reason to expect any favor from him, I told him that he had used me very ill, after I had been such a faithful servant to him for so many years; on which, without saying any more, he turned about and went away."[16]

Equiano thought he was through with the sea. To support himself, he learned to dress hair. He studied mathematics, and for entertainment he learned to play the French horn. He went to work for Dr. Charles Irving, an inventor who was perfecting a machine to make seawater fresh—an important innovation for the British Empire, which relied on long ocean voyages to connect its far dominions. In 1773 he and Dr. Irving joined an expedition to the Arctic to try to find a northwest passage and also to test the machine. After being icebound, and nearly drowned, Equiano and the expedition returned safely to England. He left Dr. Irving and sailed on a merchant vessel to Smyrna, where he saw the Greeks "kept under by the Turks, as the Negroes are in the West Indies by the white people,"[17] and to Genoa, whose grandeur was diminished in his eyes by the wretched life there of galley slaves.

Back in London, Equiano enjoyed a relatively good life, although wages on land were far below those he could earn at sea. In 1774 he prepared to ship out as a steward on a voyage to Turkey. The ship needed a cook, and Equiano recommended his friend John Annis, who immediately went on board to work as it lay at anchor awaiting its cargo. Annis had been a slave on the island of St. Kitts; his owner, a Scotsman named John Kirkpatrick, had brought him to England and now was trying to get him back to the West Indies. In 1772, England's Lord Chief Justice William Mansfield had ruled in a case involving a Massachusetts slave, James Somerset, that once a slave set foot in England, he could not be returned to slavery against his will. Thus, under English law, Annis was free. Kirkpatrick did not care much for the law. While Equiano hired a lawyer to protect his friend's rights, Kirkpatrick hired some men to kidnap Annis and take him back to the West Indies. Equiano received a letter describing Annis's final days: he was "staked to the ground with four pins through a cord, two on his wrists, and two on his ankles, was cut and flogged most unmercifully and afterwards loaded cruelly with irons about his neck." Finally, "kind death released him out of the hands of his tyrants."[18]

Equiano blamed himself for failing to protect his friend. He wanted to die himself. He thought of going to Turkey and converting to Islam, as his good life in England now seemed empty and meaningless. Feelings of sinfulness overcame him, and he sailed for Spain, reading his Bible, hating all things, and wishing that he had never been born. Thinking himself the unhappiest man who ever lived, he was convinced that God treated him better than he deserved, and wondered what his fate might be. In the Spanish port of Cádiz on October 6, 1774, he began to get a strange feeling that his life was about to change. He spent the evening reading and meditating on the Bible. Then, suddenly,

> the Lord was pleased to break in upon my soul with his bright beams of heavenly light; and in an instant, as it were, removing the veil, and letting light into a dark place, I saw clearly with an eye of faith, the crucified Saviour bleeding on the cross on mount Calvary; the scriptures became an unsealed book; I saw myself a condemned criminal under the law, which came with its full force to my conscience, and when "the commandment came sin revived, and I died." I saw the Lord Jesus Christ in his humiliation, loaded and bearing my reproach, sin, and shame. I then clearly perceived that by the deeds of the law no flesh living could be justified. . . . It was given me at that time to know what it was to be born again.[19]

John Annis's suffering and death seemed taken up in the death and resurrection of Jesus, and both redeemed Equiano. In later years, looking back on his life, Equiano would recall as equally important the date of his freedom from slavery and the date of his spiritual conversion.

Though reborn spiritually, Equiano still found it difficult to cut his ties to slavery. He returned to England to work for Dr. Irving, who now was planning a colony on the Mosquito Coast of Nicaragua. He hired Equiano as his foreman, and the two sailed for Jamaica to buy slaves to work on their plantation. Equiano reconciled himself to his new role by purchasing only Ibos, and as overseer he made sure that the slaves were well clothed and fed and not overworked, and he instructed them in Christianity. Maintaining a spiritual community on a tropical plantation was difficult. Equiano soon grew disgusted at the lack of religious devotion among the Europeans and the wild drinking bouts of the Mosquito Indians. He left Nicaragua in June 1776; and, after nearly being killed en route by an English captain, he reached Jamaica. He found Dr. Irving in Jamaica, where he had gone to buy more slaves. After Equiano had left the plantation, the new European overseer had cut the slaves' food supply and forced them to work harder. They had fled into the jungle and drowned. Dr. Irving's plantation was doomed to failure.

Equiano returned to England with the British fleet, now convoying ships in the first year of the American Revolution. He watched a British vessel destroy an American privateer, a lesson in the consequences of rebelliousness. He petitioned the Anglican Church to send him as a missionary to Africa, but his application was denied. He then settled down to a "more uniform" life, pursuing his religious devotions and working as a personal servant. Equiano might have lived out his days in the quiet role of an English servant, and never have written his book, had he not been called to action in 1783.

In November 1781 disease had broken out on the British slave ship *Zong.* Sixty slaves and seven white crew members died before the ship reached Barbados. The shipowners could collect insurance on slaves who drowned, but not on slaves who died of disease. Consequently, the captain ordered 54 sick Africans brought to the deck, had them chained together, and then thrown overboard. The next day, he had another 42 chained and thrown into the sea; and on the following day, 36 more who showed symptoms of disease were chained and forced over the side. He brought the remaining 248 Africans into port and sold them, then sailed for England to file a claim for 132 drowned slaves.

Equiano learned this story, perhaps from a sailor on the London docks. In early 1783 he told it to Granville Sharp, the British philanthropist who had helped James Somerset win his lawsuit for freedom under British law eleven years earlier. Sharp tried to stop the insurance company from paying the claim. He was unsuccessful, and the shipowners collected insurance on the murdered slaves. But this vivid demonstration of the slave trade's horrors pressed Sharp and other philanthropists to arouse public opinion. In 1784 and 1785, British antislavery advocates, including Sharp, David Ramsay, and college student Thomas Clarkson, published pamphlets attacking the inhumanity of the slave trade and the brutality of West Indian planters.

West Indian planter James Tobin responded with a vigorous defense of slavery. He argued that blacks were inherently inferior to whites and would not be suited for freedom. What would happen to the slaves of the West Indies if they became free? Would they be accepted in England as members of British society? Would they be able to work without the whites forcing them to do so? These were critical arguments, since even whites who believed slavery to be morally repugnant might see blacks as their inferiors and might doubt if the two races could live together in peace.

Equiano recognized the importance of these arguments. He also saw that white philanthropists would not effectively answer the racial charges of black inferiority. Equiano responded to Tobin in a series of letters to the British newspapers, arguing for the full equality of Africans before God and man. Equiano's solution to the supposed problem of innate racial differences was simple: whites and blacks should intermarry, in "open, free, and generous loves upon Nature's own wide and extensive plain, . . . without distinction of color of skin."[20] Intermarriage, and offspring who were neither white nor black, would ultimately make color differences irrelevant.

Equiano resumed his travels, making trips in 1785 and 1786 to New York and Philadelphia, two centers of the American antislavery movement. Both cities had large free-black communities, and Pennsylvania had become in 1780 the first American state to abolish slavery. Quaker Anthony Benezet had long argued against the slave trade and had established a school for free blacks in Philadelphia. New York's Society for Promoting the Manumission of Slaves had been formed in 1785, and a school for free blacks opened there in 1787. Equiano visited Benezet's school, and saw these free schools as models for British philanthropy. He argued that with proper education, blacks could become productive members of society. He saw the color distinction as artificial, and hence one that could be made to fade away.

British philanthropists either were less optimistic or did not see the color line as an artificial one. After the American Revolution, England's black population grew with arrivals of slaves belonging to American Loyalists and blacks who had fought against the rebellious colonists. Although free under British law, economically and socially these blacks were confined to menial positions, where it was feared they would take jobs away from poor whites. A group of philanthropists formed a Committee for the Black Poor, which hoped to improve the lot of both white and black poor people by sending the blacks to West Africa. Although Equiano opposed this proposal, as he believed black men and women could become members of British society, he agreed to serve as the expedition's commissary when the committee invited him. But Equiano discovered corruption and mismanagement in the planned expedition. The agent contracted to supply the expedition overcharged the government and failed to deliver the goods for which he had been paid. Equiano accused the agent of corruption, the agent accused Equiano of mismanagement, and Equiano was fired. He took his case to the public, was cleared of wrongdoing, and was paid for his services. (The expedition did go to West Africa and founded the colony at Sierra Leone.)

In London, Equiano joined with other Africans living in England to form the Sons of Africa. They planned to stay in England and wanted to live as Englishmen. Although they came from many different African nations, they had begun to recognize a common African identity. To improve the lives of all African people, the Sons of Africa launched a campaign against the slave trade, and on March 21, 1788, Equiano presented an antislavery petition to Queen Charlotte. He began to write his autobiography, which would be a more powerful weapon against slavery and the slave trade. Published just as Parliament began to debate the slave trade, his *Interesting Narrative of the Life of Olaudah Equiano, or Gustavus Vassa, the African* presents the story of a real man, not a distant abstraction, caught in the horrors of slavery. It shows not only that he could endure, but also that once free he had become a valuable member of society. Equiano embarked on a national tour, and for the next eight years he visited all parts of the British Isles, speaking against slavery and the slave trade and selling copies of his book. By 1790 it appeared in its third English edition, and it had been translated into Dutch; in the following year, the first American edition of his book appeared in New York.

In 1792, Equiano married Susan Cullen, who came from a small town near Cambridge, England. They had known one another since at least 1789, when she subscribed to the first edition of the *Interesting Narrative*. Their marriage was an example of the kind of open, free, and generous love that he had recommended in 1785. Their first daughter, Anna Maria Vassa, was born in 1793, and then Johanna in 1795. Susan Vassa died a few months after her second daughter's birth, and Equiano died in April 1797. Anna Maria survived her father by only a few months. Johanna lived into adulthood and collected an inheritance from her parents' estate, £950 earned from the sale of the *Interesting Narrative*.

The story of Equiano's life, recorded in his autobiography, remained a weapon against slavery and the slave trade long after his death. Written as an indictment of slavery, the book serves as testimony to one person's ability to survive and to endure against the brutality of others.

Notes

1. Olaudah Equiano, *The Interesting Narrative of the Life of Olaudah Equiano, or Gustavus Vassa, the African* [first published edition, 1789], ed. Robert J. Allison (Boston, 1995), 47.
2. Ibid., 53–54.
3. Ibid., 54.
4. Ibid., 55.

5. Ibid.

6. Ibid., 58.

7. Ibid.

8. Ibid., 61.

9. Ibid., 64.

10. Ibid., 65–66.

11. Ibid., 78.

12. Ibid., 102–3.

13. Equiano, *Interesting Narrative*, 1st American ed. (New York, 1791), vol. 2, title page.

14. Equiano, *Interesting Narrative* [1789], 116; *Georgia Gazette*, February 21, 1765.

15. Equiano, *Interesting Narrative* [1789], 139.

16. Ibid.

17. Ibid., 141.

18. Ibid., 152.

19. Ibid., 159.

20. Equiano to James Tobin, Esq., quoted in Folarin Shyllon, *Black People in Britain, 1555–1833* (London, 1977), 251.

Suggested Readings

Equiano's autobiography, *The Interesting Narrative of the Life of Olaudah Equiano, or Gustavus Vassa, the African* [first published edition, 1789], ed. Robert J. Allison (Boston, 1995), is the best source for his life. Catherine Acholonu, *The Igbo Roots of Olaudah Equiano* (Owerri, Nigeria, 1989), has fascinating information on both his family, then and now, in the village of Isseke. On slavery and the slave trade, particularly valuable are Joseph E. Inikori and Stanley Engermen, eds., *The Atlantic Slave Trade: Effects on Economies, Societies, and Peoples in Africa, the Americas, and Europe* (Durham, NC, 1992); and Patrick Manning, *Slavery and African Life: Occidental, Oriental, and African Slave Trades* (New York, 1990). Michael Craton, *Sinews of Empire: A Short History of British Slavery* (Garden City, NY, 1974) is an excellent overview. Robin Blackburn's twin volumes, *The Making of New World Slavery: From the Baroque to the Creole* (London, 1997) and *The Overthrow of Colonial Slavery, 1776–1848* (London, 1988), are compelling syntheses. On the ideology of slavery, Winthrop Jordan, *White over Black: American Attitudes toward the Negro, 1550–1812* (Chapel Hill, NC, 1969); David Brion Davis, *The Problem of Slavery in the Age of Revolution, 1770–1823* (Ithaca, NY, 1975), and his more sweeping *Slavery and Human Progress* (New York, 1984); Orlando Patterson, *Slavery and Social Death: A Comparative Study* (Cambridge, MA, 1982); and Eric Williams, *Capitalism and Slavery* (Chapel Hill, NC, 1944) are well worth reading. Folarin Shyllon, *Black People in Britain, 1555–1833* (London, 1977), looks at the status of Africans and their descendants in English society; and W. Jeffrey Bolster, *Black Jacks: African-American Seamen in the Age of Sail* (Cambridge, MA, 1997), takes a long-overdue look at the world of black sailors like Equiano.

5

Eliza Lucas Pinckney
Vegetables and Virtue

Gary L. Hewitt

Best known for her successful indigo experiments in Carolina, Eliza Lucas Pinckney (1722–1793) managed both her absentee father's plantations and later, in her widowhood, her husband Charles Pinckney's properties. Plantations thrived under her direction, although married women did not own land by law in her time and typically did not manage family businesses. Elite, but not exactly leisured, Eliza once presented the Princess of Wales with a dress of silk made from Eliza's own silkworms. In choosing to remain in Carolina after her husband's death, rather than return to England and rejoin her family, was Eliza fulfilling the duties of a deputy husband by preserving her children's inheritance, or did she also relish the opportunity to manage plantation affairs again?

As the daughter of a royal governor, Eliza Lucas had many English acquaintances. Her sons were educated in England, but they returned to Carolina and distinguished themselves as officers in the Continental Army. Why would members of the Pinckney family, who had long maintained ties throughout the empire, embrace the revolutionaries' cause? How influential was Eliza's example? As Gary Hewitt explains, she cultivated virtue and patriotism in her sons and grandsons with the same care she had applied to her garden. Pinckney family patriotism did not ensure economic prosperity throughout the Revolutionary War. Her sons remained prominent leaders, but middle-aged Eliza lost much of her own economic independence. In the aftermath of the Revolution, as a grandmother, Eliza wrote to her daughter's son, Daniel Huger Horry, in England and tried to interest him in American affairs by enclosing a copy of America's new federal Constitution. Horry settled in France, but he did change his name to Charles Lucas Pinckney Horry. Admired by George Washington, who later requested to be a pallbearer at her funeral, Eliza embodied the values of a republican mother even before there was a republic.

Gary L. Hewitt's scholarly work focuses on the political economies of South Carolina and Georgia in the early eighteenth century. He has taught at Princeton University and Grinnell College.

Eliza Lucas Pinckney's young son Tom once observed that "Mama loves long letters."[1] Despite her earlier fears that she might not have enough "matter to support an Epistolary Intercourse," Eliza's surviving letters span nearly half a century.[2] Her extensive correspondence has proved a blessing for modern historians, who have found in those long letters a tantalizing window into the world of a woman of striking intelligence, vivacity, and charm. While Eliza did not quite write her "waking and sleeping dream,"[3] as she threatened one friend, her letters touched on topics as diverse as the prices of agricultural products, local politics, neighborhood romance and marriage, and the latest novels. Her mail was directed around the globe to friends, relations, and business associates from London to New England to the West Indies, and it was accompanied by gifts to cement these cosmopolitan friendships. Eliza Lucas Pinckney's world was as far-flung as the sprawling British Empire of the eighteenth century, and she tied it together with her letters.

Eliza was from the very circumstances of her life an extraordinary woman. Her education, wealth, and status all made her decidedly atypical for Carolinians of the mid-eighteenth century. Eliza read voraciously in literature and philosophy and wrote numerous long letters during an age when a minority of Carolinians, whether male or female, free or enslaved, was literate. She was born in the West Indies, educated in England as a girl, and returned for an extended stay there after her marriage. Although most Carolinians during this era, like Eliza, had been born outside the colony, most had not experienced her wide travels. She enjoyed the leisure and comforts that came with being a member of one of the wealthiest families in the colony: not only a library filled with books but also gardens, music lessons, and a constant round of visits and entertaining. Her father was a colonel in the British army and lieutenant governor of the wealthy colony of Antigua, her husband was a prominent South Carolina politician, and her two sons were leaders of the patriot cause during the American Revolution in South Carolina—both as generals in the state militia, and one as the state's delegate to the Constitutional Convention in 1787.

Eliza Lucas Pinckney's story is noteworthy but not simply because she was a wealthy and privileged lady. Her accomplishments were unusual for a woman of her wealth and status, or perhaps for any woman in the eighteenth-century Anglo-American world. Eliza directed important family business as she managed the Lucas family's three plantations from 1739 to 1745. She possessed a keen interest in the life of the mind, as her wide-ranging and frequent letters attest. She was also an amateur, though talented, scientist. Eliza was, as she put it once, "fond of the vegetable world," and for several years she was engaged in horticultural experiments that eventually led to the successful commercial cultivation of indigo in South Carolina—a crop that quickly became a major contributor to the wealth of the colony's plantation economy.[4]

Despite Eliza Lucas Pinckney's unusual level of activity and wealth, she helps to illuminate some of the central themes of revolutionary-era American life. Her education and thinking reflect the intellectual currents of the eighteenth century. Her travels from colony to colony and two sojourns in England illustrate the interlocking sinews of the British Empire. Her management of the family plantations and agricultural innovation depict a desire for success and profit among the planters of South Carolina. As a whole, Eliza Lucas Pinckney's life helps demonstrate how fluid women's roles could be in the eighteenth century. Her opportunities were tremendous, and she took good advantage of them to participate in the world of business and of the mind. Yet, Eliza was constrained by her sex as well. She was conscious that, as "a girl," her ideas were valued differently from those of her brothers. More profoundly, Eliza's horizons shrank after her marriage and the birth of her three children. Eliza moved easily into a new role of wife and mother and left some of the intellectual vivacity of her youth behind in favor of a more sober didactic sensibility, in which the education—especially moral—of her children was most important. Her desire to instill "virtue" into her sons' breasts stands out in her numerous letters—virtue that served both Eliza and her sons well when the Revolution came to South Carolina.

Eliza Lucas had lived a cosmopolitan life before she was out of her teens. Born on the British island colony of Antigua in December 1722, Eliza spent a few years in an English girls' school and briefly returned to her birthplace before moving to South Carolina in 1738 with her father and mother, George and Anne Lucas, and her younger sister Mary (her younger brothers, George and Thomas, remained in England at school). Her far-reaching travels were the consequence of her family's wide-ranging set of transatlantic connections. Her father was an important man on Antigua: he was heir to a large sugar estate and son of an assemblyman, and by 1733 he sat on that colony's Royal Council. George Lucas also had a promising military career. Beginning as a captain of a local militia in 1722, he had purchased a major's commission in the British army by the time the family moved to South Carolina.

The Lucas family was no less important in their new home. Here, too, the Lucases were closely connected to the wealthy and powerful planters and merchants who ran South Carolina by the 1730s. These connections were hardly accidental, since Carolina had a long-standing relationship with the Caribbean. From South Carolina's beginnings in the late seventeenth century, West Indian planters had invested heavily in its colonization. The islands had gotten crowded after a half-century-long sugar boom, and opportunities for planters' sons were declining. Sugar plantations needed food, too, and Carolina was close enough to provide a reliable and cheap supply of grain and meat that many West Indian planters, in pursuit of sugar profits, refused to grow for themselves. The Lucases followed this pattern. As early as 1713, Eliza's grandfather John Lucas had acquired substantial amounts of land in South Carolina, and his holdings had grown over the years. When the Lucases arrived in South Carolina in 1738, the family owned three thriving plantations on the Wappoo, Combahee, and Waccamaw Rivers, as well as several lots in the thriving provincial capital and port city of Charles Town (now called Charleston).

Major Lucas's status within the British Empire called him to the king's service when war broke out between England and Spain, only a year after his family's arrival in South Carolina. He was promoted to the rank of colonel and appointed lieutenant governor of his native island colony of Antigua, and so was forced to leave his wife and daughters behind in the comparative health and safety of the mainland. His departure, combined with Anne Lucas's chronic illness, left his family and affairs largely in the hands of his sixteen-year-old daughter Eliza, who made the most of this opportunity to exercise her considerable talents.

The most striking aspects of Eliza's life in South Carolina was her restless activity, both mental and physical. Many days she spent on the plantation, busy from before dawn to after dark. Perhaps the best illustration of her level of activity is her description of the course of a typical day to her friend, Miss Bartlett, niece of Eliza's close friends Elizabeth and Charles Pinckney. "In general," Eliza wrote, "I rise at five o'Clock in the morning, read till Seven, then take a walk in the garden or field." After breakfast, she spent an hour practicing music, then an hour reviewing French or shorthand. Then two hours were devoted to teaching her younger sister and the two slave girls who, she hoped, would teach the rest of the family's slaves. More music followed lunch, with needlework until dark, after which time she would "read or write." Yet her life was not all fancywork and modern languages. Thursdays were reserved entirely for "the necessary affairs of the family"—which meant writing letters, either on the "business of the plantation" or to her friends. Mixed into this schedule were variations: music lessons, entertaining visitors from neighboring plantations, and on Fridays going "abroad" to visit neighbors.[5]

Although Eliza chose to live "in the Country" after her father's departure, she was by no means socially isolated on their Wappoo River plantation. In her own neighborhood, she reported, there were six "agreeable families" with whom she socialized, and she frequently visited Charles Town, just seven miles away by water. Almost all political and business affairs were settled in the provincial capital, so most prominent families had houses in town, and Charles Town became the center of social life in the colony. By the time of Eliza's arrival, it was a bustling town of almost seven thousand inhabitants and boasted a literary society, a theater, and a weekly newspaper, as well as horse races, balls, and an endless round of informal visits among the elite. Eliza, as a single, wealthy, and attractive young woman, found herself at home in Charles Town society, where she developed intimate friendships with several families with whom she stayed while enjoying "all the pleasures Charles Town affords."[6]

Charles Town was not the limit of Eliza's social circle. She maintained a broad set of correspondents far beyond South Carolina. Her letters were directed across the empire in a sort of female counterpart to her father's imperial web of connections. She could not boast a commission in the army or a governorship, but Eliza still maintained in her letters the cosmopolitan flair of her youth, corresponding with her hostess during her youthful sojourn in England, a cousin in Boston who had been a companion in both Antigua and South Carolina, and a friend from school in England, who was the daughter of the governor of Pennsylvania. Even in South Carolina, Eliza's connections had a transatlantic feel: one of her closest friends, Miss Bartlett, was a visitor from England. Many early letters described the Carolina countryside and local news to her curious correspondents. Since Eliza's family was separated across the globe—her brothers were in England, her father in Antigua, and her mother and sister with her in South Carolina—much time was spent soliciting and passing along family news.

Eliza accompanied her letters with gifts. The variety of these gifts displays not merely a generous spirit made possible by great wealth; it also helps to illustrate aspects of colonial life as diverse as young ladies' activities and the commercial needs of the British Empire. To Miss Thomas in Philadelphia, she sent a tea chest that she had lacquered; to her father she sent one of her lacquered butler's trays. Ornamental work was one employment that occupied the time of many well-to-do young ladies in London and South Carolina and, not surprisingly, Eliza participated. Eliza's other gifts reveal more. Often she sent food across the sea: "a kegg of sweetmeats"[7] and turtle meat (for turtle soup, a delicacy) to England, or potatoes to New England. She also sent larger quantities of beef, rice, and even pickled eggs to her father in Antigua. Unlike her gifts of turtle or sweet-meats, these were profitable commodities in the Atlantic world. She even hoped to establish a lucrative market in eggs in Antigua. Thus, Eliza's correspondence reflected more than young ladies' crafts: she was a messenger on the outposts of a vibrant and dynamic English commercial empire. With the public world of imperial life largely closed to her sex, Eliza Lucas created around herself a different kind of personal empire—a social circle of family and female friends, brought together with friendly moral advice and gifts of turtle meat and japanned boxes, yet also tied together by the practical sinews of commerce and business.

The most striking aspect of Eliza's letters is her constant intellectual energy. Her two hours of reading a day were spent on books as diverse as John Locke's *Essay Concerning Human Understanding,* Samuel Richardson's novel *Pamela,* and Latin pastoral poems—all of which served as the basis for a lively commentary. Eliza's thoughts, so far as her letters reveal them, appear at first glance to have traveled along fairly conventional eighteenth-century paths. Alongside the everyday sociability of her letters is a fairly commonplace concern for duty to parents, adherence to moral principles, and following the principles and observances of the established church. Yet behind this conventionality lurked Eliza's realization that her attention to the life of the mind was unusual for one her age, especially unusual for a young woman. Shadowy figures of older women appear in her letters, chiding her for getting up too early, for working too hard, for reading too much (one woman threw Eliza's book into the fire), and perhaps even for thinking too much. Since women's roles were not so confined in eighteenth-century South Carolina as they would become a century later, Eliza did not self-consciously transgress beyond women's "proper" sphere. She was not a rebel, but she lived on the fuzzy boundaries between the world of women and the world of men.

Another characteristic of Eliza's thinking was a concern for self-discipline and self-reflection, concepts that infused eighteenth-century standards of virtue and manliness. Several times she commented on the propriety of the amusements that Charles Town had to offer: card games, promenades, balls, and the theater. She believed it was acceptable to indulge, at least in moderation, in these pleasures, but still feared the consequences that overindulgence would have on her own character. When she returned from lively Charles Town to the slow-paced life of her plantation and found it "gloomy and lonesome," she gazed inward, and wondered why her isolation could no longer "sooth my . . . pensive humour." Had home changed, or had she changed? She "was forced to consult Mr. Locke" on the question of "personal Identity." Evidently, Eliza was pleased when her reading helped return her to her former "love of solitude."[8]

Yet underneath this self-reflection ran a current of lightness and self-effacement, not ponderous philosophizing and self-aggrandizement. She hoped that her correspondent (her Charles Town friend, Elizabeth Pinckney) would not "conclude me out of my Witts" or "religiously mad" because she was "not always gay."[9] Her thoughtfulness would turn neither to morbid self-reflection nor to a religious enthusiasm that led to events such as the suicide of Mrs. Le Brasures, who had killed herself to get to Heaven sooner. In addition, Eliza's moral comments were also part of the more important process of tying her social world together. This lighter side was most evident when one of Eliza's friends designed a cap for her, and named this new pattern a "whim." Eliza feared that the cap was ill-named, since she already had "so many whims before, more than I could well manage." "Perhaps," Eliza punned, the designer "thought the head should be all of a peice [*sic*], the furniture within and the adorning without the same"—that is, a whim on the head to match the whims within.[10] Nevertheless, Eliza sent the pattern along with her comment to her friend Miss Bartlett, who, Eliza thought, had not so many whims.

Eliza was as happy to give advice as patterns for caps, at least to those younger than herself. Miss Bartlett received a few moral and religious lectures, which Eliza usually turned in humorous directions. When a local planter had religious delusions, Eliza lectured on the importance of rationality in religious life, but finished her discourse with the jocular question of whether Miss Bartlett would "wish my preachment at an End."[11] Eliza changed the subject to the appearance of a comet in the Carolina sky, but quickly returned to the contemplation of whether this comet portended the end of the world, meditations on the "shortness of life," and finally the consolation regarding death that "the Christian religion affords the pious mind."[12] In general, Eliza's advice ran along less sober lines: the two exchanged poetry (and Eliza gave helpful criticism of Miss Bartlett's verses) and commentaries on the propriety of the heroine's behavior in the tremendously popular English novel *Pamela* (1741). Throughout Eliza's writings, a moral sensibility predominated; after Miss Bartlett returned to England, she asked Eliza to "write a poem on Virtue."[13] Eliza disclaimed any ability on that score—she was as likely to read ancient Greek, she said, as write a good poem on any subject—but Miss Bartlett's request says much of the relationship between the two young women and Eliza's character.

Eliza's two younger brothers, who had remained in England to complete their education, were the recipients of more sober moral lessons. The younger brother, Thomas, was gravely ill while Eliza was in South Carolina, a fact that elicited both cheerful encouragement and long meditations on mortality from his sister. George, on the other hand, was healthy and had entered the British army as an ensign at only fifteen years of age. Eliza feared the dangers her brother would encounter in the military, especially the violent passions provoked by the heat of battle and the company of soldiers. Instead, she counseled a "true fortitude," in which "rational principles" would provide him with the necessary courage to fight with honor, but not lead him to take unnecessary chances. A "composed state of mind" was what she recommended.[14] She understood that "Victory and conquest must fire your mind" as a soldier, but reminded George that "the greatest conquest is a Victory over your own irregular passions."[15] True virtue, for Eliza, allowed the rational mind to overcome desires for glory or revenge, while following the dictates of religion and conscience. While Eliza's image of man's virtue at war with his passions was by no means unusual for her era, she extended her concern for reason and virtue to both men and women. It seems, however, that she believed the stakes of male virtue were higher, even as the threats were stronger.

"But to cease moralizing and attend to business," Eliza punctuated one of her letters to her father (after describing her sisterly advice to George on the subject of virtue).[16] That Eliza would think of morality and business as separate pursuits indicates something about eighteenth-century political thought. Hers was an era before Adam Smith argued that an "invisible hand" could make individuals' pursuit of self-interest yield a public good. Rather, in her era, "irregular passions," including self-interest, threatened the virtue of Eliza's brother. For this reason, Eliza's business correspondence has a matter-of-fact quality quite distinct from her breezy social exchanges or her sober moral lessons. To be sure, Eliza paid close attention to the management of her family's South Carolina estates. She continually wrote to her father and her business associates in Charles Town about the day-to-day business of rice planting and international commerce. But Eliza usually did not make the effort to copy the text of these matters verbatim. She preferred simply to write memoranda into her letterbook noting the general subjects of her letters, or perhaps she copied them elsewhere or sent them to her father. In any event, the point remains that she considered business a separate realm, one of memoranda and ledger entries, not of personal relationships that merited word-for-word copies of letters. Of course, Eliza also had close personal attachments to most of the recipients of these letters: her father, the Pinckneys, and the other members of South Carolina's merchant elite who were also her friends. Thus Eliza might bring together these two worlds with her awkward transition from a moral concern for her brother to "attend to business."

That junction represented the outer limits of what Eliza could do as a woman in the British Empire. There were, however, times when Eliza carved a further breach in the masculine world of business, or at least exploited the blurry lines between women's and men's roles. From time to time, as she reported to her friend Miss Bartlett, she provided legal services for her "poor Neighbors" who could not afford the services of a lawyer. Eliza had a copy of an English legal handbook and used it to draw up wills for neighbors on their deathbeds. But Eliza knew when she was out of her depth—even when "teazed intolerable," she refused to draw up a marriage settlement (a sort of eighteenth-century prenuptial contract, intended to allow a bride to retain control of the property she brought to the marriage). She did finally serve as a trustee of the bride's property in that instance; this role was not an unheard-of one for a woman, but it was unusual for anyone as young as Eliza. The "weighty affairs" Eliza had on her hands led her to wonder whether she would become "an old woman before I am well a young one." Eliza understood that her attention to business and the world of "affairs," like her self-described "pensive humour" and her love of books, set her apart from most young women.[17] Perhaps for this reason, Eliza wanted Miss Bartlett to keep her lawyering a secret from her aunt and uncle, the Pinckneys.

Eliza Lucas's most famous activity during her first years in South Carolina was her agricultural experimentation on her father's plantations. "I love the vegitable world extremely," she told one friend, and her horticultural work was constant as long as she lived in South Carolina.[18] Within a year of her arrival in the colony in 1738, she began planting numerous crops in an effort to determine which ones might grow well in her new home. Many of them were common to her native West Indies: indigo, ginger, cotton, lucerne (a kind of alfalfa), and even cassava, a root crop originating in Brazil that became a staple for Caribbean slaves. None of these had been commercially successful in South Carolina, and Eliza did not always succeed. Her first crops of cotton and ginger were destroyed in a frost, and her lucerne, she reported, was "dwinderling."[19] She also experimented with Mediterranean crops and tried an orchard of fig trees. Not all of her horticultural efforts were directed toward commodities. While reading Virgil, she was struck by his descriptions of Roman gardens, which she thought might suit her own colony. So Eliza's busy mind immediately contemplated the "beauties of pure nature, unassisted by art" on her plantation.[20] She also considered how she might improve on nature, by planting a cedar grove as well as gardens of flowers and fruit trees.

Still, profit was never far from Eliza's active thoughts either. Her future husband, Charles Pinckney, accused her of having a "fertile brain at scheming," by which he meant schemes to make money.[21] Indeed, in most of her agricultural experiments, Eliza was interested in making them pay off, or at least hoped that they might "provid[e] for Posterity."[22] Her fig trees were planted "with design to dry and export them," and she carefully calculated the expenses and profits of that project.[23] She planted oaks in the hopes that they could be sold to shipbuilders. She even pickled eggs and sent them to the West Indies, hoping they might provide another source of income. In each venture, she looked for commodities that would serve as articles of trade in the dynamic commercial empire that Great Britain had created in the early eighteenth century. Just as Eliza's letters circulated around the empire, so too, did her produce.

In this context of searching for profitable export commodities, Eliza's most famous experiment developed. Indigo, a blue dye extracted from the *Indigofera anil* plant, was the object of Eliza's highest hopes and most diligent efforts. The dye had been produced in the first years of South Carolina's settlement in the late seventeenth century, but the production of rice and naval stores had quickly taken over the colony's economy. The drawbacks to these new staples had become evident by 1740. South Carolina's naval stores were of low quality and therefore price. Rice, which dominated the economy after 1730, was bulky in relation to its value, and many ships were needed to carry away the annual crop. With hostilities heating up after 1739, these ships were in danger from privateers, and insurance rates skyrocketed. War also cut off the colony's primary European markets for rice, and prices therefore dropped dramatically. By 1744, the colony was in deep recession from this squeeze on rice profits—something which, one imagines, went through Eliza's mind as she reviewed her plantation business each Thursday, or while she calculated the profits to be earned from her fig orchard. Indigo solved these problems: it was much more valuable per pound, and a year's product could be carried on a few well-armed ships. England's growing textile industry needed dyes, and so prices were high.

No wonder that Eliza, together with her father and her neighbors, invested so much time and effort in producing indigo. A great effort was necessary, since a number of logistical problems had to be overcome if indigo was to be produced profitably. South Carolina's climate was just barely suited to growing the plant, and Eliza's first crop was destroyed by frost before the plants were mature, and the second by worms. Her father sent different strains of seeds repeatedly to restart the process. More problematic, however, was the high level of technical expertise required to oversee the production of the dye itself. Turning the gold leaves of the indigo bush into cakes of almost-black dyestuff required a series of stages of fermentation, stirring, and drying, all of which needed to be closely monitored in order to produce a high-quality dye. Colonel Lucas sent a series of indigo experts to help instruct the Carolina slaves in the processing of indigo, but these experts were more interested in keeping their secrets than in sharing their knowledge. One, Eliza thought, had deliberately ruined a batch of indigo by dumping too much lime into the vat of fermenting leaves. Eventually, however, the joint efforts of Eliza, her neighbors, and their slaves succeeded; in 1744 a small amount of dye was produced, along with a sufficient quantity of seed to sell to other Carolinians eager to find a secondary crop.

Indigo cultivation spread rapidly across South Carolina after 1745, a testament to the collective efforts of Eliza and her neighbors in developing the crop. Eliza's friend and neighbor (and future husband) Charles Pinckney helped promote indigo, publishing articles in the *South Carolina Gazette* that lauded it as the answer to South Carolina's economic problems. And indigo was not just a profitable export commodity; it was also well suited to the colony's existing economy. It complemented rice planting and slavery. By 1740 the colony's economy depended utterly on slaves to do the backbreaking work of planting rice. The production of indigo, especially, fit into this slave economy. Indigo cultivation and rice cultivation could coexist on the same plantation—they demanded different kinds of land and labor at different times of the year. Rice planters could easily move into the production of indigo, and they did so. One of Eliza Lucas's legacies to South Carolina was the revitalization of plantation slavery during a decade of hard times for the colony's key crop, rice. By the end of the 1740s the value of indigo exports approached that of rice exports, and the slaves who tended both found themselves busier than ever.

Slavery, it should be remembered, was an important part of Eliza Lucas's life in South Carolina. By 1739 about two-thirds of the colony's population was enslaved and of African descent, although this fact is nearly invisible in Eliza's letters, in which she rarely mentions her family's slaves. Slaves sometimes delivered her frequent messages to her friends in Charles Town, since she referred to "Mary Ann," "Togo," and "David" as conveyors of messages. Thus, slaves both produced Eliza's wealth and helped tie together her social world. Slavery drew Eliza's attention more often because of the possibilities of slave rebellion. This focus is not surprising: the Lucases arrived in South Carolina just before the Stono Rebellion erupted there in September 1739, the largest slave rebellion to occur in that colony or all of colonial North America. About one hundred slaves, crying "Liberty," rose up against their masters and fought their way toward Spanish St. Augustine, killing about twenty white Carolinians in the process. Although the rebellion was suppressed in a few days, and far more slaves were executed than whites had perished, white society was hardly calmed. The nearly simultaneous onset of war with Spain, and the Spanish offer of freedom to Carolina's slaves that had contributed to the rebellions, only made white Carolinians more nervous about the threat that their enormous numbers of slaves posed to their dominance and safety. Fears of slave rebellion echoed for the rest of the 1740s. Eliza Lucas noted several suspected slave conspiracies early in that decade, including one that implicated one of her family's slaves.

While the South Carolina Assembly responded to the Stono Rebellion by passing a strict slave code in 1740, restricting slaves' freedom of movement and ability to congregate, it does not appear that Eliza Lucas cracked down on her family's slaves. Indeed, Eliza may have had a more humanitarian notion of how to treat her slaves, although she could not have lived on her plantation without witnessing the daily brutality of slavery. In 1741, Eliza mentioned a "parcel of little Negroes whom I have undertaken to teach to read," and later she told her father of another one of her "schemes": she wished to teach two slave girls to read, so that they could in turn serve as "school mistres's [*sic*] for the rest of the Negroe children."[24] Her purpose in educating her slaves remains unclear. Perhaps teaching her slaves was yet another outlet for her seemingly boundless energy; perhaps she had some other plan. (Slave education would not be outlawed in South Carolina until a later rebellion in 1822.)

It seems possible that Eliza was less fearful of her slaves than many Carolinians, a feeling that her account of a strange event in 1742 helps illustrate. In March a wealthy planter, Hugh Bryan, in the religious enthusiasm of the Great Awakening, began to prophesy slave rebellions and cast himself in the role of Moses in leading slaves to freedom. His attempt to part the waters of a creek, however, failed—he nearly drowned—and Bryan quickly recanted his prophecies. Many white Carolinians feared the "consiquence [*sic*] of such a thing being put in to the head of the slaves," as Eliza put it, but, for her own part, Eliza seems to have appreciated the ridiculousness of the entire story more than its danger.[25] The lesson she drew from it concerned the perils of religious enthusiasm and the importance of following natural reason even in contemplating religious matters. It is characteristic of Eliza Lucas that her mind turned quickly from the threat of slave rebellion to a didactic lesson, from fear to hope. It is also characteristic that Eliza opposed the Great Awakening's religious fervor and followed instead the mainstream Anglican theology of her friend Dr. Alexander Garden, commissary of the Church of England and opponent of religious revivalism.

In January 1744, Eliza Lucas's good friend, Mrs. Elizabeth Pinckney, died after a long illness. Four months later, Eliza Lucas married the widower, Colonel Charles Pinckney. Twenty-four years Eliza's senior, Charles Pinckney was an important man in South Carolina. In the 1730s he had served actively in the colony's Commons House of Assembly, and in 1736 he was elected speaker of the Commons House, a testament to his importance within the colony's political structure. The Pinckneys had been among Eliza's first friends in South Carolina. A close, even affectionate relationship between Eliza and Charles had emerged alongside the female friendship of Eliza, Elizabeth Pinckney, and the Pinckneys' niece, Miss Bartlett. It was Charles who lent Eliza books, assisted in her indigo experiments, and accused her of having a fertile mind for scheming. The two exchanged a continuous friendly correspondence, the breeziness and intimacy of which is striking between a single woman and a married man. Perhaps Charles was a father figure to Eliza, as he was about her father's age. Charles also may have substituted as a social companion for his increasingly ill wife—certainly, Eliza wrote far fewer letters to Elizabeth Pinckney than to Charles. In fact, Charles appears to have been the only man not a relative with whom Eliza cultivated a close correspondence.

Charles Pinckney was not the first man to fall for Eliza Lucas, although none of the earlier suitors gained her favor. When Eliza was only eighteen, two men conveyed their interest in Eliza to her father, who passed on these sentiments to the young lady. She refused them absolutely, and in characteristic form. As for the first, "the riches of Peru and Chili . . . could not purchase a sufficient Esteem for him"; the second she did not know well enough to consider.[26] She preferred to remain single. Indeed, she seemed to spend little thought on matters of the heart: "As to the other sex, I dont trouble my head about them. I take all they say to be words. . . ."[27] Matters had not changed the next year. Eliza reported a romantic "Conquest" of an "old Gentleman" to her friend Miss Bartlett several years later, but refused to provide details in her letter. Indeed, Eliza promised that Miss Bartlett's uncle (Charles Pinckney himself!), who was "much pleased" with the entire affair, would provide a "full account."[28]

On the other hand, in 1741, Eliza signed her copy of one of her letters to Charles Pinckney oddly—"Eliza Pinckney"—which was three years later to be her married name.[29] Perhaps this was a slip of her pen when she copied her letter over in her letterbook, though one must speculate in that case as to whether her subconscious was busily at work. Regardless of Eliza's thoughts that day, it is clear that Eliza and her future husband had developed a close friendship before the death of Elizabeth Pinckney. There is something in the tone of these letters that betrays a high degree of affection and intimacy between the two. The rapidity of their marriage following Elizabeth Pinckney's death was hardly unusual in the eighteenth century, but it occurred soon enough that local gossips wondered whether Eliza had denied Mrs. Pinckney medical care as she was dying. Eliza was shocked by the implication that she would do away with her friend—but Eliza's marrying one of South Carolina's wealthiest and most important men probably made envious aspersions inevitable.

Marriage in May 1744 marked a basic transformation in Eliza's life. While she still looked after her father's plantations after moving to Belmont, the Pinckney plantation north of Charles Town, her activities on that score were necessarily reduced now that she had a husband (and her own household) to attend. This transformation was surely magnified when Eliza became pregnant within a month of their marriage, and gave birth to her first son, Charles Cotesworth, in February 1745. Three more births followed over the next six years: a son, George, in 1747 (who died two weeks after his birth); a daughter, Harriott, in 1748; and a son, Thomas, in 1750. In short order Eliza had become a wife and a mother, and her inclinations toward religious and moral instruction—already evident in her relationship with her brothers—quickly rose to the occasions. Charles apparently was of one mind with Eliza, and together they worked to educate their sons and daughter. Charles Cotesworth reputedly knew his letters before he could talk. The children memorized passages from the Bible and attended church regularly. Eliza's ample energies were now focused, it seems, on her children's education and her husband's happiness, "even in triffles."[30] Her energies were not limitless, on the other hand: with three living infants, and a bout of depression following the death of George, Eliza ceased writing in her letterbook for five years.

South Carolina, despite its wealth and vibrant social life, was still a province, and Charles Pinckney believed that his sons would be best educated at "home"—that is, in England. Eliza, of course, had herself been educated in England, and since the birth of Charles Cotesworth she had hoped that the family would be able to make an extended stay in the mother country. Charles Pinckney's hopes for appointment as chief justice in South Carolina put off the trip for several years, but the position eventually went to another, and Charles put his financial affairs in order for the long visit to England. He also was appointed by the South Carolina Commons House of Assembly as the colonial agent to the Board of Trade in London, providing the family with social and professional contacts in England, as well as more financial support. With these preparations done, in late April 1753 the family of five boarded ship for the voyage across the Atlantic and arrived twenty-five days later in England.

For Eliza, this move was both gratifying and unsettling. She very much desired to return to England. Although her brothers had since departed, she still had friends from her first stay there as a girl. Yet she also "gave a wistful look" at Charles Town as she left.[31] Eliza was now thirty-two years old, and had lived about half her life—all her adult life—in South Carolina. Soon after arrival the family settled near London, and Eliza set about the task of entering English society. Friendships from her earlier stay in London were quickly renewed, and the large community of Carolinians in London supplemented Eliza's lively social scene. At the same time, Eliza maintained her connections across the Atlantic and wrote long letters to women in South Carolina, full of the news from London. With her sons deposited in boarding school and her husband busy in London, Eliza entered the social world with all her energy—with winters at Bath, frequent attendance at the theater, and visits to and from her friends.

While London offered more social opportunities than South Carolina, the narrowing of Eliza's horizons that had begun with her marriage continued in England. Certainly, Eliza's letters ceased to show the kind of vivacity and energy that they had during her single life. Perhaps the variety of social connections in England available to Eliza allowed her to show her wit and charm in drawing rooms instead of in her letters. Yet this change in the tone of her letters also reflected a change in what she herself had to do. Her activities no longer included horticultural experiments, and her moralizing was restricted while her sons were at school. Although her sons' occasional illnesses demanded a mother's attention, socializing occupied most of Eliza's time.

Charles Pinckney became homesick soon after the family's arrival in

London, but it is clear that Eliza did not share this feeling and, in fact, opposed returning to Carolina. Perhaps Eliza was less tied to the New World; the only sign that Eliza might have felt attached to America was her close attention to American affairs after the French and Indian War broke out in 1754. Her letters to South Carolina reveal no pining for that distant land. The outbreak of war, however, did dramatically change the Pinckney family's circumstances. Charles feared that South Carolina was in peril from French attack and desired to return to the colony so he could liquidate his plantations. The children would remain in the safety of English schools. Eliza was not enthusiastic about this plan. She feared the dangers of travel during wartime (her father had died in 1747 after being captured during the last war) and did not particularly want to return to South Carolina herself. Most important, she did not want to be separated from her children for the two or three years it would take for Charles to settle his Carolina affairs. Yet she submitted to her husband's wishes for the most part: Eliza and Charles left their sons in England and embarked for South Carolina in the early spring of 1758, but they took their ten-year-old daughter Harriott with them.

Separation from her sons was only the first of Eliza's trials that year. Less than a month after the couple's arrival in Charles Town, Charles Pinckney contracted malaria, lingered for three weeks, and died on July 12, 1758. Over the next month, Eliza buried her husband, began to arrange for the disposition of his estate, and went about the melancholy task of informing her sons and her family of Charles's death. In these letters, Eliza displayed her characteristic strength of character and moral sensibility, as well as her affection for her husband of fourteen years.

One can imagine how difficult it was to break this news by letter to her sons, only seven and thirteen years old. Not surprisingly, Eliza drew a potent moral and religious lesson from the untimely passing of Charles at fifty-nine years of age. His family more than ever had to depend on the strength of God, whose will was most clearly expressed in the unhappy event. She told her sons that their father's death was an exemplary one: "His sick bed and dying moments were the natural conclusion of such a life," and he "met the king of terrors without the least terror or affright," and "went like a Lamb into eternity." Eliza promised that she, as widow and mother to Charles Pinckney's children, would devote the rest of her life to honoring their father's memory by serving them. She concluded with an exhortation that her sons be "worthy [of] such a father as yours was."[32] To her mother, who had returned to Antigua after Eliza's marriage,

Eliza repeatedly described the virtues (she used the word four times in her letter) of her husband and her hopes to meet Charles in eternity.

More pressing practical business included the settlement of Charles's estate and providing for the education of the children still in England. For Eliza, both were familiar territory. She had no problem assuming the management of Charles's affairs: paying debts, arranging for probate of the will, and maintaining the family plantations, which were run down after the Pinckneys' four-year absence. One imagines that Eliza's return to the world of business must have been unhappy at first, but that, with time, planting gardens and directing affairs were pleasant tasks. "I love a Garden and a book," Eliza wrote a friend in England five years after her husband's death, "and they are all my amusement" except for raising her daughter.[33] Eliza also renewed the vivacity and charm of her youth during these years, as she continued to build and maintain the friendships that she had made across the globe and sent more potatoes, limes, and beets around the world.

Yet managing these worldly matters demanded that Eliza remain separated from her sons; Charles Cotesworth did not return to South Carolina until 1768, and Thomas not until 1772. Eliza's direction of their education accordingly had to take place across the Atlantic. Here, too, Eliza gave the same counsel as she had to her brothers: she emphasized virtue, independence, and Christian morality to her sons. She gave advice on a wide variety of subjects, from proper treatment of servants to the importance of restraining one's passions. While Eliza feared that "the morals of Youth are taken little care of" at public schools and university and she knew that London offered "temptations with every youthful passion," she had faith in her sons' ability to maintain "moral Virtue, Religion, and learning."[34]

Her counsels were given to sons who followed a typical English gentleman's education—attendance at elite boarding schools, followed by a stint at, if not a degree from, Oxford or Cambridge University, and perhaps legal training at the Inns of Court in London. The next generation of planter-aristocrats received an English liberal education. It is ironic, then, that both Charles Cotesworth and Thomas Pinckney came of age in England and partook of an English gentleman's education just as the first stirrings of Anglo-American conflict appeared. Both sons identified with their native soil from the earliest phases of this conflict, with Thomas being known as the "Little Rebel" by his English friends and Charles Cotesworth in 1766 having a portrait painted of himself declaiming against the Stamp Act of 1765.

During the convulsions preceding American independence, Eliza saw her daughter Harriott married to Daniel Horry in 1768, and her two sons return to South Carolina, marry, and take their place on Pinckney family plantations. These domestic transformations did not leave Eliza alone or idle, since she still maintained the easy sociability of the South Carolina low country, and her new son- and daughters-in-law merely expanded her social circle. Eliza spent long periods with Harriott at Hampton, the Horry family estate. It must have gratified Eliza to see Harriott follow her mother's interest in gardening and to assist in the moral and intellectual training of her grandchildren, who were born with some regularity in the years following 1768. Eliza also appears to have become something of a medical practitioner in middle age; ailments and treatments played an increasing role in her correspondence with her South Carolina acquaintances.

Eliza Lucas Pinckney had spent her life enmeshed in a web of empire-wide connections. Her father was a colonial official, she had spent long periods of time in England, and her family had even at one point planned to settle in the mother country. Her friendships extended around the Atlantic, mostly among correspondents who were also connected with imperial administration. It is ironic, then, that her family would be so closely identified with the movement for American independence in South Carolina. While Eliza made few references in her letters to the crises leading to that independence, her sons, especially Charles Cotesworth, were intimately involved with the political storms that developed during the 1770s and usually favored a vigorous colonial response to the actions of the British ministry. Soon after the battles of Lexington and Concord in April 1775, Charles Cotesworth led a raid on the colony's armory that secured the government's weapons for the patriots, and later that year he was elected a captain in the South Carolina militia. Thomas soon followed his brother into the patriots' service, and both ended the war as high-ranking officers in the Continental army, with Charles Cotesworth becoming a brigadier general.

The Pinckney sons' deep support of the patriot cause is not altogether surprising, even considering their close connections with the British Empire. Their father had been central in the development of a distinctive political rhetoric in South Carolina in the 1730s, one that emphasized the necessity of virtue and independence in government. South Carolinians repeatedly decried attempts by royal governors to limit the prerogatives of the elected assembly, either by overt action or by insidious acts of "corruption": for instance, providing government offices to assemblymen friendly to the government. Charles Pinckney Sr. had experienced corruption firsthand just before the family's trip to England, when he was denied the office of chief justice of South Carolina in favor of a better-connected man. Even after their father's death, Eliza's consistent reminders to her sons to follow the paths of virtue and independence reinforced this basic understanding of politics. When the British ministry's acts began to look corrupt in the escalating crises following the Stamp Act, the Townshend Duties, and finally the Intolerable Acts, men such as the Pinckneys were willing to put aside their loyalty to the king and follow the path that they had been taught was virtuous.

During these crises, Eliza could not be virtuous in the same way as her sons. As a woman, her political role was restricted to the sidelines. When war came to South Carolina in 1778, however, women such as Eliza had to make choices about what to do, choices that indicated their loyalty and could also provoke reprisals from the partisan forces at war. With the British occupation of Charles Town and a bitter civil war raging over the countryside, there was no neutrality. Eliza, caught in the midst of these struggles on her son-in-law's plantation outside Charles Town, chose to support the patriot cause in her way. Much of the low country where Eliza's family lived was occupied alternately by British and American troops, leaving her subject to depredations from both sides, but mostly from the British. Since Eliza would not proclaim loyalty to the king, her houses in Charles Town were occupied by British troops who paid no rent, while her stock was carried off her plantations, and her slaves ran away or were captured, leaving her plantations to produce no income at all. In 1779, Eliza complained of her "losses" and the "almost ruined fortunes" of her sons, and two years later she found herself incapable of paying a debt of £60 sterling—an amount that would have been a trifle just five years earlier.

Eliza suffered more than economic losses. Both her sons were soldiers in the cause of independence, and she was daily concerned with their health and welfare. Thomas was injured and captured by the British in 1780, leaving her quite distraught with worry. Charles Cotesworth quickly offered to share his own estate with his brother and mother after these disasters, but both refused. For Eliza, what was most grievous was the loss of her independence, her ability to be free from obligation to others and to shower her own benevolence on her children and grandchildren. Here, Eliza shared in the ideas of virtue and independence that she had impressed upon her sons: she wanted to be dependent on no one, to provide for herself.

Following the war, times did not immediately improve. The War of

Independence in South Carolina had become a bitter civil war among the colony's inhabitants, and this animosity persisted well beyond the coming of peace in 1783. Independence had thrust many poorer Carolinians into political activity, an unaccustomed phenomenon for the low-country planter oligarchy who had maintained the upper hand for so long. Sizable numbers of low-country planters had been loyal to the king or tepid in their patriotism, which made their property attractive targets for angry patriots, who pushed for bills confiscating loyalist estates and heavily taxing those whose support for the cause was less than fervent. Perhaps because Eliza Lucas Pinckney herself had no public political position—as a woman she had no formal political voice, and her husband's politics had been in the grave for nearly a quarter century—her estates (damaged as they were) could not be seized. In fact, the damage that Eliza's property received at the hands of the British probably helped demonstrate that the British did not consider her a friend. Finally, her two sons' conspicuous service in the patriot cause ensured that they would not be punished (Charles Cotesworth, indeed, sat in the state legislature). Eliza's son-in-law Daniel Horry was less lucky—his estate was punitively taxed, and a friend of the family believed that only the Pinckneys' "many Virtues" prevented it from being confiscated.[35]

Eliza spent most of the postwar years at the Horry plantation, where she continued her agricultural labors and helped oversee the education of her grandchildren. She even entertained President George Washington during his visit to South Carolina in 1791. A single letter to her grandson, Daniel Horry Jr., survives, in which she reprised for a third generation the moral and religious advice she had given her brothers and sons. A "liberal Education," a proper restraint of emotions and passions, and industriousness were the virtues she urged upon twelve-year-old Daniel, whom she saw as part of a "rising generation" whose "abilities and improved Talents" would raise the newly independent South Carolina in its "Second Infancy."[36] Eliza's basic message had not changed: virtue, restraint of passions, and self-control. To this, however, Eliza added a new message of service to one's nation. Historians have called this moral emphasis "Republican motherhood"—the notion that women, as mothers and grandmothers, could instill in their children the virtue needed to guide a nation. Eliza had been doing this job for three generations, but the political context of this work had changed in the meantime, from the world-spanning British Empire, to the independent State of South Carolina, and now to the new United States of America.

Eliza Lucas Pinckney was diagnosed with cancer in 1792, at seventy years of age. A year later she traveled to Philadelphia to consult with a famous physician, who failed to cure her. She died on May 26, 1793, and was buried the next day, with President George Washington serving as a pallbearer. (Washington had sought out Eliza during his visit to South Carolina two years earlier; he had wanted to meet the famous agriculturalist and the mother of two such conspicuous South Carolina patriots.) Eliza had lived a long and varied life. She had been the epitome of the cosmopolitan British Empire, and the mother of American patriots. She had been a society belle with extraordinary wit, charm, and manners, and had also been a devout Christian, a moralist, and an agricultural innovator. She was a vivacious single woman, a devoted wife and mother, and an industrious widow, but her life was never entirely defined by her connections to men. Her legacies lived long after her death—her descendants continued to experiment with new crops such as sugar and cotton, and the Pinckneys remained politically prominent in South Carolina. Eliza Pinckney is well remembered as the mother to this famous family; she should be remembered also in her own right.

Notes

1. Eliza Lucas Pinckney (hereafter, ELP) to Mrs. Evance, June 19, 1760, in Elise Pinckney, ed., *The Letterbook of Eliza Lucas Pinckney, 1739–1762* (Chapel Hill: University of North Carolina Press, 1972), 151. Hereafter cited as *Letterbook*. All dates before 1752 are Old Style, except that the year is taken to begin on January 1.

2. Eliza Lucas (hereafter, EL) to Miss Bartlett (hereafter, Miss B.), January 14, 1742, *Letterbook*, 26.

3. Ibid.

4. ELP to C. C. Pinckney, September 10, 1785, quoted in *Letterbook*, xxv.

5. EL to Miss B., ca. April 1742, *Letterbook*, 34–35.

6. EL to Mrs. Boddicott, May 2, 1740, *Letterbook*, 7–8.

7. EL to Mrs. Boddicott, June 29, 1742, *Letterbook*, 42.

8. EL to Mrs. Pinckney, ca. July 1741, *Letterbook*, 19.

9. Ibid.

10. EL to Miss B., ca. April 1742, *Letterbook*, 31.

11. EL to Miss B., ca. March 1742, *Letterbook*, 29.

12. Ibid., 29–30.

13. EL to Miss B., ca. May 1743, *Letterbook*, 62.

14. EL to George Lucas, June 1742, *Letterbook*, 45.

15. EL to dear Brother, July 1742, *Letterbook*, 52–53.

16. EL to Father, February 10, 1743, *Letterbook*, 59.

17. EL to Miss B., ca. June 1742, *Letterbook*, 41.

18. EL to Miss B., ca. April 1742, *Letterbook*, 35.

19. EL to Father, June 4, 1741, *Letterbook*, 15.

20. EL to Miss B., April 1742, *Letterbook,* 36.

21. Ibid., 35.

22. EL to Miss B., May 1742, *Letterbook,* 38.

23. EL to Miss B., April 1742, *Letterbook,* 35.

24. EL to Charles Pinckney, February 6, 1741, *Letterbook,* 12; EL to Miss B., April 1742, *Letterbook,* 34.

25. EL to Miss B., March 1742, *Letterbook,* 29–30.

26. EL to Colonel Lucas, ca. April 1740, *Letterbook,* 6.

27. EL to Miss B., January 1742, *Letterbook,* 27.

28. EL to Miss B., May 1743, *Letterbook,* 62.

29. EL to Charles Pinckney, February 6, 1741, *Letterbook,* 12.

30. ELP to Gov. George Lucas, ca. 1745, quoted in Marvin R. Zahniser, *Charles Cotesworth Pinckney: Founding Father* (Chapel Hill: University of North Carolina Press, 1967), 8.

31. ELP to Mary W. Wragg [?], May 20, 1753, *Letterbook,* 75.

32. ELP to Charles and Thomas Pinckney, August 1758, *Letterbook,* 94–95.

33. ELP to Mr. Keate, February 1762, *Letterbook,* 181.

34. ELP to Charles Pinckney, February 7, 1761, *Letterbook,* 158–59; ELP to Charles Pinckney, April 15, 1761, *Letterbook,* 167.

35. Edward Rutledge to Arthur Middleton, February 26, 1782, quoted in Zahniser, *Charles Cotesworth Pinckney,* 73.

36. ELP to Daniel Horry Jr., April 16, 1782, in Elise Pinckney, ed., "Letters of Eliza Lucas Pinckney, 1768–1782," *South Carolina Historical Magazine* 76 (1975): 167.

Suggested Readings

Baskett, Sam S. "Eliza Lucas Pinckney: Portrait of an Eighteenth Century American." *South Carolina Historical Magazine* 72 (1971): 207–19.

Chaplin, Joyce E. *An Anxious Pursuit: Agricultural Innovation and Modernity in the Lower South, 1730–1815.* Chapel Hill: University of North Carolina Press, 1993.

Coon, David L. "Eliza Lucas Pinckney and the Reintroduction of Indigo Cultivation in South Carolina." *Journal of Southern History* 42 (1976): 61–76.

Kerber, Linda. *Women of the Republic: Intellect and Ideology in Revolutionary America.* Chapel Hill: University of North Carolina Press, 1980.

Pinckney, Elise, ed. *The Letterbook of Eliza Lucas Pinckney, 1739–1762.* Chapel Hill: University of North Carolina Press, 1972.

———. "Letters of Eliza Lucas Pinckney, 1768–1782." *South Carolina Historical Magazine* 76 (1975): 143–70.

Ravenel, Harriott H. *Eliza Pinckney.* New York: Scribner's, 1896.

Woloch, Nancy. "Eliza Pinckney and Republican Motherhood." In *Women and the American Experience,* 51–64. New York: Alfred A. Knopf, 1984.

Zahniser, Marvin R. *Charles Cotesworth Pinckney: Founding Father.* Chapel Hill: University of North Carolina Press, 1967.

6

Benjamin Gilbert and
Jacob Nagle
Soldiers of the
American Revolution

John Shy

The Revolutionary War marked a coming of age for the new nation and for Benjamin Gilbert (1755–1828) of Massachusetts and Jacob Nagle (1762–1841) of Pennsylvania, who both served in the American military. For two ordinary men, Gilbert and Nagle left extraordinarily rich written accounts of their lives. Youths when the Revolution began, they both served in local regiments, and yet military service and travel broadened their worldview. While Gilbert provides an eyewitness account of camp life in the Continental Army, Nagle's adventures included captivity as a prisoner of war. Given the experiences of Gilbert and Nagle, was Eliza Lucas Pinckney justified in worrying about soldiers' temptations to immorality?

Gilbert achieved officer rank and reenlisted, while Nagle became a patriot privateer and later a member of the Royal Navy. In calling Gilbert a success and Nagle a failure, what is being measured? What role did chance, or family connections, play in their contrasting fates? At war's end, Gilbert left the army, married, and became a farmer in western New York and later a New York legislator. As a professional sailor, Nagle traveled to more distant and exotic places, including Australia. Both Gilbert and Nagle died as Revolutionary War heroes, even though Nagle had served much longer in the Royal Navy than in the patriot cause. As John Shy concludes, each character represents a different type of American: Gilbert, the middle-class western farmer; and Nagle, the supreme individualist.

John Shy, an expert in the military history of the American Revolution, is the author of numerous books and articles, including *Toward Lexington: The Role of the British Army in the Coming of the American Revolution* (1965) and *A People Numerous and Armed: Reflections on the Military Struggle for American Independence* (1990). He has long taught at the University of Michigan.

Wars are fought by the very young. However and wherever wars start, invariably men—and now women—barely out of their childhood do the actual fighting and most of the dying. The War for American

Independence, 1775–1783, was no exception. American political leaders, many in their forties, had mobilized opposition to British taxation and other measures that most Americans felt violated a long-standing limitation of the power of British government to rule the colonies. When this political opposition led to violence and then to open warfare in 1775, men of that same older generation, such as George Washington (age forty-three in 1775), became the generals and colonels commanding the rebel armies. Younger men, in their thirties or late twenties, were the captains who led companies of fifty or one hundred men into battle. But after the first few months of fighting around Boston, where men of every age turned out to serve briefly, the hard, dirty work of fighting for independence fell mostly on thousands of mere boys.

Eight years later, when American independence was finally won, those boys were men, hardened and changed by their experience of war. When we think of the impact of the American Revolutionary War, we usually recall the stirring words of the 1776 Declaration of Independence—"all men are created equal"—with its definition of the American cause as "life, liberty, and the pursuit of happiness." But for thousands of very young men, and a few women who disguised themselves as men, the true impact of the Revolution was in the specific way it sent their lives spinning quickly into a new orbit, with the final destination out of their control.

The experiences of two ordinary young men, Benjamin Gilbert and Jacob Nagle, both still in their teens when war erupted in 1775, allow us to see in detail how the American Revolution changed, profoundly but very differently, two lives. Both men survived the war, dying in their seventies to public praise as heroes of the American Revolution. Each, for his own personal reasons, created a careful written record of his life, accounts that have survived down to our own time and given us a rare chance to trace and assess the impact of the Revolutionary War on two ordinary yet very different lives.

Benjamin Gilbert, still in his teens, went to war the day it began in April 1775. When early on a spring morning British regular soldiers and Massachusetts militiamen opened fire on one another at Lexington, not far from Boston, Benjamin was living in the town of Brookfield, about fifty miles west of the action. But Benjamin was already a soldier in Brookfield's "minute" company—a militia unit of about fifty local men who had been training for just such an emergency and were ready to march when the news came that fighting had broken out. Within a few hours after the first reports of Lexington reached towns like Brookfield, minute companies like Gilbert's from all over Massachusetts were on the road to Boston. Brookfield's company was too far away (a good two-day march) to see any action in this first battle of what would be known as the War of American Independence, but Gilbert and his comrades joined thousands of others who surrounded the port town of Boston, where British troops had retreated after two days of bloody fighting along the road to Lexington and the nearby town of Concord, which had been their original objective.

From these first days of the war, Benjamin Gilbert may have kept a written record of his military experience. We say "may," because personal records for this early period of his military service have never been found. But we do have his diary, beginning New Year's Day 1778, that continues into the postwar years, as well as letters written by Gilbert that he copied either on blank pages in the diary or into a separate notebook. Diary-keeping as a way of tracking one's moral behavior and religious condition was an old New England custom. Many diaries kept by New England common soldiers in the colonial and Revolutionary wars have come down to us, and obviously young Benjamin Gilbert was a diary-keeping Yankee. So it seems reasonable to think that he kept a record from the very beginning, a record that has been lost. But we can roughly reconstruct what happened to him in the early years of the war from army records, and also from his own pension application, submitted to the federal government long after the war. Only in 1778, his third year at war, can we begin to learn about his life in rich detail.

Jacob Nagle, Gilbert's even younger counterpart from Pennsylvania, probably kept no such day-to-day records, although we cannot be sure. What Nagle left us was a very detailed memoir of his life, written when he was an old man. Memories often become blurry and distorted as the years pass, and so there is good reason to ask why we should trust the memory of old Jacob Nagle on events of his teens and twenties. The answer is in the details he recorded of his service in the American army, and later as a prisoner of war and at sea. These details can be checked against official records, and in virtually every case they match exactly. There is no way Nagle could have invented the stories in his memoir, because the details were buried in records that were not available to him at the time. Either he had a wonderfully clear memory, or his final, handwritten memoir (which was found among his possessions after his death) was based on other personal records, perhaps diaries like those kept by Gilbert or letters that have not survived. All we have from Jacob Nagle is the memoir, but it is at least as rich in personal insight as the diaries and letters of Benjamin Gilbert.

Gilbert, at age nineteen, was in the war first. Why? What motivated him? His deeper motives remain a mystery, but we can feel certain that his family and community figured significantly in sending him off to war. Brookfield, Massachusetts, was a fairly typical New England country town, first settled a century before the American Revolution on land cleared by previous Indian settlers. In 1675, Indians returned to Brookfield and waged one of the bloodiest wars in all American history, "King Philip's War." Brookfield, out on the frontier of English settlement, was destroyed and its site abandoned for a decade.

When Brookfield began to be resettled in the 1680s, many of the new settlers came from the older coastal town of Ipswich, and the English family name of Gilbert was prominent among them. Brookfield was not a prosperous town; most of the houses, even after the Revolution, were poorly built and unpainted. But like other towns, Brookfield taxed itself to build a meetinghouse and hire a Congregational minister, and by 1750 even to pay a "School Dame" to teach its children. Young Benjamin Gilbert attended the town school while his father and grandfather were serving in the colonial wars against the French that ended with a complete British victory in 1763. The inhabitants of Brookfield were proud to be British, but they were even more devoted to the British traditions of liberty and self-government. New British policies toward the American colonies after 1763 seemed to threaten those traditions, and though the center of agitation, protest, and resistance was Boston, Brookfield solidly supported Boston in the political battle that turned into war by 1775. Surely young Benjamin Gilbert felt the influences of his own town.

Daniel Gilbert, Benjamin's father, a veteran of the failed military campaign of 1757 to save Fort William Henry, familiar to those who have read the book or seen the film *The Last of the Mohicans,* was an officer in the Worcester County militia and also a "selectman," one of the town's elected board of managers. Despite these military and political offices, Daniel was no more than a well-off farmer, because most of the Gilbert family wealth had been inherited by Daniel's older brother Joseph. Benjamin's uncle was listed in town records as a merchant, whose sons—Benjamin's cousins—attended Yale and Dartmouth while Benjamin would make his way through life on what he had learned from the "School Dame." The family's military tradition may have been a reason for his joining Brookfield's "minute company" when it was formed in 1774 and marching to war in 1775. Desire for adventure is also normal in a young man, and maybe the New England army swarming around Boston looked to an ambitious boy like both Adventure and Opportunity.

Within days at Boston, Benjamin had enlisted in the company commanded by a Brookfield neighbor, Captain Peter Harwood, part of the regiment commanded by Colonel Ebenezer Learned. Learned's regiment was stationed at Roxbury on the far right of the American line ringing the British garrison of Boston, so when the British attacked in June at the left end of the American line at Bunker Hill, Learned's men came under fire but were not in the American line of battle, which the British finally overran after suffering enormous casualties. Although Benjamin could not possibly have reached Lexington in time for the April battle, and almost surely was not in the heavy fighting at Bunker Hill in June, his son would engrave on his father's tombstone "Lexington" and "Bunker Hill." Benjamin Gilbert would not be the first, or the last, veteran to claim to have taken part in a battle he just missed, but the third battle name on the tombstone—"Saratoga"—would be fully earned.

In March 1776 the British navy evacuated the Boston garrison, which had failed to break the American siege. Learned's Massachusetts regiment, now renamed the Third Continental, under the general command of George Washington, who had been chosen by the Congress in Philadelphia to lead the American military effort, moved with the main army to New York, the likeliest point for the next British attack. Against superior British seapower, the port of New York was essentially indefensible, but Congress and Washington, faced with a shaky American union that was still struggling to declare independence from British rule, felt compelled to make their best effort. Gilbert and the Third Continentals escaped being caught in one of the worst defeats in American military history, at Brooklyn Heights on Long Island in August, but they saw plenty of combat. In July, British warships had sailed up the Hudson, past Manhattan Island, firing at the American artillery guarding the bank. Several British shots hit the camp of Gilbert's regiment, one flying between the legs of two of his comrades, but no one was hurt.

Far more serious was Benjamin's first real battle in October, when the Third, as part of a Massachusetts brigade of about eight hundred men commanded by John Glover of Marblehead, at Pelham Bay in the Bronx, stopped a much larger British landing force trying to cut off the retreating American army. Mission accomplished, Glover's exhausted brigade marched northwest to safety and rest, leaving six dead comrades; Gilbert's new regimental commander, William Shepard, was hit in the throat by a British bullet but survived.

The little battle of Pelham Bay, one of few successful American actions in the 1776 New York campaign, was unlike anything Gilbert had experienced before. Armed with not very accurate smooth-bore, single-shot muskets that required almost a minute to reload, Gilbert and his few hundred inexperienced comrades had faced at close quarters in an open field thousands of well-trained British infantry, bayonets fixed, moving in to kill them. Little imagination is needed to realize how he must have felt. As Washington's defeated and disintegrating army straggled across New Jersey to reach the Delaware River, Gilbert stayed with Glover's brigade east of the Hudson River, part of a larger force left by Washington to guard against any British move northward, toward New England. In late November, hard-pressed and desperate for reinforcements, Washington ordered these eastern troops to join him as quickly as possible on the west bank of the Delaware.

At about the time of the traditional New England Thanksgiving in 1776, Benjamin Gilbert and his comrades were loading into boats at Peekskill, New York, and crossing the mighty Hudson River. Winter was coming, and British officers noted that the Americans they had killed or captured wore only light clothing and sometimes lacked even shoes, stockings, and blankets. As Gilbert clambered out of the boat and onto the Jersey shore, hoisting his pack and musket for the long, hilly trek to the Delaware, he was in a foreign country. Brookfield and Boston were home, but this—New York and New Jersey—was a strange land. He could not have guessed that for much of the next seven years this foreign country, the lower Hudson Valley, would become his backyard, and he would come to know it very well—a new "home."

In his application for a federal pension, submitted when he was sixty-two, Benjamin Gilbert mentioned no battles, but said that he had served the "whole" campaign of 1776, so we may assume that he was a member of Glover's brigade on Christmas night when it crossed the ice-strewn Delaware, marched nine miles down the river road in a snowstorm to Trenton, where it surprised and killed or captured almost a thousand German regulars, hired by Britain to reinforce its army in America. This small but spectacular American victory was won at just the moment when many observers thought the American rebellion had collapsed. But we cannot assume that Gilbert was present a week later, in early January 1777, when Washington won another small but politically crucial victory at Princeton, just ten miles away, because no surviving record for the regiment tells us who stayed and who left when their enlistments expired. Gilbert, like his comrades in Boston, had enlisted the previous January for exactly one year, and that year was up December 31, 1776. All the New Englanders, beaten, tired, and ill prepared for winter, wanted to go home, and many did so. Some had left before the victory at Trenton, convinced that travel time should be part of their enlisted service. Washington had begged them to stay and to reenlist for a longer term. Some stayed but very few reenlisted in Washington's army. Even John Glover, a gallant brigade commander, went home after Trenton, and his own regiment—the Fourteenth Continentals—went with him. Benjamin Gilbert may have done the same, as was his undoubted right.

Once back home, he did not pick up the plow and resume the life of a Yankee farmboy, secure in the belief that he had done his share of fighting and suffering and that some other sturdy American lad would take his place. Instead, in January 1777 he rejoined the army, this time enlisting for three years, under two family friends—Captain Daniel Shays and Colonel Rufus Putnam. Happy to recruit a seasoned combat veteran of twenty-two, they made him a sergeant in the Fifth Massachusetts Regiment, in which he would serve until the end of the war. By late spring, Putnam's men were marching, not southward to join Washington, but westward to stop a British invasion from Canada. The plan for 1777, adopted in London, to crush the American rebellion, called for the British army in New York to engage Washington in decisive battle, while another army, moving directly south from Montreal, drove a stake into the heart of the American cause. It was this army from Canada that Gilbert would face.

Fort Ticonderoga had fallen to the British advance before Gilbert and the Fifth Massachusetts Regiment joined the retreating American army in July. He was just one of thousands of soldiers coming from New England to reinforce the failing effort to stop the Canadian invasion. At the final major battle fought near Saratoga, on October 7, Colonel Putnam's regiment helped stop the British attack and then captured a supporting redoubt manned by German regulars. Several days later men from the Fifth Massachusetts were part of the force that cut off the last line of British retreat. British surrender at Saratoga brought France openly into the war as an American ally, ensuring that Britain would never be able to defeat the colonial rebels.

Benjamin Gilbert must have done well at Saratoga because he was promoted soon after to sergeant major, or top sergeant in Shays's company. Very likely he had been one of forty volunteers at Saratoga under Captain Nathan Goodale, who had captured the boats in which the British had hoped to get away, because later Gilbert was transferred to Goodale's company. From the end of 1777, we have the full, personal record of Gilbert's service to the end of the war, and of his life afterward.

While Benjamin Gilbert was helping to win the battle of Saratoga, Jacob Nagle was getting a taste of war in his home state of Pennsylvania. Like Benjamin Gilbert, Jacob lived in a small town, Reading, about fifty miles inland from a major seaport, in his case, Philadelphia. His father was a militia officer, a veteran of the last colonial war, and a local political officeholder; and like Benjamin Gilbert, Jacob had younger sisters but no brothers. Jacob's father, George, recruited a company of riflemen when the news of Lexington arrived in Reading, Pennsylvania, and he led them to Boston in 1775. The town of Reading, settled heavily by German immigrants like the Nagles in the decades before 1775, was not so outspoken in its opposition to British policies as Brookfield, Massachusetts, but, with the outbreak of war, there seemed little question as to which side the town would support. George Nagle was a blacksmith, and also the sheriff of Berks County, but in January 1776 he was appointed major of the Fifth Pennsylvania Regiment. Major Nagle took his fourteen-year-old son Jacob with him to Philadelphia, where the boy saw life in the barracks. Though sixteen was usually the minimum age for military service, some big boys lied about their age, and some officers, like Major Nagle, enlisted underage sons to serve as personal orderlies or "waiters." Enrolled as a soldier in Captain Gibbs Jones's company of Colonel Thomas Proctor's artillery regiment, Jacob became part of Washington's army in 1777, facing the invasion of his homeland by a British army that had landed in Maryland at the head of Chesapeake Bay.

Benjamin Gilbert was marching to Saratoga when young Jacob Nagle experienced defeat at Brandywine Creek, where Delaware abuts Pennsylvania. It was along the Brandywine that Washington planned to stop the British advance on the American capital at Philadelphia. The battle of the Brandywine is not one of the glorious moments in American military history. As had happened a year earlier on Long Island, Washington was badly out-generaled. But as Jacob later wrote, he could "not pretend to give a discription of the action, only where I was myself."[1] Most of the British army moved well out of sight up the Brandywine Valley to outflank the American line, but young Nagle and his comrades thought that they and their cannons were facing the main enemy attack. Jacob had eaten almost nothing for three days, and the battle opened for him when a British cannonball shot away the kettle cooking what he expected to be a "glorious" breakfast. Infantry moved back and forth across the meadowland in front of his position, and when he rested from the day's heat in the shade of a wagon, another British shot knocked off a wagon wheel. British infantry charged the position held by his father's regiment, to his right, and he saw a red-coated British officer leading the charge simply disappear in a blast from one of Captain Jones's brass cannons. He never forgot his horror when he saw soldiers hastily burying an American officer whom, for a few moments in the confusion of battle, Nagle mistook for his own father.

Soon they heard that British troops were coming down the roads behind them, and the order came to withdraw. His company abandoned their cannon when, with all the horses dead, they could not be pulled across the swampy ground. As the retreat became a rout, Jacob remembered seeing a beautiful white horse, handsomely appointed and running free, but he was too frightened by enemy fire to try to catch it. Faint from thirst, he was saved by an older comrade who pushed through fugitives crowded around a well to bring Jacob a canteen of water. A steady cold rain during the next days made the long retreat of the beaten army miserable, but Colonel Proctor gave Jacob a spare horse to ride until, "driping wet and shivering with cold," he was invited into an ammunition wagon to get warm and dry.[2] At Yellow Springs, about twenty-five miles from Philadelphia, the army encamped, and Jacob was given a "furlow" to go home to Reading. There he learned that his mother had been caring for a wounded American soldier, about his own age, who had finally died of three bullet wounds. Although he returned to army duty for a few weeks in 1777, seeing the encampment at Valley Forge, and for a few more weeks in spring 1778, Jacob Nagle had had enough of the army. Underage and the only son of a senior officer, he easily got his discharge.

In 1778, at the midpoint of the War for American Independence, the lives of our two young Americans sharply diverged. Benjamin Gilbert, a seasoned combat veteran of twenty-three, committed himself to army life. Jacob Nagle, barely sixteen, went home and stayed there for a few years. Gilbert would serve in the army to the very end of the war, in late 1783, and then build a new life, fairly prosperous and eminently respectable, far from his Brookfield home, out on the New York frontier. Jacob Nagle chose very differently. As he reached manhood, he too left home, making another contribution to the American cause, but then drifted through the turmoil of war into a long career of incredible adventure, never finding stability or security, never seeking respectability, and never avoiding trouble. It is tempting to say that Jacob Nagle, unlike Benjamin Gilbert, was a failure, ruined by the fortunes of war. But perhaps it is wiser to tell their stories, and let the reader judge.

After Saratoga, Gilbert's regiment moved down the Hudson Valley to West Point, where a massive rocky outcropping forces the river to make a sharp bend, thereby providing a natural defensive position for the American army about fifty miles north of Manhattan Island, the British headquarters. For almost six years, West Point and vicinity would be Gilbert's home base. Later travelers admired the great natural beauty of the spot, where wooded mountains plunge sharply into the river, and a plateau stretching to the point of land offers a breathtaking view up the valley. But all the beauty was lost on Gilbert. Seeing it for the first time with the eyes of a farmer, he wrote in his diary that it was "a Rough Desolate place."[3] Much later, in 1782, striving to put his impressions into elaborate language that he had picked up from reading popular eighteenth-century literature, he described West Point to his younger stepbrother back in Brookfield:

> Stationed in a concavity between two Stupendious Spercial Hills where Nature has excluded it from her most beautiful part. No Magnificent landscapes to feast my eyes nor Verdant groves to ravish my sences, or purling streams, nor mumering rivelets to cool or refresh me. . . . If I indulge my eyes to wander abroad with hopes of beholding some beautifull objects I at once perceive my hopes Blasted. Instead of beholding spacious planes, Vegetable Fields, or beautified parks, I observe one continued series of convexative Rock and prominent Clifts.[4]

Even allowing for shaky spelling and dubious word choice, we may guess that Gilbert wrote this letter when he was drunk. Elated by a recent promotion to lieutenant and participation the previous fall in the decisive Yorktown campaign that had virtually ended all British hope for victory over the rebellious Americans, Gilbert had just returned from a furlough spent at home in Brookfield. His diary records a round of visits, parties, and more than a little drinking. Other evidence strongly indicates that, during his furlough, he had also made a sexual conquest of Patience, the daughter of Colonel James Converse, one of the most prominent men in Worcester County and commander of the county militia regiment. So the letter to his stepbrother was written after enjoying a hero's welcome back home, and a few days after his depressing return to the grimy reality of military routine. No longer the boy who had gone to war as a fifer with the Brookfield minutemen in 1775, he was a fully formed man, nearing his twenty-seventh birthday, when he wrote this pompous, silly, and probably drunken description of where he had spent most of the past four years.

Skipping ahead four years, from 1778 to 1782, may seem unfair to the story, but Benjamin Gilbert's life at war after 1777 was not—with a few exceptions—very exciting or as dangerous as it had been in 1776 and 1777. With the British army fortified on and around Manhattan,

Washington deployed most of his army at least a long day's march northward, in the hills of New Jersey and near the Hudson highlands, with West Point as the central point. Here Sergeant, later Lieutenant, Gilbert did his duty and made his own life as pleasant as possible. The two armies warily watched one another, patrolling, raiding, and skirmishing across the no-man's land that separated them, making plans that usually fell through, and waiting for a chance to end the war in one decisive blow. Gilbert served in some of the American detachments that roamed down into Westchester County, hoping to ambush the enemy and trying to avoid being ambushed. He was never wounded or captured on these expeditions, although once he almost broke a leg returning to camp drunk at night, after visiting a nearby farmhouse. The rest of his time he spent training new recruits, doing army paperwork, repairing and cleaning his clothing, attending to his own bodily needs—including an occasional bath—and otherwise finding ways to pass the time. Reading, picking berries in season, playing cards and ball games, talking, and writing letters were among the ways he recorded in his diary—itself a way to fight the boredom of army life. But his most frequently noted pastimes were hunting women and drinking.

Jacob Nagle's father, colonel of the Tenth Pennsylvania Regiment in 1777, left the army in an obscure scandal and then moved his family to Philadelphia after the British gave up the city in 1778. There he later opened a waterfront tavern catering to sailors, and Jacob decided to go to sea. He offers no explanation in his memoir, but a reasonable guess is that, by then eighteen and with his memory of what happened on the Brandywine still fresh, he was strongly disinclined to be dragged back into the army. Perhaps the remembered unpleasantness of military service on land repelled him as much as the risk of being killed. Listening to the sailors' salty talk at his father's tavern also may have been a factor. It is clear from the record that he was physically strong and did not lack courage, but the sea must have looked, as it has for many other young men, the more attractive wartime alternative. And so, early in 1780 (when Benjamin Gilbert was home on leave, being promoted to officer rank, and signing up for another three years in the army), Jacob Nagle joined the tiny American navy by signing on the USS *Saratoga,* then being built in Philadelphia. When launching of the *Saratoga* was delayed, young Nagle impatiently turned to another line of sea service—privateering.

Privateers were privately owned and managed warships that contributed to the war effort by attacking British supply and merchant ships, with their crews paid in shares of whatever they captured. Many observers considered privateering as little more than legalized piracy as well as a drain on the youthful pool of manpower badly needed by the army. Nevertheless, the appeal of privateering to young men hoping to improve themselves even while fighting for American independence was irresistible, and it proved very popular as the war dragged on. For Nagle, it was the most important decision of his life.

His first ship, the sixteen-gun brig *Fair American,* sailed down Delaware Bay in May 1780, and Nagle quickly learned that the lower bay was swarming with armed enemies—not British warships, but American loyalist privateers, Tory bandits preying on every ship slower and weaker than their own. Nagle confronted suddenly what Gilbert had learned more gradually while roaming the dangerous roads of Westchester County, New York: about one American in five was bitterly opposed to the Revolution, and many of them were ready to take up arms to resist it. Nagle's ship survived the perils of Tory predators, and, out in the Atlantic, soon took numerous prizes: British merchant ships, laden with wine, dry goods, and crockery, to be sent back up the dangerous bay to Philadelphia for condemnation and sale. For sailors like Nagle, it was far more profitable than service in the army, as well as far more exciting and dangerous. Brutal and dishonest ships' officers, quite unlike the paternalistic Colonel Proctor and Captain Jones whom Nagle had known as a young artillery soldier, were frequently encountered, as were thuggish shipmates. But Nagle, almost fully grown though not a big man, was athletic, unafraid to fight when necessary, and able to take care of himself. After a few voyages he was an experienced sailor.

He could not, however, control the fortunes of war. On a voyage in late 1781 to the West Indies, his ship was captured by a British warship, and Nagle was imprisoned on the island of St. Christopher. The battle of Yorktown, just weeks earlier, had virtually decided the outcome of the American war on the mainland, but the British and French navies were still waging an all-out struggle for defense of their extremely valuable West Indian islands. A French attack on St. Christopher "liberated" Nagle, but confusion over his true identity led to his re-imprisonment. When the French and British agreed to an exchange of prisoners, Nagle was included as a "British" sailor. At the end of the war in 1783, while Gilbert was agonizing at West Point over what to do with himself when peace broke out, Jacob Nagle found himself serving on a British man-of-war, sailing "home" to Britain.

We left Lieutenant Benjamin Gilbert near the end of the war, still in the army, drinking too much, and chasing women. However we may judge what had become a distinct pattern of behavior, we can see, nevertheless, how extended service in the Revolutionary War had affected his life. Soldiers with little to keep them occupied are likely to find their own ways of releasing energy and relieving boredom. The war in Gilbert's sector during the years after Saratoga was not especially active, yet Washington did not dare move or reduce his force up the Hudson. Gilbert was part of that essential force, keeping the British garrison in New York more or less pinned down, but he was also a normal young man. Months of inactivity, broken only by occasional alarms (usually false) and one brief but dramatic journey (to Virginia and the entrapment of a British army at Yorktown in the fall of 1781), could not be a healthy situation for any young man. In the diary and letters there is more than a hint that he had adjusted well to military life, perhaps even grown attached to it, enjoying the comradeship of his fellow sergeants and officers, and in the process had become a fairly good soldier. On the other hand, he had known little except the army during his few years as an adult. And as chances offered, he fell into the behavior so typical of soldiers through the ages, drinking too much, too often, and literally grabbing any available woman. The details are clear enough in the diary; the wonder is that no one later destroyed the evidence and that it has come down to us with only a few places showing where someone had tried to erase a name or initials.

At Yorktown, where Washington swiftly brought his troops from New York with a French force marching from its base in Rhode Island, while a French fleet drove the British navy out of Chesapeake Bay, the British had lost the war, surrendering a field army just as they had four years earlier at Saratoga. Lieutenant Benjamin Gilbert, according to his 1828 obituary, had "commanded a platoon in the detachment led by the late Gen[eral Alexander] Hamilton at the storming of the redoubt at Yorktown."[5] Gilbert failed to mention this heroic act in his letters or diary, so perhaps it seemed more important to him that "the Ladies [of Virginia] are exceeding Amouris . . . and amongst the Vulgar any man that is given to concupience [that is, lust] may have his fill. The Ladies are Exceeding fond of the Northern Gentlemen, Especially those of the Army."[6] Though he may have been simply teasing an absent friend and fellow officer in a letter, the comment also suggests his state of mind in the seventh year of his military service.

Standard histories of the Revolution stress the physical hardships of the Continental Army, unpaid, badly clothed and housed, ill-fed, neglected both by Congress and the states, which were supposed to look after their own regiments. Gilbert's diary and letters record the ups and downs of life in the Continental Army. Almost never in Gilbert's record was there a question of freezing, starving, or sheer survival. Instead, extreme discomfort and neglect led to low morale, desertion, and even mutiny. A breakdown of discipline was the greatest threat to the army, but the great danger to the individual, greater even than enemy fire, was illness. Wet, cold, tired, unclean, sleeping badly, and malnourished, soldiers were prey to colds and a host of more serious ailments. Medical science was rudimentary and often worse than no treatment at all; in any case, the medical service of the Continental Army was grossly inadequate.

Benjamin Gilbert, a strong, healthy young man, suffered several bouts of debilitating illness during the war. The worst one occurred in winter 1778–79, when he had been disabled, but luckily was sheltered and cared for by the Hoyt family in Danbury, Connecticut, a major American supply base to which his regiment had marched in September. His symptoms—described in detail—included mouth sores, periodic vomiting, and general weakness, and suggest a serious vitamin deficiency, made worse by his fairly heavy drinking. He had remained an invalid for almost six months. His father had traveled more than a hundred miles from Brookfield to visit him, probably afraid that his son was dying. The following September he was laid up again for more than a week, but then he had injured himself stumbling back to camp in the dark in the wake of an all-night drunk. At the end of the war, in June 1783, desperately worried over what he would do to survive after leaving the army, he told his father, "my [physical] constitution is so far spent, that I am not able to earn the one half per Month or day that I was before the war."[7]

At one time, Gilbert talked of settling in Vermont after the war, and later he hoped to buy land near Albany, New York, that was to be sold after having been confiscated from its American loyalist owners. But a clause in the peace treaty, signed in 1783, forbade any further confiscation of Tory property, and all Gilbert knew when he finally left the army was that he would never live in Brookfield again. In September 1782, Lieutenant Benjamin Gilbert received a letter from his hometown accusing him of fathering the child that Patience Converse was then carrying. His first response, a letter to Colonel James Converse, Patience's father and a close family friend, was apologetic, even admitting that "the misfortunes that have befel your Daughter and myself are Just punishments for our unwarrantable practises."[8] But very soon after he was backing away and denying his responsibility, and in a letter to his father he even accused a friend, Isaac Cutler, of being the true father. He later brushed off a demand from Colonel Converse to return immediately to Brookfield, apparently to marry Patience, on the grounds that he could not leave the army "without relinquishing every Idea of Honour (which I hold much dearer than life)."9

Finally, in November 1783, after leaving the army for good, he settled his dispute with Patience Converse and her father. With a Worcester County warrant out for his arrest, he called on Colonel Converse and agreed to pay £30 (roughly $150, but at least ten times that today), and in return he received a written "acquittal," or receipt. There the affair ended. He had spent his last year in the army drinking more than ever and becoming a regular customer at "Wyoma," a brothel near the army's main encampment at New Windsor, just north of West Point.

Gilbert had detoured on his journey back to Brookfield, stopping at Danbury to call on the Hoyts, the family that had cared for him during his long illness five years earlier. He was on his best behavior and stayed two months. Perhaps he was putting off as long as possible the unpleasant but inevitable interview with the irate Colonel Converse. He obviously enjoyed his first postwar autumn in western Connecticut, and he also resumed an acquaintance with the family of the Hoyts' neighbor, Captain John Cornwall, whose wife and mother had taken a hand in Gilbert's nursing years before, and with whose son Francis he had played checkers to pass the time. Probably because he had been too ill to misbehave, Gilbert had made a favorable impression on the Hoyts and the Cornwalls, and they welcomed his return. There Gilbert found a wife. Mary, the daughter of Captain John Cornwall, was only fourteen in 1778, but she was a young woman when Gilbert returned. At dinners, dances, and afternoon teas, Mary Cornwall and Benjamin Gilbert fell in love.

First, Benjamin had to go home and deal with the Converse problem. He did so by December. Then, in March 1784 he traveled, not south to Danbury, but westward from Brookfield, calling on his old comrades, Captain Daniel Shays, who two years later would lead the farmers' rebellion bearing his name, and Colonel Rufus Putnam, who spent a few days teaching Gilbert the rudiments of surveying. Leaving Putnam, he traveled to Albany and the Mohawk River, where he looked first for a job and then for a farm. South of the Mohawk, toward Otsego Lake, Gilbert found what he was looking for. In the Cherry Valley, best known for a terrible Indian raid during the Revolutionary War, Gilbert took a job teaching school and bought a farm. After establishing himself and saving a little money, he journeyed back to Brookfield to see his "Dada," then on to Danbury, where he and Mary Cornwall were married.10

Their first years were not easy. Farm work was very hard for both of them, their crops did not always do well, and livestock suffered from prowling bears and wolves, which, as Benjamin reported to her father, frightened Mary. Not only did both fathers help the young couple with money, tools, affection, and advice, but Benjamin acquired a valuable patron. William Cooper, the father of the novelist James Fenimore Cooper, was the founding father of Otsego County and its seat at Cooperstown and the unofficial king of the whole region, which included Cherry Valley. In time, Benjamin became a political henchman of William Cooper and, through his patronage, a local official, county sheriff, and several terms a New York legislator, running as a Federalist in the hotly contested politics of western New York. While maintaining contact with his old friend, the rebel Daniel Shays, Gilbert climbed to the conservative side of the political fence. Mary bore eleven children, they attended the Baptist Church, and Benjamin became a pillar of the local Freemasons, which he had joined while in the army. When he died in 1828, the *Cherry-Valley Gazette* lamented the passing of a hero of the American Revolution.

Jacob Nagle's postwar life, compared to Gilbert's, was far more eventful and exciting. After being paid off for his wartime service at the British naval base of Plymouth in April 1783, Nagle did not seek the first ship "home" to Philadelphia, though there were many such ships there, as British merchants rushed to be the first back in the American market. Instead he elected to see the great city of London, and while his money lasted, he enjoyed the sights and pleasures offered by London to men of the seafaring class. A few months later, with his money gone, he rejoined the Royal Navy. Jacob Nagle had become, or was fast becoming, a professional sailor.

The sailor's life took him on the flagship of the legendary First Fleet to Australia in 1787, when the new colony was being settled. Later he served in the wars of the French Revolution and under the Mediterranean command of the greatest of all British naval heroes, Horatio Nelson, in 1796–97. During the Napoleonic Wars, Nagle would serve in the merchant marine.

Returning to England in 1795, he "took a liking to a daughter of Mr. Pitmuns," a boatwright whose three sons he had known previously, "a lively hansome girl in my eye, and maried hur."[11] They had children, how many is unknown, although he seldom saw his wife until he brought the family to Lisbon, where he was stationed, in 1802. A yellow fever epidemic swept Lisbon soon after, and within six weeks Nagle was, in his own words, "left alone."[12] Almost immediately he sold his goods in Lisbon and took ship as a cabin passenger to Norfolk, Virginia, and then to

Philadelphia. Nothing except the sequence of his narrative connects the two events—the death of his wife and children and his journey home to the United States—but the emotional connection is obvious. Nowhere else in his memoir did he mention his wife and children. In Philadelphia he found that his parents had died, but that his three sisters and many cousins were still living. To see his uncle he traveled to Reading, his birth-place, and there he received a small legacy left to him by his Grandfather Nagle. In a four-month sojourn in rural Pennsylvania and Maryland, he saw almost all of his family as well as many old friends, but what those meetings meant to him he leaves us to guess. In November he signed on a ship carrying American corn to Spain and Portugal.

Jacob Nagle had done everything sailors have done throughout time: been drunk, mugged, robbed, cheated, beaten up, imprisoned, press-ganged, flogged with a cat-o'-nine-tails, and almost killed by a cannonball. He had known whores and other easy young women, fought often with his fists and other handy weapons, deserted, and, in 1797 on a British war-ship cruising off Toulon in the Mediterranean, engaged in a mutiny for which the crew was luckily forgiven. He had escaped hanging and serious injury. Although there is no bragging in his memoir, he was clearly an exceptionally able seaman. Early in his seafaring career, his literacy, brains, and toughness won him promotion to boatswain, but he declined to serve. Later, he virtually commanded the HMS *Netley*, a sloop of war, serving as quartermaster to a capable but inexperienced commander. Nagle was offi-cer material, but clearly he had no interest in holding power and exercis-ing responsibility. He was a free spirit, and determined to remain that way. That he had never lost his national identity is also clear. When in 1808 he led fellow crewmen in demanding their pay from a stingy Scottish shipowner, the owner greeted Nagle with the words: "Well, Mr. American, how do you do?"[13]

A voyage under armed convoy to China in 1806 escaped the French privateers infesting the Indian Ocean, but not a Southeast Asian disease called "the white flux." Nagle escaped again when almost all his shipmates went down with the disease, but on his next voyage, to Nova Scotia, his luck ran out. Working in a ship's boat, when no one would volunteer to join him to free a dangerously fouled anchor cable in heavy, freezing seas off the coast of Cape Breton, he suffered a severe chill—"hypothermia" is the modern medical term—and he may never have fully recovered. He was forty-six, and even his powerful body and spirit were wearing out.

He made other voyages, especially to Latin America, but on one of them, in 1812, his health gave way, and he was left in a British hospital in

Rio de Janeiro. Whether by design or not, it was a good time for an American to lie low while his two countries fought the War of 1812. After leaving the hospital, he worked a variety of shore-based jobs, tending bar, keeping books, and skippering a pleasure boat. An abortive attempt to leave Rio landed him, alone and sick, confused and unable to speak Portuguese, at the small Brazilian town of Porto Seguro, where for one of the few times in his memoir he tells us how he felt. He sat down on some logs and began

> to reflect, in my illness, though I had traveled a good many years through the four quarters of the globe, been a prisoner twice, cast a way three times, and the ship foundering under me, two days and a night in an open boat on the wide ocion without anything to eat or water to norish us, and numbers of times in want of water or victuals, at other times in action, and men slain a long side of me, and with all, at this minute it apeared to me that I was in greater distress and missery than I had ever been in any country during my life. I fell on my nees, and never did I pray with a sincerer hart than I did at that presentime.[14]

A kindly black woman, wife of the master of a local fishing boat, fed him and gave him shelter, and he appears to have taken up fishing thereafter. Although he soon made contact with the American consul up the coast at Bahia, he stayed in Brazil until 1821, when he signed on a ship sailing for Norfolk, Virginia. He crossed the Atlantic a few more times, but after another stay in the hospital, in New York in 1824, he took ship for Baltimore, and there unpacked his seabag for the last time, at the age of sixty-two.

The last sixteen years of his life were spent trekking between eastern Pennsylvania and Maryland, and northern Ohio, seeking shelter with whatever family member would take him for a while and finding work at whatever menial or clerical job would make him a little money. In an age when the hundreds of miles between Hagerstown, Maryland, or Philadelphia at one end and Canton or Perrysburg, Ohio, at the other are easily passed in a day's drive on high-speed highways, Nagle's forlorn walks on the rutted, dusty, or muddy roads across that corrugated landscape through heat, rain, sleet, and snow, across creeks with no bridges and toward a night's destination that was never sure at the start of each day, seem poignant beyond words. People along the way were often kind to him, as the black lady in Porto Seguro had been, but once, walking from the national capital to Baltimore, he observed of Jacksonian America: "I must say this of the country, they have no respet or humanity for a person in poverty."[15] An old man, worn out, lonely, and unwanted, but unbroken in spirit, he never quit and rarely complained even as he must have felt the end coming in his final port at Canton, Ohio. When he died seven months after the last entry in his memoir, in early 1841 at age seventy-nine, he left virtually nothing, except the memories of people who had known this remarkable old bird, and a unique and marvelous record of his life. Although he had served only a short time in the American Revolution and much longer in the Royal Navy, both the *Stark County Democrat* (Canton) and the *Advertiser and Journal* of Cincinnati noted his passing under the same headline: "ANOTHER REVOLUTIONARY SOLDIER GONE!" But if old Nagle was greeted by his Maker, perhaps the better words were those spoken by the Scottish shipowner to him in 1808: "Well, Mr. American, how do you do?"

Looking back at these two young lives amid war and revolution, we readily see the great role played by what appears to be chance: service in the army, on land, kept Benjamin Gilbert physically tied to the territorial United States, while service at sea turned young Jacob Nagle into a lifelong vagabond, rootless, wandering, far more at the mercy of chance than Gilbert ever was. But there was more than chance working in their lives: Gilbert, on the verge of making a mess of his personal life in the last few years of the war, pulled himself together, married well, stopped drinking heavily and trying to seduce every young woman he met, took advantage of the opportunities offered by peace and American independence, worked hard, raised a family, was elected to public office, and died in an aura of respectability. Nagle, by contrast, given chances to return to his family and the United States after the war, never showed much interest in doing so until the death of his wife and children in 1802; he was just as likely to sign on another ship going in the other direction.

As we try to probe these two lives more deeply, we notice an important difference in the role played by their families. Gilbert's letters to his father Daniel, back in Brookfield, are frequent, respectful, and affectionate. More than once, he asked his father for help with clothing, money, or other matters. In the Patience Converse scandal, his father stood by him, and Lieutenant Gilbert's reports of the war and the army, though not free of complaint, are crafted to get his father's approval. He does not talk to his father about women and drinking, and it is clear that he cares deeply about his father's opinion. Ultimately, he shaped his own life on that of his father—farmer, militia officer, elected official, respected member of his community. Benjamin's mother had died in childbirth, in 1772, and we know little of her, or of his two stepmothers, but he wrote from the army to his young sisters, extolling the virtue of chastity and warning them against men who would steal it from them. Obviously, family mattered to him.

Family also mattered to Jacob Nagle. He remembered being on a French schooner at Martinique in 1782 (aged twenty) "walking the deck till 2 or 3 in the morning, crying and fretting for the loss of my parents, never being so long from home before, when 14 or 16 shells would be flying in the air at one time."[16] He also remembered that in 1780, returning home from his first privateering voyage, his mother at first did not recognize him, and his father had been away, out trying to warn him about the press-gang looking for sailors. Later, his mother nursed him through a fever that she thought would be fatal. To his father's reputation there clung something unsavory; he was perhaps not the best of role models. By the end of the war and during the long years after, he had lost touch with his parents and does not mention missing them or wanting to see them (his father died in 1789, his mother in 1793) or his sisters. Only when he retired from seafaring penniless and in poor health did he seek out family, a sister, a cousin, a nephew—anyone who would take in an old, broken-down, slightly disreputable sailor. He never gave up, but from his memoir comes a sense that, unlike Gilbert, family had ceased to be a focal point for his life and that he was, perhaps as much by choice as by chance, something like a seagoing version of that great figure of later American folklore—the lonesome cowboy.

In Gilbert it is easy to see how, coming through war and out of revolution, he typified the thousands of Americans who seized opportunity, moved westward, and pursued happiness to become the middle-class backbone of American democracy. But in Jacob Nagle, we see something radically different yet equally American—the brave, battered survivor, the supreme individualist for whom life is an endless challenge, the whole world is "home," and "family" is the human race.

Notes

1. *The Nagle Journal: A Diary of the Life of Jacob Nagle, Sailor, From the Year 1775 to 1841,* ed. John C. Dann (New York, 1988), 10.

2. Ibid., 10.

3. The first section of Gilbert's diary, 1778–1782, has been published as *A Citizen-Soldier in the American Revolution: The Diary of Benjamin Gilbert in Massachusetts and New York,* ed. Rebecca D. Symmes (Cooperstown, NY, 1980), 29. Hereafter cited as Gilbert Diary.

4. Gilbert letter to Aaron Kimball, April 30, 1782, *Winding Down: The Revolutionary*

War Letters of Lieutenant Benjamin Gilbert of Massachusetts, 1780–1783, ed. John Shy (Ann Arbor, MI, 1989), 56. Hereafter cited as *Gilbert Letters.*

5. Cherry-Valley [New York] Gazette, January 29, 1828.

6. Gilbert to Lieutenant Park Holland [August 1781], *Gilbert Letters,* 47.

7. Gilbert to his father [ca. June 6, 1783], ibid., 107.

8. Gilbert to Colonel Converse [September 30, 1782], ibid., 69.

9. Gilbert to Colonel Converse, March 24, 1783, ibid., 91. By that date, her pregnancy had passed its term. There is no mention in the record of actual childbirth.

10. He uses the affectionate term in a letter to Daniel Shays, September 26, 1785, *Gilbert Diary,* 77–78.

11. *Nagle Journal,* 186.

12. Ibid., 248.

13. Ibid., 278.

14. Ibid., 312–13.

15. Ibid., 333.

16. Ibid., 53.

Suggested Readings

Nothing is better than the published primary evidence for the lives of these two men. Gilbert's exists in two slim volumes. His diary from 1778 to early 1782, plus a few letters between 1785 and 1788, is available in *A Citizen-Soldier in the American Revolution: The Diary of Benjamin Gilbert in Massachusetts and New York,* edited by Rebecca D. Symmes (Cooperstown, NY, 1980). His letterbook for 1780–1783 is published in *Winding Down: The Revolutionary War Letters of Lieutenant Benjamin Gilbert of Massachusetts, 1780–1783,* edited by John Shy (Ann Arbor, MI, 1989). The second part of his diary, for 1782–1786, was discovered not many years ago and is now in the New York State Historical Association at Cooperstown, New York. It has never been published, but was used by permission in the publication of the letterbook. Some of Gilbert's political correspondence from 1793 to 1797 is in the Paul F. Cooper Jr. Archives, Hartwick College, Oneonta, New York, and was used by permission in writing this chapter. All we have for Jacob Nagle appears in one published volume, *The Nagle Journal: A Diary of the Life of Jacob Nagle, Sailor, From the Year 1775 to 1841,* edited by John C. Dann (New York, 1988). The editorial introductions and commentary as well as the illustrations in each of these three published volumes add a great deal to our understanding of Gilbert and Nagle.

For the Revolutionary War and the men who fought it, two very different books provide interesting background and comparisons: Charles Royster, *A Revolutionary People at War: The Continental Army and American Character, 1775–1783* (Chapel Hill, NC, 1979), and John C. Dann, ed., *The Revolution Remembered: Eyewitness Accounts of the War of Independence* (Chicago, 1980). Both Gilbert and Nagle applied for federal pensions long after the war, and the latter book offers a careful selection from the thousands of pension applications submitted by revolutionary veterans that are now in the National Archives.

Marcus B. Rediker, *Between the Devil and the Deep Blue Sea: Merchant Seamen, Pirates, and the Anglo-American Maritime World, 1700–1750* (New York, 1987), is a stimulating and much-discussed account of the sailor's world just before Nagle joined it. On the British navy when Nagle belonged to it, there is G. J. Marcus, *The Age of Nelson: The Royal Navy, 1793–1815* (New York, 1971); and on naval life, there is Dudley Pope, *Life in Nelson's Navy* (Annapolis, MD, 1981). Christopher Lloyd, *The British Seaman, 1200–1860: A Social Survey* (London, 1968), is a readable survey of the sailor's way of life. On privateering in the American Revolution, a valuable chapter by W. Minchinton and D. Starkey is found in *Ships, Seafaring and Society: Essays in Maritime History,* edited by Timothy J. Runyan (Detroit, 1987).

Robert A. Gross, *The Minutemen and Their World* (New York, 1976), is a highly readable, prize-winning account of the pact of the Revolutionary War on a New England town, Concord, Massachusetts, not unlike Gilbert's *Brookfield,* while a Pulitzer Prize-winning exploration of the upstate New York world in which Gilbert spent his postwar life is Alan Taylor, *William Cooper's Town: Power and Persuasion on the Frontier of the Early American Republic* (New York, 1995).

7

Absalom Jones and the
African Church
of Philadelphia
"To Arise out of the Dust"

Gary B. Nash

Absalom Jones (1746–1818) was not a revolutionary for his wartime activities, but for his role in the creation of the Free African Society, with his colleague Richard Allen, and the African Church of Philadelphia, an organization in which free blacks proclaimed their religious independence from white churches. Jones was a black Episcopal minister who had been born into slavery. After first purchasing his wife's freedom, he later, at the age of thirty-eight, bought his own independence. Given Jones's goal of freedom, why did he and his wife not seek refuge behind British lines during the British occupation of Philadelphia?

Legislators passed a gradual emancipation law for Pennsylvania in 1780, but Gary Nash demonstrates that many potential white benefactors would have preferred that free blacks worship in white churches. Such attitudes, as well as the treatment of African-American parishioners at St. George's, galvanized black goals for religious and cultural independence. Why did the Revolution's spirit of equality not lead Jones to advocate the end of racial separation in the religious sphere? Did the creation of a separate African church represent disillusionment with the rhetoric of the Revolution, or its fulfillment? The original plan lacked a denominational affiliation, but ultimately the majority of black elders favored the Episcopal Church, and, as a committed Methodist, Allen separated from the church. Did peaceful, internal differences between Jones and Allen threaten black unity, or present democratic choices between meaningful alternatives: St. Thomas's Episcopal or Bethel Methodist Church? What was the role of the independent black church in forging an African-American community? Given that white colonial churches were being disestablished in the immediate post-revolutionary era, how can the rising influence of the black church be explained?

An expert on African-American history of the revolutionary era, Gary B. Nash teaches history at the University of California at Los Angeles. He is the author of numerous articles and books, including *The Urban Crucible: The Northern Seaports and the Origins of the American Revolution* (1979) and *Forging Freedom: The Formation of Philadelphia's Black Community, 1720–1840* (1988).

In an open field outside of Philadelphia on a sultry afternoon in August 1793, about one hundred white construction tradesmen and two of Philadelphia's most important citizens sat down at long tables "under the shade of several large trees" and consumed a bounteous dinner complete with excellent liqueurs and melons for dessert. They were served by a company of Philadelphia's free blacks. Then, after the white Philadelphians arose, about fifty blacks took their places and were waited on at a second sitting of the banquet by "six of the most respectable of the white company." The occasion for this unusual display of racial reciprocity was the raising of the roof for the African Church of Philadelphia, the first free black church in the northern United States. Benjamin Rush, Philadelphia's ebullient doctor, reformer, social activist, and general busybody, toasted, "Peace on earth and good will to men" and "May African churches everywhere soon succeed to African bondage." Describing to his wife the outpouring of emotion on that hot afternoon, he wrote: "Never did I witness such a scene of innocent—nay, more—such virtuous and philanthropic joy. Billy Grey [William Gray] in attempting to express his feelings to us was checked by a flood of tears." After dinner all the blacks converged on John Nicholson and clasped the hand of the city's entrepreneur par excellence, who had lent $2,000 for the building of the church. One old man "addressed him in the following striking language: 'May you live long, sir, and when you die, may you not die eternally.' " Rush rhapsodized, "To me it will be a day to be remembered with pleasure as long as I live."[1]

Another year would pass before the African Church of Philadelphia opened its doors for religious services, but the interracial banquet in August 1793 already foreshadowed two interlocking developments that marked the entire course of black history in the early national period: first, the efforts of former slaves to construct a foundation for freedom and a community-based fortress from which to fight white hostility and oppression through the establishment of independent black churches; and second, their difficult relations with the benevolent portion of the white community whose patronage was essential to the building of black institutions in this era but whose ingrained racial attitudes and desire to maintain social control often led to misperceptions, withdrawal of support, and sometimes opposition.

To understand the birth of the African Church of Philadelphia we must recreate the situation in which the city's free blacks found themselves in the 1780s. On the eve of the Revolution the city's slave population had been declining rapidly as a result of high mortality and low fertility rates, combined with the virtual cessation of slave importations. War further diminished the black population, as many slaves fled with the British when they evacuated the city in the summer of 1778, and many others were sold by their hard-pressed masters, died in the patriot military forces, or simply ran away. By the close of the war only about nine hundred black Philadelphians remained of the fifteen hundred or so who had resided in the city in 1767.

A wartime wave of abolitionist sentiment produced thousands of manumissions that reversed this demographic trend. From Philadelphia's hinterland to the west, from Delaware, Maryland, and Virginia to the south, and from New York, New Jersey, and New England to the north and east came a steady flow of dark-skinned former bondsmen and bondswomen seeking work and the fellowship of other blacks in the premier port city of the North. By 1790 more than 2,100 of them, all but 273 free, lived in the city and its environs. By 1800, in a city where some 63,000 white Philadelphians resided, black numbers had swelled to about 6,400, of whom only 55 remained in bondage.

These gathering black Philadelphians, like former slaves in other parts of the country, had to rethink their relationship to American society in the early years of the Republic. Were they Africans in America who might now return to their homeland? Were they African Americans whose cultural heritage was African but whose future was bound up in creating a separate existence on soil where they had toiled most of their lives? Or were they simply Americans with dark skin, who, in seeking places as free men and women, had to assimilate as quickly as possible into the cultural norms and social institutions of white society? Working out this problem of identity—and choosing strategies for fulfilling the goals they had set—required close attention to the particular locale in which freedmen and freedwomen found themselves or contrived to reach, for the social climate was far from uniform in postrevolutionary America.

Outwardly, Philadelphia beckoned manumitted blacks as a haven from persecution and an arena of opportunity. The center of American Quakerism where the first abolition society in the country had formed, the city was also the location of the state government that in 1780, in the midst of war, had passed the new nation's first gradual abolition act. Philadelphia was also a bustling maritime center that promised employment for migrating African Americans, who rarely possessed the capital to become independent farmers and therefore took to the roads leading to the coastal towns in the postwar years. Philadelphia's drawing power owed something as well to the considerable sympathy among some whites for freed blacks setting out on the road to freedom.

In its internal workings, however, Philadelphia fell far short of the ideal suggested by Rush. The illiterate and often unskilled black men and women who trekked there after the Revolution had to compete for jobs with Irish and German immigrants and did not always find work. Although not disenfranchised by law, free blacks faced some white social pressure to stay away from the polls. Moreover, virtually every institution and social mechanism in the city—religious and secular, economic and social—engaged in discriminatory practices, which flowed like water from the pervasive belief in black inferiority. Against the assumption that blacks were either innately handicapped or had been irreparably degraded by the experience of slavery stood only a minority of white Philadelphians who believed that recently freed slaves could overcome the marks of birth and oppression.

For black immigrants who found their way to Philadelphia after the Revolution, overcoming patterns of behavior peculiar to slavery became a crucial matter. By its nature slavery assumed the superiority of the master class, and even the most benevolent master occupied a power relationship vis-à-vis his slaves that daily reminded them of their lowly condition. Perhaps few American slaves believed they were inferior human beings, but slavery required them to act so. "Governed by fear," as the Pennsylvania Abolition Society put it, they carried into freedom an acute understanding of the tactics of survival, which included an almost instinctive wariness. Moreover, they now had to face the dominant white culture, which was far from ready to treat them as equals and continued to demand complaisant comportment from them. The will to plan rationally, to strive for an independent and dignified existence, to confront racial prejudice, and to work for the future of their children depended upon throwing off the incubus of slavery, an institution that had perpetuated itself by exacting a terrible price for attempts at independent or self-reliant black behavior.

Free blacks also had to confront the contradictory effects of benevolence on their lives. On the one hand, humane Philadelphians, Quakers foremost among them, succored slaves and freedmen and helped them cope with their vulnerability in a racially divided society. On the other, benevolence perpetuated feelings of powerlessness and functioned to maintain white social control.

The positive side of benevolence is seen vividly in the work of Anthony Benezet, the saintly Huguenot immigrant schoolmaster and social critic who dedicated so much of his life to the Negro's cause.

Benezet's greatest contribution to black Philadelphians lay in his challenge to the deeply rooted doctrine of black inferiority. He urged his pupils to regard themselves as citizens of the world and argued doggedly, as early as 1762, that the African environment had produced notable cultures and must not be considered as a place of jungle barbarism. He taught his black students that it was the environment of slavery, not an innate condition, that turned Africans in America into degraded and disheartened human beings.

The negative side of benevolence can be seen in the attitudes of many of Benezet's fellow Quakers. The Society of Friends led the way in opposing the slave trade and in manumitting slaves, and its members played a major role in establishing the Pennsylvania Abolition Society in 1775, which had to suspend operations during the war. In 1784, Quakers began visiting black families, quietly urging them to a life of industry and morality and helping those in distress. By the late 1780s the reorganized Pennsylvania Abolition Society was urging slaveowners to free their slaves and exercise stewardship over those who were free—educating them, watching over them, and inculcating in them middle-class values of sobriety, work, morality, and religious faith.

Such services were received among blacks at a cost. "There can be no greater disparity of power," writes historian David Brion Davis, "than that between a man convinced of his own disinterested service and another man who is defined as a helpless object."[2] Even more to the point, Quaker humanitarianism was never based on a deep sense of the "likeness among all persons." Unlike the spartan-living, humble Benezet, most Quakers held themselves apart from other people, white and black. The Society of Friends, in fact, was the only religious group in Philadelphia that refused to accept blacks as members in the 1780s. Theirs was more a "doctrine of stewardship" than a true humanitarianism, and their efforts on behalf of blacks "partook more of condescension than humanitarianism."[3] Thus, Quaker benevolence sometimes perpetuated black dependence, stood in the way of mutual respect between blacks and whites, and hampered autonomous behavior among those emerging from slavery.

Only a few years out of bondage in the 1780s, Philadelphia's free blacks lived in a highly fluid situation, full of possibilities yet also full of difficulties. Included within their gathering ranks were two men who would exert an extraordinary influence on the shaping of Philadelphia's black community, especially in the creation of black churches as the vital center of African-American life. In their backgrounds Absalom Jones and Richard Allen shared much. Both were born into slavery, Jones in 1746 and Allen in 1760. Both experienced bondage in its rural and urban forms, having been raised partly in Philadelphia and partly in southern Delaware. Both lived under humane white masters and both prevailed upon their owners to allow them to learn to read and write. Both were touched by religion in their formative years, Allen by Methodism and Jones by Anglicanism. Finally, both persuaded their masters to reward faithful service by allowing them to purchase their freedom in the early 1780s.

When their paths crossed in Philadelphia for the first time, probably in 1786, Allen was Jones's junior in years but his senior in religious intensity. About 1778, bearing only the slave name Richard, Allen had been converted to Methodism by itinerant preachers in Delaware. No small part of his awakening may be related to the abolitionist stance of those he heard. For his freedom, in fact, he might have thanked Freeborn Garretson, the silver-tongued circuit rider who had convinced Allen's master that slaveholders at Judgment Day were "weighed in the balance and were found wanting."[4] Shortly thereafter, just before his twentieth birthday, Allen's master, Stokely Sturgis, proposed that Richard and his older brother buy their freedom. Taking a surname to signify his status as a free man, Allen spent the next six years interspersing work as a sawyer and a wagoner with months of riding the Methodist circuits from South Carolina to New York and even into the western Indian country. Traveling with some of the leading early Methodist sojourners, he learned to preach with great effect to black and white audiences alike. By the time he arrived, full of zeal, in the Philadelphia area, probably in February 1786, Allen seems to have completed the crucial psychological "middle passage" by which those who gained freedom in a legal sense procured as well the emotional autonomy that meant they had overcome their dependence upon whites.

No such blinding religious light had filled the mind of Absalom Jones. Born into a prominent merchant-planter family in Sussex County, Delaware, and named simply Absalom, he was taken from the fields into his master's house when he was very young. Removed from the debilitating world of field labor, he gained an opportunity for learning. Absalom later wrote that with pennies given to him from time to time, "I soon bought myself a primer and begged to be taught by any body that I found able and willing to give me the least instruction." Literacy could only have increased the distance between him and those of his age who did not live in the master's house, and hence Absalom became introspective, or "singular," as he termed it.[5] Then, in 1762, his master, Benjamin Wynkoop, sold Absalom's mother and six siblings, left his Delaware plantation, and moved to Philadelphia, taking the sixteen-year-old slave boy with him. The traumatic breaking up of his family proved to be a turning point in Absalom's life. While bereft of his kin, he had landed in the center of the nascent abolitionist movement in America and in the city where, more than anywhere else in prerevolutionary America, humanitarian reformers had created an atmosphere conducive to education and family formation among slaves. Thus, while he had to work in his master's shop from dawn to dark, Jones prevailed upon Wynkoop in 1766 to allow him to attend a night school for blacks. Soon, Jones was able to write his mother and brothers in his own hand.

In 1770, Absalom married Mary Thomas, the slave of his master's neighbor. Mary and Absalom took vows in St. Peter's Church where the Wynkoop family worshiped. Soon after this, encouraged by the abolitionist sentiment that Quakers and others had spread throughout Philadelphia, he put the tool of literacy to work. After drawing up an appeal for his wife's release, he carried it, with his wife's father at his side, to some of "the principal Friends of this city," asking for their support. "From some we borrowed, and from others we received donations," he later recounted. Thereafter, as war came to Philadelphia, Absalom "made it my business to work until twelve or one o'clock at night, to assist my wife in obtaining a livelihood, and to pay the money that was borrowed to purchase her freedom."[6]

When the British occupied Philadelphia in September 1777, Jones remained at his master's side, resisting the chance to flee with his wife to the British, as did many black Philadelphians. It took Jones years to repay the debt incurred to buy his wife's freedom. But by 1778, Absalom had discharged his obligations and was pleading with his master to allow him to purchase his own freedom. Wynkoop would not consent until October 1, 1784, six years after the first of what Absalom remembered as a series of humble requests. So Jones used his hard-won surplus to purchase a small house and lot in the city.

Probably in 1784, upon gaining his release, Absalom took the surname Jones. It was a common English cognomen, yet one that he had chosen and one that could not be mistaken for the Dutch name of his master, whom he had served until he was thirty-eight. But he acted as if he bore his master no grudges. Forbearing, even-tempered, and utterly responsible, he continued to work in Wynkoop's store. More than thirty years later, in an obituary for Jones, it was said that his master, Wynkoop, "always gave him the character of having been a faithful and exemplary servant, remarkable for many good qualities; especially for his being not only of a peaceable demeanour, but for being possessed of the talent of inducing a disposition to it in others."[7]

Allen and Jones met in Philadelphia in 1786 after the Methodist elder in the city sent for Allen to preach to the growing population of blacks and offered him St. George's Church in which to hold meetings— at 5:00 A.M. "Several souls were awakened," Allen remembered years later in relating his life story to his son, "and were earnestly seeking redemption in the blood of Christ." Impressed by the large number of free blacks drifting into the city, and aware that "few of them attended public worship," Allen began supplementing his predawn services at St. George's with daytime meetings on the commons in adjacent Southwark and the Northern Liberties. Soon he had "raised a Society . . . of forty-two members."[8] Among them was Absalom Jones, who had abandoned Anglican services at St. Peter's Church, where his former master still worshiped, in favor of St. George's. Like taking a surname, this was a step in forging a new identity.

Within months of Allen's arrival in Philadelphia, Absalom Jones and two other recently freed slaves, William White and Darius Jennings, had joined the Methodist preacher to discuss forming a separate black religious society. Religion and literacy had helped all these men achieve freedom, so it was natural that, when they looked around them to find the majority of former slaves illiterate and unchurched, they "often communed together upon this painful and important subject in order to form some kind of religious society." Shortly thereafter Allen proposed this "to the most respectable people of color in this city," only to be "met with opposition." Leading white Methodists who heard of the plan objected even more strenuously, using, Allen wrote, "very degrading and insulting language to try to prevent us from going on."[9] Nonetheless, after these deliberations, Jones and Allen decided to organize the Free African Society. Founded in April 1787, it was the first black organization of its kind in America.

Organized in the manner of white benevolent societies, the Free African Society was quasi-religious in character and, beyond that, an organization where the people emerging from the house of bondage could gather strength, develop their own leaders, and explore independent strategies for hammering out a postslavery existence that went beyond formal legal release from thralldom. The society soon began assuming a supervisory role over the moral life of the black community, working to forge a collective black consciousness out of the disparate human material finding its way to Philadelphia. In May 1790 the society attempted to lease the

Strangers' Burial Ground in order to turn it into a black cemetery under their control. In the next month the society established "a regular mode of procedure with respect to . . . marriages" and began keeping a book of marriage records. Having assumed quasi-ecclesiastic functions, the society took the final step in September 1790, when a special committee recommended the initiation of formal religious services, which began on January 1, 1791.[10]

Many of the society's enlarged functions bore a decided Quakerly stamp, reflecting the influence of Friends on many of the leading members and the Quakers' early involvement with the Free African Society. However, Richard Allen viewed the Quakerly drift of the Free African Society with concern. He made no objections when the black organization adopted Quaker-like visiting committees in late 1787, or when they instituted the disownment practices of the Friends the next year. But when the society, in 1789, adopted the Quaker practice of beginning meetings with fifteen minutes of silence, Allen led the withdrawal of "a large number" of dissenters whose adherence to Methodism had accustomed them to "an unconstrained outburst of the[ir] feelings in religious worship."[11] Allen came no more to meetings of the African Society but privately began convening some of its members in an attempt to stop the drift of the organization toward the practices of a religious group whose "detachment and introspection were not without value, but . . . did not seem to speak to the immediate needs of black people as Allen saw them."[12]

The adherence of many free blacks to Methodism is not hard to understand. As the first black historian of the African Church of Philadelphia wrote in 1862, the new Methodist preachers "made no pretensions to literary qualifications, and being despised and persecuted as religious enthusiasts, their sympathies naturally turned towards the lowly, who, like themselves, were of small estimate in the sight of worldly greatness."[13] Moreover, Methodism was far more experiential than other denominations, advocating lay preachers and lay societies, simplifying the liturgy of the Book of Common Prayer, and holding meetings in fields and forests or in the city, in sail lofts and homes. Also commending Methodism to former slaves were the well-known antislavery views of its founder, John Wesley, and the Methodist discipline and polity worked out in 1784, which attacked slave trading and slaveholding and barred persons engaged in these practices from holding church offices, as did no other religious group except the Society of Friends.

Perhaps most important, in Philadelphia the passionate preaching of Richard Allen had drawn many blacks to Methodism. Jones and others tried repeatedly to bring Allen back into the bosom of the Free African Society, but when he proved unyielding in his criticisms of their Quakerly innovations, they followed the Friends' procedure of censuring him "for attempting to sow division among us." When this had no effect, they reluctantly declared in August 1789 that "he has disunited himself from membership with us."[14]

Now the leadership of the Free African Society fell to Absalom Jones. Mild-mannered but persistent, Jones made the crucial connections in the white community that launched plans for building a black church. The ties with the Society of Friends were wearing thin by the summer of 1791, because many Quakers objected to the Sunday psalm singing by blacks in the Quaker schoolhouse. But Jones, perhaps understanding the limits of the Quaker connection, had been forging new patronage lines to one of Philadelphia's most influential citizens—the widely connected, opinionated Benjamin Rush. Over the next four years it was Rush who became the Anthony Benezet of the 1790s so far as Philadelphia's free blacks were concerned. As a young physician before the Revolution, Rush had written a passionate antislavery pamphlet at the urging of Anthony Benezet. By 1787, Rush was thoroughly converted to the free blacks' cause, becoming one of the Abolition Society's most active members and writing a friend in Boston that "I love even the name of Africa, and never see a Negro slave or freeman without emotions which I seldom feel in the same degree towards my unfortunate fellow creatures of a fairer complexion."[15]

By 1791, Jones and a small group of emerging black activists had fixed their sights on building a community, or "union," black church. It was to be formed, as Rush said, from "the scattered and unconnected [black] appendages of most of the religious societies in the city" and from an even larger number of blacks "ignorant and unknown to any religious society."[16] Lacking denominational affiliation, it would not be tied to creeds or ordinances governing most white churches. Its goal was black unity in Christian fellowship, and beyond that a concern for the general welfare of the city's blacks. Jones and his group, in fact, proposed to build a black school first and then a church, though the two enterprises were hardly separable in their minds. Their formula was to become the classic one for the black church as it would emerge in the United States, "a pattern of religious commitment that has a double focus—the free and autonomous worship of God in the way Black people want to worship him, and the unity and social welfare of the Black community."[17]

Aided by Rush, Jones and his cohorts drew up a plan for a separate black church. Attempting to cast their appeal broadly, they adopted articles of association and a plan of church government "so general as to embrace all, and yet so orthodox in cardinal points as offend none."[18] The church was to be named the African Church of Philadelphia, and it was under this title, devoid of denominational reference, that the work of raising subscriptions went forward for the next three years. Jones and his group drew Richard Allen back into the fold, and eight leaders were selected to act as the "representatives" of the African Church. In a ringing broadside appeal for support, they argued that a black church would gather hundreds of those who worshiped in none of the white churches of the city, because "men were more influenced [by] their moral equals than by their superiors . . . and more easily governed by persons chosen by themselves for that purpose, than by persons who are placed over them by accidental circumstances."[19]

This democratic argument was accompanied by another that indicated the ideology of racial separation that Jones was hammering out. "Africans and their descendants" needed their own church because of the "attraction and relationship" among those bound together by "a nearly equal and general deficiency of education, by total ignorance, or only humble attainments in religion," and by the color line drawn by custom. All of this argued for the "necessity and propriety of separate and exclusive means, and opportunities of worshiping God, of instructing their youth, and of taking care of their poor."[20] Such a decisive step toward black self-assertiveness signified the pivotal role in the life of emancipated slaves that the black church would assume in an era when the centrality to community life of the white churches, disestablished and fragmented by the Revolution, was diminishing. Black religion would be, as one historian has explained, "the one impregnable corner of the world where consolation, solidarity and mutual aid could be found and from which the master and the bossman—at least in the North—could be effectively barred."[21]

Having enunciated the concept of a racially separate, nondenominational, and socially oriented church, Jones and the seven other trustees began the work of financing its construction. Rush's suggestions for circulating a broadside appeal with subscription papers—a tried and true method of raising money in Philadelphia—had been received by the black leaders, he wrote, "with a joy which transported one of them to take me by the hand as a brother."[22] When the work of circulating the subscription papers began in the fall of 1791, Rush tried to stay in the background, convinced that "the work will prosper the better for my keeping myself out of sight." But he was hardly capable of self-effacement, and word of his role in the plans soon circulated through the city. William White, rector of Christ Church and recently appointed bishop of the Episcopal Church in Pennsylvania, accosted Rush in the streets and "expressed his disapprobation to the proposed African church," because "it originated in pride." Leading Quakers also conveyed their displeasure to Absalom Jones, and the Methodists threatened to disown any black Methodist who participated in the undertaking.[23] Paternalistic Philadelphians discovered that helping their black brothers proved more satisfactory than seeing them help themselves.

Such disapproval from Episcopalians, Quakers, and Methodists, some of whom had been active in the Abolition Society, drove home the lesson that even whites who claimed to have befriended free blacks were unwilling to see them move beyond white control. An early historian of black Methodism, reflecting in 1867 on the final separation of Richard Allen from the white Methodist Church, dwelt on precisely this point. "The giant crime committed by the Founders of the African Methodist Episcopal Church," wrote Benjamin Tanner, "was that they dared to organize a Church of men, men to think for themselves, men to talk for themselves, men to act for themselves: A Church of men who support from their own substance, however scanty, the ministration of the Word which they receive; men who spurn to have their churches built for them, and their pastors supported from the coffers of some charitable organization; men who prefer to live by the sweat of their own brow and be free."[24]

The opposition of white leaders partially undermined the appeal for building funds. Some modest contributions were garnered, including donations from George Washington and Thomas Jefferson. Rush himself contributed £25. But after six months, with money only trickling in, Jones and Allen decided to take to the streets themselves. Believing "that if we put our trust in the Lord, he would stand by us," Allen recounted, "we went out with our subscription paper and met with great success," collecting $360 on the first day.[25]

Thereafter the going got harder and much of the early optimism began to fade. The initial subscriptions proved sufficient, however, to buy two adjacent lots on Fifth Street, only a block from the Statehouse, for $450. But most blacks had only small amounts to contribute from their meager resources, and most whites seemed to have snapped their pocketbooks shut at the thought of an autonomous black church. White church leaders, who had initially responded to the idea of a separate black church as a piece of arrogance on the part of a people so recently released from slavery, now began calculating the effect on their own churches. "The old and established [religious] societies," Rush confided to a friend, "look shy at them, each having lost some of its members by the new association." Still, Rush did not waver in his conviction that "the poor blacks will succeed in forming themselves into a distinct independent church."[26]

Whatever their difficulties, the resolve of black Philadelphians to form a separate church was strengthened in the fall of 1792 in one of the most dramatic confrontations in early American church history. A number of black leaders were still attending services at St. George's Methodist Church, where the congregation had outgrown the seating capacity. When the elders decided to expand their house of worship, black Philadelphians contributed money and labor to the effort. Then, on the first Sunday after the renovations were completed, the elders informed the black worshipers who filed into the service that they must sit in a segregated section of the newly built gallery. Allen later recounted:

> We expected to take the seats over the ones we formerly occupied below, not knowing any better. We took those seats; meeting had begun, and they were nearly done singing, and just as we got to the seats, the Elder said, "Let us pray." We had not been long upon our knees before I heard considerable scuffling and loud talking. I raised my head up and saw one of the trustees, H—— M——, having hold of the Rev. Absalom Jones, pulling him off his knees, and saying, "You must get up, you must not kneel here." Mr. Jones replied, "Wait until the prayer is over, and I will get up, and trouble you no more." With that he [H. M.] beckoned to one of the trustees, Mr. L——S——, to come to his assistance. He came and went to William White [a black worshiper] to pull him up. By this time prayer was over, and we all went out of the church in a body, and they were no more plagued by us in the church.[27]

The St. George's incident confirmed what many blacks must have suspected—that there would be no truly biracial Christian community in the white churches of the city. Allen recalled that after the incident the black leaders renewed their determination "to worship God under our own vine and fig tree" and "were filled with fresh vigor to get a house erected to worship God in."[28]

By late 1792, with money coming in very slowly for construction of the African Church, the black leaders faced the prospect that they could not raise sufficient funds to build a church on the lots they had purchased. To their rescue came the unlikeliest of figures—the Welsh immigrant John Nicholson, who had blazed meteorically onto the Philadelphia scene after the war as state comptroller and high-flying speculator in western lands and revolutionary loan certificates. Not wholly accepted in polite Philadelphia circles, and uninvolved in the work of the Abolition Society, Nicholson provided what none of the established Philadelphia elite would offer—a large loan to begin construction. "Humanity, charity, and patriotism never united their claims in a petition with more force than in the present instance," Rush wrote to Nicholson in a letter hand-carried by William Gray and Absalom Jones. "You *will* not—you *cannot*" refuse their request "for the sake of Religion & Christianity and as this is the first Institution of the kind."[29]

It took two months more to execute the mortgage and another month to draw up building contracts. Finally, in March 1793, with reports of continued black rebellion in the French West Indies filtering into Philadelphia, the city's free blacks and some of their white benefactors gathered to see earth turned for the church. Writing a quarter of a century later, Allen remembered the day vividly: "As I was the first proposer of the African Church, I put the first spade into the ground to dig the cellar for the same. This was the first African church or meeting house to be erected in the United States of America."[30]

Before the two-story brick building could be completed, its humble founders had to endure additional difficulties. Like most visionaries, Jones and his cohorts had planned expansively, designing a brick church capacious enough to seat eight hundred. The cost estimates for the building ran to $3,560. Even with the $1,000 loan from Nicholson, more money had to be raised. Another kind of black movement for independence paradoxically undermined this attempt. With hundreds of French planters fleeing the Afro-French rebellion in Saint Domingue and streaming into Philadelphia with French-speaking slaves at their sides, many white city dwellers reneged on their pledges to the African Church in order to help the destitute white slaveholders now taking refuge in their city. Philadelphia's free blacks learned that even the most sympathetic white men placed the distress of white slaveowners, even those from outside the United States, ahead of the aspirations of those who had been slaves.

Nicholson again came to the rescue, lending another $1,000 in mid-August. Ten days later the black leaders staged the roof-raising banquet on the edge of the city. But even as glasses were raised in toasts, ill fortune struck again, this time delaying the completion of the church for nearly a year. It came in the form of the worst epidemic of yellow fever in the history of North America. The first victims succumbed late in July 1793; by late August the fever had reached epidemic proportions. With twenty Philadelphians dying daily of the putrid fever, shopkeepers began closing their doors, and all who could afford it commandeered horses, wagons, and carriages to carry their families out of the city. Hardest hit were the laboring poor. Living in crowded alleys and courts where the fever spread fastest, they were too poor to flee, sometimes too poor even to pay for a doctor.

By early September, the social fabric of the city was torn in pieces. Soon, with more than one hundred people dying every day, the work of tending the sick and burying the dead exceeded the capacity of the doctors and city authorities, because most nurses, carters, and gravediggers, who regarded the disease as contagious, refused to go near the sick, dying, and dead. Husbands fled wives of many years who were in the throes of death, parents abandoned sick children, masters thrust servants into the streets. Mathew Carey, the main chronicler of the catastrophe, wrote that "less concern was felt for the loss of a parent, a husband, a wife or an only child than, on other occasions, would have been caused by the death of a servant, or even a favorite lap-dog." Hundreds perished for lack of treatment, "without a human being to hand them a drink of water, to administer medicines, or to perform any charitable office for them."[31] By mid-October the poor were starving, and the dead lay everywhere in the streets, while thousands of those who could afford to had moved to the countryside.

Into this calamitous breach stepped Philadelphia's free blacks. Benjamin Rush, who played generalissimo of the relief forces, implored Richard Allen in early September to lead his people forward as nurses, gravediggers, and drivers of the death carts. Assuring Allen that the malignant fever "passes by persons of your color," he suggested that this God-bestowed exemption from the disease laid blacks "under an obligation to offer your services to attend the sick."[32]

The Free African Society met on September 5, 1793, to consider Rush's request. Much of what had transpired in the last six years might have inclined them to spurn the requests for aid—the humiliating incident at St. George's the year before, the opposition to establishing their own church, and most recently the readiness of those who had signed their subscription lists to beg off in order to aid slaveowning French planters, who arrived with their chattel property in tow and then attempted, though unsuccessfully, to overturn the state law requiring manumission of any slave brought into the state by an owner establishing residence. But much had also transpired that argued for aiding the white community's desperate plight—the encouragement they had received in planning their church, the considerable aid of the Abolition Society, and the personal solicitation of Rush, their closest adviser.

A pamphlet written by Absalom Jones and Richard Allen after the epidemic indicates that they saw this as a God-sent opportunity to prove their courage and worth and to show that they could drive anger and bitterness from their hearts. Perhaps they could dissolve white racism by demonstrating that in their capabilities, civic virtue, and Christian humanitarianism they were not inferior, but in fact superior, to those who regarded former slaves as a degraded, hopelessly backward people. The "God who knows the hearts of all men, and the propensity of a slave to hate his oppressor," they wrote, "hath strictly forbidden it in his chosen people." Philadelphia's black Christians would act as the Good Samaritan, the despised man who aided a fellow human in desperate need when all the respected men of the community turned their heads away. They would succor those who despised and opposed them, because "the meek and humble Jesus, the great pattern of humanity, and every other virtue that can adorn and dignify men, hath commanded [us] to love our enemies, to do good to them that hate and despitefully use us."[33]

On September 6, 1793, Jones and Allen offered their services to the mayor, who immediately placed notices in the newspapers notifying citizens that they could apply to Jones or Allen for aid. "The African Society, intended for the relief of destitute Negroes," wrote the best authority on the epidemic, "suddenly assumed the most onerous, the most disgusting burdens of demoralized whites." They nursed the sick, carried away the dead, dug graves, and transported the afflicted to an emergency lazaretto set up outside the city. Jones, Allen, and William Gray, under instructions from Rush, acted as auxiliary doctors, bleeding patients and administering purges. By September 7, wrote Rush, Jones and Gray were "furnish[ing] nurses to most of my patients."[34] Before the epidemic ran its course, Rush's untutored black assistants had bled more than eight hundred patients, making notes on each case for Rush as they worked through the day. At night they drove the death carts to the cemeteries.

Within two weeks, Rush's assertion that Negroes were immune to the infectious fever had proven a ghastly error. Seventy Philadelphians were dying each day, and now blacks were numerous among them. "The Negroes are everywhere submitting to the disorder," Rush wrote on September 26, "and Richard Allen who had led their van is very ill."[35] In the first weeks of October, mortality raged through the half-abandoned city like a brushfire. On October 11 alone, 119 died. Still convinced "that it was our duty to do all the good we could to our suffering fellow mortals," Jones, Allen, and the other blacks carried out their gruesome tasks.[36] By the end of the month nearly 12,000 whites, along with the national and state governments, had fled the city, and nearly 4,000 persons, including about 240 blacks, had succumbed to the fever. Not until early November did the epidemic pass.

Work on the African Church, suspended for nearly three months during the yellow fever crisis, resumed in December 1793. It took further fundraising and another six months to complete the building. In soliciting support in the white community the black leaders may have expected to draw on the credit they had accumulated through their heroic efforts during the terrible days of autumn. But even this altruism had to be defended, for Mathew Carey, the Irish immigrant publisher in the city, publicly vilified the free blacks for opportunistically charging exorbitant fees to nurse the sick and remove the dead. Carey's pamphlet, *A Short Account of the Malignant Fever,* was itself a lesson in deriving profit from mass misery. Selling briskly, it went through four editions between November 14 and December 20. Carey provided a narrative account of the terrifying epidemic and appended lists of the dead. But the city's saviors in Carey's account were the rising merchant, Stephen Girard, and other whites who organized an emergency hospital just outside the city, where they selflessly tended the sick and dying. For the black Philadelphians who drove the death carts, buried the dead, and nursed the sick in the back streets and alleys, Carey had few good words.

Carey's *Short Account* drew a shocked response from Jones and Allen. They did not deny that some opportunistic persons "in low circumstances," both white and black, charged extravagant prices to nurse or remove the infected. This behavior was to be expected, "especially under the loathsomeness of many of the sick, when nature shuddered at the thoughts of the infection, and the task was aggravated by lunacy, and being left much alone" with the sick. But Philadelphians should consider such stories, they argued, alongside those of the many blacks who asked no recompense at all, content to take whatever the patient thought proper to give. One old black woman, when asked her fee, answered, "A dinner, master, on a cold winter's day." Caesar Cranchell, a founding member of the African Society, swore he would not "sell my life for money," even though he should die, which he did in the process of tending sick whites. Jones, Allen, Gray, and most other blacks had remained in the city throughout the biological terror, while nearly twenty thousand whites, including Carey, had fled. Assured that they were immune from the disease, black Philadelphians had remained in the city, only to learn otherwise; before cold weather ended the scourge, nearly one-tenth of the black population had died, as great a proportion as among whites. "Was not this in a great degree the effect of the services of the unjustly vilified black people?" asked Jones and Allen.[37]

As workmen completed the African Church, Philadelphia's blacks gathered to make a momentous decision about denominational affiliation. A "large majority" of the black elders and deacons favored uniting with the

Episcopal (formerly Anglican) Church, with only Jones and Allen opting for the Methodists. The majority view is understandable for several reasons. The local Methodist church had insulted Philadelphia's blacks just a few years before, and the presiding white elder remained opposed to a separate black church and, recounted Allen, "would neither be for us nor have anything to do with us."[38] Moreover, Methodism, while an evangelical and popular movement, operated under an autocratic ecclesiastical structure whereby its congregants had no voice in the pastoral affairs of their church or in the church's annual conferences.

The Episcopal Church, on the other hand, had much to commend it to Philadelphia's free blacks. It was theologically flexible and tinged with evangelicalism since before the Revolution, and its authority structure was more fluid than that of the Methodists. Many black Philadelphians, both slaves and free persons, had married, worshiped, and christened their children in the city's three Episcopal churches. Furthermore, their two closest white supporters were Episcopalians—Benjamin Rush, who had converted from Presbyterianism in 1787, and Joseph Pilmore, the former Methodist who, after returning to Philadelphia as an Episcopal priest, had ministered to the Free African Society's religious meetings.

Steadfast in his conviction that "there was no religious sect or denomination that would suit the capacity of the colored people as well as the Methodist," Allen quietly withdrew again. He could not accept the invitation to be the minister of the church. "I informed them," he wrote later, "that I could not be anything else but a Methodist, as I was born and awakened under them, and I could go no further with them, for I was a Methodist, and would leave them in peace and love."[39]

With Allen declining to lead them, the deacons and elders turned to Absalom Jones. He lacked Allen's exhortatory gifts, but his balance, tenacity, education, and dignified leadership qualities all commended him. His "devotion to the sick and dying" during the terrible days of the yellow fever epidemic had also earned him affection in the black community. "Administering to the bodily as well as the spiritual wants to many poor sufferers, and soothing the last moments of many departing souls among his people," it was later written, "he became greatly endeared to the colored race."[40]

With Jones leading them, the elders and deacons of the African Church of Philadelphia began to formalize the union with the Episcopal Church in July 1794. The black Philadelphians agreed to "commit all the ecclesiastical affairs of our church to the government of the Protestant Episcopal Church of North America," while at the same time securing internal control of their church—and church property—through a constitution that gave them and their successors "the power of choosing our minister and assistant minister," provided that members were to be admitted only by the minister and church wardens, and specified that the officers of the church—the vestrymen and deacon—were to be chosen by ballot from among members of at least twelve months' standing. Finally, only "men of color, who were Africans, or the descendants of the African race," could elect or be elected into any church office except that of minister and assistant minister. With the help of Benjamin Rush, they had contrived a formula for maintaining black control of the church, while allowing for the absence of trained blacks to fill the ministry. They had "declared a conformity to our Church in Doctrine, Discipline, and Worship," wrote Bishop William White, but simultaneously they had gained the promise of ordination of their leader, Absalom Jones, while preserving the all-important rights of self-government.[41]

On July 17, 1794, the African Church of Philadelphia opened its doors for worship. The published account of the dedication ceremony indicates that most of the white ministerial opposition had melted. "The venerable Clergy of almost every denomination, and a number of other very respectable citizens were present," a witness related. James Abercrombie, assistant minister of Christ Church, officiated, and Samuel Magaw, rector of St. Paul's Church, gave the sermon from the text: "Ethiopia shall soon stretch out her hands unto God" (Psalms 68:31). The discourse was from Isaiah: "The people that walked in darkness have seen a great light"—the same epigraph that was etched in marble above the church doors (Isaiah 9:2).[42] But we may imagine that the worshipers, those who were black and those who were white, derived different meanings from this epigraph.

Magaw's sermon stressed the need for gratitude and subservience on the part of the blacks who crowded the church. They or their fathers, he preached, had come from the heathenish lands of Senegal, Gambia, Benin, Angola, and Congo, and that burden of birth had been increased by the dismal effects of slavery, which "sinks the mind, no less than the body, . . . destroys all principle; corrupts the feelings; prevents man from either discerning, or choosing aright in anything." Having providentially been brought from "a land of Pagan darkness, to a land of Gospel light," these former slaves must now maintain their gratitude to the white Christians who freed them and donated or lent money to build the church. As for their brethren still in slavery, they should pray—but not take action. He emphasized the need for black passivity and moderation in all things and warned them to suppress the pride that was on the rise among them. Instead, they should cultivate "an obliging, friendly, meek conversation." Their church, Magaw counseled, in a perfect display of white paternalism, owed its existence to the benevolent action of whites. That it had been born in strife and discrimination and had arisen only when free blacks defied the opposition of white churchmen received no mention.

How did black Philadelphians receive Magaw's message? It must have confirmed among many of them the wisdom of forming a black church, not only to worship God in their own way but as a means of proving themselves and thus achieving equality and real freedom. By setting alongside Magaw's advice the thoughts of Jones and Allen, published a few months before, we can better comprehend the social and psychological struggle of free blacks: "You try what you can to prevent our rising from the state of barbarism you represent us to be in," wrote Jones and Allen in their reply to Mathew Carey, "but we can tell you from a degree of experience, that a black man, although reduced to the most abject state human nature is capable of, short of real madness, can think, reflect, and feel injuries, although it may not be with the same degree of keen resentment and revenge, that you who have been and are our great oppressors, would manifest if reduced to the pitiable condition of a slave." This hot indictment of white oppression and denigration of blacks was followed by an insistence on the capabilities of Africans and their descendants, which echoed Benezet's views. "We believe, if you would try the experiment of taking a few black children, and cultivate their minds with the same care, and let them have the same prospect in view, as to living in the world, as you would wish for your own children, you would find them upon the trial, they were not inferior in mental endowments."[43]

One month later, Absalom Jones preached the alternative black interpretation of the words from Isaiah—"the people that walked in darkness have seen a great light." The "darkness" through which they had walked was not the land of their birth but slavery. And the "great light" they had now seen was the light of freedom as well as the light of Christianity. In recording the "Causes and Motives" for establishing the African Church, written just a month after the church opened, Jones again expressed the rising tide of black determination to find strategies that would promote strength, security, and a decent existence. They had learned, Jones wrote, "to arise out of the dust and shake ourselves, and throw off that servile fear, that the habit of oppression and bondage trained us up in." In what seems to be a direct reference to the charges of Bishop White about black "pride," Jones continued that they wished "to avoid all appearance of evil, by self-conceitedness, or any intent to promote or establish any new human device among us"; hence they had decided to "resign and conform ourselves" to the Protestant Episcopal Church of North America.[44] Nonetheless, this was to be an autonomous black church, as their constitution spelled out.

Although he did not mention it, Jones might have added that the black "pride" and determination to create their own institutions drew much sustenance from the day-to-day accomplishments of Philadelphia's blacks during the decade that followed the Revolution. Through their ability to establish families and residences, by their demonstrated capacity to sustain themselves as free laborers and artisans, and in their success at conducting themselves morally, soberly, and civilly, they must have proved to themselves the groundless and racist character of the prevalent white view that former slaves were a permanently corrupted people.

This is not to argue that the transition from slavery to freedom was without its hazards. Philadelphia in the 1790s was full of struggling black sojourners, many with limited skills, who arrived by water and land from every direction. Hundreds of them at first could not establish independent black households, many had to bind out their children, and only a minority rose above a pinched and precarious existence. But their general ability to fashion a respectable life for themselves, giving credence to the arguments of Benezet, helped to galvanize leaders and convince them of their capability to establish separate churches.

As black Philadelphians completed St. Thomas's African Episcopal Church and formalized its affiliation with the Protestant Episcopal Church, Richard Allen continued to pursue his vision of black Methodism. Successful as a carter, trader, and master of chimney sweeps, he used his own money to purchase a blacksmith shop and haul it to a site he had bought at Sixth and Lombard Streets. Renovated as a humble house of worship, it opened its doors for a dedication service led by Bishop Francis Asbury on June 29, 1794. The Reverend John Dickens, the white Methodist elder recently assigned to Philadelphia, prayed "that it might be a 'Bethel' to the gathering of thousands of souls."[45] This marked the birth of "Mother Bethel," the first congregation of what became, in 1816, the independent African Methodist Episcopal Church.

Although the sources have allowed us to follow primarily the efforts of black leaders to point the way forward by organizing separate churches, it is important to measure the response of the mass of ordinary former slaves to the establishment of St. Thomas's and Bethel because that can tell us, if only imperfectly, about an emerging black consciousness in Philadelphia.

All of the available sources indicate an extraordinary response by Philadelphia's free blacks to the establishment of separate churches where they might worship, organize themselves, and develop their own leadership apart from white supervision.

In 1794, in the year they were founded, St. Thomas's and Bethel recorded 146 and 108 members respectively; one year later they had increased their membership to 427 and 121. Besides no fewer than 548 registered members in the two churches, "a floating congregation of at least a hundred or more persons" attended St. Thomas's, according to the church's first historian, and a number of others must have done so at Bethel.[46] The proportion of black adults who joined the two churches must have been about 40 percent of the 1,500 who lived in the city. This level of church participation was probably higher than that among whites in general and perhaps twice as high as among whites of the laboring classes. These figures are all the more impressive in view of the fact that about half of the city's free blacks were living in the households of whites, many as indentured servants, and therefore were less than fully free to act autonomously, while hundreds of others were French-speaking blacks recently manumitted by their Saint Domingue refugee masters or newly arrived migrants, often destitute and old, from the South.

The independent black church movement led by Absalom Jones and Richard Allen was the first major expression of racial strength and the most important instrument for furthering the social and psychological liberation of recently freed slaves. Bishop White had been correct, though in ways he knew not, when he reacted in anger in 1791 to news that free blacks were planning their own church, charging that their plan "originated in pride." That "pride" was really a growing feeling of strength and a conviction that black identity, self-sufficiency, self-determination, and the search for freedom and equality could best be nurtured in the early years of the Republic through independent black churches.

Absalom Jones tended his flock at St. Thomas's for a quarter-century, until he died in 1818 at seventy-one years of age. He guided his parishioners through a period of intensifying white racism, helped them take January 1 as their national holiday (because in 1808 it marked the end of the legal slave trade), and led them in building schools, mutual aid organizations, and literary societies. Though unnoticed in the history books from which young Americans learn about their founding period, Jones accomplished more in a lifetime than all but a handful of white Americans to make the revolutionary credo a reality. While struggling against congealing white racism, men like Jones became, in a peculiar way, the conscience of the nation. It was they, along with a small number of white reformers, who emerged in the early nineteenth century to demand of the Constitution, as one historian puts it, "more than its slave-holding creators dared to dream, wrestling it toward an integrity that the [Founding] Fathers would not give it."[47]

Notes

1. Benjamin Rush to Julia Rush, August 22, 1793, *Letters of Benjamin Rush,* ed. L. H. Butterfield, 2 vols. (Princeton, NJ, 1951), 2:639.

2. David Brion Davis, *The Problem of Slavery in the Age of Revolution, 1770–1823* (Ithaca, NY, 1975), 254.

3. Sydney V. James, *A People among People: Quaker Benevolence in Eighteenth-Century America* (Cambridge, MA, 1963), 316–19.

4. *The Life Experience and Gospel Labors of the Rt. Rev. Richard Allen, To Which is Annexed The Rise and Progress of the African Methodist Episcopal Church in the United States of America* (Nashville, TN, 1960), 17.

5. "Sketch of Jones," in William Douglass, *Annals of the First African Church in the United States of America, now styled the African Episcopal Church of St. Thomas* (Philadelphia, 1862), 118–21.

6. Ibid.

7. *American Daily Advertiser* (Philadelphia), February 19, 1818.

8. *Autobiography of Richard Allen,* in R. R. Wright Jr., *Bishops of the African Methodist Church* (Nashville, TN, 1963), 53–54.

9. Ibid., 54. The quotation about "often communed together" is from the preamble to the constitution of the Free African Society, in Douglass, *Annals,* 15.

10. Douglass, *Annals,* 18–41, where extracts of the Free African Society's minutes, no longer extant, are recorded.

11. Ibid., 18–23.

12. Carol V. R. George, *Segregated Sabbaths: Richard Allen and the Rise of Independent Black Churches, 1760–1845* (New York, 1973), 57.

13. Douglass, *Annals,* 9.

14. Ibid., 24.

15. Rush to Jeremy Belknap, August 18, 1788, *Letters of Rush,* 1:482.

16. *Extract of a Letter from Dr. Benjamin Rush, of Philadelphia, to Granville Sharp* (London, 1792), 6–7.

17. Gayraud S. Wilmore, *Black Religion and Black Radicalism: An Interpretation of the Religious History of the Afro-American People* (Garden City, NY, 1972), 114.

18. *Extract of a Letter from Rush,* 4.

19. "Address of the Representatives of the African Church," in ibid., 6–7.

20. Ibid.

21. Wilmore, *Black Religion and Black Radicalism,* 106.

22. Rush to Julia Rush, July 16, 1791, *Letters of Rush,* 1:599–600.

23. George W. Corner, ed., *The Autobiography of Benjamin Rush* (Princeton, NJ, 1948), 202.

24. Benjamin T. Tanner, *An Apology for African Methodism* (Baltimore, 1867), 16.

25. *Autobiography of Allen*, 55.

26. Rush to Jeremy Belknap, June 21, 1792, *Letters of Rush*, 1:620.

27. *Autobiography of Allen*, 55.

28. Ibid.

29. Rush to John Nicholson, November 28, 1792, *Letters of Rush*, 1:624.

30. *Autobiography of Allen*, 57.

31. Mathew Carey, *A Short Account of the Malignant Fever* (Philadelphia, 1794), 23.

32. Rush to Richard Allen, [September 1793], Mss. Correspondence of Rush, Library Company of Philadelphia, 38:32.

33. Absalom Jones and Richard Allen, *A Narrative of the Proceedings of the Black People, During the late Awful Calamity in Philadelphia, in the year 1793* . . . (Philadelphia, 1794), 24–25.

34. J. H. Powell, *Bring Out Your Dead: The Great Plague of Yellow Fever in Philadelphia in 1793* (Philadelphia, 1949), 96–98; Rush to ———, September 7, 1793, *Letters of Rush*, 2:654.

35. Rush to Julia Rush, September 13, 25, 1793, *Letters of Rush*, 2:663, 683–84.

36. Jones and Allen, *Narrative of the Black People*, 15–16; *Minutes of the proceedings of the Committee* . . . (Philadelphia, 1794), 204.

37. Jones and Allen, *Narrative of the Black People*, 7–16.

38. *Autobiography of Allen*, 57–58.

39. Ibid., 58–59.

40. George F. Bragg, *Richard Allen and Absalom Jones* (Baltimore, 1915), unpaginated.

41. The constitution is in Douglass, *Annals*, 96–99. White's statement is quoted in Edgar L. Pennington, "The Work of the Bray Associates in Pennsylvania," *Pennsylvania Magazine of History and Biography* 58 (1934): 22.

42. Samuel Magaw, *A Discourse Delivered July 17th 1794, in the African Church of Philadelphia, on the occasion of opening the said Church and holding public worship in it for the first time* (Philadelphia, 1794), reprinted in Douglass, *Annals*, 58–81.

43. Jones and Allen, *Narrative of the Black People*, 23–24.

44. Absalom Jones, "Causes and Motives for Establishing St. Thomas's African Church of Philadelphia," in Douglass, *Annals*, 93–95.

45. *Autobiography of Allen*, 59.

46. Douglass, *Annals*, 110.

47. Vincent Harding, "Wrestling toward the Dawn: The Afro-American Freedom Movement and the Changing Constitution," *Journal of American History* 74 (1987): 719.

Suggested Readings

Recapturing the life of African Americans in the revolutionary era takes patience and resourcefulness because the printed record is very thin. Jones himself wrote only a few pages about his life, published in the first history of Jones's church by a later minister, William Douglass. Only in a short newspaper notice of his death in 1818—hardly a proper obituary—can one find details about his career. Jones wrote and delivered many sermons from the pulpit, but only a few of them were published. His most distinct footprints, in written form, are in *A Narrative of the Proceedings of the Black People, During the late Awful Calamity in Philadelphia, in the year 1793* . . . (Philadelphia, 1794).

Jones can be brought from the shadows only by reconstructing the city in which he spent most of his life and reconstructing the life of African Americans in Philadelphia through the records of the Pennsylvania Abolition Society, newspapers, city directories, municipal records, deed books, and the like. The fullest treatment of black Philadelphia in the era of Absalom Jones is Gary B. Nash, *Forging Freedom: The Formation of Philadelphia's Black Community, 1720–1840* (Cambridge, MA, 1988). Also important is Billy G. Smith, *The "Lower Sort": Philadelphia's Laboring People, 1750–1800* (Ithaca, NY, 1990); and Carol V. R. George, *Segregated Sabbaths: Richard Allen and the Rise of Independent Black Churches, 1760–1845* (New York, 1973). For a broader view of African Americans in the American Revolution, see Benjamin Quarles, *The Negro in the American Revolution* (Chapel Hill, 1996 [1961]).

8

Rebecca Dickinson
A Life Alone in the Early Republic

Marla R. Miller

While Eliza Pinckney lived life with republican motherhood at its center, Rebecca Dickinson, her near contemporary, followed quite a different path. Born in modest circumstances in western Massachusetts, she resided there her whole life. Although she at least twice had the opportunity to marry, she never did. Unlike most women of her day, she was neither wife nor mother; instead she carved out a distinctive and independent life for herself as a skilled artisan. Through her extensive diary, we learn that her work as a gownmaker necessarily kept her in contact with her clients, which, along with her interaction with her mother and extended family, spared her a life of complete isolation. She led an at times lonely life, but she harbored decidedly mixed feelings about her singleness. She alternately despaired at her solitude and relished her liberty to set her own course, but she always took comfort in the continuing presence of God in her life. In an era when notions about American women were evolving from the ideal of republican motherhood to the cult of true womanhood, Rebecca Dickinson chose a road less taken, but one not without its satisfactions.

Marla R. Miller is assistant professor of history at the University of Massachusetts-Amherst, where she teaches classes in public history and early American history. Her 1997 Ph.D. dissertation, completed at the University of North Carolina at Chapel Hill, won the Organization of American Historians' Lerner-Scott Prize for outstanding work in women's history.

"Too is better than one for if one [Should] fall the other can lift him up but i must act my Part alone."[1] When Rebecca Dickinson (1738–1815) penned these words in the summer of 1789, she had spent many hours just like this one, alone in the chamber of a weather-beaten red saltbox just across from the meetinghouse in Hatfield, Massachusetts. An evening at the home of her brother had put the diarist in an especially thoughtful mood. Henry Dodge, an old bachelor who had courted her sister Irene more than fifteen years ago, had also been visiting there that night. Irene had long since married, but Henry had not. "He appeared to sit by her and i belive he has never forgot her," Dickinson mused. Dodge's plight was, to the aging spinster, only too familiar: "How great the loss is to loos the Pardener of our life for in the beginning tha was made male and feemale . . . there is great need of the help of Each other through the jorney of life . . . but i must act my part alone . . . alone in a world where tha goe too and too male and female."[2]

On the evening she wrote these words, diarist Rebecca Dickinson was forty-nine years old, and she, like Dodge, had never married. She was born in rural western Massachusetts in 1738. Dickinson's single status, more than any other factor, shaped her experience as a woman in early New England. A "bullock unaccustomed to the yoke" of spinsterhood, Dickinson recorded to her journal the rabblement of emotion her life alone evoked. Referring to herself as a "fish out of water," a "gazing stock," a "cat on a roof," a "sparrow alone on a rooftop," she was clearly aware of nothing so much as her own aberration: "How oft tha have hissed and wagged their heads at me," she wrote, "by reason of my Solotary life."[3] Her manuscript—four sewn gatherings of foolscap containing nearly five hundred entries written between July 1787 and August 1802, discovered tucked in the garret of her home some eighty years after her death—preserves the difficult "journey of life" of a woman struggling to "act her part alone."

In a society where marriage was nearly universal, Dickinson wrote that her "story frights half the women of the town." But hers is not the story of a village outcast. Evidence apart from Dickinson's own record paints a very different picture of her place among Hatfield citizens. Surviving recollections suggest that Dickinson was indeed a loved and respected member of her community. In his history of Hatfield, Daniel Wells records that "as she travelled from house to house about her work [gownmaking] . . . she acquired a fund of information concerning her neighbors that was unequalled by any other person. A gift for pithy, epigrammatic remarks caused her to be regarded as something of an 'oracle.'" Samuel D. Partridge, a lifelong resident of Hatfield, remembered Dickinson from his boyhood as a "very intelligent woman" whose sayings "were frequently repeated" by townspeople. Another woman recalled her as "Aunt Beck, it being the habit in those days to call single women who were loved by that community title, and Aunt Beck was well-liked by all." Nineteenth-century Hatfield historian Margaret Miller's research (Miller first brought the diary to public attention after its discovery in the 1890s) suggests that Dickinson indeed achieved at least the outward appearance of grace: "To old people who remember her," Miller wrote, "or knew her by hearsay she was a 'Saint on Earth,' a 'marvel of piety.'" Others remembered her as the "most industrious woman that ever lived."[4]

If some contradiction exists between Dickinson's sense of herself as an anomalous, even outcast, member of her community and other accounts of a village figure "well liked by all," that apparent discrepancy only mirrors other tensions that run through this complex text. Dickinson used the pages of her journal to express (and then lock away, literally, and perhaps figuratively as well) mounting concerns that she had been deservedly "cast out from the Peopel." Here she examined "how it Came about that others and all in the world was in Possession of Children ad frinds and a hous and homes while i was So od as to Sit here alone."5 Yet, at the same time, Dickinson's journal hints that the diarist found attractions in her single status—attractions that she herself could barely admit. This text tells a tale of both shame and satisfaction, and it is in that very contradiction that the meaning of singlehood for early American women lies. Like other women offered no viable social role outside marriage, Dickinson nevertheless carved one out and bore the social and psychological costs of that struggle.

Dickinson's journal is an exceptional source for historians, not least because so few personal testimonies of never-married women exist. Personal writings of this type vary greatly in purpose and content. As windows into the past, their clarity depends upon the view we seek. Vast differences, for example, distinguish Dickinson's diary from that of her neighbor and client Elizabeth Porter Phelps. The two women were roughly the same age and lived on opposite sides of the Connecticut River; on Sundays after church meeting both women bent over their respective journals. But Phelps's text is an accounting of the social life and work activities that shaped life on the large farm of her politically and socially important family. She noted the text of the Sunday sermon but devoted the bulk of her energies to recording the comings, goings, and activities of friends, family, servants, and artisans. Whereas Phelps often lamented her little opportunity for contemplation, in contrast, Dickinson's was "a life full of self-reflecttion."6 The difference between the manuscripts each woman produced is perhaps best illustrated by the fact that, although Rebecca Dickinson was a skilled gownmaker, almost nothing of her work can be gleaned from her own journal. If one seeks to study the trade of rural Massachusetts needlewomen, then Phelps's diary, which records the work performed by the artisans and domestic servants she hired, is a better source than Dickinson's own, more meditative text.

In her diary, Dickinson searched for ways in which to understand her place in the world. Small remarks by neighbors reverberated in the diarist's mind; in her journal they were turned over, reexamined, challenged, internalized, in prose so painfully unreserved that the reader can almost feel her reddening blush, the hairs rising on her burning neck as she encounters the tacit or declared reproach of her neighbors. At other times, the loneliness seems more than she can bear:

> About Dusk or the Edge of the evining Set out to Come home to this lonely hous where i have lived forty nine years lonesome as Death. . . . Came home Crept into my window and fastened up my rome neeled Down by my bed and after a Poor manner Commited my Self to god but not with that thankfull heart as i aught to have had o my god my Poverty and my leanness my Poverty as to the things of time when other Peopel are a Seeing there Children rejoicing with one another im all alone in the hous and all alone in the world a most wicked and Sinfull thought which makes me Cry o my leanness how Poor those Souls are who have there Portion in this life i am ashamed to Call god my father and to Complain the want of any thing.[7]

A young woman whose "mind was stored with Poetry" when she began to keep a journal, probably in the 1760s, Dickinson wrote through the dramatic decades of revolution and nation-building, years of political and social turmoil in Hatfield as elsewhere. But the summer of 1787 (while Congress hammered out the Federal Constitution in Philadelphia) found her burning those earlier, too-temporal quires. On July 22, 1787, Dickinson began the new diary, which survives today. She rededicated her writings to the state of her soul. The first half of that year had been especially difficult, and part of the significance of and motivation for these surviving pages lies in the months immediately prior to their opening. That summer, Dickinson grieved the loss of two close companions, Lucretia Williams and Elizabeth Alver, both of whom had died not long before. "This Sommer has stripped the[e] of all thy acquaintences. More precias than fine gold has thy friends been to the[e]." Without her companions, Dickinson was not simply lonelier, but more cognizant of her own aging, her own mortality, and the increasing likelihood that she would endure it all alone. Now, she wrote, "the world wears a difirent face."[8]

Other evidence of the ebb and flow of life was surely on Dickinson's mind about that time as well. As she approached fifty, the diarist had likely just passed or was passing through menopause, confronting the reality that, whether or not she would ever "change her name," no children would take care of her in her old age. "What Shall i do or where Shall i gow with whoom Shall i live when old and helpless"—uncertainty tore at her peace of mind. "This summer has given me a Sight of myself," she wrote at the close of that painful season; in a spirit of both resolve and despair she declared that "there is no hope for me in the things of time"—and hence all "the more need of Sending all my hopes to the heavenly world."[9]

Apart from these pages, little record of Rebecca Dickinson survives. She was the eldest daughter of Hatfield farmer and dairyman Moses

Dickinson and farmwife Anna Smith Dickinson. Throughout Rebecca Dickinson's life, the population of her thriving farming community along the Connecticut River hovered at about eight hundred. The 1790 census reports 103 houses in the village and surrounding countryside; ten years later, just 20 more had been added. When Yale president Timothy Dwight passed through in 1797, he described Hatfield as a town where the "inhabitants have for a long period been conspicuous for uniformity of character. They have less intercourse with their neighbors than those of most other places . . . an air of silence and retirement appears everywhere. Except travelers, few persons are seen abroad besides those who are employed about their daily business. This seclusion probably renders them less agreeable to strangers, but certainly contributes to their prosperity. Accordingly, few farming towns are equally distinguished either for their property or their thrift."[10]

Rebecca's father, however, was distinguished neither for property nor thrift; tax and probate records show that he was a man of average means in the community, producing mostly grain on about 15½ acres of land and operating a dairy. As the eldest child, Rebecca surely helped raise her younger sisters and brother. By Rebecca's eighteenth birthday, Anna had given birth to five more children: Samuel, Martha, Miriam, Anna, and Irene. In time, each of these married. Martha moved seventy miles north, to Bennington, Vermont, and Anna left for Pittsfield, Massachusetts. Irene and her husband went to Williamsburg, a town set off from Hatfield lands, while Samuel and his wife Mary moved just over the Hatfield line to Whately and continued in the dairy line. Miriam remained closest, moving just a few doors south to the tavern owned by her husband, Silas Billings.

Meanwhile, Rebecca remained in the house in which she had been born. At some point, probably around the age of twelve, she was sent "to learn the trade of gownmaking." Through the years, she worked at her trade, helped with her siblings, and generally remained active in the "busi scenes of life," all the while passing gradually beyond the usual age of marriage, about twenty-three for Anglo women in eighteenth-century rural New England. Then, when it seemed that she should have a chance finally to "change her name," she felt the "bitter blow" that "robbed her hopes" for marriage, a family, and a home of her own. Gradually, what had seemed unthinkable in her teens and twenties came to haunt her thirties and forties and was, on the eve of her fifties, a grim reality.

Fortunately for Dickinson, and unlike most of her contemporaries, she enjoyed the benefits of a marketable skill: gownmaking. In her diary she frequently mentioned "invitations" to work in surrounding Hampshire County towns, suggesting that she had no need to solicit clients. In addition to simple tailoring and the occasional making of stays, Dickinson produced women's better garments: gowns of silk and taffeta for Sunday worship and special occasions, such as the garments rendered on that August afternoon she spent "at Sister bilings to fix Patte Church and Bets Huntinton for the we[dding reception] of oliver hastings," or the dark brown ducape gown in which Hadley gentlewoman Elizabeth Porter married Charles Phelps. Other clients included the wives and daughters of the so-called River Gods, members of the seven interrelated families who wielded the lion's share of political, economic, and ecclesiastical authority in the towns of the Connecticut River Valley through most of eighteenth century. That Dickinson was entrusted to create important gowns for prominent members of the local aristocracy suggests that she was sufficiently trained and talented to secure the patronage of the area's leading families.

Dickinson gratefully acknowledged the benefits of her marketable trade. Following a visit by the widow Catherine Graves, Dickinson wrote, "She began the world with me wee went together to learn the trade of gown making which has been of unspeakable advanta[g]e to me but of no Servis to her." Dickinson's suggestion that Graves's apprenticeship had been of "no Servis" refers to Catherine's subsequent marriage to Moses Graves, a man thirty-seven years her senior. Graves's income plus the raising of her six new stepchildren probably made taking in needlework unnecessary, if not impossible. Without husbands to provide for them, single women largely depended on the largess of male relatives for their maintenance. Dickinson enjoyed the benefit of her father's home, but she provided her own day-to-day expenses. Craft skills meant that she did not to have to appeal to any family members for necessities, much less for small luxuries like her silk gloves or her looking glass.[11]

Still, Dickinson recognized the trade's pitfalls. She frequently bemoaned the sporadic nature of the work and the threat that slack periods posed to her security. "How times vary with me," she noted one November afternoon, lamenting "how hurried [she] was formerly at this Season of the year." The pronounced seasonal variation of the clothing trades typically produced, for both tailors and gownmakers, months of complete unemployment broken by times of extreme overwork. The effect of this seasonality is captured in the lines of a character (who, like Dickinson, was an unmarried laborer) in one eighteenth-century drama:

"What a present is mine, and what a prospect is my future. Labour and watchings in the busy season—hunger in the slack—and solitude in both."[12] This irregularity of employment, from season to season or year to year, proved stressful to Dickinson, who as her own sole source of support could ill afford time away from her needle. Once, while eagerly anticipating a visit from her sister Martha and her children, Dickinson wrote: "I Shall be glad to see them i hope to be at home when tha Come to town which makes me at a loss about going [to Hadley] but my daily bread depends upon my labour." Torn between readying her home for anxiously awaited guests and "imploy for her hands," Dickinson chose the latter.[13]

As she grew older, Dickinson's anxiety over her income mounted. Some years in the past, she wrote in 1787, she had been "hardly too scared to walk too miles afoot," but now, she fretted, "old age has Crept up" on her. As her geographical range necessarily narrowed, so too did the range of potential clients. Sickness also threatened her income, and apprehension over her recurrent bouts with the "Collick" caused much concern. During the following winter, Dickinson found herself "Distressing ill." She tried diligently to carry on, but her "Physick overdoing" finally caused her to faint. Alone in the house, she took to her bed, but this infirmity only produced panic over her fragile finances: "Have had an invitation to goe to Hadley to work but no Strength to move and must be Content with what is ready earnt by me since my health and my Strength is gon i would beg of god that my Estate may be a comfort to me now in the time of old age."[14]

Whether this "estate" refers to some security she received following the death of her father in 1785, or to some amount of money she was able to set aside after fulfilling her own fiscal obligations, is not clear. At the time of his death, Moses Dickinson provided equally for each of his daughters, bequeathing "the sum of sixty six pounds thirteen shillings and four pence of silver money what I have advanced to each of them to be accounted as part thereof the remainder to be paid by my son Samuel in two years after my decease." Despite Rebecca's unmarried status (at forty-seven), Moses' will made no special provisions for her welfare. In 1780, Moses had given Rebecca seventy acres of land in nearby Williamsburg. If the gift was intended to serve as potential income to be converted to cash at some later date should she find it necessary, that would suggest one way in which Moses acknowledged his daughter's need for support. Perhaps she rented the land to a Williamsburg farmer, drawing steady income from the property. Moses' decision not to allocate to her in his will greater resources than to his married daughters may also suggest that she was faring fairly well on her own.[15]

Whatever the actual state of Dickinson's finances, apprehension over security invaded her consciousness both day and night. Once, for example, she was "awaked by a dream i thought that i had Stole from mrs hurberd but knew my Self to be innocent but my Credit was a going." Dreaming she had been reduced to stealing from her friend, local innkeeper Lucy Hubbard, she pleaded that God spare her that humiliation and protect her soul from transgression. Elsewhere she sighed, "God has in great mercy this Summer back given me work he heard my Cry and has sent imploy for my hands the god who heard my Cry has given me work."[16]

Dickinson's "Cry" is understandable: over time she had ample opportunity to witness the precarious economic states other unmarried women endured. Without husbands and children, elderly single women were housed, fed, and clothed only as the generosity of others allowed. Dickinson knew what such dependence could mean. In the fall of her forty-ninth year, she noted the death of a thirty-year-old spinster who "was Driven from one brother to another and lived with her Sisters Some of the time." On another occasion she noted her own good fortune: "When i Compare my life with many of my acquaintences i am Content and well i may be there is no unmaried woman who has a hous to Shelter my goods in when others run from Place to Place not knowing where to goe nor what to Do."[17] Never-married women, Dickinson well knew, shuttled from place to place, wherever they were most needed or least underfoot.

Despite her own comparatively stable living situation, Dickinson knew that since she was without title to her home, any change in the family's circumstances could dramatically alter her own. She constantly anguished over the looming possibility that her aging mother would die, prompting her brother, who stood to inherit the property, to sell the Hatfield house. "What Should i Doe was it not for this old hous it is a Safe Retreat from troble"; "the Winter is Comming on when there will be no rome for me"; "tha will put me where tha please who have the care of me"—passages such as these regularly mark Dickinson's text, pointing up her sense of vulnerability, her awareness that her hold on that "Safe Retreat" was tenuous at best.

Dickinson's journal is so filled with her sense of being alone in the world that it would be easy to forget the important role her family played—apart from her sense that her eventual fate lay in their hands—in shaping her day-to-day life. And yet they, like her trade, proved sources of both comfort and concern. In the eighteenth century, as today, family caregiving was primarily ascribed to women, and especially to unmarried women, who without husbands or children to look after were perceived to have fewer competing obligations. Like many single women, Dickinson was assigned and assumed the role of caregiver for infirm family members, in this case both her elderly mother, Anna, and her "feeble" nephew, Charles. These responsibilities both mitigated and exacerbated aspects of her life alone.

Charles Dickinson, born in April 1779 to Samuel and Mary Dickinson, was a "poor weekly boy who has never been well," given to "fits." It is possible that Samuel and Mary placed their son with his childless aunt in the hope that he would be a help to her (perhaps also he was of little use on Samuel's farm). But it seems likely too that the "feeble" eight year old was placed with Rebecca so that she might keep a watchful eye on a young boy who, despite his frailty, managed to cultivate a "mischeavous disposition."

In addition to her nephew, Rebecca also assumed much responsibility for the care of her elderly mother. Dickinson's mother arrived each fall to spend the winter with Rebecca and departed each spring to her "other house in the woods," probably Samuel's home in Whately. One might expect that such an arrangement would have provided both women with companionship and care in their advancing age. Widowed in 1785, Anna may have turned to Rebecca for care and support, and Rebecca may have gained a friend and companion no longer bound by the needs of her own family. But Dickinson's journal does not suggest that these two women enjoyed a particularly close relationship. Though at times Rebecca seemed to regret her mother's departures, she also expressed a certain vexation at her return. Loath to shirk her responsibility, her utmost concern was "my Duty to my aged Parent." One winter, even as she longed to travel to Bennington, Vermont, to stay with Martha and her family, Dickinson maintained "my greatest Scrupel has been on my mother's account." Presented with this opportunity a second time, she again was "confounded between" her "schemes" and her "Duty."[18]

Family caregiving, a function legitimized by society, enabled Dickinson to participate vicariously in the traditional nurturing aspects of marriage and motherhood, perhaps easing her sense of uselessness. But if she did derive satisfaction from these duties, she did not record it. Instead it seems that the care of her mother proved emotionally and physically exhausting. In October 1787, when her mother returned after an absence of several months, Rebecca wrote, "We have Set up housekeeping one time more [though] how we are to live i Cant See." Just two weeks later, her nerves frayed and patience exhausted, Dickinson expressed her complete exasperation: "My mother Seventi five years of age not able to take Care of herself in a Pusseling [puzzling] fit broke my Specticles a great loss to me for tha Suted me So well that 1 ginny [a guinea was a coin of high value] should not have bought them out of my hand."[19]

As she aged, Dickinson's own illnesses aggravated her frustration. Each fall after she reached forty, Dickinson was plagued with a few weeks of serious illness. In fact, a "most distressing Collick" had confined her during the same week in which her mother underwent the "Pusseling fit." Although she "gained ease" after the local physician opened a vein, Dickinson commented, "how Sad to be Sick" when there was "no one to Doe the least kind offis." Anticipating yet another bout with her illness, she declared, "I Cant be Sick i wont be Sick there is none of my fellow being to Show me the least kind offis . . . my mother near eighty as Stuped as Can be [and] a litel feble boy Charls and my body in Sore distress." Her patience at an end, she fumed, "How Can the Stupid world not know my trobles no one from my brothers hous have been here but a boy ten years of age after a great many words by me."[20]

One can only imagine the tension of this scene: Rebecca, already exhausted and feeling unappreciated, pleaded with her brother and sister-in-law for some assistance in caring for Samuel's mother and son Charles. To her dismay, they responded by sending their ten-year-old son Moses, clearly more to assess the situation than to provide care. The added burden of her mother's arrival was apparently simply more than Rebecca could bear, as she later remarked, "Wee was too feeble to help one another i thought i had better be in the hous alone." Dickinson constantly bemoaned her lack of companionship, yet preferred solitude to responsibilities she felt she could not shoulder. Perhaps it is no wonder that after Anna's departure she wrote, "My mother has been gone five weeks tomorrow and Sweet Content has Crouned every Day."[21]

Dickinson's family, like their nineteenth- and twentieth-century counterparts, thought unmarried women like Rebecca, without husbands and children to attend to, had ample time and energy for childcare, nursing, or help with housekeeping. Singlehood strained her relations with members of the family in other ways as well. In 1792, English author Mary Wollstonecraft observed that "when the brother marries . . . [the unmarried sister] is viewed with averted looks as an intruder, an unnecessary burden on the benevolence of the master of the house and his new partner. . . . [The wife] is displeased at seeing the property of her children lavished on a helpless sister."[22] Consistent with observations like Wollstonecraft's, Rebecca and Samuel's wife, Mary, enjoyed a less than cordial relationship. Mary's reluctance to travel to Hatfield to care for Anna, Rebecca, or even her own son Charles, suggests the discordant perceptions that characterized Dickinson's relationship with her family. Mary suspected Rebecca of exaggerating her need while Mary herself had a whole household to run; for her part, Dickinson described Mary as "the most unhappy of the Daughters of Eve She is Pashanate Covetous jellous Sordid no love for her husband mean as the Dirt . . . what a tryal She has been to me."[23] With so much family authority vested in her brother, this tense relationship with his wife must have been a cause of concern for Rebecca as she looked toward an uncertain future.

Dickinson's discussion of her family points up one of the ways in which her actions sometimes belied her words. Despite her real sense of lonesome vulnerability, Dickinson herself engineered her solitary residence in the Hatfield home, requesting that she retain the house after Moses' death rather than move in with a sibling or have one of them with their families move in with her. Her desire to gain or retain an independent existence—in spite of an abiding loneliness—is striking. Luckily, her family was disposed both financially and temperamentally to accede to her request. Her life alone there, she concluded, was both "ordered of god as well as Contrived by myself."[24]

Dickinson also made this choice in full light of her belief that her neighbors "hissed and wagged their heads" at her "Solotary life." And her sense that her situation drew comment among her neighbors was not mere paranoia: notice of her solitary life *was* publicly taken. One summer, for example, she passed a pleasant evening in the house of her minister. Visiting there was Lydia Lyman Peck, an old friend of Rebecca's who herself had married late in life. After the guests had shared their conversation and tea, as Dickinson was making her exit, Lydia followed her to the door and blurted out that "she Could not bare to have me Come to this hous alone." Momentarily dumbfounded, Dickinson replied, "not So lonesome as the grave," but she "wondered after i Came home wether i was rite to give Such an answer how i must look in the eyes of the world."[25] The startled spinster had risen quickly to her own defense, but she acknowledged privately that her situation was bound to elicit comment and concern, if not outright censure. While Dickinson was in Bennington, her tentative effort to join the household of her sister Martha was crushed when, in a similar incident, a stranger asked her how it was that she had never married. "Thunderstruck," Dickinson again retorted, "my affairs might be in a worse order," but she abandoned her planned move and raced home, where her situation was less likely to prompt new inquiry.

In eighteenth-century Europe and America, singlehood invoked an interlacing set of implications. In essence, of course, an "old maid" was a woman who had failed to marry. From that fact followed a set of attendant assumptions. Older single women were often looked on with suspicion and derision as observers guessed reasons for their plight. Often, at least in parodies of the day, "old maids" were accused of pridefully declining reasonable proposals of marriage while they held out for the better offer that never came. Thus, a certain fastidious, finicky quality was often ascribed to the stereotypical old maid. Meanwhile, because sex outside of marriage was strongly discouraged by both social mores and religious doctrine, the reproductive potential of unmarried women of all ages was forever untapped. Of course, women violated prescription—and often—but never-married women were, at least publicly, presumed virgins. As historian Lee Chambers-Schiller suggests, since early American conceptions of womanhood were constructed around biology, "the misuse, or disuse, of those functions proved cause for concern." Permanent celibacy then carried with it a vague scent of decay, of withering organs and soured spirits. Finally, without in-laws and subject to the dearth of gainful occupations for women, the old maid remained, at least in theory, dependent on her family of origin and so perpetually, if artificially, "immature," no matter how advanced in age. In short, the old maid, according to one 1790 satire, was "one of the most ill-natured, magotty, peevish, conceited . . . censorious, out-of-the-way, never-to-be-pleased, good for nothing creatures."[26]

Given the general severity of scorn and ridicule heaped upon women who did not marry, and Dickinson's acute feelings of vulnerability and constant loneliness, the sources of her singlehood become all the more curious. As voiced by another young woman in 1762, when Dickinson was twenty-four years old, "The appellation of old Made . . . I don't believe one of our sex would voluntarily Bare."[27] What circumstances, then, led Dickinson to her life alone? Was the appellation involuntarily borne?

Certainly in Hatfield, demographic pressure reduced every woman's chances to obtain a mate. As fewer men moved into Massachusetts and greater numbers migrated westward, the proportion of men to women shrank. Midcentury warfare also took its toll. Britain's continuing effort to eject France from North America drew numbers of eligible men off to war, some of whom inevitably did not return. Though estimates vary, women outnumbered men in Massachusetts by at least the 1760s. In 1772 (when Dickinson was thirty-four) essayist William Gordon numbered the "excess" women in Massachusetts at 5,665. Gradually, the proportion of never-married women "grew from 9% for families formed between 1700 and 1759, to 12% among daughters whose parents married 1760–1774, to nearly 15% for those marrying 1775–1799."[28]

In Hatfield, as elsewhere, women hoping to marry were caught in a demographic bind. Dickinson was sixteen when the Seven Years War reached Hampshire County. The continued settlement of outlying villages in the 1760s and 1770s, when she was in her twenties and thirties, removed more men from the immediate community. The statistical probability of entering into marriage was decreasing during Dickinson's lifetime; and at least a dozen area women roughly contemporary to Dickinson remained single throughout their lifetimes. Moreover, that estimate probably represents just a fraction of the true number.

But Dickinson did not perceive her singlehood to be the result of broad social forces; instead, she pointed toward a single act, a "stroke which mowed down [her] earthly hopes." That phrase seems to indicate that the "appellation of old Made" was indeed involuntarily borne; however, other evidence suggests that her singlehood was not altogether without design. The truth, in other words, is probably somewhere in between. Although Dickinson often attributed her singlehood to one defining moment, in fact, she considered a variety of explanations, with sources in both the temporal and the eternal. For New England Calvinists, adversity—in this case Dickinson's lack of a husband, home, and children—was welcome evidence that God was sufficiently concerned with the state of one's Soul to send useful calamities: "It is good to be sick it is good to be afflicted for thereby i have learned to keep thy Commands." In denying her the comforts of family life, God had protected her soul from competing temporal interests. With "no children no grand children no house no land" to distract her from her faith, Dickinson was free to achieve the highest measure of devotion.[29]

But that same sense of divine intervention also carried with it an implied criticism, that her poor spiritual state required chastening. After much reflection, Dickinson determined that it was "vile idollatry" of the "things of time" that doomed her to a solitary life. Hoping to quiet rising resentment at another evening alone, she wrote, "It is the will of god Conserning me no other Place would Doe to Cure me of my Pride and to wean me from the world." "How Can i quarel with the government of god who has witheld nothing from me which would have been for my good," she asked, "for what is all the gratification of this life to a Sure belief that our name is written in heaven[?]" If she failed to seize this opportunity—

to be "so recluse and get no more good by it"—the consequences were dire: "What a Sad thought to be so miserable here and tormented in the world to Come."[30]

If we cannot test her thesis about divine intent, we can examine her assertion that it was this "bitter blow" that put her on the solitary path. She no doubt experienced the event that so haunted her, but was it the cause of her singlehood? Although Dickinson claimed so, she may have adopted this explanation—consciously or unconsciously—as an acceptable one, the jilted lover being one of the few "scenarios" available to eighteenth-century women to explain a failure to marry. William Hayley's 1786 *Philosophical, Historical and Moral Essay on Old Maids,* for example, urges the never-married woman, "whenever she has occasion to speak of the nuptial state, to . . . represent her own exclusion from it, not as the effect of choice, arising from a cold irrational aversion to the state in general, but as the consequence of such perverse incidents as frequently perplex all the patterns of human life[.]"[31]

To be sure, Dickinson represented her singlehood, "not as the effect of choice," but as the consequence of a "perverse incident" revealed in subtle clues throughout her text. The first comes in an entry recording the events of the previous evening at her sister Miriam's home. Dickinson noted the presence of Jesse Billings, who, she wrote, "put those Sad thoughts into my mind." She returned home and "lited no Candel for the Darkness of my mind was beyand the Darkest Dungin there was no hope for me in the things of time." That night, she had a "Strange Dream": "I thought i was on a jorney with jesse billings mare with one rein of my bridle broke my Self lost entagled among horses where i had to lead the Creture rather than have any Servis from her my Desire was to gow to meeting but was not able to find the way."[32] That this encounter produced such sorrow, fear, and confusion suggests that Billings was the source of her disappointment.

Moreover, in October 1790, Dickinson reflected on the mind's inability to "forget" pain, musing "the Soul or thinking Part will remember[.] Some sorrow of the mind which was twenti years Past is more fast on my mind then the Pain [the colic] which i felt the week back." Twenty years earlier, in March 1770, Billings had married Rebecca's second cousin, Sarah Bardwell.[33] Although by then Dickinson was already thirty-two, Sarah Bardwell was just twenty-seven; the women's age difference suggests that Dickinson could have reasonably entertained notions of marriage to Billings (whose age is unknown). Billings's blacksmith shop, just south of Miriam and Silas's tavern, would have provided ample opportunity for her to encounter Billings, and it was he who maintained her sewing tools.

Whatever did or did not occur in the past, even later, when presented with opportunities to marry, Dickinson was not desperate enough to choose "any match to avoid the reproach of having none." In April 1789, Dickinson recorded the death of Charles Phelps, whom she noted had once offered her his hand. Although Dickinson described Phelps as "a Person well lerned," she regretted he "knew too litel of himself . . . he was very great and very Small." Dickinson's assessment matches other accounts of a difficult man whose ambition exceeded his social and political savvy. Phelps eventually abandoned Hadley for the wilderness of the New Hampshire Grants. There Phelps channeled his considerable combative energies toward the fledgling government of what became the state of Vermont. Phelps's tenacious, if futile, battle to resist state authority ultimately resulted in his imprisonment. At the close of his life, Charles Phelps's health—physical, emotional, and financial—lay in ruins. It is little wonder that Dickinson concluded, "[I] have lived better than i Could have lived with him for the last ten years of my life."[34]

In 1788, fifty-year-old Rebecca received another proposal, from Dr. Moses Gunn of Montague. "He was more agreable than i Could think of," she wrote, "he would Doe if he was the right one but i Shall never Change my name i really belive there will alwais be a bar in the way." Perhaps she found the fact that Gunn had lost a leg "by a fit of Sickness" distasteful or the twenty-mile move to Montague unappealing. Reluctance to alter her lifestyle to accommodate the unknown trials of matrimony when she was at this time beyond her childbearing years may also have contributed to her decision, as marriage could no longer produce children who would care for her in her old age. But perhaps the "bar in the way" meant here, as elsewhere, her own "Stubborn Heart," that is, a general disinclination to marry. Whatever the reason, Rebecca accepted full responsibility for her fate, saying, "Tho i have no home may it be on my mind that today i have had the offer of one."[35] In the almost five hundred journal entries extant Dickinson repeated the phrase "here again in this old hous alone" more than one hundred times. Yet she chose that life, again and again.

On good days, Dickinson saw her way clear to a positive view of singlehood: "My bou[g]hs have been trimmed of[f] but the tree is not hurt . . . [though I] look not like the rest of the trees yet my mounten Stands Strong." In fact, God would "surely bring [her] feet to the gate of heaven" through singlehood. "There is a great many family blessings i know nothing of," she wrote in the spring of 1788, "but the gifts of time alwais bring Sorrow along with them a numirous family and a great Estate bring a great Consern upon the minds of the owners more than a ballence for all the

Comfort that tha bring." Throughout life, Dickinson struggled to cling to that insight, to look at a neighbor and conclude that "she has her fortun i mine very different and both right."[36]

Dickinson's craftwork played no small role in the formulation of both her public and private assessments. Her artisanal skill enabled her to fend off the poverty so often associated with singlehood, to withstand the loneliness and sense of purposelessness that she battled daily, and to turn down offers of marriage when she found the overall situation disadvantageous. It may well have been her skill with shears, needle, and pins that permitted, or even encouraged, Dickinson to resist offers of marriage and to find a positive role in her community—"Aunt Beck," as she came to be known—contrary to the title of "old Made," which she did not like.

Dickinson's text may also reflect increasing ambivalence toward women alone in the New Republic. As scholars studying women's lives in the nineteenth century have noted, singlehood became an increasingly necessary and viable option in the quarter century following the Revolution. In the words of historian Mary Beth Norton, "In the years after the war [women] started to dispute, in tentative fashion, perhaps the most basic assumptions of all: that marriage was every woman's destiny." For single women, "Republican Motherhood"—a term historians have coined to denote the role offered women in the New Republic, encouraging women to accept civic duties (surrounding the raising of good citizens) rather than political rights—offered a more abstract conception of motherhood, one that enabled women such as Rebecca Dickinson to carve new roles for themselves as cultural custodians at large.[37] Over the first half of the nineteenth century, a "Cult of Single Blessedness" emerged, as increasing numbers of women embraced independence and voluntarism and consciously chose to remain single. The abolitionists and suffragists of the nineteenth century were the first prominent beneficiaries of that new mode of thinking. More than once, Dickinson "wondered what i was made for," insisting, if uncertainly, that "there is Surely Some thing for me to Doe in the world."[38] Decades later, she might have found an answer in the antislavery or suffrage movements, in settlement house work, or any one of a host of reform efforts; in late-eighteenth-century Hatfield, however, her choices were more circumscribed.

Yet, if demographic upheaval, economic exigency, and new currents of republicanism eventually eased (though by no means eliminated) longstanding hostilities toward the never-married, these shifts were in ideology and circumstance of which Rebecca Dickinson was at best but dimly aware. A product of her own culture, Dickinson shared the beliefs and assumptions of the society in which she lived. She understood herself and others according to established, available definitions. The result was a series of disjunctures between the negative attributes ascribed never-married women and her own positive sense of herself. That discrepancy between her private and public identity is in part an artifact of the sources themselves. As students of journal keeping often observe, the cathartic function of personal writing produces a skewed picture of an author; only some aspects of a person's character find themselves projected into permanence in the pages of a journal. Few of us would want to be known exclusively by the pages of our journals, but that is the only way we can now know Rebecca Dickinson. At the same time, however, the disjunctures that characterize this text reflect a tension *within* Dickinson's private identity, as she struggled to reconcile competing evaluations of singlehood provided by her religion, her community, popular culture, and her own observations and experiences.

At the throne of her God, for whom she ultimately kept this journal, Dickinson was not an old maid, but simply another penitent soul, striving toward heaven. "My days glide quietly along," the aging artisan wrote in the summer of 1794. Dickinson, "found in the spirit of thy holy day," rededicated herself "to live in the light of Spiritiall life hopeing waiting doeing gods will to the end of my mortal life is the Desire of rebeca Dickinson." "I Should never have [lived] through So many Storms," she wrote, "had it not been for the hope of heavenly things." Eventually, the elderly aunt moved into the home of her nephew Joseph and his family, and it was there, in the twilight hours of 1815, that Rebecca Dickinson left behind the storms of singlehood and perhaps found some comfort in heavenly things. "Ever tending toward that land of Promise," she finally gained admittance to the one place "where tha never marry nor are given in marriage but are like the angels of god."[39]

Notes

1. Rebecca Dickinson, Diary, June 1789, Memorial Libraries, Deerfield, MA, 108.

2. Lacking less pejorative terms, I occasionally employ the most familiar words that currently connote both never-marriedness and the opprobrium attached to it: spinster and spinsterhood. The word "spinster" did not come into its contemporary usage, however, until the nineteenth century, "old maid" being the usual term in Dickinson's lifetime.

3. Dickinson, Diary, September 22, 1787, 23.

4. Daniel White Wells, *History of Hatfield*, Massachusetts (Springfield: F. C. H. Gibbons, 1910), 205, 256; Partridge and Miller are quoted in Margery Howe, *Deerfield Embroidery* (New York: Charles Scribner's Sons, 1976), 62.

5. Dickinson, Diary, August 20, 1787, 12.

6. Ibid., October 21, 1788, 88.

7. Ibid., August 22, 1787, 9.

8. Ibid., September 2, 1787, 12.

9. Ibid., August 12, 1787, 4.

10. Timothy Dwight, "Journey to the White Mountains," in *Travels in New England and New York,* vol. 2, ed. Barbara Solomon (1821; Cambridge, MA: Belknap Press of Harvard University Press, 1969), 35.

11. Dickinson, Diary, September 26, 1787, 24; Hampshire County Hall of Probate, box 48, no. 37, Northampton, MA.

12. Dickinson, Diary, November 22, 1787, 36; Krishna Gorowara, "The Treatment of Unmarried Woman in Comedy from 1584–1921" (Ph.D. diss., Glasgow University, 1961), 322.

13. Dickinson, Diary, September 5, 1787, 17.

14. Ibid., September 5, 1787, 17; November 1787, 35–37.

15. Ibid., September 10, 1787, 20.

16. Ibid., September 28, 1788, 82; April 26, 1789, 102; June 21, 1789, 110; September 10, 1787, 20.

17. Ibid., July 3, 1789, 117; September 13, 1787, 21; June 8, 1788, 58.

18. Ibid., December 2, 1787, 38; July 14, 1788, 66.

19. Ibid., October 26, 1787, 33; November 15, 1787, 34.

20. Ibid., November 21, 1790, 137–138.

21. Ibid., November 21, 1790, and July 3, 1791, 151.

22. Mary Wollstonecraft, *Vindication of the Rights of Woman* (1792), reprinted in Bridget Hill, *Eighteenth Century Women: An Anthology* (London and Boston: Allen and Unwin, 1984), 131.

23. Dickinson, Diary, June 29, 1794, 200.

24. Ibid., August 12, 1787, 4.

25. Ibid., October 1787, 29.

26. Lee Chambers-Schiller, *Liberty, A Better Husband: Single Women in America: The Generations of 1780–1840* (New Haven: Yale University Press, 1984), 159; Dickinson, Diary, July 25, 1787, 1; and June Sprigg, "Women's Everyday Lives in Eighteenth-Century America" (master's thesis, University of Delaware, 1977), 57.

27. Sally Hanschurst to Sally Forbes, 1762, Sally Hanschurst Letterbook, miscellaneous manuscripts, Library of Congress, as quoted in Terri Premo, *Winter Friends: Women Growing Old in the New Republic, 1785–1836* (Urbana: University of Illinois Press, 1990), 75.

28. Gloria Main, "Gender, Work and Wages in Colonial New England," *William and Mary Quarterly* 51 (1994): 65 n 91.

29. Dickinson, Diary, end of October 1790, 136 ff.; May 3, 1789, 103.

30. Ibid., August 20, 1787, 7; September 25, 1787, 25; August 12, 1787, 4; March 30, 1788, 50.

31. William Hayley, *A Philosophical, Historical and Moral Essay on Old Maids* (London: T. Cadell, 1786), 7–9.

32. Dickinson, Diary, October 20, 1790, pp. 136 ff.

33. Dickinson, Diary, October 30, 1790, 136 ff.; Wells, *History of Hatfield,* 372.

34. Dickinson, Diary, April 19, 1789, 101.

35. Ibid., October 3, 1788, 84.

36. Ibid., August 12, 1792, 172 (from Psalms 30:7); May 31, 1794, 194.

37. Mary Beth Norton, *Liberty's Daughters: The Revolutionary Experience of American Women, 1750–1800* (Boston: Little, Brown and Co., 1980), 239.

38. Dickinson, Diary, ca. November 3, 1787, 34; May 25, 1788, 57.

39. Ibid., August 3, 1794, 206; September 2, 1787, 12; and June 1789, 108.

Suggested Readings

The manuscript diary of Rebecca Dickinson is owned by Memorial Libraries in Deerfield, Massachusetts, and is in generally good condition. Page numbers given in the notes correspond to a typescript prepared from a photocopy of the manuscript, also in Deerfield's Memorial Libraries. In this essay, Dickinson's original spelling and punctuation have been maintained, though in cases where her style impedes easy reading of the text, spelling has been corrected and words or letters have been added in brackets. As a whole, however, Dickinson's hand, if not her spelling and punctuation, is clear and consistent, and the original text quite readable. The diary of Elizabeth Porter Phelps was published in consecutive issues of the *New England Historical and Genealogical Register* between 1964 and 1968.

The most thorough treatment of never-married women in early America remains Lee Chambers-Schiller's *Liberty, A Better Husband: Single Women in America: The Generations of 1780–1840* (New Haven: Yale University Press, 1984). Chambers-Schiller's articles about single women in the nineteenth century pursue several of these themes; see in particular "Woman Is Born to Love: The Maiden Aunt as Maternal Figure in Ante-Bellum Literature," *Frontiers* 10 (1988): 34–43; and "The Single Woman: Family and Vocation among Nineteenth-Century Reformers," in *Woman's Being, Woman's Place: Female Identity and Vocation in American History,* ed. Mary Kelley (Boston: Hall Publishers, 1979), 340–342. A related work is Terri Premo's engaging study of aging women in early America, *Winter Friends: Women Growing Old in the New Republic, 1785–1836* (Urbana: University of Illinois Press, 1990). An excellent overview of women's lives before the Revolution can be found in Carol Berkin's book *First Generations: Women in Colonial America* (New York: Hill & Wang, 1996). The standard works on women's experiences surrounding the American Revolution remain Mary Beth Norton, *Liberty's Daughters: The Revolutionary Experience of American Women, 1750–1800* (Boston: Little, Brown & Co., 1980); and Linda Kerber, *Women of the Republic: Intellect and Ideology in Revolutionary America* (Chapel Hill: University of North Carolina Press for the Institute of Early American History and Culture, 1980).

Finally, for further insight into diary keeping in early America, consult Suzanne L. Bunkers and Cynthia A. Huff, eds., *Inscribing the Daily: Critical Essays on Women's Diaries* (Amherst: University of Massachusetts Press, 1996); and Steven E. Kagle, *American Diary Literature, 1620–1799* (Boston: Twayne Publishers, [1979]). Mary Moffatt and Charlotte Painter discuss the cathartic function of journal keeping in their anthology of personal writing, *Revelations: Diaries of Women* (New York: Vintage Books, 1984). Williams Andrews's edited collection of women's writings, *Journeys in New Worlds: Early American Women's Narratives* (Madison: University of Wisconsin Press, 1990), provides both the text of several diaries and critical analyses of those texts.

9

Sacagawea
A Historical Enigma

Laura McCall

Sacagawea is probably the best-known Native American female in history. A Lemhi Shoshone, she was the teenaged wife of Toussaint Charbonneau,
an interpreter on the Lewis and Clark expedition through the Northwest to the
Pacific Ocean in the early years of the nineteenth century. She was no mere
passenger on the journey, however. Her survival skills, her knowledge of the
terrain through which the exploring party passed, her language proficiency,
and her dexterity in acting as a diplomatic go-between for the explorers and
the Natives they encountered, all proved indispensable to the venture's success. The relatively minor place she occupies in the journals kept by the white
men on the trip says less about the value of her services than it does about
gender relations and attitudes regarding ethnicity that characterized the time.
Historians continue to argue not only about her role in the expedition itself but
also about her place in the clash of cultures that afflicted Native
American–white relations in the West for more than a century.

Laura McCall is professor of history and member of the honors faculty at
Metropolitan State College, Denver, Colorado. Her publications include *A
Shared Experience: Men, Women and the History of Gender* (1998), coedited
with Donald Yacovne.

In 1804, Meriwether Lewis and William Clark hired Toussaint Charbonneau to serve as an interpreter for their epic journey up the Missouri
River, across the Rocky Mountains, to the Pacific Ocean, and back. Charbonneau was a forty-five-year-old French Canadian who had lived in
Indian country for at least ten years. He had many shortcomings but
could interpret the languages of the river tribes: the Mandan, Arikara,
Hidatsa, and Sioux.[1] With him was his fifteen-year-old pregnant wife,
Sacagawea (ca. 1788 or 1789–1812, 1869, or 1884), whom he had either
purchased from her captors or won in a game of chance.

Sacagawea, a Lemhi Shoshone, became an indispensable member of
the Corps of Discovery and was essential to its success. At opportune

Laura McCall wishes to thank James Drake, Stephen J. Leonard, John Monnett, and
Katherine Osburn for comments on an earlier draft.

moments, she acted as a guide, and without "her services as a translator, the expedition would have failed." As sister to Shoshone chief Cameahwait, she enabled the corps to obtain the horses needed to cross the Rocky Mountains and fostered cordial relations between Lewis and Clark and her people. She assured the safety of the group on numerous occasions because "her mere presence, with her baby, was a guarantee to strange Indians that this was not a war party."[2] She foraged for food when the corps was starving and, in less desperate times, supplemented their carnivorous diet with roots and berries. Without Sacagawea, the men of the Lewis and Clark Expedition would have either perished or been forced to turn back and the history of the United States could have been significantly different.

Sacagawea is one of the few historical actors widely recognized by the general public. *Collier's Encyclopedia* (1976) calls her "a national heroine; there are more statues [erected] to her than to any other American woman." Gary Moulton, one of the premier scholars of the expedition, proclaims Sacagawea "the most famous member of the party after the two leaders themselves."[3] She is the first woman after Susan B. Anthony to be depicted on a U.S. coin.

Despite her popular renown, Sacagawea remains an enigma. Although volumes crowd library bookshelves and she is beatified in novels and film, she is chronicled only in the writings of expedition members whose journals are extant. The academic community debates the spelling, pronunciation, and precise meaning of her name. Etymologists and historians accept Sacagawea; novelists prefer Sacajawea; inhabitants of the Dakotas favor Sakakawea. In the Hidatsa language, the word means Bird Woman. In Shoshone, it means Boat Pusher or Boat Launcher.[4]

Sacagawea is rarely named in the journals but instead is referred to as "the Squar" or "the Indian woman." Patrick Gass, who produced two lengthy and detailed logs, was uninterested in Sacagawea—he never mentioned her by name and called her only "the interpreter's wife." Gass failed to recount Sacagawea's heroic efforts when the flagship of the expedition nearly overturned, referring only to "the men who had been on board." He overlooked the incident when Sacagawea identified moccasins foreign to her people as well as the two occasions when Sacagawea fell gravely ill. On June 29, 1805, when Clark, Charbonneau, Sacagawea, and her infant, Jean-Baptiste, nearly perished in a flash flood, Gass merely described "another heavy shower of rain" after which Captain Lewis returned to camp, "drenched with rain." Gass passed over Sacagawea's remarkable meeting with her brother. On November 8, 1805, when several of the men and Sacagawea became ill while crossing a bay, he wrote, "Some of our men got sea sick, the swells were so great."[5] How could a voyager who was in daily and close contact with the only woman on the expedition be so detached and indifferent?

The other chroniclers responded similarly. Sacagawea is most often described in relation to her usefulness to the Voyage of Discovery—she saved precious instruments, gathered food, recognized important geographical signposts, interpreted on numerous occasions. With few exceptions, the diaries reveal little about her opinions, personality, or character. Rarely do her thoughts, feelings, or reactions to the journey surface. Sacagawea essentially lacks her own voice.

Some of this omission is owing to the nature of the expedition and the primary purpose of journal keeping. Even though William Clark regarded the corps as his "Band of Brothers," this voyage was not conducted for male identification, and rarely do any of the journals display deep introspection or ruminations about personality and character. Sacagawea was not the only member of the expedition about whom scholars know painfully little. The French engagés—men who signed on as guides, translators, and hunters—also received scanty attention.[6] This was the Age of Enlightenment, not Romanticism; the chroniclers were gathering scientific data and ethnographic information about Native Americans while attempting to establish trading networks. The general tone in these journals is clinical, not sentimental. Sacagawea was born in 1788 or 1789 in present-day Idaho within the shadows of the Continental Divide. Little is known about the lifeways or culture of her people, for prior to Lewis and Clark, their only contact with Euro-Americans had been indirectly with the Spanish to the south.

Meriwether Lewis recorded contradictory impressions about Lemhi women: Although the men "treat their women but with little rispect, and compel them to perform every species of drudgery, . . . [the] women are held more sacred among them than any nation we have seen and appear to have an equal Shere in all conversation, which is not the Case in any other nation I have seen."[7]

Demitri Shimkin, who studies the Eastern Shoshone, reports that a young woman's marriage was arranged "shortly after menarche." Her relatives "sought a good hunter, a stable and reliable although often much older man." Lewis reported similarly. Infant daughters were promised to grown men or "to men who have sons for whom they think proper to provide wives. . . . the girl remains with her parents until she is conceived to have obtained the age of puberty which with them is considered to be about the age of 13 or 14 years. the female at this age is surrendered to her sovereign lord and husband agreeably to contract." Sacagawea, a Northern Shoshone, had been promised before her capture and before "she had arrived to years of puberty. the husband . . . was more than double her age and had two other wives. he claimed her as his wife but said that as she had had a child by another man, who was Charbono [Charbonneau], that he did not want her."[8]

When Sacagawea was ten or eleven, members of her tribe ventured to the Three Forks region in present-day Montana, where a band of armed Hidatsa (Minitari or Gros Ventres) warriors launched an attack. Sacagawea later told Meriwether Lewis that the Shoshone braves, who were outnumbered and without guns, "mounted their horses and fled as soon as the attack began. The women and children, who had been berry-picking, dispersed, and Sacagawea, as she was crossing a shoal place, was overtaken in the middle of the river by her pursuers." Sacagawea dwelled with the Hidatsa until she was purchased or won by Charbonneau. The couple was living in the Mandan village in present-day North Dakota when Lewis and Clark decided to construct nearby Fort Mandan for their winter headquarters. On November 4, 1804, the captains and Charbonneau entered into a verbal arrangement by which the French trader would interpret among the Hidatsa. Later *Journal* entries indicate the interpreter's wife would translate for the Shoshone.[9]

On February 11, 1805, Sacagawea gave birth to Jean-Baptiste Charbonneau, "the indestructible baby," who would accompany the expedition across the continent and back. In the first detailed reference to Sacagawea, Captain Lewis observed that "one of the wives of Charbonneau was delivered of a fine boy. It is worthy of remark that this was the first child which this woman had born, and as is common in such cases her labor was tedious and the pain violent."[10] A scant two months later, the young mother and her sturdy infant departed on a seventeen-month journey that took them to the shores of the Pacific and back. Assessing Sacagawea's role in the Lewis and Clark Expedition remains the subject of lively debate. Perceptions of her significance have waxed and waned over the past two hundred years and have often reflected prevailing attitudes toward women. In the renderings of late-nineteenth- and early-twentieth-century scholars and during a period when the women's rights movement was in ascendance, Sacagawea directed Lewis and Clark across the Northern Plains and Rocky Mountains. As interpreter, guide, and ambassador to several Indian nations, she single-handedly ensured the success of the Corps of Discovery.[11] She thus provided feminists with a symbol of the strong, accomplished woman.

Mid- to late-twentieth-century scholars of the expedition, however, are not so favorably inclined. In their opinion, Sacagawea's service as a guide was minimal and that of interpreter was limited to a few specific incidents. She was an unessential member of the corps, which would have succeeded without her contributions.[12] The journals, however, indicate otherwise.

On May 14, 1805, for example, the flagship containing most of the corps's irreplaceable possessions filled with water and nearly overturned. On board were the papers, instruments, books, medicine, seed specimens, gunpowder, and culinary implements—in short, "almost every article indispensibly necessary to further the views, or insure the success of the enterprize in which we are now launched to the distance of 2200 miles." Sacagawea, in rapidly rushing and frigid waters and with her baby in tow, managed to catch and preserve most of the staples that were washed overboard. Lewis, who never warmed to Sacagawea, on this day ascribed to the "Indian woman . . . equal fortitude and resolution with any person on board at the time of the accident." Were it not for her alacrity and with "the essentials of their equipment lost, they would have had to turn back."[13]

Consider Sacagawea's contributions to the men's diet and health. The Corps of Discovery was in the wilderness, burning calories from exertion and cold and periodically on the verge of starvation. Sacagawea provided food on numerous occasions. On April 9, 1805, Lewis noted that "when we halted for dinner the squaw busied herself in serching for the wild artichokes which the mice collect and deposit in large hoards. this operation she performed by penetrating the earth with a sharp stick. . . . her labor soon proved successful, and she procurrd a good quantity of these roots." They were Jerusalem artichokes, strong perennials, but neither artichokes nor from Jerusalem. Also known as the Canada potato, they were one of the edible tubers widely cultivated by North American Indians.[14]

As historian Stephen Ambrose has observed, these roots were "welcome" because the expedition's hunters had been unable to procure meat. On April 30, 1805, Clark noted that "the Squar found & brought me a bush Something like the Current, which She Said bore a delicious froot and that great quantities grew on the Rocky Mountains." On May 8, "the Squar Geathered on the Sides of the hills wild Lickerish, & the white apple . . . and gave me to eat, the Indians of the Missouri make great use of the white apple dressed in differnt ways." In July, while at the Three Forks of the Missouri, Lewis saw where the natives had peeled the bark off the pine trees, upon which "the indian woman with us informs that they do to obtain the sap and soft part of the wood and bark for food."[15]

Sacagawea's foraging enabled the group to supplement their virtually all-meat diet and thereby prevent scurvy and other forms of malnutrition. On August 16, 1805, Joseph Whitehouse noted that the Indian woman "gathered a pale full [of service berries] & gave them to the party at noon." John Ordway declared they were "the largest & best I ever Saw." Sacagawea was also a fisherwoman. On at least one occasion, while recovering from a serious illness, "she has been walking about and fishing."[16]

At Fort Clatsop, Oregon Country, the corps spent a particularly miserable winter, cherishing a mere twelve days without rain and only six days of sunshine. Food was scarce and often moldy. So was their leather clothing, which was literally disintegrating off their backs. Sacagawea helped the men mend their old clothes and moccasins and tan leather for new attire. She relinquished her precious belt of blue beads for two otter skins. On November 30, 1805, she generously gave Clark "a piece of bread made of flour She had reserved for her child and carefully Kept untill this time, which has unfortunately got wet, and a little Sour—this bread I eate with great Satisfaction, it being the only mouthfull I had tasted for Several months past." On December 3, Clark twice recorded that after the marrow from the shank bones of an elk had been extracted, "the Squar chped the bones fine boiled them and extracted a pint of Grease, which is Superior to the tallow of the animal" and necessary for oiling boots and guns.[17] On Christmas Day, she bestowed upon Clark two dozen white weasel tails.

During the return journey, "Sahcargarmeah geathered a quantity of the roots of a speceis of fennel which we found very agreeable food, the flavor of this root is not unlike annis seed." Clark reported similarly on the same day and on May 18, 1806, wrote that the "Squar wife to Shabono busied her Self gathering the roots of the fenel Called by the Snake Indians Year-pah for the purpose of drying to eate on the Rocky mountains. those roots are very paliatiable either fresh rosted boiled or dried and are generally between the Size of a quill and that of a mans fingar and abut the length of the latter." The men, who had been complaining of headache and intestinal gas, found that these roots "dispell the wind . . . and adds much to the comfort of our diet." On June 25, 1806, Clark remarked that "the squaw collected a parcel of roots which the Shoshones Eat. it is a small knob root a good deel in flavour and consistency like the Jerusolem artichoke." Not only had Sacagawea again provided a nutritious supplement to the corps' edibles, but she also brought a new botanical item to the attention of the captains. As Gary Moulton points out, the "species was unknown to science at the time, and Lewis collected the type specimen two days later." On August 9, 1806, Clark reported that the "Squar brought me a large and well flavoured Goose berry of a rich Crimsin Colour, and deep purple berry of the large Cherry of the Current Speces."[18]

Her skills as an interpreter merit greater recognition. Clearly, Lewis and Clark recruited Charbonneau because Sacagawea could converse with the mountain tribes and thereby assist in obtaining horses. Her importance as a prospective translator was clearly revealed when, on June 16, 1805, she fell gravely ill. Clark bled her and Lewis gave her a mixture of bark and laudanum. In a telling journal entry, Lewis expressed his selfish anxieties as to whether she would recover and lead them to the Shoshone. Her indisposition "gave me some concern, as well for the poor object herself—then with a young child in her arms—as from the consideration of her being our only dependence for a friendly negotiation with the Snake Indians, on whom we depend for horses to assist us in our portage from the Missouri to the Columbia River."[19]

On August 13, Lewis and his band encountered sixty warriors including the Shoshone chief, Cameahwait. Sacagawea, traveling with Clark, was not reunited with her people until the morning of August 17. She first greeted Jumping Fish, who had received her name while bounding across a stream to escape the Hidatsa in the raid that captured Sacagawea. Their tearful reunion was cut short by an impatient Meriwether Lewis, who needed horses and petulantly called the "interpretress" into council. There she began to translate from Shoshone into Minnetaree, Charbonneau from Minnetaree into French, and François Labiche (half French and half Omaha) into English for the captains. Suddenly, she sprang up in astonishment. In one of the most remarkable reunions in history, she recognized her brother, Cameahwait. "[S]he jumped up, ran & embraced him, & threw her blanket over him and cried profusely."[20] They visited briefly before the resumption of negotiations.

At Cameahwait's village, Sacagawea confirmed through the translation chain that the crossing to the Pacific was going to be arduous and would require Shoshone horses and a guide. On August 25, Lewis learned from Charbonneau that Sacagawea had overheard her brother tell members of the tribe to prepare for travel to the buffalo country east of Lemhi Pass rather than help the corps portage west across the mountains. Had that happened, "Lewis and his men would have literally been left high and dry, halfway up Lemhi Pass, with only a dozen or so horses, and no guide for the Nez Perce trail." Lewis shamed Cameahwait into keeping his original promise, although, over the next several days, the price of horses rose precipitously.[21]

Sacagawea's interpreting skills proved unexpectedly invaluable while the group wintered in the Pacific Northwest. During a visit with the Walla Walla Indians and their chief, Yellept, the captains were, thanks to Sacagawea, able to parley in ways other than sign language. As Clark reported on April 29, 1806, "We found a Sho Shone woman, prisoner among those people by means of whome and Sah-cah-gah-weah, Shabono's wife we found means of Converceing with the Wallahwallars. We Conversed with them for Several hours and fully Satisfy all their enquiries with respect to our Selves and the Object of our pursute. they were much pleased." With the aid of Sacagawea's translations, Lewis learned that several members of the tribe required medical assistance. He treated a man seriously afflicted with rheumatism, another with a broken arm, and many with sore eyes. In return, the expedition left with twenty-three horses, most of them "excellent," and a shortcut that saved them approximately eighty miles.[22] Once more, Sacagawea had served them well.

Between May 14 and June 10, while in the company of the Nez Percé, the captains again benefited from Sacagawea's interpretive skills. In an almost daylong meeting, a young male Shoshone captive enabled the parties to communicate in a translation chain that tediously passed through Nez Percé, Shoshone, Hidatsa, French, English, and back. The captains explained to the principal chiefs "their intention of establishing tradeing houses for their relief, their wish to restore peace and harmony among the nativs, the Strength welth and powers of our Nation &c." Lewis concluded that "they appeared highly pleased."[23]

Although she was enlisted as an interpreter, Sacagawea inadvertently served the corps as ambassador and guide. On July 22, 1805, her abilities as a keen observer first emerged: "The Indian woman recognizes the country and assures us that this is the river on which her relations live, and that the three forks are at no great distance. this peice of information has cheered the sperits of the party who now begin to console themselves with the anticipation of shortly seeing the head of the missouri yet unknown to the civilized world." Four days later, the voyagers camped at the site of Sacagawea's capture. On August 8, Lewis reported that "the Indian woman recognized the point of a high plain to our right which she informed us was not very distant from the summer retreat of her nation on a river beyond the mountains which runs to the west. . . . she assures us that we shall either find her people on this river or on the river immediately west of it's source; which from it's present size cannot be very distant. as it is now all important with us to meet with those people as soon as possible."[24]

Sacagawea's perceptive guiding came none too soon, for the weather was getting cold. In the days that followed, Sacagawea continued to assure Lewis and Clark they were in her country. She also provided critical geographical information and confirmed they were nearing the headwaters of the Missouri and thus the Continental Divide, where they encountered Cameahwait's band.

Why Sacagawea accompanied the expedition to the western coast remains unclear. Neither Lewis nor Clark alludes to the reasons for her continuation, and it seems odd she would leave her people after less than three weeks. No one anticipated that her interpretative services would be needed after the corps passed through the mountains with their Shoshone guide, Toby. Nor could she recognize any landmarks. Anthropologist Clara Sue Kidwell asserts that as "a captive and the wife of a white man, she no longer had a place within the social structure of her own tribe." Charbonneau and the corps "were now Sacagawea's main reference points. Having been removed from her tribe, she could not go back; indeed, she may have chosen freely not to go back." Anthropologist Rayna Green surmises that a "good" Indian woman "must defy her own people, exile herself from them, become white, and perhaps suffer death." Stephen Ambrose, in contrast, speculates "that the question [of] whether she should stay with the expedition never came up, that she was by now so integral a member of the party that it was taken for granted that she would remain with it."[25]

Nevertheless, Sacagawea proved invaluable on this leg of the journey. While floating down the Snake and Columbia Rivers, both captains commented upon how Sacagawea's presence calmed the fears of the Northwestern tribes. During the second week of October, Clark attributed the Indians' sudden friendliness to the "wife of Shabono our interpetr [who] we find reconsiles all the Indians, as to our friendly intentions a woman with a party of men is a token of peace." On October 19, 1805, Clark recounted a mildly tense moment that was mitigated when Sacagawea appeared and the Walla Walla "immediately all came out and appeared to assume new life, the sight of This Indian woman, wife to one of our interprs. confirmed those people of our friendly intentions, as no woman ever accompanies a war party of Indians in this quarter."

On their eastward return, Sacagawea unquestionably proved her value as a guide. When the corps reentered Shoshone country, she was the first to orient and confirm they were on the right trail. On July 6, 1806, John Ordway noted that "our Intrepters wife tells us that She knows the country & that this branch is the head waters of jeffersons river &C. we proceeded on down the branch." Clark reported that "the Indian woman wife to Shabono informed that she had been in this plain frequently and knew it well that the Creek which we decended was a branch of Wisdom river and when we assended the higher part of the plain we would discover a gap in the mountains in our direction to the Canoes, and when we arived at that gap we would See a high point of a mountain covered with snow in our direction to the canoes. . . . The Squar pointed to the gap through which she said we must pass which was S. 56° E. She said we would pass the river before we reached the gap."

On July 13, 1806, in what is now southwestern Montana, William Clark had to decide between Flathead and Bozeman Passes. Sacagawea recommended the latter and better choice—Bozeman Pass is lower—and she earned Clark's praise: "The indian woman who has been of great Service to me as a pilot through this Country recommends a gap in the mountain more South which I shall cross."[26]

In the following month, the Lewis and Clark Expedition descended to the Mandan village, where, on August 17, Sacagawea, Charbonneau, and Jean-Baptiste parted with the Corps of Discovery. Charbonneau was paid $500.33. Sacagawea, who had been far more useful, received nothing except a few revealing compliments from William Clark. In a letter thanking Charbonneau for his services, Clark recognized Sacagawea's importance when he commended "your woman, who accompanied you that long and dangerous and fatiguing route to the Pacific Ocian and back, deserved a greater reward for her attention and service on that route than we had in our power to give her at the Mandans."[27]

In 1810, Charbonneau and Sacagawea moved to St. Louis, obtained property, and attempted to settle down. The restless Charbonneau transferred his lands to Clark and returned to the wilderness, where he served as an interpreter and purveyor. He died in the early 1840s.[28]

Jean-Baptiste, whom Clark affectionately referred to as Pomp or Pompey, was educated in St. Louis, traveled through Europe in the 1820s as the protégé of Prince Paul of Württemberg, and came back to America in 1829 fluent in German, French, Spanish, and English. He returned to the West, where he served as a hunter, trapper, guide, and excellent cook. Sources place his death in Oregon in 1866 or Wyoming in 1885.[29]

After Charbonneau's departure from St. Louis in 1810, Sacagawea's life clouds. The most widely accepted theory has her accompanying her husband up the Missouri River and dying in childbirth in 1812 at Manuel Lisa's trading post in present-day South Dakota. A second hypothesis asserts Sacagawea was killed near Glascow, Montana, in 1869 during an

Indian skirmish. A man claiming to be her grandson testified "in open council where other Indians could hear and correct his story."[30]

The third version, derived from Shoshone oral tradition, describes an elderly squaw named "Sacajawea" or "Porivo" who had knowledge of minute details of the Voyage of Discovery. According to this rendition, Sacagawea separated from Charbonneau after he wed a Ute woman while the couple was living in the Southwest. Sacagawea joined the Comanche and married a warrior named Jerk Meat. The Nez Percé attest that after his death in battle, she made her way back to Fort Washakie on the Wind River Shoshone Reservation in Wyoming and settled with her adopted son, Bazil. She died on April 9, 1884.

According to the Shoshone, Jean-Baptiste died in 1885. Bazil, who died the following year, was buried with papers purportedly proving that the woman who died in 1884 had accompanied the Lewis and Clark Expedition. When his body was exhumed in 1925, the evidence had decomposed.[31]

Even in death, therefore, Sacagawea remains a mystery. The exact timing and placement of her demise, however, provide historians with another issue for further study. As Americans approach the bicentennial of this pathbreaking journey, interest in Sacagawea and her fellow voyagers will most likely intensify. Along with the renewed curiosity are debates within the profession regarding the use of oral history as valid historical evidence.

Many scholars dismiss Native American oral traditions because they are not part of a written record, are often not arranged in a linear fashion, can be recited decades after the events under scrutiny, and do not "conform to Western standards of historical analysis and writing." Yet as Dakota scholar Angela Cavender Wilson observes, students of Native American studies need to "understand the power of the spoken word and to incorporate native oral traditions into American history." Wilson describes the vigorous and extensive training required of youth as they assume the task of preserving the stories of their people, concluding that "the ability to remember [and verbalize those memories is as much] an acquired skill" as is the white ability to record.[32] The precise placement of Sacagawea's death provides historians with an opportunity to ponder the validity of oral history.

A serious question for feminist scholars concerns the cultural baggage the expedition's journalists carried with them to the Far West. Were their judgments of Native American women informed by attitudes toward white women, such as the colonial helpmate, the "republican mother" of the Revolutionary era, or the true woman of the early nineteenth century?

Were their points of view influenced by stereotypes of Native American women, which included the enchanting princess or the degraded squaw?[33] Although the chroniclers commented upon the various Native American women encountered on their journey—they were particularly interested in their dress, their physiques, their sexual customs, and their work habits—in these respects they were mysteriously silent about Sacagawea.

Their reticence merits analysis. Her proximity made her the perfect ethnographic study, but they did not turn her into a specimen. Had the young wife and mother taken on a human form? Were they protecting this unique individual from intense future scrutiny? Whereas they could generalize about the anonymous men and women whom they briefly visited, Sacagawea lived with the corps for one and one-half years. She fed them, translated for them, provided gifts for some, and assured the safety of all. Did they come to care for her?

Two illustrative incidents occurred when the corps reached Oregon. In the first, the captains had to decide whether to build their winter stockade near the soggy coast or farther upriver. In an unusual move, they put the decision to a vote. Clark registered the opinions of every member of the party, including his slave York and Sacagawea, whom he affectionately called Janey. At Fort Clatsop, the corps learned that a whale lay beached on the shores of the Pacific. A party of a dozen men made preparations for the five-day journey, and Sacagawea insisted upon going. "She observed that She had traveled a long way with us to See the great waters, and that now that monstrous fish was also to be Seen. She thought it verry hard that She Could not be permitted to See either (She had never yet been to the Ocian)." She "was therefore indulged."[34] Sacagawea's ability to have her way reveals her power and agency. This episode not only illustrates her assertiveness but marked recognition on the part of the men—they knew they owed her for her innumerable contributions.

Finally, can modern-day analysts reasonably blame or credit Sacagawea for the opening of the West to white settlement? In 1905 in Portland, Oregon, Susan B. Anthony lauded "the assistance rendered by a woman in the discovery of this great section of the country." Anna Howard Shaw termed her a "forerunner of civilization." Eva Emory Dye claimed she "led the way to a new time. To the hands of this girl . . . had been entrusted the key that unlocked the road to Asia." In 1942, Donald Peattie credited Sacagawea with adding five stars to the American flag.[35] Donna Kessler, in her intriguing book *The Making of Sacagawea*, hints at evidence that potentially holds Sacagawea responsible for, or at the least a major actor in, the opening of the West to white settlers, soldiers, and traders. Had it not been for Sacagawea, the mission most likely would have failed.[36] How would that have affected the status of the Oregon Country, which was simultaneously claimed by Great Britain, Russia, and the United States? How does this square with the "legacy of conquest" theories of the New Western Historians, who accuse rapacious whites of sundering native cultures? How does their revisionist model account for the possibility that a Native American woman participated in the opening of the West?

Clara Sue Kidwell contends that "Indian women were the first important mediators of meaning between the cultures of two worlds. . . . Explicitly, their actions led finally to the loss of Indian land and to destructive changes in Indian culture. But implicitly, they acted from motives that were determined by their own cultures."[37] Native American women served as intermediaries between their own tribes and others, often deciding the fate of captives and entrusting them to their care. Thus, it was only natural for women to serve as central agents in the fur trade, providing white men with important entrées into their tribes and ensuring male success through female labor and diplomacy. Sacagawea's essential assistance to Lewis and Clark was an extension of this intermediary role.

The year 2005 will mark the bicentennial of the meeting between Lewis, Clark, and Sacagawea. Considering all that has been written and filmed about this extraordinary woman, what do scholars actually know? She is not self-defined but described through others. Her name is in dispute. So, too, are the time and place of her death. Why have scholars underplayed her important contributions to the expedition? Is it valid to hold a fifteen-year-old Native American woman responsible for the opening of the West, the destruction of tribal ways of life, and environmental degradation? Was she, like Christopher Columbus, merely the first? If she had not lent her assistance to the expedition, would someone with comparable abilities have? Or were her myriad skills—as a food gatherer, interpreter, guide, and symbol of peace—unsurpassable and unmatchable? Sacagawea compels us to ponder these questions.

Notes

1. Irving W. Anderson, "A Charbonneau Family Portrait," *American West* 17 (March–April 1980): 4–13, 58–64.

2. Sacagawea was a member of the Lemhi Shoshone, who lived on the Montana-Idaho border near present-day Salmon, Idaho. The Shoshone were also known as the Snake. Gary Moulton, ed., *The Journals of the Lewis and Clark Expedition,* 9 vols. (Lincoln: University of Nebraska Press, 1983–1997), 3:328; 5:85; Ella E. Clark and Margot Edmonds, *Sacagawea of the Lewis and Clark Expedition* (Berkeley: University of California Press,

1979), 1; Harold P. Howard, *Sacajawea* (Norman: University of Oklahoma Press, 1971), 62; John Bakeless, ed., *The Journals of Lewis and Clark* (New York: New American Library, 1964), 211 n.

3. Clark and Edmonds, *Sacagawea,* 1; and Moulton, *Journals,* 3:3, 229.

4. Howard, *Sacajawea,* 16; John Logan Allen, *Lewis and Clark and The Image of the American Northwest* (New York: Dover, 1991), 221 n; Allen's book is a republication of *Passage through the Garden: Lewis and Clark and the Image of the American Northwest* (Urbana: University of Illinois Press, 1975).

5. Carol Lynn Macgregor, ed., *The Journals of Patrick Gass: Member of the Lewis and Clark Expedition* (Missoula, MT: Mountain Press Publishing Co., 1997), 94, 107, 148.

6. "Appendix A: Members of the Expedition," in *Journals,* ed. Moulton, 2:509–12.

7. Bernard DeVoto, ed., *The Journals of Lewis and Clark* (Boston: Houghton Mifflin, 1953), 208, 218; Demitri B. Shimkin notes a different paradox among the Eastern Shoshone: "On one hand, women were socially subordinated to men. . . . On the other hand, women possessed critical skills in plant gathering, household crafts, household transportation, child care and other areas." Shimkin, "Eastern Shoshone," in *Handbook of North American Indians,* William C. Sturtevant, general editor, vol. 11, *Great Basin,* ed. Warren L. D'Azevedo (Washington: Smithsonian Institution, 1986), 311.

8. DeVoto, *Journals,* 207; Shimkin, 312–13.

9. Moulton, *Journals,* 3:206–07; Clark and Edmonds, *Sacagawea,* 7–8; Moulton, *Journals,* 3:3; DeVoto, *Journals,* 63, 73, 85, 92–94.

10. Bakeless, *Journals,* 118; John Bakeless, *Lewis and Clark: Partners in Discovery* (New York: William Morrow and Co., 1947), 156.

11. The dissemination of this view into the popular imagination was a result of the fictional treatment of Sacagawea in Eva Emery Dye, *The Conquest: The True Story of Lewis and Clark* (Chicago: A. C. McClurg and Co., 1902); Grace Raymond Hebard, *Sacajawea: A Guide and Interpreter of the Lewis and Clark Expedition, with an Account of the Travels of Toussaint Charbonneau, and of Jean Baptise, the Expedition Papoose* (Glendale, CA: Arthur H. Clark Co., 1932).

12. The chief detractors include C. S. Kingston, "Sacajawea as Guide: The Evaluation of a Legend," *Pacific Northwest Quarterly* 35 (January 1944): 2–18; Ronald W. Taber, "Sacajawea and the Suffragettes: An Interpretation of a Myth," *Pacific Northwest Quarterly* 58 (January 1967): 7–13; and Allen, *Image of the American Northwest,* 211–12.

13. DeVoto, *Journals,* 110, 147; Bakeless, *Lewis and Clark,* 190; Moulton, *Journals,* 4:2; Stephen E. Ambrose, *Undaunted Courage: Meriwether Lewis, Thomas Jefferson, and the Opening of the American West* (New York: Simon and Schuster, 1996), 225.

14. Ambrose, *Undaunted Courage,* 212; DeVoto, *Journals,* 93; Norman Taylor, ed., *Taylor's Encyclopedia of Gardening,* 4th ed. (Boston: Houghton Mifflin, 1961), 620, 1180.

15. Ambrose, *Undaunted Courage,* 212–13; Moulton, *Journals,* 4:89, 128, 403.

16. Ambrose, *Undaunted Courage,* 223; Reuben Thwaites, ed., *Original Journals of the Lewis and Clark Expedition,* 8 vols. (New York: Dodd, Mead, 1904–1907), 7:134–35, cited in Macgregor, *Journals of Patrick Gass,* 239 n; Moulton, *Journals,* 4:318.

17. DeVoto, *Journals,* 312; Moulton, *Journals,* 6:97, 106–07; Clark and Edmonds, *Sacagawea,* 52.

18. Moulton, *Journals,* 7:264–65, 270, 286, 8:52 n, 286; DeVoto, *Journals,* 410; Clark and Edmonds, *Sacagawea,* 73.

19. E. G. Chuinard, "The Actual Role of the Bird Woman: Purposeful Member of the Corps or Casual 'Tag Along'?" *Montana, The Magazine of Western History* 26 (Summer 1976): 18–29; Ambrose, *Undaunted Courage,* 187; Clark and Edmonds, *Sacagawea,* 15; Bakeless, *Journals,* 188.

20. Ambrose, *Undaunted Courage,* 255–56; Moulton, *Journals,* 5:109–16; 8:161, 279, 305; Bakeless, *Lewis and Clark,* 250; Nicholas Biddle, *The Story of the Expedition under the Commands of Captains Lewis and Clark* (Philadelphia: Bradford and Inskeep, 1814), cited in Ambrose, *Undaunted Courage,* 277.

21. Ambrose, *Undaunted Courage,* 280–83; Moulton, *Journals,* 5:165.

22. Moulton, *Journals,* 7:178–80; Ambrose, *Undaunted Courage,* 359.

23. Moulton, *Journals,* 7:244; Ambrose, *Undaunted Courage,* 362–65.

24. Cited in Gunther Barth, *The Lewis and Clark Expedition: Selections from the Journals Arranged by Topic* (Boston: St. Martin's Press, 1998), 68–69; Moulton, *Journals,* 5:59.

25. Clara Sue Kidwell, "Indian Women as Cultural Mediators," *Ethnohistory* 39 (Spring 1992): 101–02; Rayna Green, "The Pocohontas Perplex: The Image of Indian Women in American Culture," *Massachusetts Review* 27 (Autumn 1975): 698–714; Susan Lobo and Steve Talbot, eds., *Native American Voices: A Reader* (New York: Longman, 1998), 185; Ambrose, *Undaunted Courage,* 285.

26. DeVoto, *Journals,* 249–50; Moulton, *Journals,* 5:268, 305; 9:331; 8:167, 180.

27. Thwaites, *Original Journals,* 7:134–35; and Howard, *Sacagawea,* 141–42.

28. Moulton, *Journals,* 3:228–29 n; Bakeless, *Lewis and Clark,* 454–55.

29. Albert Furtwangler, *Acts of Discovery: Visions of America in the Lewis and Clark Journals* (Urbana: University of Illinois Press, 1993), 221–22; Bakeless, *Lewis and Clark,* 454; Moulton, *Journals,* 3:291 n.

30. Irving Anderson strongly believes that Sacagawea died in 1812 and that later sightings were cases of "mistaken identity." Anderson, "Probing the Riddle of the Bird Woman; How Long Did Sacajawea Live; Where and When Did She Die?" *Montana, The Magazine of Western History* 23 (1973): 2–17; James P. Ronda, *Lewis and Clark among the Indians* (Lincoln: University of Nebraska Press, 1984), 258; Moulton, *Journals,* 3:171, 229; despite the title, Blanche Schroer's, "Boat Pusher or Bird Woman? Sacagawea or Sacajawea?" *Annals of Wyoming* 52 (1980): 46–54 focuses almost exclusively on the debates surrounding Sacagawea's death and favors the 1812 version; Clark and Edmonds, *Sacagawea,* 105–06; Bakeless, *Lewis and Clark,* 455.

31. Bakeless, *Lewis and Clark,* 456; Clark and Edmonds, *Sacagawea,* 144, 115, 128; Howard, *Sacagawea,* 154–62; Moulton, *Journals,* 3:229.

32. Angela Cavender Wilson, "Power of the Spoken Word: Native Oral Traditions in American Indian History," in *Rethinking American Indian History,* ed. Donald L. Fixico (Albuquerque: University of New Mexico Press, 1997), 102–04.

33. Sherry L. Smith, "Beyond Princess and Squaw," in *The Women's West,* ed. Susan Armitage and Elizabeth Jameson (Norman: University of Oklahoma Press, 1980), 63–75.

34. Moulton, *Journals,* 6:83–84, 168–72.

35. Cited in Clark and Edmonds, *Sacagawea,* 94–96; Chuinard, "Bird Woman," 20.

36. Donna J. Kessler, *The Making of Sacagawea: A Euro-American Legend* (Tuscaloosa: University of Alabama Press, 1996), 26–27, 29, 43, 47, 60–1, 89–90, 101.

37. Kidwell, "Indian Women," 97–98.

Suggested Readings

The few primary sources include the journals of Meriwether Lewis, William Clark, John Ordway, Joseph Whitehouse, and Patrick Gass; manuscript collections housed at the Missouri State Historical Society; and oral histories collected by Grace Raymond Hebard.

Relatively complete journal collections begin chronologically with Nicholas Biddle, ed., *The History of the Expedition under the Commands of Captains Lewis and Clark*, 2 vols. (Philadelphia: Bradford and Inskeep, 1814); Elliot Coues, ed., *History of the Expedition under the Command of Lewis and Clark*, 4 vols. (New York: Francis P. Harper, 1893); Reuben Gold Thwaites, ed., *Original Journals of the Lewis and Clark Expedition*, 8 vols. (New York: Dodd, Mead, 1904–1907); Donald Jackson, ed., *Letters of the Lewis and Clark Expedition* (Urbana: University of Illinois Press, 1962, rev., 1978); and Gary Moulton, ed., *The Journals of the Lewis and Clark Expedition*, 9 vols. (Lincoln: University of Nebraska Press, 1983–1997).

Historical monographs of the Lewis and Clark Expedition include but are not limited to John Bakeless, *Lewis and Clark, Partners in Discovery* (New York: William Morrow and Co., 1947); Bernard DeVoto, *The Course of Empire* (Boston: Houghton Mifflin, 1952); John Allen, *Passage through the Garden: Lewis and Clark and the Image of the American Northwest* (Urbana: University of Illinois Press, 1975); James P. Ronda, *Lewis and Clark among the Indians* (Lincoln: University of Nebraska Press, 1984); Albert Furtwangler, *Acts of Discovery: Visions of America in the Lewis and Clark Journals* (Urbana: University of Illinois Press, 1993); Stephen E. Ambrose, *Undaunted Courage: Meriwether Lewis, Thomas Jefferson, and the Opening of the American West* (New York: Simon and Schuster, 1996). The Lewis and Clark Trail Heritage Foundation of Portland, Oregon, publishes a journal devoted to the expedition entitled *We Proceeded On*.

Book-length studies of Sacagawea include Grace Raymond Hebard, *Sacagawea: A Guide and Interpreter of the Lewis and Clark Expedition, with an Account of the Travels of Toussaint Charbonneau, and of Jean Baptiste, the Expedition Papoose* (Glendale, CA: Arthur H. Clark Co., 1932); Harold P. Howard, *Sacajawea* (Norman: University of Oklahoma Press, 1971); Ella E. Clark and Margot Edmonds, *Sacagawea of the Lewis and Clark Expedition* (Berkeley: University of California Press, 1979); and Donna J. Kessler, *The Making of Sacagawea: A Euro-American Legend* (Tuscaloosa: University of Alabama Press, 1996).

For fictional treatments, consult Eva Emery Dye, *The Conquest: The True Story of Lewis and Clark* (Chicago: A. C. McClung and Co., 1902); and Anna Lee Waldo, *Sacajawea* (New York: Avon Books, 1979).

10

Peter P. Pitchlynn
Race and Identity in
Nineteenth-Century America

Donna L. Akers

Peter P. Pitchlynn was an opponent and victim of Indian removal. To that end, he supported tribal unity but was unsuccessful in realizing that goal. As an individual of mixed heritage, Pitchlynn laid claim to two worlds that increasingly were at war with one another: that of the Choctaw and that of the Euro-American. Nonetheless, Pitchlynn was unable to bridge the divide or mediate that conflict. He and others of mixed heritage occupied a unique position in American society. Although highly literate and articulate, Pitchlynn was considered inferior by Euro-Americans. Yet he, like most white Americans in the Age of Jackson, valued his individuality and pursued wealth. Pitchlynn's life, not surprisingly, was fraught with conflict and contradiction. Although he was bicultural, he was never accepted by, or felt fully part of, Choctaw or Euro-American society. Successful at moving between these two worlds, he never considered himself wanted in either. An ardent opponent of removal, he finally acquiesced in its inevitability and successfully led two parties to Indian Territory. The victim of racism, Pitchlynn owned slaves and spent the better part of his postremoval life in Washington, DC. Pitchlynn's life vividly illustrates the immense difficulties that people of mixed heritage faced, and how they negotiated their way through the terrains of white and Indian culture.

Donna L. Akers, a member of the Choctaw Nation of Oklahoma, teaches Native American history at Purdue University, West Lafayette, Indiana. She is the author of "Removing the Heart of the Choctaw People: Indian Removal from a Native Perspective," *American Indian Culture and Research Journal* 23 (1999): 63–76; and "Removing the Heart of the Choctaw People: Indian 'Removal' in Its Spiritual Context," in Clifford E. Trafzer, ed., *An Anthology of American Indian History* (forthcoming). She is currently finishing a book on the Choctaw people of the nineteenth century.

In 1806, in a crude cabin in the backwoods of what would one day be Mississippi, in the midst of the Choctaw Nation, a baby was born. His father, John Pitchlynn, paced the boards of the porch outside. He was a white trader who had come to the Choctaw Nation before the American Revolution and spent his entire adult life among the Choctaw. Inside, female relatives who were members of the large and influential Choctaw clan assisted the baby's mother. Safely delivered, the baby began to squall. His first cries would come to be echoed throughout the whole of Choctaw lands.

The boy was called Ha-tchoc-tuck-nee (Snapping Turtle), but he had a white name, too: Peter P. Pitchlynn. Therein lay one of the defining elements of his life. Peter Pitchlynn had claims to two very different worlds: that of the Choctaws and that of Euro-Americans. Most Choctaws accepted him as one of them, despite his white father. Choctaw society was based upon matrilineal kinship, a system of clans in which the mother's lineage defines the children's identity. Maternal relatives were considered one's only close kin, so fathers and all other Choctaws were members of other clans and were not considered close relatives. Therefore, that Peter had a white father was largely irrelevant to the Choctaws. Peter and other children of these mixed Choctaw-white unions were, in fact, Choctaw to these Native American people.

Conversely, most Euro-Americans did not accept Pitchlynn and others of mixed heritage as equal members of their society. Even though as an adult Pitchlynn spoke English well and could appear and behave as a white man and, indeed, was the son of one, he nonetheless was a "half-breed" or "mixed blood" to Euro-Americans. Over his lifetime, he successfully functioned in both worlds. But his life among whites was always circumscribed by their racial attitudes.

Pitchlynn and other people of mixed Native American and Euro-American heritage occupied a strange and unique position within American society and thought. Among Euro-Americans, they were categorized as nonwhite and inferior. In the system of racism that developed in the United States during the eighteenth and nineteenth centuries, Indians initially were relegated to a level somewhere between that of whites and blacks. Because "mixed bloods" often had lighter skin than did "full bloods," they occupied a special niche in the racial order—closest to whites of all the people of color.

Pitchlynn's life reflected a syncretic identity—although he was bicultural, while he was in either society he was still a part of the other. In Washington, he never forgot that he was Choctaw. And in the Choctaw Nation, he continued to be aware of the lure of power in the halls of Congress. Mindful, too, of the lack of education of the Choctaw people, Pitchlynn was infected with the materialism and individualism of Euro-American society. Though he continued to assert his identity as "Choctaw" throughout his life, his identity was not that of the traditional people of the Choctaw Nation. He blended ideas from both worlds, creating in the process a new identity.

Like other people of mixed heritage, Pitchlynn tried to prove himself in two very different worlds. He was adept biculturally—that is, he was able to function well among whites in Washington society as well as among his native people in the Choctaw Nation. His agility in successfully navigating through both white and native worlds came with a price, however. At times he felt unwanted in either world. To some Choctaws, his ability to understand the white worldview made him suspect. That he spoke English, was educated and literate, and was accepted in white society caused some Choctaws to reject him. Euro-Americans also saw him as tainted—able to function and pass as one of them, but not truly one of them. People of mixed heritage in race-conscious America indeed traveled a difficult path. At times, they were excluded from the inner councils of both sides. But, for the most part, people like Pitchlynn combined and blended their cultural heritage into an identity from which they found comfort and belonging. From his experiences, perhaps we can gain a better understanding of the people of mixed heritage in nineteenth-century America.

The Choctaw peoples' ancient homelands consisted of some twenty-three million acres in what later became the states of Mississippi and Alabama. Unlike the accepted stereotype, Choctaws and most other southeastern native peoples were not nomadic; American Indians were sedentary agriculturists, who lived in towns dispersed throughout a defined territory. They raised corn, squash, beans, and other crops for their own use, occasionally trading any surplus to native groups living nearby.

In the first two decades of the nineteenth century, the U.S. government obtained millions of acres of Choctaw lands through a treaty process. These transfers were not what they seemed: an exchange of Indian lands for money through a course of action in which both parties were equally powerful. Instead, most of the large land cessions were obtained through fraud, intimidation, and threats of force on the part of the government and its representatives. By the 1820s, the Choctaws had been forced to cede more than twelve million acres of land, and still the whites wanted more.

At the same time that U.S. political leaders aggressively sought more and more Choctaw land, they also engaged in aggression of a different nature. The U.S. government sought to transform and civilize Indians into whites through education. Of course, by the lights of their own culture, Native American people already were civilized. Yet whites believed passionately that Euro-American culture and religions were superior to all others—certainly to those of American Indians. Euro-Americans believed that all peoples progressed through different stages, beginning with a state of savagery, and moved through a series of conditions until they achieved civilization. Having themselves reached this stage, Euro-Americans considered all peoples of color to be primitive.

This philosophy was both complex and convincing. Pitchlynn and other Native American people who attended white schools or were exposed to white culture were inculcated with these beliefs. During the first quarter of the nineteenth century, the great southeastern Nations of native people were particular targets of white propaganda. Their societies were not closed. They offered built-in mechanisms for dealing with change and incorporating new ideas or behaviors from external sources. For centuries they had absorbed alien societies into their confederations, tolerating a degree of dissimilar beliefs in exchange for political or economic fealty. Eventually, some alien beliefs found their way into the main culture.

The Choctaws, Cherokees, Muscogees, Chickasaws, and others of the Southeast selectively imported and integrated ideas, behaviors, technologies, and material items from Euro-Americans and their societies. Peter Pitchlynn and others of mixed parentage successfully encouraged the Nations to incorporate some of these changes. For example, the Choctaws came particularly to value education and literacy. They asked white missionaries to set up schools within the Nation in 1818 and eventually erected their own education system that was the envy of many whites in backwoods areas.

Choctaw leaders turned to people of mixed heritage to institute new mechanisms within traditional forms to deal with a changing world. For that reason Pitchlynn's biculturalism made him useful in dealing with the changing cultural circumstances of the Choctaws during this period. For instance, alcohol was disrupting and destroying the foundation of Choctaw society. Government officials used it in treaty negotiations and did little to halt its illegal importation into Indian Nations. Choctaw leaders had to invent new mechanisms to deal with this external threat. Pitchlynn's maternal uncle, Mingo Mushalatubbe, was chief of the district and as such had a great deal of power. When Pitchlynn was only eighteen, Mushalatubbe appointed him captain of the Lighthorse, a new institution within the Choctaw Nation. The Lighthorse was an internal police force whose sole mission was to halt the illegal importation of alcohol by whites into the Nation. Pitchlynn's appointment not only demonstrated his uncle's confidence in him but also Peter's ability to lead Choctaws and deal with whites.

During the first two decades of the century, Americans shared a fairly broad consensus favoring eventual Indian assimilation into white society. But after 1820, the price of cotton rose sharply on the world market, making the rich southern lands of the Choctaws extremely attractive to white land seekers. Demands for Indian "removal" became the universal cry in the backwoods, and state and federal politicians changed U.S. policy to reflect the new goal.

In 1828, Andrew Jackson, the leading proponent of Indian dispossession, was elected to the presidency. For years, he had been calling for the repudiation of the treaty agreements in which the United States recognized the rights of Native Americans to possess their lands; now he had the power to implement these ideas. When Jackson became president, Georgia and Mississippi, anxious to obtain the rich farmlands of the native people within their borders, passed legislation that would unconstitutionally extend state laws over native Nations. This legislation made it criminal for a Native American chief or captain to lead his people. Peaceful assemblies of native people were outlawed. Anyone professing to be a Choctaw leader or following Choctaw law was subject to arrest and imprisonment. Indians were not allowed to defend themselves in the state court system, so any white who brought suit against them automatically won. White Mississippians invaded the homes and farms of the Choctaws and took them by force—expelling Choctaw families into the swamps. If Choctaws resisted, they were arrested for assault.

President Jackson sent negotiators to the Choctaws demanding that they sign a treaty giving up the remainder of their lands in Mississippi and Alabama in exchange for undeveloped lands west of the Mississippi River. Jackson sent word that the federal government did not intend to uphold its treaty obligations to the Choctaws, nor would it stop the state governments from illegally extending their laws over them. Pitchlynn and other Choctaw leaders were outraged by the prospect of dispossession. Yet they saw that the Nation had only two choices: stay and fight or agree to a removal treaty. No longer a military threat to the United States, they would lose any prolonged armed confrontation. Leaving their homeland was also not an option; it was a death warrant. Pitchlynn and others struggled futilely to craft a third alternative, but the government left them none.

As this realization dawned, many Choctaws grew dispirited. Pitchlynn traveled from town to town, giving speeches, trying to ward off complete despair. Nonetheless, with white encroachment on their lands, crops could not be planted, tended, or harvested. Invading whites stole cattle and other

Choctaw livestock. The men feared leaving the women and children to go hunting. The people's ability to procure food was completely disrupted. Whiskey poured through the Nation, and many dispirited Choctaws welcomed the relief of a drunken stupor. Many towns descended into confusion and chaos. Despite Pitchlynn's efforts, Choctaw society virtually stopped functioning.

Despite pressure from the national government and white encroachments, almost all members of the Nation stood fast. In October 1830, Choctaw representatives gathered at the treaty grounds refused to sell their land. Tribal tradition recounts that clan Mothers—the leaders who controlled all the Nation's lands—refused to allow the sale of another foot of Choctaw land. At an impasse, Americans declared that negotiations were over, and most tribesmen left the treaty grounds and returned to their homes. Unknown to them, however, a handful of Choctaws remained behind. Bribed by the Americans, they signed the "Treaty of Dancing Rabbit Creek." Although negotiators later told Congress that the Choctaw National Council approved the sale, fewer than twenty-five Choctaws signed this document.

Pitchlynn fought vigorously against the ratification of the treaty. He expressed outrage and shock that the Americans would break all their former treaty agreements and dispossess the Choctaws of their birthright through fraud. Choctaws and their white allies sent dozens of protests, documenting that the Choctaw signers were not authorized to sell any of the land. Despite their remonstrations, the Senate ratified the treaty on February 25, 1831. Peter Pitchlynn immediately called for the ousting of the three district chiefs, who, he said, cooperated "with the intruding enemies of our country in their plans and schemes to swindle us of the little store of wealth which we possessed." These "enemies" had corrupted the old chiefs and led them astray. With their help, the United States had procured a treaty "without the consent or knowledge of the people of the Nation."[1]

Indian removal was more than a policy; it was a human tragedy, a spiritual and physical disaster. To Choctaws, their land was not a commodity, something to be bought or sold, or traded for a similar stretch of land. Their land was held communally by all the Choctaw people. The land was assigned to the care of the clans. Any member of the Nation could use the land for hunting, farming, fishing, or other activities, but no one person actually "owned" any of it. More importantly, it was also sacred ground, given to them by the Great Spirit. Land was the essence of their identity, the Mother, the life-giver of the Choctaw people. Choctaw spiritual life and traditions centered on the Great Mother, a sacred mound that the Nation revered, called Nanih Waiya. Most importantly, Choctaw spiritual beliefs and traditions informed them that if they left the bones of their ancestors, the hunters would find no more meat, disease would come, and the Nation would die.

The U.S. government gave the Choctaw people only three years to move the entire nation out of their homelands. Federal agents were to make the arrangements for this massive endeavor, and preparations for "removal" were begun immediately. Under the strain the Choctaw Nation again sank into chaos. Factions formed and reformed, anarchy reigned, and no one could bring sense out of the madness. White observers reported that the cries of the women and children echoed night and day throughout towns and villages. The Nation literally went into mourning.

Rejecting the leadership of those who sold the Nation's lands and sold out the Nation, the people of his district asked Peter Pitchlynn to lead them west. Pitchlynn led two parties. Through his able leadership and administrative skills, most of his charges escaped the worst. His old uncle Mingo Mushalatubbe and his hundreds of followers were not so lucky. Cholera repeatedly struck their party. Exceptionally bad winter weather—largely unknown in the region in which they traveled—snowed under the defenseless travelers, delaying them at one point for two weeks in a storm without tents or blankets. Dozens of his party died. Another group of Choctaws got separated from their main party and became lost in a huge swamp when a vicious winter snowstorm struck. When they were finally rescued several days later, one American described seeing hundreds of the Choctaws' horses standing in the swamp water up to their chests, frozen in place.

From the moment of its hasty inception to its grim conclusion, removal was an unmitigated disaster for the Choctaw people. They died in the thousands as a result of government neglect and bureaucratic ineptitude. American merchants and entrepreneurs preyed upon the Choctaws at every opportunity, providing them with rotten and underweight provisions. Owing to a lack of proper supplies, such as tents, blankets, and clothing, exposure killed many of the babies and the old ones. By the time the Choctaws reached their destination, over twenty percent of the Nation had died. Finally, a majority of the surviving Choctaws arrived in their place of exile. It consisted of what is today the southern half of the state of Oklahoma. Pitchlynn began to build a cabin and clear fields. Unfortunately, his choice of locations posed the danger of malaria and fevers from the low-lying riverbed nearby. That year, the Arkansas River flooded in a massive, extraordinary flood unlike any known before. Pitchlynn and many other Choctaws lost what little they had left. Many other Choctaws were, like Pitchlynn, trying desperately to get on their feet and provide themselves with a subsistence existence in this unfamiliar land. Pitchlynn assisted several members of his clan to relocate near him, even carving out claims for them before they arrived from Mississippi.

Pitchlynn's now elderly father, John, wrote that his mother refused to leave the spirits of her dead children. The Choctaws believed that people had two spirits—one that traveled west to the Land of the Dead and one that remained where death had occurred. The spirits of the dead watched over their remains and became offended if they were not treated with respect. They wrought terrible calamities on the descendants who neglected their sacred duty to the dead. Peter's mother therefore refused to leave the spirits of her dead children behind. John remained with her. Peter's father, however, frequently expressed his hope that before he died, all of his children would be together in the new land, "with their own people."[2]

Although once an enthusiast and supporter of assimilation, Peter began to look at Euro-American society in a different light after these experiences. Dispossession and exile convinced Pitchlynn that no matter how "white" Indians became, they would never be accepted fully by Americans. Their political and economic rights would always be a subset of, and vulnerable to, those enjoyed by people of the dominant majority. The racial hierarchy that permeated every facet of American life demanded the subordination of all people of color. Pitchlynn and many of the Native people of Indian Territory turned their faces from the whites and concentrated on rebuilding a new Choctaw society.

In 1836, Pitchlynn was instrumental in drawing up a new Choctaw Constitution. Ironically, it was modeled after those of the United States and its various states. Nevertheless, many Choctaw traditions and societal norms were also incorporated. In December 1841, Choctaw chiefs asked Pitchlynn to travel to Washington on tribal business. He left the following month. There he represented the Nation on matters of education, claims by Choctaws against the government, land rights, and representation for the Indian Territory in Congress. He returned to the Nation the following spring, and that summer Pitchlynn ran unsuccessfully for a seat on his district's council. He returned to Washington again in 1847 to represent the Nation to Congress. In 1853 the Choctaw council appointed Pitchlynn and three others as delegates to settle by treaty "all and every claim and interest of the Choctaw people against the United States."[3]

Because the Choctaws and other Indian Nations in the Territory were isolated and far away from the centers of U.S. power on the East Coast, the Choctaws and their Indian neighbors entered progressively into an illusion of independence and sovereignty, a false sense of security that Americans would not come after their lands again. From the 1830s until 1860, Americans rapidly settled the lands all around Indian Territory to the west. Pitchlynn, who was in Washington much of this time, along with other representatives from the Indian Nations, fought off repeated attempts to force a territorial government on Indian Territory, a necessary prelude to confiscation of the Indians' communal lands.

After his appointment in 1853, Pitchlynn continued to live primarily in Washington, with occasional visits back to his farm and family in the Choctaw Nation. In his absence his brother, his sons, a son-in-law, and his slaves ran his farm for periods of time. The Choctaw form of slavery was quite different from the institution in the antebellum South. Slavery among the Choctaws grew out of a long tradition. From time immemorial, captives taken in war had become slaves for a period of time. Eventually, most were adopted by a clan, at which point they became Choctaw. After that point, no differences could be discerned in their acceptance by the Choctaws. By contrast, American slavery was hereditary and permanent.

Pitchlynn's slaves were treated more like servants. They were free to move about, pursue economic engagements, and keep any earned income for themselves. Often Pitchlynn would leave a leader of the slaves, Solomon, to run the farm, and he would write to Pitchlynn in Washington about the conditions on the farm, the crops, the weather, and his own private financial endeavors. After the Civil War, Pitchlynn's former slaves remained on his farm as tenants or sharecroppers, continuing to live in the small communities they had built on his land during the antebellum era.

During the 1850s, while Pitchlynn was in Washington, life began to deteriorate in the Choctaw Nation. Disorder among the Choctaws and gangs of white outlaws who fled to Indian Territory to escape U.S. justice contributed to the chaos. All of it centered on the ambiguous legal relationship of the Nation to the United States. The Choctaw Nation had exclusive legal jurisdiction over crimes committed in Indian Territory involving only Choctaw people. If a white person was involved, the United States had jurisdiction. The nearest federal court, however, was outside Indian Territory—at Fort Smith, Arkansas. For people living in remote areas of Indian Territory, travel to Arkansas was expensive and difficult. Leaders of the Choctaw Nation and the other Indian Nations in Indian

Territory complained frequently and with increasing urgency about the remote site of the court, the ambiguity of conflicting jurisdictions, the intrusion of white law enforcement personnel, and the outlaw intruders living in the Choctaw Nation—to no avail.

Once again, Peter Pitchlynn stood at the crossroads of this cultural conflict. In 1856, two of Pitchlynn's sons were arrested and charged with assault with intent to kill a white man. Two traveling white men had come to the Pitchlynn homestead with whiskey, obviously feeling the effects of it. Leonidas Pitchlynn came out and saw that one of the men's horses was near death. He requested that the white man take his horse and move on before it died, since Pitchlynn did not want to have to "hunt up oxen" to haul it away if it died on his property. The white man replied, insultingly, "You are too saucy for a damned Indian," and he refused to comply with Pitchlynn's request to move on. A fistfight ensued. Pushmataha Pitchlynn, another of Peter's sons, rushed out of the house with a gun and, in order to break up the fight, fired his gun over the heads of the two struggling men. Just as he shot, however, the white man threw one of his hands up and the bullet took off one of his fingers. The grand jury issued an indictment based solely on the word of the white men, and the Pitchlynns were arrested.

After the Pitchlynns made bail, one of the white men offered not to appear at their trial for a certain sum of money. They refused and were subsequently convicted of assault with intent to kill. Had Peter Pitchlynn not had connections in Washington, his sons would have gone to the penitentiary for three years. The boys' maternal uncles wrote an appeal for their pardon to President James Buchanan. One of the justifications was that "The two young Pitchlynns are themselves *almost white men*—had no prejudices or ill feeling toward white men, and they, as well as their Father, were proverbially hospitable and kind to citizens of the United States who traveled through the Choctaw Nation."[4]

The appeal thus in part hinged on the assertion of near-whiteness. As their uncles had it, these were not a couple of dark-skinned, ignorant savages, but rather men who were close to the level of whiteness—and civilization—of the men with whom they scuffled. The unwritten assumption was that the president, like most Americans of the day, would assess the Pitchlynns' worthiness of a pardon based at least in part on the color of their skin. The boys' uncles, in their appeal to the president, knew that "race" would play an important role in the president's decision.

The wording of the request for the pardon casts new light on the experience of nonwhite peoples who became subject to the jurisdiction of the

U.S. system of justice in antebellum America. What becomes obvious is that a system of racism informed the administration of justice in the United States. The grand jury and the federal court had taken the word of the white men who were themselves directly involved, with no other witnesses present. The appeal that the boys were "almost white men" goes to the very core of the problem created by the system of racism institutionalized in America in the nineteenth century. It also reveals how far removed Choctaws remained from being tolerated by, much less assimilated into, American society in the 1850s.

Although with the boys' uncles' help Peter Pitchlynn successfully obtained a pardon for his sons, the experience was a bitter one. From this point on, he steadfastly railed against and opposed the operation of U.S. society and its legal system. "What can be more unjust than that we should be dragged to distant points for trial, far beyond the reach for witnesses and friends, for every alleged infraction of the white man's rights," Pitchlynn complained, "and placed in the power of a Judge, as my children were, where every prejudice is against us, and every sympathy in favor of the whites—let them never be so degraded?" But in an ironic twist he hoped that in the future, white allies of the Indians would see that U.S. law would be extended to Native American people. In that case, whites who had invaded Indian Territory and were living there illegally would "be no longer free to rob, despoil, and trample upon us and then laugh in our faces."5

Unhappily for Pitchlynn's family and the Choctaws, lawlessness came to typify their experience in Indian Territory. Some of the more remote areas became havens for vicious criminal gangs, including the notorious Ned Christie, Belle Starr, and the Quantrill gang. Dozens of other outlaws and renegades also lived in the Indian Territory, terrorizing Indian and white alike. But whites were not the only renegades during this era. Choctaw young men no longer had warfare and traditional male rituals with which to prove their manhood, so they often turned to alcohol and violence. Time and again fighting broke out even among friends during drinking bouts, and many personal disputes were settled with gunfire. A Choctaw Lighthorse killed Pitchlynn's youngest son, Lee, for attempting to evade arrest for the murder of another Choctaw. Pitchlynn's grandson was killed in broad daylight by two white outlaws with whom he had had a dispute. Violence became part of the warp and weft of the Nation's life in their new homeland.

As the Choctaw people struggled to find solutions to this seemingly unending circle of violence, the Civil War intervened. The war that challenged the perpetuity of the Union presented an opportunity for the Choctaws. It served both as an outlet of aggression for the young men and provided a diversion that forced the attention of everyone in the Nation to focus on the survival of the United States. Although Pitchlynn was a slave-holder, he was opposed to the Confederacy and believed that the Choctaws should remain loyal to the Union. But the Choctaws were not allowed the luxury of choice. They came to discover that they would not have the option of remaining neutral as Pitchlynn and many others favored.

The dilemma of the Indian nations of Indian Territory during the Civil War could not have been greater. On the one hand, although some Choctaws owned slaves and practiced a style of slavery seen on southern plantations, especially along the Red River, they were a tiny minority of the Nation. The Choctaw economy did not depend on slavery, and the ruin of all those who held slaves would have had very little, if any, impact upon most Choctaw people. On the other hand, the geographical location of the Choctaw Nation placed it just across the Red River from Texas, a state whose involvement with, and dependence on, plantation slavery was paramount. During the years leading up to the Civil War, Texans and Arkansans often crossed into the Choctaw Nation to "persuade" Choctaws that their interests lay with the South, often through acts of violence and intimidation. The Choctaw decision to side with the Confederacy came as a result of the withdrawal of all federal troops from Indian Territory. The troops left to fight to preserve the Union. Their departure, however, left the Choctaws and other Native people vulnerable to raids and assaults by Texans, Arkansans, and southern partisans in Kansas, who terrorized those Indian people who they thought were pro-Union.

Taking a different, less violent tack, the Confederate government sent agents to try to entice the Choctaws into an alliance with and incorporation into the Confederacy. They promised full legal representation in the Confederate legislature, guaranteed to honor all treaty agreements between the United States and the Choctaws, and promised the Indians that they would have full political rights in the Confederate States of America. Despite their many misgivings, Choctaws declared the Nation free and independent of the United States and joined the Confederacy. They remained loyal to the South throughout the Civil War.

Ironically the Choctaw people turned to Pitchlynn, who had returned to Indian Territory to oppose an alliance with the South, for leadership during the Civil War. He was elected Principal Chief and served the Nation until the end of the conflict. Pitchlynn's astute leadership of the

Nation during and after the war kept the impact of the conflict and its aftermath at a minimum. Most of the Indian Territory and its Nations were devastated during the conflict. The territory served as the stage for another civil war among the pro-Union and pro-Confederacy factions of the Cherokee and Muscogee Nations. Damage to the Choctaw Nation was not nearly so severe. Even so, the Choctaws never recovered from the devastation of the war. Worse yet, the U.S. government forced the Choctaws to give up half their lands in Indian Territory as punishment for siding with the South.

In the years after the Civil War, Pitchlynn continued to represent the Choctaw Nation in Washington. His main activity was trying to secure a resolution to Choctaw claims resulting from the treaty of 1830. Pitchlynn died on January 17, 1881, without having succeeded in persuading Congress to honor the agreement. Yet a month after his death, the House of Representatives passed legislation to implement the agreement. Five years later, the Supreme Court awarded the Choctaw Nation over three million dollars. It took fifty years and continuous negotiations and lobbying for the United States to fulfill its obligations under the Treaty of Dancing Rabbit Creek of 1830.[6]

The experience of Peter Pitchlynn and other Native Americans of mixed heritage allows us a glimpse into the complexity of their lives and how they negotiated difficult paths in both the white and Indian worlds. In Pitchlynn's case, he never forgot or tried to deny his Choctaw identity. Nonetheless, Peter probably would not have been able to do so, even if he had so desired. The United States had embarked on a disastrous course of racism that no one individual could overcome. The experience of Native American people, African Americans, Mexicans, and other people of color illustrates the enormous effects of racism on American history.

Seen from a non-Eurocentric perspective—seen from Peter Pitchlynn's point of view—the story of the United States turns into a story that is less unique than universal, and far more believable than mythic. We find a place and time in which the skin color of individuals and groups limited their rights and hedged their opportunities. We can experience and perhaps understand the rage and frustration of people excluded unjustly from the possibilities of American life. We gain an understanding of the behavior and motives of both oppressors and oppressed. American history is sometimes not a very pretty or admirable tale. Instead, it is a human story, with which we can empathize, and from which we can learn. Indian people know the past is always with us. It is never over. The story of America is the story of all of us.

Notes

1. Peter P. Pitchlynn, transcript of speech to the Nation, 1830, Cyrus Kingsbury Collection (Thomas Gilcrease Museum, Tulsa, OK).

2. John Pitchlynn to Peter P. Pitchlynn, November 23, 1832, and John Pitchlynn to Peter P. Pitchlynn, April 5, 1835, Peter P. Pitchlynn Collection (Western History Collection, University of Oklahoma, Norman). John also wrote with great anger and disgust of the invading hordes of shiftless white folks who invaded and claimed the old Choctaw lands. He charged them with stealing everything he had and cheating the few remaining Choctaws out of their land. He averred that he could no longer stand any white man—that they were all out to get land or wealth no matter what the cost to their souls. He was infuriated and astonished at the lengths to which intruding whites went to cheat the Choctaws and to take advantage of their great distress.

3. Annie Hanie, interview with author, May 1992, notes in possession of author; W. David Baird, *Peter Pitchlynn: Chief of the Choctaws* (Norman, OK, 1972), 61–63, 67–69, 97 (quotation). A skillful amalgamation of Choctaw and Euro-American ideals was blended in some of the legislation adopted by the Choctaws. For example, the Choctaw passed a law barring the murder of witches and wizards without a fair trial before the chiefs or four captains. But if any person found the entrails of a witch "going from or returning to the body," the body could be put to death, cut open "by a proper person," and examined "to see whether it has in it any entrails." The framers of the law complied with Euro-American ideas of due process but also accommodated and recognized the beliefs of traditional Choctaws that witches were a very serious threat to the people and should be killed when discovered among them. Angie Debo, *The Rise and Fall of the Choctaw Republic* (Norman, OK, 1934), 46–47.

4 . Sampson Folsom and James Gamble to James Buchanan, President of the United States, June 29, 1857, Peter P. Pitchlynn Collection.

5. Peter P. Pitchlynn, Washington City, to Messrs. Walker and Green, Van Buren, October, 1857, ibid.

6. Shortly following Peter Pitchlynn's death, the United States gave in to demands of whites for the lands of the Native American peoples in Indian Territory. Despite all its treaty promises guaranteeing that no state or territory would ever be allowed to assert its sovereignty over the Native American peoples of Indian Territory and that their landholdings would be guaranteed forever, the United States passed the Dawes Act and other legislation in the 1880s and 1890s and seized the lands of native Nations in Indian Territory. The United States dissolved their governments over the vociferous protests of the tribes.

Suggested Readings

Catlin, George. *North American Indians.* Edited and with an introduction by Peter Matthiessen. New York, 1989.

DeRosier, Arthur H., Jr. *The Removal of the Choctaw Indians.* New York, 1970.

Jennings, Francis. *The Invasion of America: Indians, Colonialism, and the Cant of Conquest.* New York, 1976.

Martin, Joel W. *Sacred Revolt: The Muskogees' Struggle for a New World.* Boston, 1991.

Rogin, Michael Paul. *Fathers and Children: Andrew Jackson and the Subjugation of the American Indian.* New Brunswick, Canada, 1995.

Stannard, David E. *American Holocaust: The Conquest of the New World.* New York, 1992.

Swanton, John R. *Source Material for the Social and Ceremonial Life of the Choctaw Indians.* Birmingham, AL, 1993.

11

Hosea Easton
Forgotten Abolitionist "Giant"

George R. Price

One of the great and tragic ironies of the Jacksonian era is that while white males were increasingly asserting their equality with one another and participating in ever larger numbers in the political arena, they did so by pushing other groups to the margins of American society. Native Americans were one such group; African Americans were another. In the early republic, although racism was prevalent and segregation increased throughout the North, African Americans, relying on self-help and uplift to lay claim to respectability with whites, contested the "color line." Hosea Easton's experiences and writings suggest, however, that by the 1830s modern racial essentialism was becoming all-pervasive. Skin color, not talent or respectability, became the fault line in American society. Easton's life bridged both of those eras and embraced the central assumptions of African American thought characteristic of each. The son of a mixed-heritage activist, Easton championed black solidarity and self-improvement in the late 1820s. After a series of riots destroyed black churches and schools throughout the Northeast and lower Midwest, Easton became convinced that the oppressors—not African Americans—had to be transformed and that whites shouldered the burden of promoting equality. His activism and uncompromising moral critique of white society would anticipate and echo throughout the civil rights movement of the 1950s and 1960s.

George R. Price is adjunct instructor in the Departments of Native American Studies and African American Studies at the University of Montana, Missoula. He is the coauthor, with James Brewer Stewart, of *To Heal the Scourge of Prejudice: The Life and Writings of Hosea Easton* (1999).

The sit-ins of the 1960s civil rights movement were not the first such protests in American history. One hundred and sixty years earlier, a Revolutionary War veteran of black-Indian heritage, James Easton, his wife, Sarah, and their seven children, used the sit-in tactic as a protest against segregated seating arrangements in two different Massachusetts churches in 1800. After they purchased a pew in the whites-only section of one of those churches, the congregation plastered their pew with tar. The family returned to the church the following Sunday, hauling their own benches in their wagon, to replace the tarred pew. When the irate white church members threw their benches out the door, the Eastons took their seats on the bare floor. Eastons repeated such protests on at least six different occasions between 1800 and 1827.[1]

Around the year 1812, Easton and his older sons established their own iron works and foundry in North Bridgewater, Massachusetts, where they manufactured various tools and the frameworks for some major construction projects. They also created a school within their factory to provide both industrial skills and an academic education to young men of color. This school was one of the first of its type in the United States, established about ten years before the manual labor education movement began nationwide. After nearly sixteen years of struggle against substantial racist opposition to their existence, both the factory and school were forced to close. James Easton died soon after in 1830. Like other leading free men of color of his generation such as James Forten and Prince Hall, Easton would not—could not—be content with anything less than equal opportunities and rights for all colored citizens of the nation that they had fought for and helped to build with their labor.[2]

Hosea Easton, the youngest child of James and Sarah, was born into this conflicted social environment of hope and struggle. By the late 1820s he had become prominent as a leader in the fight for human rights and liberty in the United States. With a family background rich in inspiration and courage upon which to draw, Hosea worked passionately and incessantly throughout the course of his brief life for the cause and against the world that he had inherited.

In March 1828, Hosea Easton was called upon to chair "a large and respectable meeting of the people of Colour" held in Boston at the Colored Methodist Episcopal Church. The purpose of that meeting was to reaffirm a commitment among the people of the community to support *Freedom's Journal,* the nation's only newspaper published by African Americans. One of the speakers at that meeting was David Walker, who published his inspirational and controversial *Appeal to the Coloured Citizens of the World* the following year. In June 1828, Easton's first published work, *An Appeal to the Christian Public, in Behalf of the Methodist Episcopal Church,* appeared.[3]

Shortly thereafter, on November 27, 1828, Easton delivered a powerful and revealing Thanksgiving Day address to the "coloured population" of Providence, Rhode Island. He had not intended to publish the lengthy speech, but, as he recalls in the introduction, "by the ardent request of a Committee chosen for that purpose, by the Coloured Population of Providence, he was influenced to yield to their solicitation." The *Address* articulated the grief and pain of discrimination, as well as the liberating hope of equality through "uplift"—self-improvement efforts by the victims of racism. Because the occasion of this speech probably coincided with the agonizing closure of the Easton family business, in which Hosea Easton had been deeply involved, Easton's words reveal how widespread racism deeply wounded and exasperated him.[4]

The speech began with a patriotic giving of thanks for the greatness and prosperity of America. But this tone soon took an ironic, almost sarcastic turn, as Easton described how some American citizens were excluded systematically from the benefits of liberty and prosperity. He fervently declared his belief that only in a state of true liberty can the human mind and spirit develop their full potential. "The voice of Liberty calls the energies of the human soul to emerge out of nature's darkness, and to explore divine spiritual principles," Easton declared. "How admirable it is, that the higher the soul arises by being expanded by intelligent perception, the more it breathes forth praise and thanksgiving to God." To him, the ultimate crime issuing from slavery and discrimination was that an entire segment of the community effectively was robbed of the experience to develop and manifest its full humanity.[5]

In the course of this address, Easton also described the violent atrocities committed within the institution of slavery; the day-to-day realities of segregation, racism, and lack of true liberty for "free" people of color in the North; the "diabolical" evil—as he saw it—of the colonization movement; and, finally, the hope of victory through "uplift" combined as it was with divine intervention.[6] This latter aspect of Easton's thought, with its emphasis on the responsibility of the victims of racism to transform their limiting circumstances, would develop in a radically different direction during the next decade of his life.

Soon after the closing of James Easton and Son's factory and school, Hosea Easton moved to Boston and became a leader in one of the most significant developments of the abolitionist movement of the 1830s: the National Convention of Free People of Color. Several years before William Lloyd Garrison established his antislavery newspaper *The Liberator* in 1831 (which is often given as the beginning of the abolitionist movement), leaders of free, colored communities in the urban areas of the North had been coming together with increasing frequency and in growing numbers to take up the causes that were in the common interests of their people. These issues included the abolition of slavery; opposition to the American Colonization Society; the education and advancement of free people of color; the organization of their own churches; the promotion of *Freedom's Journal;* and, generally, the search for other ways to oppose effectively segregation and racism. The National Convention of Free People of Color was, therefore, both a result and culmination of the growing need for such leaders to unite to achieve their common goals and fight their common enemies.[7]

The first National Convention of Free People of Color was held in Philadelphia in June 1831, and "Rev." Hosea Easton was selected as one of the four delegates from Boston. The agenda for the convention included such issues as healing divisions and strengthening the ties between the people of color, the feasibility of emigration to Canada, and how to defeat the work of the American Colonization Society. The issue of emigration to Canada surfaced as a reaction to the white race riots in Cincinnati in 1829, when hundreds of African Americans were driven out of the city and many fled to Canada. Now other people of color were contemplating a similar emigration as a means of escaping white American racial hostility.[8]

Delegates to the convention denounced the American Colonization Society because it promoted a plan that would rid the United States of free African Americans by shipping them to Africa, thereby removing the most significant indigenous threat to the institution of slavery. The mere presence of the thousands of free blacks in the South was an inspiration to slaves to seek freedom. In the North, free people of color were spearheading the abolitionist movement. The audacity of the society to promote its plan either under the guise of benevolence or even as an antislavery program proved offensive to the African American community.[9]

Perhaps the most exciting issue raised at this first convention for Hosea Easton was a proposal put forth by three radical white abolitionists—William Lloyd Garrison, Arthur Tappan, and Simeon Jocelyn—who had recently resigned in protest from the colonization society. They submitted a proposal "that a College be established at New Haven, Connecticut . . . for the liberal education of Young Men of Colour, on the Manual Labour System." This resolution raised the possibility of reviving the work begun by Easton's father some twenty years earlier but on a much grander scale. The project would require $20,000 to complete. A "benevolent individual" (most likely Arthur Tappan) had already donated the first $1,000; convention delegates were responsible for raising the remainder. The proposed college, which had the potential to be a powerful tool for the cause of "uplift," was reason for hope. So, too, was the inclusion of white allies—however small in numbers—in the movement for liberty and equality. These allies could bring more white influence and resources to the overwhelming task of eradicating racism.[10]

White abolitionists, however, were and would remain an extremely small minority in antebellum America. Society in the Age of the Common Man was becoming ever more racist and its climate less tolerant of any dissent from the ideology of white supremacy. As the nation expanded west and south, it encountered more Indians and brought more Africans— enslaved and free—into newly opened lands. White Americans collectively came to the conclusion that lines had to be drawn regarding who could participate in, and reap the economic benefits of, territorial and industrial expansion. This consensus demanded that white social domination should remain the first priority when considering issues of social inclusion. People of color, therefore, would only be included in American society where they would serve the needs and interests of the white majority. That way of thinking was the impetus for both the movement to colonize free African Americans to Africa and the Indian Removal Act of 1830. The momentum of this social development of exclusion would negate attempts at uplift, social elevation, and equal inclusion for nonwhites—even when initiated or promoted by whites.[11]

Clearly, there was no room for a "Manual Labor College for Young Men of Colour" in such a society. Reports of the proposed college reached New Haven late in the summer of 1831. A town meeting was held in September, during which delegates made many speeches against the establishment of a "colored college." Several speakers claimed to be against slavery and for the "improvement" and education of blacks, but, nevertheless, they would not allow such a school to be built in their town. The request to permit the college to be built was defeated, 4 to 700, effectively ending the possibility of the school coming into existence. It, however, did not restore New Haven citizens' sense of well-being, security, or civility. A series of inflammatory newspaper editorials followed, each criticizing the city's "unwholesome colored population." By early October, white mobs were rioting in the black section of town and pelting Arthur Tappan's home with garbage. This and similar violent reactions to black attempts at uplift, education, and any other form of self-help throughout urban areas in the North during the 1830s had a profound effect on Hosea Easton.[12]

Easton continued to participate in the annual National Convention of Free People of Color through 1834, both as chaplain, often leading prayers, and as a delegate proposing and seconding various resolutions. Between conventions, Easton worked fervently to develop antislavery sentiments, lecturing at churches and halls all over New England. Apparently, Easton was called away from the convention of 1833, since his name does not appear in the minutes after the first day. His mother, Sarah, died a couple of weeks after that convention, so he may have left to spend time with her. Sometime later in 1833, Hosea, his wife Louisa, and their two children moved to Hartford, Connecticut, where he pastored two churches and resided for the rest of his brief life.[13] Easton's first ministry was the Talcott St. Congregational Church, which had been established as a primarily African American congregation in 1819. Easton's position was not unique. After the turn of the nineteenth century, more and more free colored Christians in New England chose to start their own churches rather than suffer the demeaning experience of being forced to sit in the segregated "negro pews" and balconies in the white churches.[14]

African American churches also became meeting places for the growing number of uplift-related societies and organizations. Not long after Easton's arrival in Hartford, he joined with several local black leaders to form the Hartford Literary and Religious Institution. In January 1834, Easton was appointed the institution's "general agent." He traveled throughout New England to raise funds by speaking to churches and to sympathetic abolitionists. Unfortunately, at this same time another wave of racist-inspired mob violence spread throughout the urban Northeast, leading the members of the institution to "call him home." White race riots broke out in Boston, New York City, Utica (New York), Pittsburgh, and Hartford during the years 1834 to 1836. Easton was no longer safe to travel—especially for the cause that he was espousing.[15]

According to Edward Abdy, an English gentleman traveler and writer, Hartford in the 1830s was particularly racist. "Throughout the Union," he claimed, "there is, perhaps, no city, containing the same amount of population, where the blacks meet with more contumely and unkindness than at this place. Some of them told me it was hardly safe for them to be in the streets alone at night. . . . To pelt them with stones, and cry out nigger! nigger! as they pass, seems to be the pastime of the place."[16] Riots in Hartford in 1834 and 1835 hit Hosea close to home. In 1834 a group of white youths attacked one of the parishoners of Easton's church as the man left the building one evening. A black neighbor, Jack Blackson, defended the victim by firing a round of buckshot that hit four of the youths. White mobs responded by brawling in Easton's neighborhood for three consecutive nights, during which time they tore down Blackson's house and several other homes of free people of color.[17]

A similar event occurred in June 1835. A gang of whites again gathered outside the Talcott St. Church, shouting taunts and epithets at the congregation while they were holding a religious service. When the service was over, the mob attacked the congregation as it left the building.

Although the ensuing riot lasted only two days, even the local press expressed outrage at the rioters' behavior, especially at how the incident started. In 1836, Easton founded and began to pastor a second church in Hartford, the Colored Methodist Episcopal Zion Church. It was burned to the ground that same year.[18]

During these years of racial discord and at great personal risk, Easton resumed traveling and pleading for the abolition of slavery and of discrimination. After the fire, Easton had added to his speeches a plea for funds to rebuild the church. But an even more significant change occurred. Instead of speaking of and for the uplift and self-improvement of African Americans to mixed audiences, Easton began to preach increasingly and aggressively to predominantly white audiences. He exhorted them to renounce their racism and bring a healing to American society, as he was now certain that only their actions could bring such a reconciliation. The events of the mid-1830s had convinced Easton that not only did black attempts at uplift fail to bring the desired social change, they apparently provoked an almost unimaginable Afrophobic hysteria. At the time he wrote his Address in 1828, Easton had only sensed the futility of African American self-improvement and uplift. Nine years later, he fully realized it. The defenders of slavery and racism needed to change, not the victims. Still a man of profound Christian faith, the Reverend Easton was now convinced that the ultimate hope for colored Americans lay in God's power to lead white racists to repentance and transformation. He saw himself playing the role as one of God's agents working in the vineyards to realize that vision.[19]

Easton's *A Treatise on the Intellectual Character, and Civil and Political Condition of the Colored People of the U. States; and the Prejudice Exercised Towards Them,* published four months before his death in 1837, was the crowning achievement of his brief life. It was his supreme and final attempt to reach white Americans with a message that he now believed they needed to hear. Within its fifty-four pages, the *Treatise* unfolds as a philosophical and theological discourse on the subject of race and racism. As such, it is arguably of greater scope and depth of analysis than anything else previously written on this topic by an American—white or black.[20]

Easton began his treatise in a manner appropriate for a Christian minister writing on the topic of race. He argued for the original oneness of humanity and coupled it to a biblical and historical account of the loss of that original God-ordained oneness. The first sentence of Easton's introduction offered a powerful counterpoint to all of the conflict and disharmony that he described throughout the remainder of the *Treatise.* "One great truth is acknowledged by all Christendom," he wrote, "viz.—God hath made of one blood all nations of men for to dwell on all the face of the earth." Easton then went on to give an environmental, though para- doxically Christian, explanation for the physical variety within the human species. That was followed by a biblical-historical account of the divergent paths taken by the descendants of Noah's sons who populated Africa and Europe, and thereby he provided an explanation for variety in cultural and intellectual development among different human groups.

At this point, the *Treatise* takes on an Afrocentric focus that is more apparent than real. Although not the first to do so, Easton extolled the glo- ries of ancient African civilization by repeatedly making references to the glories of Egypt. In contrast, Easton described how the descendants of Noah, who eventually settled in Europe, became brutal and cruel barbar- ians. Easton attributed Europe's eventual ascendancy in technology and domination over Africa and the rest of the world to a combination of brute force and the adaptation of African cultural refinement. Yet the point of Easton's historical survey was not to make any sort of argument for innate African cultural, spiritual, or intellectual superiority over Europeans. Rather, Easton was attempting to reveal an environmental, cause-and- effect relationship between worldwide historical events and the degrada- tion of all of humanity, which eventually and inevitably shaped the abysmal state of interracial relations in antebellum America.[21]

The final four chapters of the *Treatise* deal with the damage done to the victims of slavery; the nature of racial "prejudice" and the means by which it is passed on from generation to generation; the effects of racism on the so-called free people of color in the North; the failure of the U.S. govern- ment to extend its promise of life, liberty, and the pursuit of happiness to all of its citizens (including colored veterans of two of the nation's wars); and, Easton's very biblical, radically Christian solution to these problems.

Several slights that Easton himself suffered growing up in Massa- chusetts, as well as experiences in his adult life traveling throughout New England, clearly influenced the chapter that details the ways in which racism is taught and passed through generations. Based on his own life, Easton was able to provide a number of firsthand examples of racist instruction. He related stories and common sayings told to children. Easton noted the frequent use of the terms "negro" and "nigger" as slurs. He recalled to his readers visual reminders of black degradation that took the form of public posters insulting blacks. Finally, Easton noted the neg- ative but instructive effect of segregated public facilities, including, of course, the "negro pews" in the churches.[22]

Easton also made a claim for the economic motivation that perpetuated racism in the North and that correspondingly supported slavery in
the South. "Cotton, rice, indigo, tobacco, and sugar, are great blessings to
the world, say they, and [the enslaved Africans] may as well be made to
make them as not," he observed. "But to come at the truth, the whole system is founded in avarice. I believe the premises to be the production of
modern philosophy, bearing date with European slavery; and it has been
the almost sole cause of the present prevailing public sentiment in regard
to the colored population." One of the profound strengths of the *Treatise*
is Easton's consistent effort to tie the viability of the institution of slavery
in the South to the "prevailing public sentiment" of racism in the North.
Throughout his treatise, he clearly demonstrated how both sections of the
country profited from slavery and the perpetuation of racism. Neither
antislavery colonizationists nor even some sincere abolitionists escaped his
condemnation.[23]

Easton was similarly critical of the Christian clergy for its complicity
in the perpetuation of racism. "It becomes the interest of all parties, not
excepting the clergy, to sanction the premises [of racism], and draw the
conclusions, and hence, to teach the rising generation," he declared. "'The
love of money is the root of all evil'; it will induce its votaries to teach lessons to their little babes, which only fits them for destroyers of their
species in this world, and for the torments of hell in the world to come.
When clergymen, even, are so blinded by the god of this world, as to witness the practice of the most heinous blasphemy in the house, said to be
dedicated to God . . . without raising their warning voice to the wicked, it
would not be at all surprising if they were to teach their children . . . that
a negro is not like a white man, instead of teaching them his catechism."[24]

His parents' resistance to segregated seating in the church gave meaning to Easton's phrase "most heinous blasphemy." Though he certainly was
attempting to appeal to the conscience, he by no means tried to appease
whites' sensibilities. Rather, he was serving as God's prophetic voice, warning a people doomed for eternity if they did not repent.[25] He even envisioned the form that their repentance should take, and he found it in the
biblical example of the Good Samaritan. "New York emancipated her
slaves, after beating them several hundred years, left them, half dead,
without proscribing any healing remedy for the bruises and wounds
received by their maltreatment," Easton scorned. "But the good Samaritan
had quite a different view of the subject." Easton then elaborated on what
it meant to be a Good Samaritan in the early nineteenth-century United
States, calling for affirmative, remedial action on the part of white

Americans to heal the wounds of people injured by their avarice: "Emancipation embraces the idea that the emancipated must be placed back where slavery found them, and restore to them all that slavery has taken away from them. Merely to cease beating the colored people, and leave them in their gore, and call it emancipation, is nonsense. Nothing short of an entire reversal of the slave system in theory and practice—in general and in particular—will ever accomplish the work of redeeming the colored people of this country from their present condition."[26]

Of course, when Easton, a staunch anticolonizationist, observed that those emancipated must be placed back where slavery found them, he was not referring to Africa. He was alluding to the restoration of an elevated human condition—what, in Easton's perception, the captive Africans had once been.[27]

Easton considered slavery to be the root cause of the physical and psychological damage of African Americans. It was also the source of the oppressive social circumstances—North and South—in which they were forced to live. At several points in the *Treatise,* Easton emphasized not only the devastation wrought by slavery on human life but how its cumulative effects carried over from generation to generation to create an ever-worsening human condition. Its effect upon whites who supported the institution was no less significant. Easton described it as primarily spiritual, manifesting itself in a degradation of their moral character and thus endangering their eternal souls. For blacks, to the contrary, the effects were physical, mental, moral, and psychological. They increased in severity in direct proportion to the amount of time that individuals and their ancestors spent under slavery's degrading power. Easton asserted that slaves who had come more recently from Africa and freedmen or escapees who were born in Africa (and had spent relatively little time under slavery) were in a more "elevated" state. By making this point of comparison, Easton hoped to persuade his audience that the effects of the institution and white prejudice—not inherited traits—shaped and defined their perceptions and characterizations of the negative personal characteristics and faults that they claimed to find in nearly all of the colored population.[28]

Easton also argued that the human damage inflicted by the institution was so severe that slaves and ex-slaves could not be rehabilitated through their own efforts. Therefore, whites bore the primary responsibility for their recovery and restoration. In making this argument, Easton employed several illustrations that, taken out of their carefully constructed context, could easily be found offensive. Descriptions of actual and alleged African American physical characteristics, which whites had claimed were all examples of personal and racial defects, were repeated by Easton. To his credit, he attempted to sort out those characteristics that were the result of slavery and those that were part of God's intended "variety in nature." In neither case were they inherent shortcomings.

Combined with his descriptions of the psychological damage done to African Americans by slavery, Easton portrayed an image of slave degradation and helplessness that must have been particularly unsettling at best, and offensive at worst, to those who had recently escaped from slavery. By preaching white responsibility and the need for the oppressors to encourage and promote racial healing and redemptive thought and action throughout American society, Easton ran the real risk of offending both whites and blacks, including some key figures within the abolitionist movement. It was a risk Easton was willing to take; nonetheless, his critique had a direct effect on how he and his work were remembered or, rather, forgotten, by those who came after him.

Two key reasons explain why later abolitionists ignored and neglected Hosea Easton and his *Treatise*. The first involves the changes in personnel and tactics within the movement that began shortly after his death. In the early 1840s the colored leadership in the movement shifted from primarily free people of color, such as the Eastons who had been free for generations, to men and women who until recently had been slaves themselves. Besides Easton, the former group included such figures as William C. Nell, John T. Hilton, and Samuel Cornish. The latter group comprised better-known activists such as Frederick Douglass, Henry H. Garnett, Martin Delany, and William Wells Brown. With Frederick Douglass's advent on the abolitionist speaking circuit in 1841, abolitionist leaders like William Lloyd Garrison and Wendell Phillips decided that an effective tactic would be to promote dignified former slaves skilled in oratory, such as Douglass and Brown. This strategy would have the effect of making the institution of slavery appear even more dreadful for limiting the potential and abusing the talents of such nonstereotypical African Americans. Although some whites within the antislavery movement preferred and referred to the image of the helpless, debilitated slave, many gladly welcomed this shift in tactics. It kept the focus squarely on slavery in the South instead of on the unpleasant, uncomfortable, and troubling topic of racism in the North, which Easton had tried to force them to address.

Subsequent to this tactical shift and related to it, slave narrative autobiographies, which had been infrequently published before this time, soon became a profusion. How, then, could passages from the *Treatise* that argue that slavery had a completely debilitating and dehumanizing effect upon the slaves either aid the new abolitionist tactical approach, or be received as anything but an affront to the dignity and pride of people like Douglass, Brown, Harriet Tubman, and Sojourner Truth? Easton believed that the slave was metamorphosed into a machine and thus "lost all the innate principles of a freeman." When slavery ceased to act upon the slave, Easton concluded, "he is left a mere out-of-use wreck of machinery." Ultimately, the freedman would be left alone and exposed to "the withering influence of the pelting rain of wickedness." Douglass, Brown, Tubman, and Truth gave lie to that belief.[29]

Although Garrison and others often had quoted from Easton's *Thanksgiving Day Address* and several of his speeches and convention resolutions, the *Treatise* received little notice after 1840. Most notably, the name of Hosea Easton was omitted from several histories of the African American movement for freedom and equality written by members of this new black abolitionist leadership. Such works as Martin Delany's *The Condition, Elevation, Emigration, and Destiny of the Colored People of the United States* (1852), which even omits Easton from a list of the founding members of the National Convention of Free People of Color, and William Wells Brown's *The Black Man: His Antecedents, His Genius, and His Achievements* (1869), which also contains many minibiographies of colored American leaders and accomplished persons, make no mention of Easton.

The second reason for Easton's neglect is simply and prosaically timing. He died of an unnamed brief illness in July 1837, just four months after the publication of the *Treatise*. Therefore, he was not alive to debate or defend its tenets, much less to publish a modified version. Had Easton lived to revise slightly another edition of his *Treatise,* he might have left out the more excessive descriptions of slave degradation. Conversely, he might have included the experiences of some of the former slaves whom he knew personally to be individuals of high ability and noble character. In that case, he would probably have been much better remembered. As it was, Easton probably believed that it was necessary to magnify the helplessness of the enslaved population for the purpose of convincing his primary intended audience—potentially sympathetic whites—that the needed redemptive, restorative work could not be done without their help.[30]

Despite the controversial and potentially inflammatory content of the Treatise and its author's negligible legacy, Easton did not offend all, and neither did all forget him. The Reverend Amos G. Beman, a well-known black abolitionist whom Easton mentored at the Talcott St. Church, asserted in 1859, "We have had the instruction of some of the best minds of our race which the country has produced. Dr. Hosea Easton, a giant in his day, as many remember, lectured and wrote much." After the Civil War, he proclaimed, "Long will the name of Rev. Hosea Easton, whose powerful mind knew no superior among the colored people of the country, be remembered."[31] Evidently, twenty to thirty years after Easton's death, Beman still knew many people, such as the accomplished black abolitionist William C. Nell, who remembered and thought well of Easton.[32]

As a result of the neglect of Easton and his work, an important and articulate voice of opposition to racism and a significant piece of African American writing was nearly lost. Neither the man nor his work had the impact on antebellum race relations—particularly, on white American social and theological thought—it possibly might have. Yet, considering its eloquent, uncompromising, moral critique of white American society both North and South, its Afrocentric account of world history, and, finally, its prophetic call for racist Christians to repent, it most likely would not have found much popular interest. Just a glance at the full title of the *Treatise* would have offended most Americans. By 1837, a majority of Americans in the free states had made up their minds about the "intellectual character, and . . . condition of the colored people." The history of these decades too clearly proves that they did not want to hear anything about "the prejudice exercised toward them"—certainly not from any "Rev. H. Easton, a colored man."

Notes

1. William C. Nell, *Colored Patriots of the American Revolution* (Boston, 1855), 33–34; Barbara M. Van Amburg Delorey, ed., *A Copying Out of ye Olde Recordes, Beginning with ye 4th Church of Christ in Bridgewater—1740* (Brockton, MA, 1980), 418–19, 459, 572, 662; Bradford Kingman, *History of North Bridgewater, Plymouth County, Massachusetts, from its first settlement to the present time* (Boston, 1866), 95, 96. The only twentieth-century historians to mention James Easton and his church-seating protests are James Oliver Horton and Lois E. Horton, *Black Bostonians: Family Life and Community Struggle in the Antebellum North* (New York, 1979), 39; and George R. Price and James Brewer Stewart, eds., *To Heal the Scourge of Prejudice: The Life and Writings of Hosea Easton* (Amherst, MA, 1999), 3–6.

2. Nell, *Colored Patriots*, 34; Hosea Easton, *A Treatise on the Intellectual Character, and the Civil and Political Condition of the Colored People of the U. States; and the Prejudice Exercised Towards Them* (Boston, 1837), reprinted in Price and Stewart, *To Heal the Scourge of Prejudice*, 110, 111; Benjamin F. Roberts, "Our Progress in the Old Bay State," *The New Era* 31 (1870); Kingman, *History of North Bridgewater*, 379.

3. *Freedom's Journal,* April 25, 1828; David Walker, *Appeal . . . to the Coloured Citizens of the World,* ed. Charles Wiltse (1830; reprint ed., New York, 1965); Hosea Easton, *An Appeal to the Christian Public in Behalf of the Methodist Episcopal Church* (Boston, 1828).

4. Hosea Easton, *An Address: Delivered Before the Coloured Population of Providence, Rhode Island, on Thanksgiving Day, November 27, 1828, by Hosea Easton of North Bridgewater, Mass.* (Boston, 1828).

5. Ibid., 3–5.

6. Ibid., 7. Even though Easton concludes with a lengthy exortation on the importance of uplift, there is a hint in an earlier section of the speech that uplift and efforts at self-improvement may not be enough. In one instance, while dealing with the problem of lack of opportunity for higher means of employment, Easton describes the futility experienced by young people of color, like the students from the Easton's school, when they tried to apply their skills in the job market only to find closed doors. "When they have obtained their education," he observed, "they know only to feel sensible of their misery. Their minds being expanded, their perception brightened, their zeal ardent for promotion; they look around for business, they find that custom cuts them off from all advantages."

7. *The Anglo-African,* quoted in Howard Holman Bell, ed., *Minutes of the Proceedings of the National Negro Conventions, 1830–1864* (New York, 1969), 5, 6.

8. Ibid.; Richard H. Wade, "The Negro in Cincinnati, 1800–1830," *Journal of Negro History* 39 (1954): 49–51; John M. Werner, "Race Riots in the United States in the Age of Jackson, 1824–1849" (Ph.D. diss., University of Indiana, 1973). This was the second time on record in which Easton was referred to by the title of "Reverend," but there is no record of him pastoring a church until two years later, in Hartford.

9. Easton had described this ploy very accurately in a section of his *Address:* "Our ancestors were stolen property, and property which belonged to God. This is well known by our religious community; and they find that the owner is about to detect them. Now if they can slip away those stolen goods, by smuggling all those out of the country, which God would be likely to make an instrument of, in bringing them to justice, and keep the rest in ignorance; by such means, things would go on well with them, and they would appease their consciences by telling what great things they are doing for the coloured population and God's cause. But we understand better how it is. . . . They will steal the sons of Africa, bring them to America, keep them and their posterity in bondage for centuries . . . then transport them back to Africa; by which means America gets all her drudgery done at little expense. . . ." Easton, *Address,* 9–10. Garrison and other abolitionists repeated the charge. William Lloyd Garrison, *Thoughts on African Colonization* (1832; reprint ed., New York, 1968), part 2, 63–64.

10. Bell, *Minutes,* 6–7.

11. Ronald Takaki, *Iron Cages: Race and Culture in 19th-Century America* (New York, 1990) 103, 80–144; Russell Thornton, *American Indian Holocaust and Survival: A Population History since 1492* (Norman, OK, 1987), 113–18; Angie Debo, *A History of the Indians of the United States* (Norman, OK, 1970), 117–49.

12. Robert A. Warner, *New Haven Negroes: A Social History* (New Haven, CT, 1940), 50–55; Michael Kuczkowski, "One Blood: The Lost Legacy of a Radical Black Activist Who Was Ahead of His Time," *Hartford Advocate,* February 5, 1998.

13. Bell, *Minutes;* Kingman, *History of North Bridgewater,* 498; Carter G. Woodson,

Free Negro Heads of Families in the United States in 1830 (Washington, DC, 1925), 72.

14. Rev. King T. Hayes, "A Historical Profile of Fifteen Black Churches of Hartford, Connecticut" (unpublished and undated in Special Collections of the Hartford Public Library, Hartford, CT), 2–5; *Sesquicentennial Celebration of Metropolitan A. M. E. Zion Church, Hartford, Connecticut* (Hartford, CT, 1983), 3–5; Ellsworth and Marion Grant, *The City of Hartford, 1784–1984* (Hartford, CT, 1984), 60.

15. *The Emancipator,* February 17, 1835.

16. Edward Abdy, *Journal of a Residence and Tour in the United States of North America, April, 1833–October, 1834,* 3 vols. (London, UK, 1835), 3: 206–207.

17. John W. Steadman, *Scrapbooks on Hartford, Connecticut History,* 4 vols. (Collections of the Connecticut Historical Society, Hartford, CT).

18. *Hartford Courant,* June 15, 1835. No report on the fire could be found in the local papers, and the brief mentions by Easton and *The Liberator* do not state the fire's cause.

19. Easton, *A Treatise,* in Price and Stewart, *To Heal the Scourge of Prejudice,* 122, 123; *The Concord New Hampshire Observer,* reprinted in *The Liberator,* April 14, 1837; Jennie F. Copeland, "Mansfield in Other Days," *Mansfield News* (Massachusetts), March 27, 1937.

20. For a more thorough analysis of Easton's *Treatise,* see Price and Stewart, *To Heal the Scourge of Prejudice.* This book includes reprints of both the *Treatise* and Easton's 1828 *Address* as well as a biographical introduction with analysis by the editors.

21. Easton, *A Treatise,* in Price and Stewart, *To Heal the Scourge of Prejudice,* 67–82.

22. Ibid., 104–7.

23. Ibid., 107–8.

24. Ibid., 108.

25. Ibid.

26. Ibid., 119.

27. Ibid., 118–20.

28. Ibid., 83–89, 111–12, 118–20.

29. Ibid., 118; James Brewer Stewart, *Holy Warriors: The Abolitionists and American Slavery* (New York, 1996), 41–42; Charles T. Davis and Henry Louis Gates Jr., *The Slave's Narrative* (New York, 1985), xv–xvii, 319–27; David W. Blight, ed., *Narrative of the Life of Frederick Douglass, an American Slave, Written by Himself* (Boston, 1993), 2–20.

30. Easton's obituary appeared in *The Liberator,* July 14, 1837, written by the Rev. Jehiel C. Beman, an "old guard" leader from Connecticut, and father of the Rev. Amos G. Beman. For more on the Rev. Henry Drayton and the Vesey conspiracy, see Peter P. Hinks, *To Awaken My Afflicted Brethren: David Walker and the Problem of Antebellum Slave Resistance* (University Park, PA, 1997), 26–27, 38, 63, 97, 104. Ironically, Easton wrote an obituary for Henry Drayton in *Zion's Watchman,* June 2, 1837, just a little over a month before his own death. On the Easton family's emancipation, see Easton, *A Treatise,* 26; and Price and Stewart, *To Heal the Scourge,* 3, 4, 40n.

31. Amos G. Beman Scrapbooks (Beinecke Library, Yale University, New Haven, CT), vol. 2.

32. Nell, *Colored Patriots,* 34, 333–36. Several lengthy passages from Easton's *Treatise* are quoted in Nell's book. Significantly, none of the passages that Nell cites dealt with slave degradation; rather, they focused on issues of equal rights for American citizens of color, especially veterans, and the systemic denial of those rights due to white racism.

Suggested Readings

Curry, Leonard. *The Free Black in Urban America, 1800–1860.* Chicago, 1981.

Davis, David Brion. *The Problem of Slavery in the Age of Revolution, 1770–1823.* New York, 1975.

Fredrickson, George. *The Black Image in the White Mind: The Debate on Afro-American Character and Destiny, 1817–1914.* New York, 1971.

Hinks, Peter P. *To Awaken My Afflicted Brethren: David Walker and the Problem of Antebellum Slave Resistance.* University Park, PA, 1996.

Hodges, Graham R. *Slavery and Freedom in the Rural North: African Americans in Monmouth County, New Jersey, 1665–1865.* Madison, WI, 1997.

Horton, James Oliver, and Lois E. Horton. *Black Bostonians: Family Life and Community Struggle in the Antebellum North.* New York, 1979.

———. *In the Hope of Liberty: Community and Protest among Northern Free Blacks, 1700–1860.* New York, 1997.

Melish, Joanne Pope. *Disowning Slavery: Gradual Emancipation and "Race" in New England, 1780–1860.* Ithaca, NY, 1998.

Nash, Gary B. *Forging Freedom: The Formation of Philadelphia's Black Community, 1720–1840.* Cambridge, MA, 1988.

Nash, Gary B., and Jean Soderlund. *Freedom by Degrees: Emancipation in Pennsylvania and Its Aftermath.* New York, 1991.

Price, George R., and James Brewer Stewart, eds. *To Heal the Scourge of Prejudice: The Life and Writings of Hosea Easton.* Amherst, MA, 1999.

Saxton, Alexander. *The Rise and Fall of the White Republic: Class Politics and Mass Culture in Nineteenth-Century America.* London, 1990.

Takaki, Ronald. *Iron Cages: Race and Culture in 19th-Century America.* New York, 1990.

White, Shane. *Somewhat More Independent: The End of Slavery in New York City, 1770–1810.* Athens, GA, 1991.

Winch, Julie. *Philadelphia's Black Elite: Activism, Accommodation, and the Struggle for Autonomy, 1787–1848.* Philadelphia, 1988.

12

Laura Wirt Randall
A Woman's Life, 1803–1833

Anya Jabour

Women, like African and Native Americans, insisted that white Americans accept fully the political principles of liberty and egalitarianism. Yet they too suffered from restrictions—political, social, and cultural—that barred their full participation in a male-dominated society. Moreover, at roughly the same time that Indian removal and discrimination against African Americans increasingly marginalized and segregated these nonwhite groups in the late 1820s and early 1830s, white women similarly faced new, additional barriers to their claims to equality. As the family became the focal unit of American society, women were expected to devote their time and energy to the private sphere of the home, not the public arena of politics and business. Laura Wirt Randall's troubled marriage proves that freedom of choice in selecting a mate (in that open market) and the supposedly elevated status of motherhood did not necessarily translate into individual happiness. Laura's unconventional education, which was encouraged by her father, embraced a wide range of intellectual pursuits and spoke to the possibility that women might liberate themselves from a "woman's proper sphere." Unhappily, her parents also pressured Laura into a conventional and ultimately hollow marriage that more accurately reflected the "proper" role that women were to play. Her conflicted life embraced the outer limits to, and ultimate constrictions on, a woman's personal freedom in this Age of the Common Man.

Anya Jabour is an associate professor of history at the University of Montana, Missoula, where she teaches courses in U.S. women's history, American family history, and the history of the American South. She is the author of *Marriage in the Early Republic: Elizabeth and William Wirt and the Companionate Ideal* (1998) and is currently at work on a reader in U.S. family history to be published in 2003.

Y ou can be equal to any girl in . . . the United States, if you choose to be so: and why should you not strive to be so," wrote William Wirt to his daughter, Laura, when she was ten years old.[1] When Laura read these words in the early nineteenth century, she was encouraged to expand her intellectual horizons and to strive for constant self-improvement and public achievement. Only later did Laura become aware of the contradictions in her father's words. As an adult, Laura would learn that while she might strive for personal success and fulfillment, her opportunities would continue to be limited by her gender. Despite William's enthusiasm for his daughter's ability to "be equal to any girl in the United States," her life would provide an answer to his rhetorical question, why she "should not strive to be so": she was a woman in the early nineteenth-century United States.

The compelling life story of Laura Wirt Randall sheds light on the experiences of women in the early republic. Her life and writings spanned the exciting first three decades of the nineteenth century, from 1803 to 1833. In this formative era new ideas about women's education, relationships between men and women, and women's rights flourished. Women's lives and work were shaped by the rise of industrialization in the North and the entrenchment of slavery in the South. Laura, the daughter of Virginia slaveholders who lived in border cities along the Mason-Dixon Line, witnessed these changes from a unique vantage point. She felt both the new sense of possibility that northern women gained in the new nation and the stifling restrictions that southern women continued to experience in the Old South. Laura Wirt Randall's life serves to demonstrate the limited possibilities open even to a well-educated and talented woman in the new American nation.

Laura Henrietta Wirt was born in Richmond, Virginia, on September 3, 1803, the first child of Elizabeth and William Wirt. The Wirts were prominent, well-to-do members of southern society. Elizabeth was the oldest daughter of a respected Richmond merchant, Robert Gamble; William, the orphaned son of immigrant tavern-keepers, earned wealth and renown as a lawyer and author. Although comfortably well off, the Wirts were not members of the planter class; they derived the bulk of their income from William's professional work and business investments. Elizabeth supplemented the family's income by supervising the Wirts' slaves—a work force that ranged from five to ten adults—in domestic work and household production.

Like most southern parents, Elizabeth and William lavished love on their newborn. Elizabeth breast-fed Laura, and William implored his wife to send him lengthy descriptions of Laura's first words when business called him away from home. For Laura and her parents, love between parents and children was not only an end in itself but also a source of discipline. Like other parents of their generation, the Wirts expected that earning her parents' love would be Laura's chief motivation to meet their expectations. "Jewels and diamonds cannot make you happy," William reminded Laura when she was six years old, "but the love of your parents can always do it."[2]

One of the most important ways that the Wirts expected Laura to earn their love was by applying herself to her studies. Shortly after Laura's birth, William resolved to give his firstborn extraordinary advantages in education, informing his friend Dabney Carr that "if . . . her mind fulfills the promise of her face, I will spare no pains" in raising her. William was as good as his word. Like many other Americans in the new nation, Laura's father believed that educating women would enable them to participate in the democratic republic indirectly, as wise counselors to their husbands and as capable teachers of their sons. With this goal in mind, William designed an ambitious plan of education for Laura, refusing to limit his hopes because she was a girl. "I have a notion of making my daughter a classical scholar," he decided. William's plan for Laura included Latin, French, Italian, Spanish, and English grammar and composition, and he urged her to excel in all of them. William succeeded in spurring his oldest daughter to academic achievement. By the time she was six, Laura, with her mother's help, was writing letters to William assuring him that "I will try to learn very fast to please my dear Father."[3]

As she grew older, William continued to urge his daughter to earn his love by dedicating herself to intellectual improvement. "I hope to hear from your mother that you are a fine, sweet girl and are very industrious in your studies," he reminded Laura shortly before her seventh birthday, because such attention to duty "is the only way to make your parents happy and to make them love you dearly. . . ." At the same time that William urged his daughter to be "very industrious" at her lessons, he confided to his friends that despite the classical curriculum he planned for Laura—the same offered to boys who were expected to enter the professions or politics—her education was different because she was a girl. Eventually, he remarked to Carr, Laura would "enter the world"—that is, make her debut and begin a search for a suitable husband.[4]

In accordance with his assumption that Laura would enter society and marry, William made some modifications to his plan to make her a "classical scholar." He included traditional feminine accomplishments such as dancing, painting, and piano in the list of subjects he designed for Laura. He also occasionally reminded his daughter that she should avoid unfeminine pride in her intellectual accomplishments. Most importantly, William set a date for Laura to finish her studies. "Laura ought to have her education by the time she is sixteen," he reminded Elizabeth when their oldest daughter was only six; "that is little enough for all the acquirements I wish her to possess."[5] Although he was willing to postpone Laura's debut, William assumed that at seventeen Laura would leave the schoolroom to "enter the world," and that by the time she was twenty she would marry and devote herself to her husband and children. Her education would not prepare her for an alternative to marriage but would make her a better wife and mother.

The most consistent message Laura received from her parents between ages six and sixteen, however, was to strive for higher and higher levels of intellectual cultivation. William even suggested that Laura might aspire to fame as an author. He assured her that her intellectual growth would bring her the approval not only of her parents but of all she met. "Go on writing in this way, and pursue all the studies, to which you are directed, with persevering spirit," he advised, "and when you grow up, you will be the pride and ornament of your parents, and a blessing to society—and if you add to your studies, the fear and love of Heaven, you will be an ornament to the church and a blessing to the world."[6]

When Laura was fourteen, William accepted President James Monroe's invitation to serve as U.S. Attorney General, and the family moved from Richmond to Washington. As she entered her teens, Laura remained eager to continue her studies. "I am determined to study very hard after I get to Washington," she promised her father. Laura continued her schooling, including Latin, first at one of the female academies that were then appearing in cities and towns across the nation and later at home under the direction of her father and private tutors. After a bout of scarlet fever when she was sixteen, Laura went to the Virginia plantation of her aunt, Elizabeth's sister Nancy, for the summer of 1819. Nancy's husband, William H. Cabell, promised to "keep her to her books following the course [her father] shall prescribe" alongside her cousin, Louisa Elizabeth Cabell.[7]

Laura and Louisa already were well acquainted with each other because of the Wirts' habit of spending summers at the Cabell plantation. The cousins' friendship intensified during the months they spent together completing their formal schooling. Nineteenth-century women commonly formed close relationships with other women while away at school in their teens. At a time when many Americans perceived men and women as being endowed with wholly different personal qualities that suited them for their different "spheres"—the private world of the home for women and the public world of work for men—it was natural for young women to look for understanding and affection from members of their own sex. "To you, Louisa, I have always spoken my whole heart," Laura once confided to her cousin, and *you know me*."[8]

Despite the romantic and even erotic overtones that characterized female friendships in nineteenth-century America, most women found that what historians call homosocial relationships served as preparation for, rather than alternatives to, heterosexual relationships. Particularly in the South, where such friendships tended to overlap with kinship, scholars have found little evidence that female friendship offered women alternatives to conventional marriage. Nonetheless, relationships between women could pose an obstacle to marriage because these intense attachments taught women to look for more understanding and equality than was typical of nineteenth-century marriages.

It was difficult for men and women to attain the candid self-revelation and mutual affection that characterized Laura and Louisa's friendship. Despite a new ideal of love and respect within "companionate marriage," conjugal mutuality was difficult to achieve in the nineteenth-century United States. Women married at the cost of their legal identity; under common law, husbands took possession of the money their wives earned or inherited. In addition, men's experience of the world, education, wage-earning ability, and physical strength usually exceeded that of their wives. These limitations on true companionship characterized the whole nation. Southern women additionally had to contend with exaggerated age differences and the continuing popularity of the patriarchal image of the family in which a man ruled over his dependents—wife, children, and slaves. Small wonder that after parting from Louisa, Laura wrote many letters to her cousin detailing "how much I feel the want of a companion—of such a companion as you. . . . O! my dear Louisa, you cannot conceive how much I miss you!"[9]

Laura and Louisa made a solemn promise to each other to remain single. The two friends planned to found an "Old Maid's Hall" where, together with other like-minded women, they would "live and die in single blessedness." Laura vowed her own eager anticipation of life in this "Charming happy society." "Oh! Louisa, does not your heart dance at the thought of the pleasures which await our *honourable body?* Who so happy as we shall be! at our charming 'Retreat' at View Hill."[10]

Quite possibly Laura and Louisa were acquainted with literature of the time that encouraged a positive reassessment of single life for women. Whereas previous generations had considered single women to be objects of scorn, or at best pity, the postrevolutionary generations, who learned to value companionate marriage so highly, began to advance the idea that marriages that did not measure up to the exacting standards of companionate marriage—mutuality rather than male dominance—should be actively avoided. Instead of making a loveless match, antebellum writers advised, women should embrace the potential happiness and fulfillment of the single life, devoting themselves to their own intellectual or creative growth, to service to their family or community, and to reform. Laura and Louisa followed the advice of such authors when they vowed to share a life of "single blessedness" that they would devote to music making and other "refined delights," such as literature and self-improvement, and to "promot[ing] the happiness" of others.[11]

Laura was soon left to search for a life of single blessedness on her own when in 1820 Louisa decided to marry. While Laura assisted Louisa in wedding preparations, her parents made their own preparations for Laura to follow in her friend's footsteps. Although Laura planned to return quickly to Washington "because I could not spare so much time from my studies," her mother had other plans. It was time, she wrote, for Laura to *"turn in"* and acquaint herself with "the *minutia* of housekeeping." William, too, made it clear that despite Laura's education, it was time for her to learn specifically female accomplishments. "To make yourself pleasing," he admonished his daughter, was "the sweetest charm" of "your sex." An intelligent woman "may be admired," admitted William, "but she will never be beloved."[12] Laura's formal education was at an end.

Laura, who had enjoyed her studies and hoped to continue her intellectual pursuits as an adult, lamented the new responsibilities that interfered with academic work. In 1823, she complained that "the empty frivolities of the Beau Monde" made intellectual improvement impossible. Washington's season of balls and parties was antithetical to intellectual seriousness, she grumbled. Responding to her brother Robert's "uncivil observation" on her comments on literature, Laura indignantly informed him "that women have sometimes some faint glimmerings of intellect, & often a taste more nice & discriminating that that [that is, than that] of your own lordly sex . . . tho', Lord keep them! They are obliged, of necessity, to confound their wee bit of native sense with such an imbroglio of ribbons, laces, gauze tassels, &c &c &c as wd. strike Newton himself 'all of a heap.' "[13]

Laura was no more pleased with the housewifery skills that her mother attempted to teach her. When she was fifteen, Laura admitted to her grandmother that despite "Mama's insisting upon it yesterday that I must learn to ply my needle with more industry," she undertook the task "very reluctantly" and found many excuses to interrupt her progress. The next year, Laura moaned to Louisa that "I kept house today and am to do so for this week, besides mending and making my clothes!—darning stockings, and all the other disagreeable occupations that you can imagine."

Elizabeth identified the source of her daughter's discontent when she described keeping house as "the necessary, tho *un*intellectual, duties of domestic life."[14]

By the winter of 1820–21, seventeen-year-old Laura was ready for a full-fledged debut, which involved attending formal teas, balls, and parties during the capital city's winter "season." "I had no notion that Laura had in reality and bona fide *turned out,*" her brother Robert wrote in February 1821. "But I see it is the case and wish her success with all my heart:— admonishing her at the same time to be ambitious, and not to be contented with any thing less than a member of congress, or—a soldier."[15]

Robert's 1821 comments made it clear that from that point on, Laura's considerable ambitions were to be trained on a specific and limited goal: finding a good husband. William had pushed his precocious daughter to become "a classical scholar," attaining a level of education that would have prepared her, had she been a boy, to enter the professions. But as a woman in the early nineteenth-century South, there was little Laura Wirt could do with her excellent education. Although increasing numbers of women in the urban Northeast were delaying or avoiding marriage and embarking on new careers as writers and reformers, marriage was the usual destiny of women throughout the United States, and especially in the South, where the ratio of men to women was high and the defense of slavery forestalled efforts at reform.

Laura spent the next six years struggling with the conflict generated by her superior education and her limited opportunities. Trained from her childhood to exercise her mind to its fullest extent and to seek the applause of everybody she knew, Laura discovered that as a woman, the only way she could become, as her father had urged her, "the pride and ornament of your parents, and a blessing to society," was to marry and devote her life to domestic duties.[16]

Laura hesitated for six years before relinquishing her single status and her studies in favor of marriage and domestic duties. Between 1823 and 1824, she rejected three suitors: Thomas Randall, a lawyer and former army captain; Henry Middleton, a neighbor; and Mr. Lear, a family friend. On the eve of her twenty-first birthday, Laura had been out in society for nearly five years without making a match. She had many reasons to avoid marriage. The companionate ideal urged women to find true love or not to marry, and Laura had not yet met a "companion" to replace Louisa. "What put it into your head that I was in love? I assure you I am not," she wrote to Louisa in July 1824. "I do not fall in love," she maintained.[17]

Furthermore, Laura may well have had misgivings about the institution of marriage itself. Marriage in the early-nineteenth-century United States was a nearly irrevocable step that deprived women of a legal identity of their own, subjecting them to the whims of their husbands. Even women with model husbands spent most of their married lives bearing and caring for children and managing a household—activities Laura had disparaged earlier as "disagreeable occupations."

Laura also feared the dangers of childbirth and the burden of caring for sickly children as the inevitable aftermath of marriage. Heavily burdened by the onerous duties of childcare on a secluded plantation, Louisa warned Laura not to marry in 1822, causing Laura to demand "the real opinions of my friends, *pro and con,* as the lawyers say." Soon thereafter Laura had a vivid reminder of some of the possible negative consequences of marriage and childbearing when her recently married friend Ann Middleton was struck by a terminal illness just after bearing her first child. When Ann finally died, Laura was both fascinated and repulsed by the ravages the long illness had wrought on her friend. "Oh, Louisa, how fearfully was she changed by disease and death!" cried Laura. "She looked like an old woman of sixty. . . . Her once tender and snowy skin was now stretched like yellow parchment tightly over the bones, and her cheek, once brilliant with health, sunken, hollow and livid. . . . Poor, poor Ann!"[18] Knowledge of the dangers marriage and childbirth posed to women's health and happiness reinforced Laura's schoolgirl resolve to avoid marriage.

Laura's activities while she resisted her suitors' pressure for an engagement also indicated that she had not surrendered her dreams of single blessedness. In 1823, as she approached her twentieth birthday, Laura announced to Louisa that she was making it her special project to become "an exemplary domestic character." Laura's purpose was not to prepare for marriage but to investigate a possible route to respectable independence as the author of a textbook on household management. "I have made a great many discoveries in the culinary art," she boasted in July 1824, "and intend some time hence to put forth a Book on the subject."[19]

Not surprisingly, considering Laura's previous negative judgments on housekeeping, her interest soon waned. Her next project, teaching her younger sisters, seemed more promising. Laura exhibited "a great deal of enthusiasm . . . and most surprising perseverance" for her latest project, which offered both intellectual stimulation and a respite from the pressure to marry.[20]

Soon, however, Elizabeth and William Wirt became concerned about their daughter's disposition to "rusticate at home." Considering twenty-two-year-old Laura's "time of life," they worried in 1825 that they were not doing "our duty as parents in relation to our daughter"—that is, the duty to assist her in finding a husband. With eight other living children, William was anxious to ensure his children a secure future. Because there were few opportunities for respectable and remunerative employment for women, William believed that his daughter would need a "natural protector"—a husband.[21] Correctly perceiving Laura's activities as schoolmistress as an obstacle to her marriage, the Wirts began to lay plans to reenter their reluctant daughter into society.

While Laura traveled with her father and her cousin Emma to the Virginia Springs in August and September, Elizabeth took steps to ensure that her oldest daughter would not return to her previous occupation as spinster schoolmistress. Over Laura's protests, she enrolled all the younger girls at a local school. Although she placated Laura by assuring her they could be withdrawn on Laura's return, they never were. She also urged Thomas Randall—now called Colonel Randall after a year's appointment as Special Minister to the West Indies—to resume his attentions to Laura upon her return to Washington. William also encouraged the relationship, even suggesting that Elizabeth hint to Randall "that Laura without knowing it, herself, is partial to him." "The truth is," William felt, "that if she does not love him she loves no body."[22]

William may have been correct in his assessment of his daughter's feelings for Randall. By the spring of 1826, Laura was corresponding with him regularly during a stay with her grandmother in Richmond. But when she returned to Washington in June and Randall proposed a second time, after "a long and painful" conversation Laura rejected him and requested him to cease his visits for the time being, apparently giving as her reason Randall's lack of a secure income. She revealed other motives in a letter to her friend Louisa immediately after rejecting Randall. Her own character, Laura stated, was not suited to the demanding but tedious role of housewife. "Monotony kills me as dead as a door nail," she pronounced. "It will never do for me to be married."[23]

Despite her rejection of his proposal, after a while Laura requested Randall to call on her, which he did almost daily. Laura's contradictory behavior suggests that she had at last fallen in love but that her misgivings about marriage persisted. Apparently Laura never told her parents she did not wish to marry, and they grew impatient with their "coquet[t]ish" and "fickle" daughter's inability to "be sure of her affections and of her own fixed resolve" in the affair.[24]

Meanwhile, Randall continued to visit every evening, until by late

June the whole town was buzzing with the rumor that Laura was engaged. Under these circumstances, her parents' anxiety and impatience grew still more. "I told her to day that she was sealing her own doom, beyond her own control," Elizabeth worried to her husband, "and whether for better or for worse she would be obliged to marry the man that she thus palpably encouraged[.]" If it was not already too late for "retreat," Elizabeth admonished Laura, she must either cease seeing Randall immediately, or else "marry at once and take all the consequences." Concerned with the danger posed to their own and their daughter's reputation by the increasingly unfriendly gossip about Laura's conduct, Elizabeth and William pressured their daughter to make an engagement. "I am strongly inclined to doubt whether it wd. not be better for her to marry at once—than to go on as she is going," concluded William.[25]

For Laura, who had been raised to value her parents' approval and social acceptance so highly, the pressure to marry must have been agonizing. She searched desperately for convincing explanations for her "coquettish" behavior and for an escape from social and parental pressure to marry Randall. In late July and August, Laura accompanied her father and two of her sisters to the Virginia Springs. She told her father that she was unwilling to make a decision about Randall until she had news of his success or failure in his bid for a clerkship at the Supreme Court. Privately, Laura told her mother that she hoped that her sojourn in Virginia would imply to the Washington gossip mill that she herself wished to marry Randall but was forbidden by her parents. Such a rumor would have had the double advantage of placing the censure for a late rejection on Laura's parents, rather than herself, as well as offering her a socially acceptable reason for refusing any future suitors and retiring into confirmed singlehood.

Recognizing Laura's plan as detrimental to their own reputations, Elizabeth and William responded with still more displeasure with their wayward daughter. Because of the difficulty of achieving economic or social security as a single woman, Laura would have needed the support of fellow single women or her family, or both, to realize her dreams of single blessedness. But Laura's closest female friend had married, and Laura's own parents, with the best of intentions, frustrated their daughter's attempt to find a niche as a spinster teacher in their home. They withdrew the rewards of parental approval that had been so effective in directing Laura toward academic achievement, and they refused to aid her in her final attempt to find a socially sanctioned reason to refuse Randall. Marriage was now the only way for Laura to win her parents' favor and society's blessing. With her own feelings and her parents' obvious preferences both pushing her toward Randall, Laura was soon exchanging messages with him through her sister Catharine.

Although no record exists of another formal proposal, by mid-August the entire family, including Laura, assumed that an engagement had taken place. William was soon consulting Elizabeth on how best to ensure their daughter's financial security in her marriage to a poorly paid lawyer. He proposed to Elizabeth that they assist the newlyweds by giving them land and slaves to begin a plantation in the newly opened Florida territory, as well as to use his influence to obtain a position for Randall as one of the three judges of the Florida supreme court. "I have never said a word to Laura upon the subject—and dont know how she wd. take it," he added as an afterthought.[26]

Laura reacted to the news with dread, fearing that the move would mean that she would never again see her friend Louisa or the rest of her family. "I cannot endure the thought! The very prospect breaks my heart!" she exclaimed in early October. "My Uncles John and Robert [Gamble] contemplate a removal thither very soon; and they, as well as Father . . . are of opinion that it would be the best thing Col. Randall could do, at present, to remove thither also, and acquire that wealth which there seems to be no hope of in this part of the world—and without which they have taken up a notion that there is no existing for me. If it is so, they must know me better than I know myself. I think I could be very happy without it."[27]

Laura found that her own preferences had little weight against her male relatives' eagerness to achieve the fabled wealth of the frontier, and she allowed new love to blur the harsh outlines of this inequity of power. The compulsion of love that had earlier pushed Laura to achieve now dictated surrender of her hopes to her husband's wishes. "It would go very hard with me to be transplanted to this new country," she confided to Louisa, "and there is but one man under the moon for whose sake I would consent to it. I should be glad, however, that he would not make so cruel a proof of my affection." Laura concluded, however, with the thought that her love for her husband demanded the sacrifice. "If it is so much for his interest as it is thought, I ought to consent, I suppose, without murmering [*sic*]."[28]

The following fall, on August 21, 1827, Laura Wirt and Thomas Randall said their wedding vows before a group of their relatives. Laura's sister Catharine described the wedding as a happy and lavish affair, with six bridesmaids and six groomsmen in attendance. Laura's uncle, Robert Gamble, made a more sobering remark. "The Judge is obliged to hold court at Tallahassee in October on the first Monday," he observed, "which will compel him to set out early next month—Laura goes with him[.]" By the fall of 1827, it was clear that Laura's new husband would indeed "make so cruel a proof of [her] affection." Despite her resolve to submit to her husband's wishes "without murmuring," Laura could not help confiding her trials to Louisa. With her husband ill upon arrival in their new home, where Laura found "a destitution of everything like comfort," she admitted, "I am disappointed in everything."[29]

One of Laura's disappointments was her relationship with Thomas Randall, whom she still referred to as "my husband" or "Colonel Randall," indicating she had not achieved the intimacy she had hoped for with her husband, who had "lost" the "charms" he had displayed while courting Laura. "I never was less happy in my life than the two first months of my marriage," Laura admitted to Louisa. Rather than attribute her unhappiness to the circumstances of nineteenth-century marriage or to her husband's refusal to exhibit the proper spirit of mutuality, Laura concluded that her hopes of wedded bliss had been mere "charming illusions." She would "learn to be happy under the change of circumstances," she told Louisa, by lowering her expectations and devoting herself to her duties as a wife and mother.[30]

Disappointed in her hopes of a marriage in which romantic love would overcome all the obstacles to true companionship between husbands and wives, Laura also found that her earlier fears that marriage would mean a limited and arduous life of housekeeping and childcare were correct. The "regular and unvarying routine" of housekeeping was interspersed only with illness and childbirth. In 1827 or 1828, Laura Wirt Randall suffered a miscarriage. Still weak from that miscarriage, Laura bore her first child, Elizabeth, in the summer of 1828; the next summer, in *"perilously delicate"* health, she took opium to avoid a second miscarriage while she awaited the birth of her second child, Kate. By 1831, Laura had borne yet a third child, named Agnes. Laura's letters to Louisa after her marriage suggested that she was both physically exhausted and emotionally despondent. "The cares of maternity, and of housekeeping fall very heavily upon your humble servant, and truth to say I am almost as tired of one as of the other. Three babies in less than three years are enough to make one tired of babies, I think: at least, so I generally say when my feeble health makes me feel the toil of nursing and the loss of rest with peculiar heaviness."[31]

Despite her weariness, Laura took joy in her children as well. She wrote enthusiastically of her three daughters' "striking" beauty and early signs of "intellectual" capacity. Yet she concluded with the thought that her children's demands were greater than she could meet: "I am blessed in . . . my children, poor little *picanines.* Tho' they *are* so troublesome, and I feel as if I were ungrateful in repining at the only thing really hard in my lot. The rapid increase of their number. If I could only enjoy health and strength proportioned to the demands they make on me, I should have no right to complain even of that. But they decline, as is usually the case, in an inverse ratio to the increase of my family," Laura lamented.[32]

Laura's comments on motherhood suggested the limited gains that nineteenth-century women made in controlling their fertility. Although white women's birthrates nationwide dropped dramatically in the nineteenth century, contraception methods were unreliable. Consequently, women could control their childbearing only with their husbands' cooperation. Thomas Randall apparently was unwilling to suspend sexual activity in order to preserve his wife's increasingly fragile health.

It was an uphill struggle for Laura to maintain her marriage as well as to cope with housekeeping and mothering. "I am now," remarked Laura in 1831, "as my husband declares 'the most miserable, poor, good-for-nothing woman he ever saw,' which compliment comes with an ill grace from him at all events." In the face of her own poor health and her husband's lack of appreciation for her efforts to meet the demands of housekeeping and motherhood, Laura struggled for optimism. "I am blessed in my husband and children," she insisted.[33] Laura did not write to Louisa again. She died on December 17, 1833, after giving birth to yet a fourth child, another daughter, who died soon afterward.

Laura Wirt Randall's brief life illustrates the limited nature of women's gains under the conditions of legal and economic inequality that prevailed in the early American republic. Laura's life was shaped by contradictions. Trained by her father to constantly expand her intellectual horizons in classical study, she devoted her adult years to childbearing and to what her mother called "the unintellectual duties of domestic life." Marrying at a time when romantic love and "companionate marriage" was the ideal, she found herself in a relationship characterized by emotional distance. Although as a child Laura strove to be "equal to any girl in the United States," as an adult, she learned that all her efforts could only succeed in making her a "miserable, poor, good-for-nothing woman." Thus, Laura's life suggests both the changes and the continuities in American women's lives in the early American republic.

Notes

1. William Wirt to Laura Wirt, October 28, 1813, William Wirt Papers, Maryland Historical Society, Baltimore, MD.

2. William Wirt to Laura Wirt, July 14, 1810, ibid.

3. William Wirt to Dabney Carr, June 8, 1804, William Wirt Letters to Dabney Carr, 1803–1831, Library of Virginia, Richmond, VA; William Wirt to Dabney Carr, December 21, 1809, William Wirt Papers; Laura Wirt to William Wirt, June 15, 1810, ibid.

4. William Wirt to Laura Wirt, July 14, 1810, William Wirt Papers; William Wirt to Dabney Carr, December 21, 1809, ibid.

5. William Wirt to Elizabeth Wirt, September 11, 1809, ibid.

6. William Wirt to Laura Wirt, October 21, 1813, ibid.

7. Laura Wirt to William Wirt, November 24, 1817, ibid.; William Wirt to Elizabeth Wirt, ca. April/May 1819, ibid.; Laura Wirt Randall Papers, preface, Virginia Historical Society, Richmond, VA.

8. Laura Wirt Randall to Louisa Cabell Carrington, March 26, 1828, Laura Wirt Randall Papers.

9. Laura Wirt to Louisa Cabell Carrington, September 12, 1822, ibid.

10. Laura Wirt to Louisa Cabell, November 4, 1819, ibid.

11. Ibid.

12. Laura Wirt to Elizabeth Wirt, April 29, 1820, ibid.; Elizabeth Wirt to Laura Wirt, May 26, 1820, William Wirt Papers; William Wirt to Laura Wirt, May 23, 1820, ibid.

13. Laura Wirt to Robert Wirt, January 20, 1823, ibid.; Laura Wirt to Robert Wirt, January 12, 1823, ibid.

14. Laura Wirt to Catharine Gamble, May 24, 1818, ibid.; Laura Wirt to Louisa Cabell, May 3, 1819, Laura Wirt Randall Papers; Elizabeth Wirt to William Wirt, November 22, 1824, William Wirt Papers.

15. Robert Wirt to Elizabeth Wirt, February 26, 1821, William Wirt Papers.

16. William Wirt to Laura Wirt, October 21, 1813, ibid.; Elizabeth Wirt to William Wirt, November 22, 1824, ibid.

17. Laura Wirt to Louisa Cabell Carrington, July 10, 1824, Laura Wirt Randall Papers.

18. Laura Wirt to Louisa Cabell Carrington, April 27, 1822, ibid.; Laura Wirt to Louisa Cabell Carrington, November 27, 1822, ibid.

19. Laura Wirt to Louisa Cabell Carrington, February 14, 1823, ibid.; Laura Wirt to Louisa Cabell Carrington, July 10, 1824, ibid.

20. Elizabeth Wirt to William Wirt, May 6, 1825, William Wirt Papers.

21. William Wirt to Elizabeth Wirt, May 20, 1825, ibid.; William Wirt to Dabney Carr, November 17, 1828, William Wirt Letters to Dabney Carr.

22. William Wirt to Elizabeth Wirt, August 12, 1825, William Wirt Papers.

23. Elizabeth Wirt to William Wirt, June 11, 12, 13, 1826, ibid.; Laura Wirt to Louisa Cabell Carrington, June 13, 1826, Laura Wirt Randall Papers. On the couple's correspondence, which has not been preserved, see Elizabeth Wirt to William Wirt, May 23, 1826, Catharine Wirt's postscript to Rosa Wirt to William Wirt, [May 1826], all in William Wirt Papers.

24. William Wirt to Elizabeth Wirt, June 13, 1826, William Wirt Papers; Elizabeth Wirt to William Wirt, June 14, 1826, ibid.

25. Elizabeth Wirt to William Wirt, June 24, 1826, ibid.; William Wirt to Elizabeth Wirt, June 30, 1826, ibid.

26. William Wirt to Elizabeth Wirt, August 31–September 1, 1826, ibid.

27. Laura Wirt to Louisa Cabell Carrington, October 8, 1826, Laura Wirt Randall Papers.

28. Ibid.

29. Catharine Wirt to Emma Cabell, September 8, 1827, Carrington Family Papers, Virginia Historical Society; Robert Gamble (1781–1867) to James Breckinridge, August 16, 1827, Breckinridge Family Papers, Virginia Historical Society; Laura Wirt Randall to Louisa Cabell Carrington, n.d., ca. 1827–1828, Laura Wirt Randall Papers.

30. Laura Wirt Randall to Louisa Cabell Carrington, March 6, 1828, Laura Wirt Randall Papers.

31. Laura Wirt Randall to Louisa Cabell Carrington, March 6, 1828, ibid.; Laura Wirt Randall to Louisa Cabell Carrington, May 27, 1829, ibid.; Laura Wirt Randall to Louisa Cabell Carrington, May 23, 1831, ibid.

32. Laura Wirt Randall to Louisa Cabell Carrington, May 23, 1831, ibid.

33. Ibid.

Suggested Readings

Bleser, Carol, ed. *In Joy and in Sorrow: Women, Family, and Marriage in the Victorian South, 1830–1900*. New York and Oxford, 1991.

Cashin, Joan E. *A Family Venture: Men and Women on the Southern Frontier*. New York, Oxford, 1991.

———. " 'Decidedly Opposed to the Union': Women's Culture, Marriage, and Politics in Antebellum South Carolina." *Georgia Historical Quarterly* 78 (1994): 735–59.

Censer, Jane Turner. *North Carolina Planters and Their Children, 1800–1860*. Baton Rouge, LA, 1984.

Chambers-Schiller, Lee Virginia. *Liberty, a Better Husband: Single Women in America: The Generations of 1780–1840*. New Haven, CT, 1984.

Clinton, Catherine. *The Plantation Mistress: Woman's World in the Old South*. New York, 1982.

Cott, Nancy F. *The Bonds of Womanhood: "Woman's Sphere" in New England, 1780–1835*. New Haven, CT, 1977.

Farnham, Christie Anne. *The Education of the Southern Belle: Higher Education and Student Socialization in the Antebellum South*. New York, 1994.

Fox-Genovese, Elizabeth. *Within the Plantation Household: Black and White Women in the Old South*. Chapel Hill, NC, 1988.

Jabour, Anya. *Marriage in the Early Republic: Elizabeth and William Wirt and the Companionate Ideal*. Baltimore, MD, 1998.

Kerber, Linda K. *Women of the Republic: Intellect and Ideology in Revolutionary America*. Chapel Hill, NC, 1980.

Lebsock, Suzanne D. *The Free Women of Petersburg: Status and Culture in a Southern Town, 1784–1860*. New York, 1984.

Lewis, Jan. *The Pursuit of Happiness: Family and Values in Jefferson's Virginia.* Cambridge, MA, 1983.

Lewis, Jan, and Kenneth Lockridge. " 'Sally Has Been Sick': Pregnancy and Family Limitation among Virginia Gentry Women, 1780–1830." *Journal of Social History* 22 (1988): 5–19.

McMillen, Sally G. *Motherhood in the Old South: Pregnancy, Childbirth, and Infant Rearing.* Baton Rouge, LA, 1990.

Norton, Mary Beth. *Liberty's Daughters: The Revolutionary Experience of American Women, 1750–1800.* Boston, 1980.

O'Brien, Michael, ed. *An Evening When Alone: Four Journals of Single Women in the South, 1827–67.* Charlottesville, VA, 1993.

Scott, Anne Firor. *The Southern Lady: From Pedestal to Politics, 1830–1930.* Chicago, 1970.

Smith, Daniel Scott. "Family Limitation, Sexual Control, and Domestic Feminism in Victorian America." In *A Heritage of Her Own: Toward a New Social History of American Women,* edited by Nancy F. Cott and Elizabeth H. Pleck, 222–45. New York, 1979.

Smith-Rosenberg, Carroll. "The Female World of Love and Ritual: Relations between Women in Nineteenth-Century America." In Carroll Smith-Rosenberg, *Disorderly Conduct: Visions of Gender in Victorian America,* 53–76. New York, 1985.

Stowe, Steven M. "Intimacy in the Planter Class Culture." *Psychohistory Review* 10 (1982): 141–64.

———. " 'The Thing, Not Its Vision': A Woman's Courtship and Her Sphere in the Southern Planter Class." *Feminist Studies* 9 (1983): 113–30.

Wishy, Bernard. *The Child and the Republic: The Dawn of American Child Nurture.* Philadelphia, 1968.

13

Caroline Healey Dall
Transcendentalist Activist

Helen Deese

Caroline Healey Dall's experience reminds us that even though law and custom circumscribed women's potential and opportunity, the nineteenth century was a time of ferment in women's lives and in their relations with men and the larger community. Well-educated and keenly intelligent, Dall seemed destined to live the life of the mind, although she could not have predicted precisely the course that life would take. An inappropriate marriage left her essentially a single parent, and she was thus forced to earn her own way. She did so by becoming a public intellectual. She taught, lectured, and wrote articles and books. But she directed this work largely toward an ideological purpose: the liberation of women from the constraints society imposed upon them. Although she never became a leader in the women's rights movement in an organizational sense, she made her mark through the formulation of ideas. Much of her work and argumentation have a modern ring, and in some ways Dall resonates more with modern feminists than with her contemporaries.

Helen Deese is professor emerita at Tennessee Technological University in Cookeville. She has published *Jones Very: The Complete Poems* (1993) and articles on the Transcendentalists. She is currently preparing a three-volume edition of the journals of Caroline Healey Dall, to be published by the Massachusetts Historical Society.

Caroline Healey Dall (1822–1912) was not an ordinary woman. Only the fickleness of human fame and the vagaries of history enable us to treat her as such, for certainly the name of this nineteenth-century American reformer has been largely forgotten. Yet in her day she made her mark as a pioneer, playing a leading role in the women's movement in its early decades, a role that even recent historians of the movement have overlooked. Caroline Dall was, as far as she knew or as can be confirmed, the first woman to preach in Unitarian pulpits. The first Boston woman to give public lectures in that city, she was a founder and longtime officer of the American Social Science Association. Simultaneously, she lived out

Helen Deese is grateful to the Massachusetts Historical Society for permission to quote from the Dall Papers and to Tennessee Technological University for support for this project.

a poignant and in some senses tragic personal life. Her story is instructive as a revelation of some of the limits and strictures common to a woman of her time and place, even one so extraordinarily talented and educated as Caroline Dall.

Caroline Wells Healey was born to wealth and privilege in Boston, but the wealth was new and, as it turned out, unstable, and the privilege distinctly narrowed by her gender. Mark Healey, a self-made East India merchant and investor, had risen to the presidency of the Merchants' Bank of Boston by the time his daughter Caroline was a young woman. She was the oldest of eight children to survive infancy. Lacking formal education himself, Mark Healey nevertheless valued it highly and provided an excellent private education for his daughter through governesses, tutors, and private schools. He also demanded and expected great things of her; she was "bred and brought up," she later wrote, to be a literary woman. Before Caroline was ten, father and daughter were spending the evenings discussing literary, political, religious, and philosophical questions. By the time Caroline was thirteen, she had begun her attempt to fulfill his expectations by writing novels, publishing translations, and contributing short homilies to the *Christian Register*, a Boston Unitarian weekly.

Caroline's hunger for the love and approval of both her parents, and her perceived failure at achieving either, is a constant theme of her teenage journals. Her extraordinary relationship with her father came at the expense of a close bond with her mother, Caroline Foster Healey, who (almost constantly involved with childbearing) suffered depression and even in her well moments saw little use in her daughter's literary efforts. Not surprisingly, the daughter identified with her father rather than her mother. However, Caroline, as the focus of her father's attention, had to struggle to fulfill his expectations. Even her precocious writing activities did not satisfy him. He particularly disapproved of the increasingly religious tenor of her work: "I had become devotional—he wished me—to become *literary*—He never said it—but I could see it."[1]

Caroline Healey's formal schooling was cut off at age fifteen. Though such an abbreviated education was not unusual for daughters even of the most aristocratic families, Caroline was surprised and bitterly disappointed to be removed from school. If Caroline had been male, there is little doubt that she would have attended Harvard (as did her only brother to reach adulthood) and that she would have become a minister. As it was, she had to satisfy herself with being a regular observer at Harvard exhibitions, class days, and commencement exercises, and with engaging in discussions of theological questions and practical religion with the young ministerial students who were her colleagues in church-sponsored classes. The likeliest explanation for her curtailed formal education (in addition to her being female) is the beginning of a serious financial crisis for Mark Healey, who was eventually forced into bankruptcy in the aftermath of the panic of 1837. At first unaware of her father's precarious situation, Caroline continued her studies on her own and was intensely engaged in teaching and charitable activities associated with Boston's fashionable West Church, the Unitarian church that her family attended, and with missions to children in poor neighborhoods.

Dall's early association with and her education by the Transcendentalists further set her life's course on a track of idealism and self-reliance, providing her with nontraditional role models and introducing her to the world of organized reform of the Boston abolitionists. Transcendentalism, an intellectual movement that involved a number of the most distinguished Boston-area writers, thinkers, and reformers from the 1830s to the 1850s (including among others Ralph Waldo Emerson, Henry David Thoreau, Margaret Fuller, A. Bronson Alcott, Theodore Parker, and Elizabeth Palmer Peabody), held that human beings are essentially good and can find truth through their own intuition, a truth transcending that which can be learned through the senses. At the age of eighteen, Caroline Healey came under the influence of one member of this circle, the remarkable Bostonian Elizabeth Palmer Peabody. Scholar, critic, educator, and businesswoman, Peabody, who was twice Healey's age, had just opened a bookstore that became a center for Unitarian and Transcendentalist writers and thinkers. Healey was awed by the foreign publications that Peabody carried and even more by the character of the proprietor herself. She was scholarly, enthusiastic, and a more than willing mentor to Healey. Although for several years Healey had been sitting in various public halls and Unitarian churches listening to lectures and sermons by male Transcendentalists, it was Peabody who provided her entrée into their circle. In 1841, Peabody recruited Healey for a series of conversations directed by Margaret Fuller, who four years later published the groundbreaking *Woman in the Nineteenth Century*. This group was heady company indeed for an eighteen year old; Ralph Waldo Emerson was among the distinguished participants. Despite Healey's sense that Fuller did not like her, she always considered this a key experience of her life, and Fuller her most important role model. At the same time that she attended Fuller's conversations, Healey was absorbing the preaching of the iconoclastic Transcendentalist minister Theodore Parker, whose radical theology she found unsettling but ultimately convincing. Never an uncritical disciple, she wrote Parker frankly about her objections to his use of what she considered shock tactics. He responded to her criticism without condescension, as if she were an equal. Parker became another significant mentor of Healey, particularly in his commitment to social reform.

When Caroline Healey was nineteen, she met and fell in love with Samuel Foster Haven, a widower sixteen years her senior. A noted scholar, Haven was librarian at the American Antiquarian Society in Worcester, Massachusetts. The budding relationship foundered, however, when, with most unfortunate timing, Mark Healey's bankruptcy occurred. In order to contribute to the family income, specifically to pay for her younger sisters' education, Caroline looked for work. She found a suitable position as vice principal of the exclusive Miss English's School for Young Ladies in Georgetown (District of Columbia). There, in exile from family, friends, and church, worried about her father, heart-broken at Samuel Haven's silence, she was vulnerable to the attentions of a visiting young Unitarian minister, Charles Henry Appleton Dall. Dall ministered to the poor in Baltimore and must have seen in Caroline, who already had a long history of charitable activities in Boston, the perfect helpmate. After having been in each other's company for only a few days and carrying on a correspondence for a few weeks, they became engaged. A year later they were married and settled in Baltimore.

Charles Dall's American pastorates, however, were all to be notably brief. Within a year, with Caroline pregnant, the couple moved in with her parents in Boston and Charles did "supply" preaching in the area. After the birth of William Healey Dall in 1844 they moved to Portsmouth, New Hampshire, where Charles was again involved in a short-lived ministry-at-large. After another period of filling in at vacant pulpits, Charles accepted a pastorate in the rural town of Needham, ten miles from Boston, in 1847. Here Caroline gave birth to a stillborn child and then to a daughter, Sarah Keene Dall, in 1849. After three years in Needham, Charles was once again forced to move, this time accepting a position in Toronto. Caroline and the children followed the next spring.

After their move to Toronto, Caroline was desperately homesick, as the city was at that time a far cry from the cultured mecca of Boston. The Dalls scarcely had enough to live on, and Caroline's father, in response to her appeal, agreed to help only on the condition that she give up all anti-slavery activities. For some time, Caroline had been associated with the Garrisonian abolitionists, and in Canada she helped distribute aid to fugitive slaves from the States. Unhesitatingly, she refused to accede to her father's demand. As the months passed, she became happier in Toronto, making friends and attracting the intellectual elite of the city. She also developed a deep affection for a young man in her husband's congregation who eventually boarded in their household. To John Patton, an English china importer with a scholarly penchant, Caroline Dall's education and her association with the luminaries of Boston made her unlike any woman he had known. He was fascinated and devoted, and she gratefully received such unaccustomed adulation. Simultaneously, the Dalls' marital relationship began to cool. The first ten years of their marriage had been a struggle with poverty and Charles's limited success. Yet they were for the most part happy, Caroline devoted to domestic duties and child care and supportive of her husband. Now, Charles came to resent Caroline's strength and she to resent his weakness. In the wake of a serious illness that Caroline described as "brain fever," Charles suffered an apparent emotional breakdown and became hostile to his wife. There was a reconciliation, but Charles was forced to resign his pastorate, move the family back to the Boston area, and once more look for work. He finally managed to solve several problems at once, though his solution created a new set of problems for Caroline: he decided, without asking the counsel of his wife or inviting her or his children to accompany him, to become a missionary to Calcutta. For the next thirty-one years Charles lived there, returning home at approximately five-year intervals.

Suddenly, at age thirty-two and with children aged five and nine, Caroline Dall found herself adrift in a sea with few markers. She faced an economic and vocational crisis, to say nothing of the devastating personal implications of Charles's leaving. She was still a wife, but she could hardly count on the moral and emotional support of a husband. Her sense of duty and loyalty made her determined to remain a wife, even a supportive one, but she never got over her sense of having been abandoned by her husband. The portion of her husband's salary that was directed to her was insufficient. It was only with the greatest difficulty that Caroline Dall, although a woman of superior gifts, could translate her talents into economic rewards. Over the next twenty-three years (until the death of her father, when her financial situation was substantially improved) she supplemented her meager income by taking in boarders, teaching private classes, giving public lectures, and writing. She published literary criticism, children's fiction, biography, personal reminiscence, and religious and reform works. These strategies were generally more successful in helping Dall to establish a new identity than in meeting the financial needs of the family. There was periodic and often humiliating recourse to her father's sometimes generous, sometimes grudging, help. Nevertheless, as the years passed, despite her resentment that Charles seemed to be more dedicated to Hindu children than to his own, Caroline came to the point that she did not want him home. Difficult as her life was, it would in all likelihood have been much more frustrating and the forging of her own identity much more problematic if Charles Dall had stayed at home and played the traditional role of head of the household. His few visits proved traumatic for them both and must have caused Caroline privately to be thankful for his absences, in which she had managed to find meaningful work, a certain amount of fame, and a sense of herself. Thus, there was a certain freedom that she gleaned from her nontraditional marital arrangement.

Nevertheless, Caroline Dall's freedom was fraught with perils. She was after all a product of Brahmin Boston, and she, like the society that had shaped her, placed a high premium on respectability. She defined herself to a large degree by her religion and her role as mother, thus abhorring any hint of scandal. Her dilemma went far beyond the fact that she was not free to follow her heart and marry the man with whom she was doubtlessly in love. As a woman who took to the pulpit and the lecture platform and spoke in revolutionary terms of women's rights—and who did not live with her husband—she invited association in the popular mind with advocates of free love. As a matter of fact, Dall's radicalism never extended as far as the overhaul of the marital relationship, and she held to conventionally moral positions on sexual matters. Predictably, she did attract personal innuendo, most notably in the Orthodox religious paper *Boston Recorder*. Even her old mentor, Elizabeth Peabody, took exception to the frankness of Dall's lectures, writing to her that she would not wish to be in the audience in the company of a gentleman. Dall's unconventional marriage, combined with her advanced position on the woman question and with her public role (a flagrant breaching of the traditional woman's sphere), made vulnerable her equally prized roles as mother, church member, and lady.

Dall had begun her engagement with the woman question several years before Charles Dall's departure. In 1849 the *Liberator* published her first article on the topic. In the mid-1850s she wrote for and helped edit (with Paulina Wright Davis) the women's rights newspaper *Una*, probably the first such publication in the country. After Charles's departure for India her involvement in the movement intensified. She was active in a number of early women's conventions, including the Boston convention of 1855, over which she presided. Three years later she delivered a landmark address advocating woman suffrage before a committee of the Massachusetts state legislature, and in 1859, Dall spoke along with Susan B.

Anthony and other leading reformers at the Women's Rights Convention, in New York City. In the late 1850s and early 1860s she took her message to the lecture platform, repeatedly delivering four different formal series of lectures in Boston and surrounding areas.

As a public lecturer in mid-nineteenth-century New England, Dall subjected herself to scrutiny and criticism of not just her oratorical skills and the style and substance of her lectures but also her appearance, dress, marital status, and lifestyle. On one occasion she was attacked for being conceited and presuming, for thinking she knew more than anyone else, and above all for wearing a dress that was deemed too short. After a published attack on her character, the committee sponsoring her next lecture asked for several items of documentation to allay their qualms: a recent letter from her husband to prove that they had never been separated; a volume of the works of Dr. William Ellery Channing, a revered Unitarian clergyman, to establish that someone else respectable thought highly of Mary Wollstonecraft (the British women's rights advocate); and the lecture itself to be read in advance by the committee to ensure that it did not advocate free love. Such demeaning treatment went with the territory for a woman in Dall's situation. Other less personal challenges she took as opportunities: she made her own arrangements for advertising her lectures, printing tickets, and hiring her lecture hall, although she had, she noted, male friends who would have been glad to take care of these business matters. She insisted on performing such tasks herself because she wished, as she said, "to make all business thoroughfares comfortable for women."[2]

Dall's use of the lecture platform to advocate women's rights met with a mixed reception. Most reviews were favorable, but many of them were written by friends. Her audiences varied from one thousand in East Boston to only five in Boston itself on a January night in which she described the city as having its worst weather within memory. For Dall, lecturing was not really a money-making proposition. Though she does record occasions in which she took in more than twice as much money as had been promised, more typical was her experience at the end of four weekly lectures in Boston: Dall totaled up her accounts to discover that she had just about broken even. It was fortunate that Dall's primary motivation was always the cause rather than the financial reward. When someone asked her whether she would give up lecturing if her father would wholly support her, she quickly answered no; she had done it long enough to believe that she had a God-given talent for it and that her message would do the world good. She also in time thrilled to the spectacle of the "excited human faces" of her audience turned toward her, "all wrought up—all with kindled eyes."[3]

With a view to disseminating her message more widely, Dall turned her lectures into publications: *Woman's Right to Labor* (1860), which won the Hovey Prize, endowed by a Boston philanthropist to support reform causes; *Woman's Rights under the Law* (1861); and her capstone work (its publication delayed by the self-imposed moratorium on the women's movement during the Civil War), *The College, the Market, and the Court: or, Woman's Relation to Education, Labor, and Law* (1867). This last publication incorporated the material in the two earlier titles with her lectures on education. In all these works, Dall's approach was closely reasoned and logical, her careful documentation of women's oppression supporting an intellectual appeal for equality. It was an appeal that relied on moral suasion, but moral suasion buttressed by hard facts. Dall's research into women's wages, her surveys of opportunities in higher education open to women, her reports on her own visits to such schools as Oberlin, Vassar, and Antioch, and her careful examination of women's property rights and other legal positions differentiated her from earlier reformers or those who were contemporaneous with her work. Dall's method looked forward to the "scientific" approach that came to characterize reform movements in the latter part of the century.

In her writings, Dall articulated a basic theoretical foundation for the women's movement in America (expressed thus in the *Liberator*: "We believe that no faculty has ever been developed in any man, which has not been, or might not be, equally developed in some woman, and we believe such development intended by God"); she then urged specific applications of the theory for contemporary society. In effect, Dall took Margaret Fuller's basic premise that a woman should be able to develop her own nature, whatever that nature might be, and made it practicable in antebellum and postbellum America. Whereas by the time of the publication of *The College, the Market, and the Court*, Susan B. Anthony, for example, primarily focused her efforts on suffrage, Dall recognized that there were also major and equally crucial battles to be fought in the marketplace and educational arena. Her fundamental critique of women's economic role anticipates the work of such later writers as Charlotte Perkins Gilman. Indeed, Dall's perspective is remarkably modern. She observed that history, largely written by men who view women as inferior, simply reflects and validates male prejudices. On the economic front, she argued that women's labor should be valued at the same rate as men's. She sympathetically portrayed the lot of prostitutes, whose only choices often were, in her words,

"death or dishonor." She encouraged women of means to become entrepreneurs: "Now I should rejoice," she wrote, "to see a large Lowell mill
wholly owned and operated by women."[4] She suggested an early version
of temporary-employment agencies. And she looked forward to a (somewhat romanticized) era of dual career couples: "Such marriages as I can
dream of,—where, household duties thriftily managed and speedily discharged, the wife assumes some honorable trust . . . ; while the husband
follows his under separate auspices! Occupied with real service to men and
each other, how happily will they meet at night to discuss the hours they
lived apart, to help each other's work by each other's wit, and to draw vital
refreshment from the caresses of their children!"[5]

Dall was also one of the earliest practitioners in the field of women's
studies in the country. In her *Una* articles (many of which were repub-
lished in *Historical Pictures Retouched*, 1860) she scrutinized history for
instances of overlooked, suppressed, or maligned women of intelligence,
independence, and virtue. Not content with simply highlighting the work
of such figures as Margaret Fuller and Mary Wollstonecraft, she reread in
a favorable light some of the female pariahs of male-written history—
Aspasia, for example, the reputed courtesan who caused Pericles to leave
his wife and family. She "retouched" the portraits of these figures—that is,
she took the known facts and showed how they could be reinterpreted in
a way favorable to these women, whom history had thus far read in the
least sympathetic light or simply ignored. In response to a popular series
of lectures by Transcendentalist Ralph Waldo Emerson entitled
"Representative Men," Dall crafted a "Representative Women" lecture fea-
turing Fuller, Wollstonecraft, Charlotte Brontë, and Lady Sydney Morgan.

These works made Dall a reformer of national stature. The publication of *The College, the Market, and the Court* was generally considered a
major event in the American women's movement. It was widely reviewed,
from New England to New York to San Francisco to London. In 1868,
Elizabeth Cady Stanton wrote to Dall that she had been empowered to
choose "some half dozen of our most distinguished" women to be featured
in a chapter on the women's rights movement and added, "As from your
literary ability you rank first, you must be one of the six."[6] A decade later,
in honor of Dall's achievement, Alfred University awarded her a doctorate
of laws (LL.D.), probably the first honorary degree granted to an American woman.

Yet Dall's role in the women's movement faded from the record in the
last quarter of the nineteenth century. In Stanton, Anthony, and Gage's
three-volume *History of Woman Suffrage,* Dall's work is very nearly ignored.

In the chapter "Women in Boston" in Justin Winsor's *Memorial History of Boston* (1881), Caroline Dall's name is simply never mentioned. That was hardly an accidental oversight, since Dall's work was concentrated in the Boston area, and since a childhood friend of Dall's, Ednah Dow Cheney, wrote that chapter. Several reasons account for Dall's being dropped out of the history of the women's movement. Personal conflicts and jealousies were a primary cause, as the circumstances of her exclusion from the New England Woman's Club illustrate. Dall saw herself as having paved the way for the public roles of a number of Boston friends and acquaintances, including Caroline Severance, Julia Ward Howe, and Ednah Dow Cheney, all three prime movers in the 1868 founding of the Woman's Club. Dall, surprised to hear of the organization of this society without her knowledge, was then stunned to learn that she had been blackballed from membership. She never recovered from this blow, delivered by the very women whom she felt that she had enabled and with most of whom she attended church. It was perhaps the major reason that she essentially dropped out of the women's movement. Why would these "friends" have turned on her? The Woman's Club women told a friend of Dall's that it was "because [she] *always* had *led* everywhere—& always would!"[7] There is no question that Dall had a controlling personality and a lifelong history of unwittingly offending people. The result seems to be that some of those whom she had offended wrote her out of the history of the women's movement systematically. A rather obvious reason that Dall's contemporaries, in these later accounts, minimized her role was her essential abandonment of the women's movement. No doubt she would have said it the other way around, but the effect was the same.

But Dall did not abandon reform. Far from it. In 1865 she was one of the founders of the American Social Science Association, an organization that studied and attempted to improve prison conditions, the treatment of the insane, public health, and education. As a member of countless committees of this organization, Dall traveled extensively to examine and report upon conditions in prisons, asylums, and factories. All manner of issues affecting the poor, sick, or disadvantaged commanded her attention, ranging from lodging houses for women in cities to the purity of milk. So Dall's place in the women's movement was obscured later in the century partly because she was now identified, as she now identified herself, with a different reform movement.

As a reformer, Caroline Dall clearly had her limitations. Primary among them was her inability to work well with other strong women. Perhaps she does not deserve a place of eminence in the history of the women's movement if one views it from the limited perspective of organized political action. She was an idea woman, not an organization woman. But her true and crucial role was to foster what historian Gerda Lerner has called a "feminist consciousness," an enhanced awareness of woman's potential, of her marginalization by society, and a sense of connection with great women of the past.[8] The political branch of the movement built upon this consciousness.

Dall lived out the last thirty-four years of her life largely retired from active reform work, though she continued to hold an office in the American Social Science Association. In 1878 she moved to Washington, where her son, who had become famous as an explorer and author on Alaska, was building a career as a naturalist at the Smithsonian Institution. She also made extended visits to her daughter, who had married Josiah Munro, a successful businessman in Buffalo, New York. Dall's life in Washington only partly revolved around her son and her grandchildren, for she became the friend of political and scientific luminaries, the intimate of First Lady Frances Cleveland, the leader of a reading group for young women, and a well-known hostess. She also wrote for newspapers and magazines and occasionally published books on a wide variety of topics—from Shakespeare to her journey to California to theology.

In Dall's late years she recognized that the period of her young womanhood in the Boston area had been no ordinary time, and she felt an obligation to preserve her own record of it. In the 1890s she made arrangements to leave her journals (which already covered more than sixty years) and other papers to the Massachusetts Historical Society. In addition to this private contemporary record that Dall realized would not be tapped until after her death, she turned to publishing recollections and interpretations of the Transcendentalist movement and its participants. In 1895 Dall published her transcription of the Margaret Fuller conversation series that she had attended in 1841, *Margaret and Her Friends*. It remains the fullest and best contemporary record of those sessions. In the same year she delivered in Washington a lecture that she published two years later as *Transcendentalism in New England: A Lecture*. When she gave this lecture, Dall was nearly seventy-three years old. She could easily have used the stores of her memory and her journals to produce an entertaining talk filled with personal anecdotes of the celebrated Transcendentalists. But she was speaking before the Society for Philosophical Enquiry, and she aimed to be more than entertaining. Instead of telling after-dinner tales, Dall undertook to construct a revisionist interpretation of the movement, an unabashedly feminist one. The Transcendentalist movement began and ended, Dall asserted, with a woman. Its history "stretched along two hundred years," from the Puritan rebel Anne Hutchinson to Margaret Fuller. Hutchinson was banished from the Massachusetts Bay Colony as a result of her Antinomian beliefs emphasizing the conviction that the divine spirit is immanent in human beings and that its guidance should take precedence over men's laws. Dall's designation of Hutchinson, the very earliest eminent New England woman, as a foremother of Transcendentalism is a bold stroke of revisionist interpretation. Furthermore, Dall's contention for the centrality of Margaret Fuller's role in the Transcendentalist movement is a corrective to most nineteenth-century and, until recently, twentieth-century depictions of the movement.

The extraordinary life of Caroline Healey Dall, a pioneering reformer, a public lecturer and sometime preacher, an associate of the great and famous, was balanced and complemented by an ordinary life. This ordinary life was marked on the one hand by the frustration of her need for love, the failure of her marriage, the difficulties of single motherhood, the shame of personal innuendo, the pain of rejection, and on the other hand by the fulfillment made possible by her work. There is a sense, of course, in which the extraordinary life could not have been lived without the ordinary one. For it was at least in part these difficulties that brought Dall face to face with the reality of women's limited opportunities and severely restricted economic and political power and that led her to imagine and champion new paradigms for women's lives. Hers is the compelling human story of a woman whose uncommon background and education and opportunities combined with her all too ordinary failures and misfortunes to create an effective advocate for the powerless. In this sense her life story is as important a legacy as what she would have called her "work."

Notes

1. Letter to Charles Henry Appleton Dall, February 22, 1843, Caroline Dall Papers, Massachusetts Historical Society.

2. Manuscript Journal, November 11, 1858, Dall Papers.

3. Manuscript Journal, March 10, 1873, Dall Papers.

4. *The College, the Market, and the Court; or, Woman's Relation to Education, Labor, and Law* (Boston, 1867; [Memorial Edition], 1914; New York: Arno Press, 1972), 364.

5. Ibid., 208–09.

6. Stanton to Dall, February 29, 1868, Dall Papers. In the end there were fourteen "Champions of the Women's Rights Movement," including Dall, in the volume *Eminent Women of the Age*, ed. James Parton, Horace Greeley, T. W. Higginson, J. S. C. Abbott, James M. Hoppin, William Winter, Theodore Tilton, Fanny Fern, Grace Greenwood, and Mrs. E. C. Stanton (Hartford, CT: S. M. Betts, 1869).

7. Manuscript Journal, January 28, 1869, Dall Papers.

8. Gerda Lerner, *The Creation of Feminist Consciousness* (New York: Oxford University Press, 1993).

Suggested Readings

No published monograph on Dall exists. The most useful general biographical account is Stephen Nissenbaum, "Caroline Wells Healey Dall," in *Notable American Women 1607–1950*, ed. Edward T. James, 3 vols. (Cambridge, MA.: Harvard University Press, 1971), 1:428–29. Gary Sue Goodman's dissertation, "'All about Me Forgotten': The Education of Caroline Healey Dall, 1822–1912" (Stanford University, 1987), analyzes Dall's life from birth to age eighteen. Barbara Welter's "The Merchant's Daughter: A Tale from Life," *New England Quarterly* 42 (1969): 3–22, the first consideration of Dall by a women's historian, is hardly sympathetic. Rose Norman, "'Sorella di Dante': Caroline Dall and the Paternal Discourse," *A/B: Auto/Biography Studies* 5 (1990): 124–39, deals with Dall's depiction of herself in certain autobiographical writings. Dall as a reformer is treated in Howard M. Wach, "A Boston Feminist in the Victorian Public Sphere: The Social Criticism of Caroline Healey Dall," *New England Quarterly* 68 (1995): 429–50; William Leach, *True Love and Perfect Union: The Feminist Reform of Sex and Society* (New York: Basic Books, 1980). Dall's relationship to Transcendentalism is the subject of several articles by Helen R. Deese: "Caroline Healey Dall," in *Biographical Dictionary of Transcendentalism*, ed. Wesley T. Mott (Westport, CN: Greenwood Press, 1996), 60–62; "'A Liberal Education': Caroline Healey Dall and Emerson," in *Emersonian Circles: Essays in Honor of Joel Myerson*, ed. Wesley T. Mott and Robert Burkholder (Rochester, NY: University of Rochester Press, 1996): 237–60; "Tending the 'Sacred Fires': Theodore Parker and Caroline Healey Dall," *Proceedings of the Unitarian Universalist Historical Society* 33 (1995): 22–38; "A New England Women's Network: Elizabeth Palmer Peabody, Caroline Healey Dall, and Delia S. Bacon," *Legacy: A Journal of American Women Writers* 8 (Fall 1991): 77–91; and "Alcott's Conversations on the Transcendentalists: The Record of Caroline Dall," *American Literature* 60 (March 1988): 17–25. Dall's writings on Margaret Fuller are considered in Joel Myerson, "Caroline Dall's Reminiscences of Margaret Fuller," *Harvard Library Bulletin* 22 (October 1974): 414–28, and "Mrs. Dall Edits Miss Fuller: The Story of *Margaret and Her Friends*," *Publications of the Bibliographical Society of America* 72 (1978): 187–200. Although there is no comprehensive twentieth-century history of Transcendentalism, the best starting point for research on the movement and its major figures is Joel Myerson, ed., *The Transcendentalists: A Review of Research and Criticism* (New York: Modern Language Association of America, 1984).

14

George Washington Harris
The Fool from the Hills

John Mayfield

Restless ambition, so typical of the nineteenth century, characterized the life and work of George Washington Harris. Born in Pennsylvania, he moved to Knoxville, Tennessee, at the age of five and lived there most of his life. Harris was a jack-of-all-trades (metalworker, steamboat captain, journalist, railroader, farmer, and politician), but the master of none. Harris raised a family, held a pew in a Presbyterian church, worked hard, but always remained among the middling sort. He also strongly upheld states' rights, supported the South's secession from the Union, and backed the Confederacy throughout the Civil War. He was viscerally anti-Lincoln, anti-Grant, anti-Republican, and anti-Reconstruction. To say that he was a racist is to understate the truth. Yet this ordinary man created one of the most extraordinary figures in all nineteenth-century literature: Sut Lovingood, a self-proclaimed "nat'ral born durn'd fool." A product of the culture of the Old South, Sut was also a keen critic of its pretensions. Anarchic, irreverent, he challenged the self-importance and posturing of the slaveholding class. His tales, delivered in dialect so obscure that one editor actually "translated" it, concern violence, religion, politics, patriarchy, and sex with a candor and frankness not seen in other writings of his time. Sut is the ultimate subversive, a character who delights in his own imperfections and who shrewdly and pitilessly observed the society around him. Through him we gain a fresh perspective on the Old South.

John Mayfield is professor of history at Samford University in Birmingham, Alabama. He is a former member of the editorial board of the *Journal of the Early Republic*. Professor Mayfield is the author of *Rehearsal for Republicanism: Free Soil and the Politics of Antislavery* (1980); and *The New Nation: 1800–1845* (1982). He is writing a book about Southern humor.

Let us consider Fools and their uses. Fools hold a special place in every culture's history, and they come in all kinds of guises. In the medieval and Renaissance eras, Fools, court jesters, served an official function. They were virtually the only persons allowed to lampoon a king to his face. Kings kept them around, in fact, to keep a grip on reality. Fools pop up at carnivals, at Mardi Gras, and at circuses. Since the age of print, they have become fixtures in literature, and now they have moved into film. A Fool laughs at society, and, importantly, he laughs at the laugher, so that no one walks away feeling superior or unchanged. Fools keep us from taking ourselves too seriously, and that helps us keep going. They live in the borderlands between life and art; they break down the barriers between what is proper and what is absurd.

Americans, however, are often uncomfortable with Fools. Perhaps it is a manifestation of our business culture or our inclination to take ourselves too seriously. We were, after all, the "city on the hill" all the way back to the colonial era—out to show the world how it is done right—and we are incorrigible reformers. The British are much better at accepting things as they are than Americans, who still hope to improve everything. For that reason, English humor tends to farce while Americans excel at irony. Only occasionally do we let a true Fool take the stage.

Then there is Sut Lovingood, a southerner of no fixed address or occupation. He is virtually unknown outside a few circles, yet he may be the original and best American Fool of all. An east Tennessee businessman, George Washington Harris, created Sut in a series of yarns written chiefly during the 1850s and 1860s.[1] Sut describes himself as a "nat'ral born durn'd fool," without "nara a soul, nuffin but a whisky proof gizzard," with "the longes' par ove laigs ever hung tu eny cackus." His sole purpose in life is getting drunk, getting girls, and getting "intu more durn'd misfortnit skeery scrapes, than enybody, an' then run outen them faster, by golly, nor enybody" (172). When challenged to justify himself, his answer is direct and simple: "Yu go tu *hell*, mistofer; yu bothers me" (232).

Sut Lovingood exists for the practical joke. Anything—rich, poor, male, female, animal, human, old, young—is fair game. So, we have Sut slipping two live lizards up a circuit preacher's pants leg just to watch him scream. "Brethren, brethren . . . the Hell-sarpints *hes got me!*" he hollers, and strips and runs naked through the mostly female crowd (56). Or we have Sut breaking up Mrs. Yardley's quilting bee, for no reason beyond sheer maliciousness, by tying a clothesline row of quilts to a horse's saddlehorn, then splintering a fence rail over the poor animal " 'bout nine inches ahead ove the root ove his tail' " (143). The horse manages to knock down just about everything in sight, including Mrs. Yardley, who dies either from being run over or from the shock of losing a nine-diamond quilt, depending on who tells the story. Sometimes we find Sut at the receiving end, as when he lusts a little too openly after Sicily Burns ("Sich a buzzim! Jis' think ove two snow balls wif a strawberry stuck but-ainded intu bof on em" [75]). Sicily, no virgin she, slips him raw baking soda as a "love potion." As the gas comes frothing out of Sut's "mouf, eyes, noes, an' years" he thinks, "*Kotch agin, by the great golly!* . . . same famerly disper-sishun to make a durn'd fool ove myse'f . . . ef thar's half a chance. Durn dad evermore, amen!" (81).

How do we explain a creature such as this? Sut Lovingood is not from the business culture; he is outside modern sensibilities. He comes from a world of physical—not psychological—pain and deprivation, and he responds accordingly with violent and uncompromising energy. Maybe, we hope, he is the voice of the forgotten poor. In the preface to his yarns, for example, Harris lets Sut explain that he will be happy if he can give a laugh to "eny poor misfortinit devil hu's heart is onder a mill-stone, hu's ragged children are hungry, an' no bread in the dresser, hu is down in the mud, an' the lucky ones a'trippin him every time he struggils tu his all fours, hu has fed the famishin an' is now hungry hisself, hu misfortins foller fas' an' foller faster, hu is so foot-sore an' weak that he wishes he were at the ferry" (ix). Ultimately, though, this explanation does not work, at least not in any traditional way. Poor people come in for his pranks just as surely as rich ones. There is no irony to his life, no expectations. He knows he's worthless and so lives entirely for the moment. He was born a Fool from a Fool. He will die that way, probably from a clean shot to the heart from some young woman's husband.

Still, Sut is not alone in American humor. He has his peers among the bear-eaters and ripsnorters of Davy Crockett's time and in the rough humor of the frontier West, where physical cruelty and practical joking were the norm. A Fool exactly like Sut, however, could only come from the South—the prosperous and poor, proud and humiliated antebellum South that has been the genesis of so many of our national dreams and night-mares. He could not have originated in the North or Midwest. The dry business culture there simply could not sustain a creation such as Sut. Moreover, he could only have been created by a particular type of south-erner, one who was fiercely devoted to his region—even to the point of supporting secession without stint or reservation—and who knew the South's customs, proprieties, and expectations to the letter. Only one who knows what is not foolish can create a perfect Fool.

George Washington Harris created the Lovingood stories in a series of newspaper and magazine sketches that began in the 1840s and culminat-ed in a book, *Sut Lovingood's Yarns*, published in 1867. Were it not for the yarns, history would have passed him by, and it almost did. He was born in western Pennsylvania in 1814. Little is known of his parents, except that George was named after his father and that his mother had been married once before and had a son, Samuel Bell, who was Harris's half-brother.

Samuel Bell moved to the small town of Knoxville, Tennessee, a few years after Harris was born and brought the young boy with him shortly thereafter. No one knows what happened to George's parents; they may have gone to Tennessee or they may have died.[2]

Harris spent his early years learning skills and developing ambition. Samuel Bell was a trained metalworker who specialized in first-rate small arms, such as pistols, knives, and swords. He taught Harris the trade in a shop in Knoxville, and Harris kept one hand in the profession for most of his life. But George Washington Harris seems to have been a mobile, restless youth who was not entirely happy with the limitations of his half-brother's style of life. He was a small man, reputedly quick and agile, who briefly rode jockey in local quarter races. Like most young men, he was eager to set out on his own. The opportunity came when he was only nineteen. A company took him on as captain of a steamboat making the run from the port of Knoxville along the Tennessee River to the Ohio, and Harris stayed in the job for five years. In 1838, he helped transport Cherokees out of the Tennessee Valley and on to the Trail of Tears to their new homes in Oklahoma. He was apparently good at his job, maintained discipline, and took care of his equipment.

What would have been a lifetime dream for many young men was, for Harris, the first of many jobs. In 1835 he married the daughter of the inspector of the Port of Knoxville (who also owned the local racetrack) and began a family. Whether he grew tired of life on the river or whether his family and father-in-law pressured him to settle down is not known. Whatever the motive, in 1839, he took out a loan, bought a substantial farm near the Great Smoky Mountains, and settled into apparent respectability. He listed his occupation as "manufacturer and trader"— which meant that he probably farmed some, traded some, and made or fixed things. He had a nice house, carpets, books, china, a bay mare, and three slaves, plus a wife and three children. By any measure he had moved, young, into what would later be called the Victorian middle class. He had also contracted that most middle-class of burdens, a large debt. He could not maintain it. By 1843 the farm and house and carpets and at least one of the slaves were gone, and Harris took his family back to Knoxville.

There he opened a metal shop, like his half-brother, and began to settle down in earnest. The shop was large and could handle both delicate jobs and heavy machinework, but the venture did not last. By the end of the decade, Harris had signed on as superintendent of a glass factory (more likely a large shop), while he continued to do some silversmithing on the side. He apparently needed to work two jobs, for Harris still tried to maintain a large household, including two slaves and a washerwoman. If there was any consistency to his career thus far, it seems to be in his capacity for hard work and constant debt in the pursuit of the image of prosperity. During the 1850s, Harris went through an astonishing number of job changes for someone of his age and respectability. He was a steamboat captain again in 1854 and a mine surveyor the next year. The year after that he borrowed money to start a sawmill, which failed, then became for a short time a postmaster, then a railroad conductor. During the Civil War, he moved around, living for a while in northern Alabama and then Georgia. After the war he went back to Tennessee to work for the railroads again. He was still in that line when he died in 1869.

Sometime in the 1840s this fairly unremarkable man, who had had only a year-and-a-half of schooling in his life, began to write. He may have done some newspaper work for the Democratic *Knoxville Argus* in the mid-1840s, but his first attributable stories were for a national magazine, the *Spirit of the Times,* published out of New York by William T. Porter. Porter catered to sporting men from the northern and southern gentry, and his magazine recorded horse racing, fox hunting, and other pursuits of the leisure class. It also fielded some of the best and most original humor of the times, with a preference for southern tales about coon hunts, wrasslin' matches, quaint folkways, and generally weird backwoods characters. Most of the major humorists of the Old Southwest published stories in the *Spirit* at one time or the other, and most followed the formula of having a genteel narrator introduce a colorful character who then entertained the company with a story in dialect. The *Spirit* was a natural place for Harris to start, and his first stories read pretty much like the rest of the magazine's submissions: folksy characters out making fools of themselves for the rich folk to snort at.

Except even these stories suggest something different, something really anarchic, at work. His first story of any worth, "The Knob Hill Dance," is in most respects an ordinary tale of a hillbilly hoedown. For sexual references and sheer irreverence, however, it pushed the limits for its time. Girls come to the dance "pourin out of the woods like pissants out of an old log when tother end's afire" wearing everything from homespun to calico—but not silk. Any girl who wore silk would "go home in her petticotetale sartin, for the homespun would tare it off of hir quicker nor winkin, and if the sunflowers dident help the homespuns, they woudn't do the silk eny good." Translation: What the dancing did not wear out, the bushes would. Everybody drinks, dances, eats, rolls on the bed, and the whole thing ends in a glorious brawl. The narrator describes walking home with his girl, and a "rite peart *four-leged* nag she is. She was *weak* in *two* of hir legs, but t'other two—oh, my stars and possum dogs! they make a man swaller tobacker jist to look at 'em, and feel sorter like a June bug was crawlin up his trowses and the waistband too tite for it to get out."[3] He wants to marry her, or so he says. Porter's magazine was one of the few, perhaps the only, outlet for innuendos such as these, but on at least one occasion during these early years even Porter had to reject one of Harris's stories as too salty.

Harris's output was erratic until 1854, when he discovered Sut Lovingood. The original was probably Sut Miller, a local from somewhere around Ducktown, Tennessee (Harris was working there as a mine inspector). Harris added "Lovingood"—sexual reference no doubt intentional—and put him in the saloon of Pat Nash (also a real person), talking to a gentlemanly narrator named, wouldn't you know, "George." The first story, published in the *Spirit* and revised later for Sut Lovingood's *Yarns,* was a knockout: "Sut Lovingood's Daddy, Acting Horse."

It is unlike any other story of its time. Sut rides up to Pat Nash's saloon on the spindliest horse ever born and begins right away to explain that this nag is "next to the best hoss what ever shelled nubbins or toted jugs," his lamented Tickytail, who is now dead. "Yu see, he froze stiff; no, not that adzactly, but starv'd fust, an' froze arterards" (20). From that unlikely introduction, Sut jumps cleanly into an explanation of how Tickytail's death prompted Dad to act hoss. The whole family—sixteen kids plus a "prospect"—has lazed through the winter, "hopin sum stray hoss mout cum along." It never happened, so Dad lies awake one night "a-snortin, an' rollin, an' blowin, an' shufflin, an' scratchin' hisself, an' a-whisperin at Mam a heap—an' at breckfus' I foun' out what hit ment" (22). Dad will pull the plow himself, act hoss.

He is pretty good at it, maybe too good. Dad gets Sut and Mam to fashion him a harness from pawpaw bark and a bridle from an umbrella brace, and he runs around on all fours practicing snorting and kicking up his heels and trying to bite someone. Mam "step'd back a littil an' were standin wif her arms cross'd a-restin' 'em on her stumick, an' his heel taps cum wifin a inch ove her nose. Sez she: 'Yu plays hoss better nur yu dus husban'.' He jes run backards on all fours an' kick'd at her agin, an'—an' pawd the groun wif his fis" (23). So Sut leads him off to the field, and they do get into it nicely. Dad snorts and pulls, Sut begins dreaming of the corn crop they will get in (and the whiskey it will produce), and then Dad charges straight into "a ball ho'nets nes' ni ontu es big es a hoss's hed, an' the hole tribe kiver'd 'im es quick es yu culd kiver a sick pup wif a saddil blanket" (24). Dad tears off like, well, a scared horse through bushes and then seven panels of fence. He loses the harness, his clothes, everything except the bridle and "ni ontu a yard ove plow line sailin behine, wif a tir'd-out ho'net ridin on the pint ove hit" (25). When he gets to the bluff overlooking the river, he jumps in. While he bobs up and down trying to get free of the hornets, Sut begins mocking him. "Switch 'em wif yure tail, dad. . . . I'll hev yer feed in the troft, redy; yu won't need eny curyin tu-nite will yu?" (26, 27). Dad cusses him back so bad that Sut leaves for the mines for a few days. "Yere's luck tu the durned old fool," he toasts, "an' to the ho'nets too" (28).

That broke the mold. Never mind that Harris's comic imagery and use of language was far ahead of anyone else writing in the field; those are subjects in themselves. He had created a comic masterpiece from a most un-southern, un-Victorian, un-middle-class subject—a father's total humiliation. If he could do that, he could savage every other sacred cow (or horse) in the culture, and he did. The rest of the yarns, published in bits and pieces over the next dozen years and then carefully, painstakingly revised into a book, went after preachers, virgins, marriage, sentimentality, the home and hearth, anything that came within Sut's reach.

Therein lies the incongruity. How could tales this anarchic, this crude, this foolish, come from the pen of an ordinary, debt-ridden small-businessman and devoted family man from what should have been one of the most socially conservative parts of the country? One would expect him to come up with the kind of overblown heroics and sticky romantic goo that made for quick contracts and high-volume sales. Instead, he created a Fool. It all seems incongruous, but perhaps only such a man could have written such tales.

Despite the constant debt and the frequent career moves, Harris was firmly rooted in the culture and politics of a particular place—east Tennessee. It was a place where several of the South's subcultures came together. There were mountain folk and river folk, and Harris had met them on his travels. There were townsmen and businessmen passing through, and Harris had dealt with those, too. There were slaveholders, not the cotton snobs from south Alabama or Mississippi, but slaveholders nonetheless with a claim to all that implied in the complex social relations of the South. There were the rich and the frightfully poor, and Harris saw them. His whole environment, in fact, was a mosaic of often contradictory ideals.

So was Harris. Consider, for example, his religious convictions. Harris was a solid, traditional Presbyterian. For years the First Presbyterian

Church of Knoxville had a Harris family pew, and one of Harris's sons was named for the pastor there. Harris's devotion to his church was no mere social formality. Friends called him a "blue Presbyterian," which meant simply that he took his church seriously, did not work on Sunday, and raised a strict household. The religious culture around him was a good deal more diverse. East Tennesseans worshipped through established churches, circuit preachers, evangelical and holiness groups, revivals, tent meetings, and virtually anything else that prayed or sang. Some parts of the church-going population stayed strictly to themselves; others moved in and out of these religious expressions as the spirit—and opportunity—moved them. Still other parts preferred to have nothing to do with the whole scene, considered preachers frauds and hymn-singing noise, and saved Sunday mornings for the hangover. Harris pretty certainly was familiar with all these practices and shades of opinion; as a riverboat captain and railroad man, he must have seen it all. At the core, however, he was a proper man.

He was also a southern fire-eater. Harris began and ended life a staunch southern Democrat. He supported James Buchanan in 1856, wrote a rather bad political satire about the Republican and Know Nothing candidates, and got rewarded with the postmaster job. That same year, Harris was elected a city alderman. More important, in 1856, Harris went to Savannah for the Southern Commercial Convention—a loose cover for the crazier secessionists of the time. In 1859 he went to Nashville for the Democratic state convention and got appointed to the state central committee. His politics became more and more extreme. After Lincoln's election the following year, Harris wrote three vicious parodies of the new president, comparing him to a dried-out frog nailed to a board. This sort of thing was more popular in west Tennessee, where secessionists held a majority, than in unionist east Tennessee, so Harris left Knoxville. After the war, Harris wrote more nasty satires—this time on Grant, abolitionists, and radical Republicans. These satires were not his best work.

The convergence of Harris's middle-class propriety and his rabid, arrogant sectionalism is suggestive. In real life, Harris was a fairly ordinary, proper townsman with a business to run, a family to raise, and a house to maintain. His record of successes, failures, ventures, and losses was not radically different from his peers in towns all over the country, South and North, or indeed over western Europe and England. Like it or not, Harris was a member of the urban middle class and partook of its Protestant ethics.

What Harris fancied himself to be may have been something different. His failed attempt at living the life of a country squire during the late 1830s and 1840s is intriguing, because it is at that point in his careers where he acquired both debt and slaves. Given the cost of slaves, even young ones, the two were intimately connected. Moreover, he kept slaves—as many as he could—even after his move to the city made servants a luxury he could not afford. The possession of slaves more than anything else defined status in the antebellum South. It was the entry card to the elite, the connecting link to the planter class. Like members of this planter class, Harris dabbled in horse racing, delighted in telling stories and generally being sociable, and fancied himself a rising politician. With a twist of luck here or there, Harris might have moved in the same circles as the great slave-owning class. With or without that twist of luck, he certainly knew what that class expected of its members. At the same time, he knew from daily experience what was expected of a Presbyterian businessman in a small southern town.

Harris, then, lived in the borderland between two worlds, two sets of values, two elaborate codes of behavior. On the one hand was the work ethic of the urban middle class, driven by respectability, self-discipline, commercial diversification, and success. On the other was the southern beau ideal—the leisured world of the gentleman planter with his slaves, horses, great and usually costly generosity, and touchy sense of honor. At points, these worlds crossed over, to be sure. The southerner's racism cut across occupations and class lines, and both the townsman and the planter were businessmen living off the profits of their enterprises. Moreover, it is arguable that the planter's real life was not leisured and hardly ideal. But as ideals, as something to strive for, the two styles were powerful—and essentially antagonistic. They could not coexist indefinitely. The Civil War destroyed the planter's hegemony, and in that sense the townsman won and created the New South. Before that happened, however, life was a good deal complicated for someone like Harris. Who should he be?

Alone among the great southern humorists, Harris rose up from nothingness, worked for a living at whatever came his way, and suffered the consequences of his mistakes directly, with no family safety net to cushion the blow. He also wrote when time was running out. The Lovingood yarns first appeared as newspaper and magazine articles during the 1850s, and Harris probably revised his material during the war years. These were precisely the years when the planters' dependence on slavery ripened into secession, when their sense of personal honor became translated into a sense of regional honor, when their cocky indifference to death and their penchant for violence got field-tested in humiliation and war. Harris, with his fire-eating secessionism and rabid hatred of Republicans and reformers, was right there with them, in spirit if not status.

Harris was a small businessman, however, and he came from a unionist part of this South, where the dominance of the planter and his style was just weak enough to let reality creep in. This was the area that produced Andrew Johnson. The slaveholding "aristocracy" was not popular among these nonslaveholders, who during the war refused to fight in the Confederacy and sometimes sent draft agents home across a horse. Still, slaveholders, even here, wielded great power. Harris was neither a fully independent townsman nor a slaveholder; he tried to be both, and he tried to do it in a particular place where the tensions between progressive South and planter South were acute, even deadly.

The range of pretensions and hypocrisies open to Sut's/Harris's mocking rage was sizable. Consider the properly Protestant side of Harris's South, the one that would surge through the New South like a collective atonement after the Civil War and turn Baptists into businessmen and Methodists into rich businessmen and crowd the whisky-drinking Episcopalians onto the golf courses and leave them there. Here Sut's favorite target was the self-sanctifying, meddlesome, predatory preacher. It is not that Parson Bullins, who gets the lizards up his pants leg, is a bad man. He is just an irritating windbag with an eye for women who has humiliated Sut by catching him in the bushes with a girl and then tattling to the girl's mother. So Sut goes to the service, full of repentance and lizards, to hear the parson work the women into a fever with the fear of Hell-serpents. "Tole 'em how they'd quile [coil] intu thar buzzims, an' how they *wud* crawl down onder thar frock-strings . . . up thar laigs, an' travil *onder* thar garters, no odds how tight they tied 'em, an' when the two armys ove Hell-sarpents met, then—That las' remark *fotch 'em*." (53).

At this point the women are screaming, the preacher is waving his hands, and the lizards start their own travels up *his* garters. It is particularly satisfying to Sut that this preacher, who has seduced half the girls in the county, literally gets exposed. "Passuns ginerly hev a pow'ful strong holt on wimen"; says Sut, "but, hoss, I tell yu thar airn't meny ove em kin run start nakid over an' thru a crowd ove three hundred wimen an' not injure thar karacters *sum*" (58). In other tales, Sut extended the same treatment to lawyers and sheriffs—anyone who pretended to be a pillar of the community.

The pretensions of the slaveholding class presented more of a challenge, yet Sut was up to the job. It may be difficult for modern readers to understand just how ingrained the idea of honor was to southerners. One's honor was a subtle, powerful combination of family name and social class, all expressed through an elaborate code of etiquette that made language, gesture, and appearance matters of life and death. To call someone a name, tweak his nose, or leer at his lady would bring instant and violent response. Above all, honor was about being manly. A gentleman had manners and poise; a common man was rough and plain. Each defended his honor among those of his social status. Gentlemen dueled and gave gifts; common men fought and bought each other drinks. Slaves were literally not men in this strutting culture, because they had no way to defend their honor and no gifts to give. A manly man did not fear death and would rather die—in a fight, in a duel, in a war—than be humiliated. Humiliation, in fact, separated men from not-men. Those who endured humiliation (and that included failed businessmen and people who work the retail trade, which is a daily exercise in fielding insults and snubs) may have qualified as Christian saints. They would not have made it as men in the Old South.[4]

Humiliation is central to the Lovingood tales. Sut does not just violate every rule; more to the point, he takes himself outside the rules. He humiliates himself but makes himself the central, most energetic and important part of the story. In that sense he negated the whole code of southern manhood. "I'm no count, no how. Jis' look at me! Did yu ever see sich a sampil ove a human afore? I feels like I' be glad tu be dead, only I'se feard of the dyin. I don't keer for hearater, for hits onpossibil for me to hev ara soul. Who ever seed a soul in jis' sich a rack heap ove bones an' rags as this? I'se nuffin' but sum newfangil'd sort ove beas'. . . a sorter cross atween a crazy ole monkey an' a durn'd, wore-out hominy mill. I is one ove dad's explites at makin cussed fool invenshuns. . . . I blames him fur all ove hit, allers a-tryin tu be king fool" (106–107). In that one paragraph, Sut rejected most of what was essential to a southerner's manhood. He admits to being ugly, poor, afraid of dying, of dubious lineage and parenthood, indifferent to God and duty, and vengeful of his father. What is worse, he is actually proud of it.

The list goes on. Where true southern men were generous and offhand about taking on a friend's debts, Sut simply steals. Where no man would stand for being called a liar, Sut announces to the world that he is a great liar, one of the best in creation. Where bearing and deportment were concerned, and no man could stand to be "unmasked" as fearful or even human, Sut unmasks himself, literally and physically (in one sketch he tries on a starched shirt, can't stand it, and ends up jumping buck naked from a sleeping loft). His kind of "duel" is to kick a dandified stranger in the rump and then run 119 yards between shots when the fop unexpectedly pulls a two-barrel derringer on him. Nothing in the code of southern honor fits Sut.

When it came to women, Sut violated every rule and mocked every ideal set forward by both Presbyterians *and* planters. The whole culture had made ice queens of women and put them on pedestals. Sut looked up the skirt. In "Rare Ripe Garden Seed" a man marries, then leaves for Atlanta after helping his young bride put in a garden of "rare," fast-growing seeds bought off a Yankee peddler. When he comes back, four and a half months after the wedding, she presents him with a newborn baby girl. He can count at least to nine on his fingers and is beginning to express some doubts, but his mother-in-law takes him in hand. It was eating the produce of the rare garden seed that made Mary develop so fast, she explains. "This is what cums of hit, an' four months an' a half am rar ripe time fur babys, adzackly," she says. "Tu be sure, hit lacks a day ur two, but Margarit Jane wer allers a pow'ful interprizin' gal, an' a yearly [early] rizer" (236). The real father, incidentally, is the local sheriff, whom Sut and the husband humiliate in a later tale.

More explicitly, Sut rated unwed women like horses. Young girls were fine, and old maids could be tamed, but widows were best. "Hits widders, by golly, what am the rale sensibil, steady-goin, never-skeerin, never-kickin, willin, sperrited, smoof pacers. They cum clost up tu the hoss-block, standin still wif thar purty silky years playin, an' the naik-veins a-throbbin, and waits fur the word, which ove course yu gives, arter yu finds yer feet well in the stirrup, an' away they moves like a cradil on cushioned rockers, ur a spring buggy runnin in damp san'. A tetch of the bridil an' they knows yu wants em to turn, an' they does hit es willin es ef the idea wer thar own" (141).

It is misogynist cant, but at least it is sincere cant. It utterly lacks the patronizing tone nineteenth-century men used to describe women, and one has to choose which attitude is worse. Sut's at least has a certain simple directness. "Men," he announces, "wer made a-purpus jis' tu eat, drink, an' fur stayin awake in the yearly part ove the nites: an' wimen wer made tu cook the vittils, mix the sperits, an' help the men du the stayin awake" (88). A woman who stepped outside that role, who wanted to take command and not simply cater to men, was greatly to be feared. "They aint human; theyse an ekal mixtry ove stud hoss, black snake, goose, peacock britches—and d——d raskil. They wants tu be a man; an ef they cant, they fixes up thar case by bein devils."[5] This comes from a writer who was devotedly married to one woman for thirty-two years, until her death, and whose second wife was reputedly every bit as bright, intelligent, and assertive as he was. Harris was ever the devoted family man.

And that brings us back to Dad. Dad, of course, is the fool's Fool, the creator of Fools, the original of Fools. He is the antithesis of a Southern patriarch and the whole manly social order built thereon. Lineage—breeding, if you will—was so vital to the South's social order that marriages were made on it, unlikely names came from it (for example, St. George Tucker), and whole genealogies were constructed around it. It is said that one never asks a true Southerner who someone is when all you want is the name. Who you are goes back generations and out to fifth cousins. But Sut's dad is just Hoss, and when he dies, Sut and his Mam borrow a shingle cart for a hearse, ride the body around the field a few times, then drop it into a convenient crack in the ground, rather like dumping waste. Later that night, Mam says " 'oughtent we to a scratch'd in a littel dirt on him, say?' 'No need, mam,' sed Sall [Sut's sister], 'hits loose yeath, an' will soon cave in enuff.' 'But, I want to plant a 'simmon sprout at his head,' sed mam, 'on account ove the puckery taste he has left in my mouth.' "[6]

Harris wrote that particular story after the Civil War, and arguably it is his final comment on the collapse of the Old South. Probably not. The story is entirely appropriate to the Fool that Harris had constructed before the war intervened and exploded the myth of southern superiority. Nothing that Sut Lovingood ever did was intended to support or even to reform the established order of the American South. He was anarchic, chaotic, irreverent, and true to his sense of self. He was a Fool. This may be what Faulkner meant when asked why he liked Sut. "He had no illusions about himself, did the best he could; at certain times he was a coward and knew it and wasn't ashamed; he never blamed his misfortunes on anyone and never cursed God for them."[7] It was probably George Washington Harris's best epitaph.

Notes

1. George Washington Harris, *Sut Lovingood: Yarns Spun by a "Nat'ral Born Durn'd Fool," Warped and Wove for Public Wear* (New York, 1867). Except where noted, all quotes from the tales are taken from this original edition.

2. The best biography of Harris is Milton Rickels's fine book (which also explores the notion of Sut as Fool, although from a different perspective). Milton Rickels, *George Washington Harris* (New York, 1965).

3. George Washington Harris, *High Times and Hard Times,* ed. M. Thomas Inge (Nashville, TN, 1967), 47, 52.

4. The literature on Southern honor is large and growing. Two places to start are Bertram Wyatt-Brown, *Southern Honor: Ethics and Behavior in the Old South* (New York, 1982); and Kenneth S. Greenberg, *Honor & Slavery: Lies, Duels, Noses, Masks, Dressing as a Woman, Gifts, Strangers, Humanitarianism, Death, Slave Rebellions, The Pro-Slavery Argument, Baseball, Hunting, and Gambling in the Old South* (Princeton, NJ, 1996).

5. "Sut Lovingood's Chest Story," in Inge, *High Times and Hard Times,* 120.

6. "Well, Dad's Dead," ibid., 211.

7. Quoted in Rickels, *Harris,* 95.

Suggested Readings

Blair, Walter. *Native American Humor.* 1937. Reprint, San Francisco, 1960.

Cohen, Hennig, and William B. Dillingham, eds. *Humor of the Old Southwest.* 1964. Reprint, Athens, GA, 1994.

Day, Donald. "The Life of George Washington Harris." *Tennessee Historical Quarterly* 6 (1947): 3–38.

Greenberg, Kenneth S. *Honor & Slavery: Lies, Duels, Noses, Masks, Dressing as a Woman, Gifts, Strangers, Humanitarianism, Death, Slave Rebellions, The Pro-Slavery Argument, Baseball, Hunting, and Gambling in the Old South.* Princeton, NJ, 1996.

Harris, George Washington. *Sut Lovingood: Yarns Spun by a "Nat'ral Born Durn'd Fool," Warped and Wove for Public Wear.* New York, 1867.

———. *High Times and Hard Times, Sketches and Tales.* Edited by M. Thomas Inge. Nashville, TN, 1967.

———. *Sut Lovingood's Yarns.* Edited by M. Thomas Inge. New Haven, CT, 1966.

Kuhlmann, Susan. *Knave, Fool, and Genius: The Confidence Man as He Appears in Nineteenth-Century American Fiction.* Chapel Hill, NC, 1973.

Lynn, Kenneth S. *Mark Twain and Southwestern Humor.* 1959. Reprint, Westport, CT, 1972.

Mayfield, John. "The Theater of Public Esteem: Ethics and Values in Longstreet's *Georgia Scenes.*" *Georgia Historical Quarterly* 75 (1991): 566–86.

McClary, Ben Harris, ed. *The Lovingood Papers.* Knoxville, TN, 1962.

Meine, Franklin J., ed. *Tall Tales of the Southwest: An Anthology of Southern and Southwestern Humor, 1830–1860.* New York, 1930.

Rickels, Milton. *George Washington Harris.* New York, 1965.

Shields, Johanna Nicol. "A Sadder Simon Suggs: Freedom and Slavery in the Humor of Johnson Hooper." *Journal of Southern History* 56 (1990): 641–64.

Wyatt-Brown, Bertram. *Southern Honor: Ethics and Behavior in the Old South.* New York, 1982.

Yates, Norris W. *William T. Porter and the Spirit of the Times: A Study of the Big Bear School of Humor.* 1957. Reprint, New York, 1977.

15

Sgt. Peter Welsh
"Is That Not Worth Fiting For?"

Steven E. Woodworth

The story of Peter Welsh, a common soldier of the Civil War, illustrates the experience of the more than one million Northern men who went off to fight for the Union. Welsh was also an Irish immigrant, and he faced difficulties in a new land that at times received this culturally and religiously alien population with something less than open arms. Indeed, the Irish presented the primary ethnic problem of pre–Civil War Northern cities.

In this chapter, historian Steven E. Woodworth incorporates vivid excerpts from Welsh's letters home in depicting what life was like for those in the lower tiers of American Society—and the military—during the Civil War period. Woodworth is an associate professor of history at Texas Christian University, Fort Worth, Texas, and the author of *Jefferson Davis and His Generals* (1990) and *Davis and Lee at War* (1995).

Although business leaders produced and profited, politicians talked, and generals planned and tried to lead, private soldiers actually fought the Civil War. Some two million of them served before the conflict was over. Their motivations varied yet remained strong enough to keep them in the ranks through times when those who really wanted to desert usually succeeded in doing so. They found war a far cry from the romantic pictures of waving flags and battlefield glory most of them had envisioned at the time of enlistment. It was instead a cold, wet, muddy, filthy, boring, hungry, and often sickening business, but, for whatever reasons, most stuck it out. "A soldier is not a hero in fighting alone," observed one of their officers, "his patience under hardship, privation and sickness is equally heroic; sometimes I feel disposed to put him on a level with the martyrs."[1] The great masses that filled the ranks of both sides were made up of individuals with hopes, dreams, families, and life stories of their own—stories that are often overlooked in the discussion of the great events of the war.

Among the soldiers of both sides were Irish Americans. Large numbers of them had come to America during the late 1840s and throughout the 1850s, driven by famine and a certain degree of oppression in their homeland. They were poor peasants for the most part, unacquainted with

American ways, and they were not always welcome. Their poverty and their different customs led many native-born Americans to think them dirty, fractious, and ill mannered, and their Roman Catholicism worried many Protestants who wondered about the "foreign" religion's effect on the body politic. Such concerns sparked the creation of the short-lived Know-Nothing Party during the 1850s, with its anti-immigrant agenda. In the large urban areas where the Irish tended to settle, they occupied the bottom rung of the socioeconomic ladder, had the least money, and did the most undesirable jobs.

When the Civil War began in April 1861, most Irishmen felt no particular call to fight for the Union. They had had little time and, it would seem, less motivation to develop much in the way of abstract patriotism. Beyond that, many of them tended to be racist in their view of blacks, for unlike many residents of the North, they were in direct competition with the free blacks in the job markets of Northern cities. The economic rivalry brought bitter feelings, and the more the war looked like something done on behalf of the African Americans, the less the Irish Americans wanted anything to do with it. The prospect that the conflict might even free substantial portions of the slaves—to migrate to Northern cities, perhaps, and increase the already tough economic competition—was still less welcome. Yet despite all this, many Irishmen did fight for the Union, raising interesting questions of motivation. This is the story of one of those men.

Peter Welsh was born June 29, 1830, in Charlottetown, Prince Edward Island, to Irish immigrant parents. Some years later his family migrated to the United States and settled near Boston, Massachusetts. We know little of his youth, but we do know that in 1857, he and Margaret Prendergast were married at Saint Mary's Church in Charlestown, Massachusetts, with the Reverend Aloysius Janalick presiding. Margaret was as Irish as Peter. Indeed, she had been born in the Emerald Isle, in Athy, county Kildare, one of seven children of Patrick and Margaret O'Toole Prendergast.

Not long after their wedding, the young couple moved to New York City. Peter was a carpenter but found it hard to make a living in the great city, for times were hard after the financial panic of 1857 and work was scarce. As he later admitted, it was not a happy time in their marriage, at least partially because Peter sometimes went on binges of heavy drinking.

By the summer of 1862, with the war already more than a year old, Peter Welsh was still trying to make a hardscrabble living as a carpenter in New York and letting others handle the fighting. About that time, however, a dispute arose among various members of his family still living in

Boston, and Peter traveled there to see if he could help them work things out. However, both of the squabbling factions turned on him instead, and he became depressed and began drinking again, using up every cent he had brought with him. When the spree ended, Peter was deeply ashamed of his lack of self-control as well as the fact that he had squandered what little money he and Margaret could spare. In his humiliation, he felt he could not face his family again, much less ask them for money to get back to New York. So in nearby Charlestown, where Company K of the Twenty-eighth Massachusetts Volunteer Infantry Regiment was recruiting, Peter rather impulsively decided to enlist.

The Twenty-eighth Massachusetts was a virtually all-Irish outfit. In the early months of the war, Thomas Francis Meagher, a fiery Irish nationalist forced into exile a decade and a half before by the British authorities in his homeland, had set out to raise a brigade of his fellow Irish Americans to fight for the Union. As unlikely as that prospect seemed, Meagher's own participation seemed stranger still because his previous pro-Southern proclivities were fairly well known. Still, there was a great rush to the colors in the immediate aftermath of the Confederate firing on Fort Sumter, and going to war was the manly thing to do. There were a great many Irishmen in the United States, times were hard, and—at least as stereotype would have it—the Irish needed no special cause to draw them into such a purely enjoyable recreation as fighting. Fighting—for whatever cause—was said by some to have appeal enough. Such was the way Anglo society thought about them in that age and indeed the way many of them thought about themselves. In fact, some of the Irishmen who enlisted did so to gain military training and experience for possible future use against the hated British in Ireland.

Whatever the motivation of the recruits, Meagher succeeded in raising three regiments in New York City—the Sixty-third, Sixty-ninth, and Eighty-eighth New York. He had plans to enlist two other regiments, one from Philadelphia and the other from Boston, but those goals were not immediately realized. The latter two regiments did not join what was then known as the Irish Brigade until the fall of 1862. The Boston regiment was the Twenty-eighth Massachusetts, in which Peter Welsh would soon march as a private in Company K.

It was September 3, 1862, when Welsh enlisted, and he and his new comrades were soon trained and on their way to Washington. By the time they arrived there, the rest of the regiment had already departed for the front. Things were not going particularly well for the Union in Virginia at that time. Four days before Welsh's enlistment, Federal forces under Maj.

Gen. John Pope had suffered a severe defeat at the hands of Confederate general Robert E. Lee and his trusty lieutenant Thomas J. "Stonewall" Jackson at the Second Battle of Bull Run. Lee had then decided to follow up his advantage and cross the Potomac River into Union-held Maryland, seriously threatening both Washington, DC, and Baltimore. In response, Union authorities had rushed every possible reinforcement to the army, now commanded by George B. McClellan in place of the disgraced Pope. Among those who went were the soldiers of the Twenty-eighth Massachusetts, currently attached to Maj. Gen. Ambrose Burnside's Ninth Corps rather than the intended parent unit, the Irish Brigade of Maj. Gen. Edwin V. Sumner's Second Corps.

Welsh and his batch of fellow recruits caught up with the regiment September 13, near Frederick, Maryland. He was pleased that he had been able to stand the long, hard marches of the previous week and felt stronger than ever, though many of his comrades had given out along the way.

The next day the new men had their baptism of fire as the regiment went into action at the Battle of South Mountain. Three days later an even more stern encounter awaited them on the banks of Antietam Creek in a struggle that was the bloodiest single day of the war. Peter never said much of what he saw there, but it must have been a harrowing experience. One of the recruits who had come down with him from Boston less than two weeks before fell dead nearby, and Peter's tentmate (Civil War soldiers usually lived two to a tent while in the field), "a very nice man with a wife and famely," lost his right arm.[2]

After the battle, Peter continued to enjoy good health: "Never was so hearty in my life," he wrote his wife, "exercise in the open air agrees with me better then anything else."[3] He did worry, though, about Margaret, especially about her poor health. He wanted to make sure she was getting the small stipend that the state of Massachusetts had authorized for the support of the families of its soldiers and was disappointed to learn that it was only four dollars per week rather than eight dollars as he had thought. He sent her all the money he could from his pay and urged her to keep their furniture so that they would be able to set up housekeeping again more easily when he got out of the army at the end of the war. That, he reckoned, had to be less than six months off. Still, he assured his wife that even if the war lasted another year, he was better off in the army. The pay was more than he could have gotten as a carpenter in New York, even if he could find steady work. Most of all, he admonished her, "do not fret and worry yourself so much."[4]

The Army of the Potomac slowly followed the beaten Confederates back into Virginia. Early in November, Peter proudly reported to Margaret that he had been promoted to corporal. Later that month the Twenty-eighth transferred from the Ninth Corps to the Second Corps's Irish Brigade, for which it had originally been raised, and the troops camped just north of the Rappahannock River, opposite the picturesque little town of Fredericksburg, Virginia. Peter assured Margaret that no battle would be fought in the near future, newspaper reports notwithstanding. The first snow fell on December 5, and he predicted that the army would soon go into winter quarters.

About that he was mistaken. On Thursday, December 11, reveille sounded at 4:00 A.M. in the camps of the Irish Brigade. Their officers had them eat a quick breakfast, pack their things, leave their knapsacks piled in camp with a detail to watch them, and march toward the Rappahannock. They left camp about daybreak to the ominous rumble of distant cannon, but after two hours of marching, they halted along the hills that overlooked the Rappahannock from the north while other Union troops tried to force their way across the river. They were up again the next morning at four and under way at daybreak, this time marching across a pontoon bridge into Fredericksburg. Throughout the day, they expected to be sent into battle at any moment, but the order never came, though the artillery thundered on. That night, they camped in ankle-deep mud. Peter and some of his comrades succeeded in finding pieces of boards on which to lie, and there he "slept as sound I think as ever I slept in my life."[5]

When the officers awakened them at four the next morning, Saturday, December 13, Peter found a thick layer of frost on the blanket under which he had slept so soundly. After he and his comrades finished their usual breakfast of hardtack, salt pork, and coffee, the officers ordered them into line of battle in one of Fredericksburg's streets, ready for action. There they stood, shoulder to shoulder in two ranks, and waited while Confederate gunners on a ridge called Marye's Heights, about a mile outside town, spotted them from across an open plain and opened fire. The Southern artillerists soon had the range all too well, and Union men started falling. Right beside Peter a shell cut down two men, one standing behind the other.

When the order to advance came, it was almost a relief—until the men saw where they were supposed to advance. Across a wide, smooth plain that sloped very gently upward, they could see that Marye's Heights was crowned with thundering Confederate cannon. At the foot of the ridge, Southern infantrymen, sheltered in a sunken road behind a stone wall, could sweep the plain with their rifle fire. Another Federal brigade had already attempted to storm the ridge, and its dead and wounded littered the ground over which the Irishmen would have to advance. The artillery tore into their ranks at once. "The storm of shell and . . . canister was terrible," Peter wrote to Margaret, "mowing whole gaps out of our ranks and we having to march over their dead and wounded bodies." However, he added, "we advanced boldly despite it all."[6] And so they did. The charge of the Irish Brigade was the admiration of both sides that day and one of the war's most amazing displays of raw courage. The five regiments moved forward with steady tread and solid ranks, five U.S. flags flying, one with each regiment. In the center marched the Twenty-eighth Massachusetts, the only unit in the brigade that day to carry its regimental flag into action; it was a green banner displaying a harp as a symbol of Ireland. Terrible and magnificent to those who watched, the charge was only terrible for those who took part. They had hardly cleared the town when Peter's captain, Captain Sanborn, went down, shot in the foot. Then, Company K's only other officer, 2d Lt. John Sullivan, fell dead a few feet from where Peter was marching on the right side of the company. Only Peter and one other man came through unwounded in that part of the line. Overall, 12 of the 37 men the company had taken into battle were killed or wounded. A total of 490 from the Irish Brigade fell that day.

The desperate attack failed, of course, as did the assaults of several other brigades that came soon after. Defeated, Burnside pulled the Army of the Potomac back to the north bank of the Rappahannock. The weeks that followed the lopsided Union defeat at Fredericksburg were a time of discouragement for the men of the Army of the Potomac, just as they were for much of the rest of the nation. The war seemed futile, the expense in blood and treasure enormous. Many, especially among the Irish, hated Lincoln's Emancipation Proclamation and told themselves that most of the nation's troubles were the result of abolitionist "fanatics" and the incompetence—or worse—of the Lincoln administration. Peter thought so too.

In many ways, however, he was a remarkably contented soldier. He lived in a wooden shanty that he and his comrades had built for their winter quarters that year. He had a cracker-box for his writing desk, and writing letters to his beloved Margaret was his favorite occupation when he was not involved in regular drills and other duties. The shanty's chimney, as was typical of such structures, drew very poorly, and the interior was often full of smoke, but Peter minded little. He thrived on the diet of hardtack, salt pork, dried or "dessicated" vegetables, supplemented with beans and rice when available, and he admitted that army regulations banning the sale of liquor to the soldiers were wise. He worked hard and attributed his steady, robust health to all the outdoor exercise and plain food. He even liked his strict but fair commanding officer.

His one grief was Margaret. He missed her terribly, worried often about the health problems of which she complained, and was also pained at her attitude toward the war and, especially, his participation in it. She said she cared nothing for the nation: What had it ever done for her? She objected to Peter's use of soldier's stationery with patriotic pictures and poems on it and to his protest that the Union cause was divinely sanctioned. She replied indignantly that she thought God had nothing to do with the war. Bitterly, she reproached Peter for having caused her little but unhappiness in their married life. Hers were not letters to boost the spirits of a soldier far from home.

Margaret's complaints elicited from the simple Irish American carpenter an eloquent defense of the cause for which he was pledged to fight. True, he admitted, the immediate occasion for his enlistment had been that unfortunate drinking spree in Boston, but he now felt that a larger purpose had brought him to fight for the Union cause. Why must *he* fight for it? What was it to *him*? "This is my country as much as the man that was born on the soil," he explained, "and so it is with every man who comes to this country and becomes a citezen." This he claimed not as a charter of privileges but as a solemn responsibility. "This being the case I have as much interest in the maintenence of the goverment and laws and the integrity of the nation as any other man," he continued.[7]

He then tried to express to his wife the meaning of the war in words that were remarkably similar to those used by the president whose policies he generally opposed. "This war with all its evils with all its errors and missmanagement," he wrote, "is a war in which the people of all nations have a vital interest. This is the first test of a modern free government in the act of sustaining itself against internal enemys and matured rebellion. All men who love free government and equal laws are watching this crisis to see if a republic can sustain itself in such a case. If it fail then the hopes of milions fall and the designs and wishes of all tyrants will suceed. The old cry will be sent forth from the aristocrats of europe that such is the comon end of all republics. . . . The giant republic has fallen."[8]

He admitted to feeling that the Lincoln administration had mismanaged the war, mishandled the army, and, worst of all, freed the slaves, but if slavery was in the way of the Republic's survival, then so much the worse for slavery as far as this Irishman was concerned. Think, he urged Margaret, of what a beacon America was to the oppressed of the world, a place where they could live in freedom and eat the fruit of their labor.

"What would be the condition to day of hundreds of thousands of the sons and daughters of poor opressed old erin [Ireland] if they had not a free land like this to emigrate to? . . . The same may be said of thousands from other lands." Though he was a member of a nationality supposedly victimized by severe discrimination in America, Peter Welsh then put the case plainly in terms that still resonate more than a century later: "Contrast the condition of the masses of this with any other country in the world and the advantages we enjoy will stand out boldly so that the blindest can see them. Here there is no bloated peted [petted] rascals or what is called in monarchial countrys the aristocracy. . . . Here the poorest mother may look with joy and satisfaction on her ofspring if she only gives him a proper training in his tender years . . . and from that [he] takes his start with all the honours and the hiest position that a great nation can bestow open before him."[9] Nancy Hanks's son often said the same—and with but little greater eloquence.

"Is this not worth fiting for?" Peter concluded. He answered his own question: "It is our duty to do our share for the comon wellfare not only of the present generation but of future generations. Such being the case it becomes the duty of every one no matter what his position to do all in his power to sustain for the present and to perpetuate for the benefit [of] future generations a government . . . which is superior to any the world has yet known."[10]

Margaret would not be persuaded and continued to complain about the Union cause and Peter's absence. Her husband, still very concerned about her health, offered advice and urged her to see a doctor, avoid overwork, and try not to worry.

On Saint Patrick's Day 1863, General Meagher presided over a full day of festivities in the camps of the Irish Brigade. A good time—and quite a bit of whiskey—was had by all. Festivities stopped abruptly, though, when word came of significant skirmishing several miles up the Rappahannock at Kelly's Ford, and Meagher ordered the brigade into line, ready for battle. Peter's company was now the color company, responsible for bearing the national and regimental banners. The company fell into line, and Captain Sanborn, by now recovered from his Fredericksburg wound, was startled to see that the green flag was missing. Where was it? The bearer could not say. Turning to Welsh, who may have looked more sober than the other noncommissioned officers, Sanborn ordered him to find the colors and get into line with them. When Peter did, Sanborn made him the permanent bearer of the green flag. The next day the decision was made official, and Welsh received the accompanying promotion to the rank of sergeant. "I shall feel proud to bear up that flag of green, the emblem of Ireland and Irish men," he wrote Margaret, "and espesialy having received it on that day dear to every irish heart, the festivel of St Patrick."[11]

The much-depleted size of the Irish Brigade earned it a reserve role at the Battle of Chancellorsville that May, and it saw only brief fighting with few casualties. Still, it had just as much hard marching to do over roads that became bottomless mud when heavy rains came the day after the battle. And the men experienced just as much discouragement when the army retreated after what the soldiers could only conclude had been another defeat. Back on the north side of the Rappahannock, camp life resumed, and Peter, along with Company K's first sergeant, built themselves "the purtyest little shanty in this army."[12] As usual, he was content and healthy.

The quiet routine was broken again on Sunday evening, June 14, 1863, just as the Irish Brigade was coming off a two-day picket-guard detail. Orders came to march immediately, and march they did, all night and most of the next day. Days of long, hard marches followed, now in smothering heat and choking dust, now in torrential rains and calf-deep mud. Lee had slid around the Army of the Potomac's right flank and was racing northward. The Federals followed, keeping themselves between Lee and Washington. Two weeks into the campaign, on Monday, June 29, the Second Corps, of which the Irish Brigade was part, marched thirty-two miles from Frederick to Uniontown, Maryland, "the greatest march ever made by any part of our army," Peter thought.[13] Thousands of exhausted and footsore soldiers fell out along the roads, unable to go on without rest, and later hobbled along to catch up with their regiments as best they could throughout the night. In Company K, Twenty-eighth Massachusetts, Peter was one of the handful who kept up the pace all day, and he was the only man with enough energy left to light a fire and boil a pot of coffee (the soldiers' ubiquitous favorite beverage) before retiring that night.

On Wednesday, July 1, the Second Corps was marching northward again, crossing into "Pencilvenia" while listening to the angry muttering of artillery somewhere off to the north near the town of Gettysburg.[14] The next day, they formed into battle lines near the center of the army. A mile away across rolling farmland, the rebel army remained strangely quiet throughout the morning.

Then, at about four in the afternoon, the Confederates struck hard at the left end of the Union line, and the Irishmen could judge by the gradually approaching roar of battle that things were not going well for the Federals there. Not long after five o'clock, the call for reinforcements came. Among the Second Corps troops sent in response was the Irish Brigade. When the men were ordered to form into line and prepare to march toward the steadily rising crescendo of battle on their left, Catholic chaplain William Corby of the Eighty-eighth New York asked the brigade commander, Patrick Kelly, if he could give the men absolution. Kelly agreed and had the troops called to attention. The chaplain climbed atop a small boulder and told the men his purpose. The soldiers knelt and uncovered their heads while Corby recited in Latin the formula of absolution, then concluded with the reminder that the "Catholic church refuses Christian burial to the soldier who turns his back upon the foe or deserts his flag."[15] Thus encouraged and challenged, the men rose and took their places in line.

Marching in the center of the division's front line, the Twenty-eighth advanced through a thin skirt of forest called Trostle's Woods, across a farm lane, and out into a field of ripening wheat. On the far side of the field rose a wooded hill that everyone seemed to remember most for the thickly strewn boulders that covered its slope and concealed the Confederate riflemen who blazed away at the advancing Irishmen. On went the Irish Brigade, only some six hundred–strong now, once again making a magnificent charge under their five flags of green—one borne by Peter—and five of red, white, and blue. They pressed in and fought at close quarters with the rebels among the rocks, forcing the Southerners to flee down the back side of the hill. Their success was short-lived, however. New brigades of Confederates came up on both the left and right, the ones in front rallied and came on again, and the Irish Brigade was driven rapidly back across the hotly contested wheat field, barely escaping being surrounded and cut off. A third of their scant numbers had fallen, including half the men of the Twenty-eighth Massachusetts.

The following day brought a noisy artillery bombardment, but its chief aim (and that of the Confederate infantry assault that followed) was another sector of the Union line, and the Twenty-eighth escaped unharmed. Lee retreated, and the Army of the Potomac followed at a far more leisurely pace than when it drove north. Months of desultory and inconsequential camping and campaigning followed in Virginia.

Throughout this period Peter continued to enjoy excellent health, but Margaret's health and state of mind both deteriorated. She was frantic enough in her loneliness to contemplate traveling down to Virginia to visit him, but he had to explain to her that that was simply not possible. Under the steady assault of his wife's complaints, his dedication to the cause began to flag late in 1863. He said that he wished he could be promoted to the rank of commissioned officer so that he could resign and go home. Failing that, he hoped for a furlough—but furloughs could be had only by reenlisting, in effect extending his term of service from the fall of 1865 to early 1867, if he and the war both lasted that long.

In the end, Peter signed on for another term and in exchange took thirty-five days of leave in New York. "The time sliped by on lightning wheels," he later wrote, "it seemed verry short to a man after being a year and a half from home."[16] He returned to the regiment in early April 1864 as the army, now operating under the orders of the more resolute and skillful Ulysses S. Grant, was preparing for its spring offensive against Lee.

"The Twenty-eighth Massachusetts Volunteer Regiment broke camp at Stevensburg, Va., at dark on the evening of May 3, 1864," wrote Capt. James Fleming in his report as senior surviving officer of the regiment several weeks later.[17] They marched all that night and crossed the Rapidan River the next morning, moving into an area of dense woods known as the Wilderness. Battle was joined May 5, but the Twenty-eighth saw mostly skirmishing duties and suffered only a dozen or so casualties. Still, the experience was what Peter called "a pretty rough time," with "8 days constantly fighting."[18]

By May 12 the tide of battle had carried the contending armies to a hamlet named Spotsylvania Court House, near the edge of the Wilderness area. There, Lee had succeeded in blocking Grant, and on that morning, Grant made his bid to break Lee's lines in a massive predawn assault spearheaded by the Second Corps. Initial results were good, with Confederate entrenchments overrun and dozens of guns and thousands of soldiers captured, including Confederate general Edward Johnson, taken by one of the Irishmen of the Twenty-eighth.

Somewhere in this first stage of the fighting, Peter Welsh took a bullet in the left arm. "A flesh wound in my left arm," he described it, "just a nice one to keep me from any more fighting or marching this campaign." It had been "the greatest battle of the war," he told Margaret, and "we licked saucepans out of them."[19]

"Slight" was what the doctors at the Second Corps field hospital had called the wound. But on May 14 the surgeon at Carver Hospital in Washington determined that the bullet had shattered the bone in Peter's forearm and was lodged there still. Three days later, doctors operated to remove the bullet, along with some bone fragments. All went well for another three days. Margaret arrived from New York, and was at his bedside well before May 20, when his condition became more serious. The wound hemorrhaged, and although attendants stopped the bleeding, pyemia (blood poisoning) set in within days. Knowledge of antiseptic practices was virtually nil among Civil War surgeons, and infections carried off thousands of soldiers who would otherwise have recovered from their wounds. Now infection went to work on Peter. The wound drained an alarming discharge, nausea and chills set in, and he could no longer eat. By May 28, he was delirious, and before the day was over, the infection had claimed the life of this soldier who had always been so healthy.

"He is dead and will be in New York in morning," Margaret wired her uncle in that city.[20] The army records tell us she took his effects with her—his blanket, cap, two shirts, trousers, and boots. She never remarried.

Peter had once written that the war would be "a powerfull purifier" for the nation. Perhaps, had he been able to see it through to the end, it might have purified him of his racism, as it did at least in part for many Northern soldiers who witnessed the way black troops fought and who came to know some blacks personally. Perhaps he might have seen that the newly freed slave as well as the recent Irish immigrant both had "a stake in America," an interest in the same freedom, and the same chance of bettering himself for which he had fought. For either of them and for the rest of America, that was indeed something "worth fiting for."[21]

Notes

1. John William De Forest, *A Volunteer's Adventures: A Union Captain's Record of the Civil War*, ed. James H. Croushore (New Haven, CT: Yale University Press, 1946), 151.

2. Peter Welsh, *Irish Green and Union Blue: The Civil War Letters of Peter Welsh, Color Sergeant, 28th Regiment Massachusetts Volunteers,* ed. Lawrence Frederick Kohl and Margaret Cosse Richard (New York: Fordham University Press, 1986), 28. For historical accuracy and flavor, Welsh's spelling, punctuation, and syntax have been preserved in this and all succeeding quotes.

3. Ibid., 20–21.

4. Ibid., 24.

5. Ibid., 42.

6. Ibid., 43.

7. Ibid., 65.

8. Ibid., 65–66.

9. Ibid., 66–67.

10. Ibid., 67.

11. Ibid., 80.

12. Ibid., 98.

13. Ibid., 109.

14. Ibid.

15. Harry W. Pfanz, *Gettysburg: The Second Day* (Chapel Hill: University of North Carolina Press, 1987), 268.

16. Welsh, *Irish Green and Union Blue*, 152.

17. U.S. War Department, *The War of the Rebellion: Official Records of the Union and Confederate Armies*, 128 vols. (Washington, DC: U.S. Government Printing Office, 1881–1901), series 1, vol. 35, pt. 1, p. 388.

18. Welsh, *Irish Green and Union Blue*, 156.

19. Ibid.

20. Ibid., 157.

21. Ibid., 67, 70.

16

Winfield Scott Hancock
"The Knightly Corps Commander"

Ethan S. Rafuse

Although it was the private soldiers, such as Peter Welsh, who fought the battles, men of higher rank usually directed their actions and thus exercised an influence on the course of events far out of proportion to their numbers. Those of the highest rank, the great commanders such as Robert E. Lee and Ulysses S. Grant, gained immense fame, becoming well known—if sometimes little understood—by vast numbers of Americans. Yet between army head-quarters and the men in the ranks who did the fighting and most of the bleeding were several layers of officers whose job was to turn their commanders' ideas into realities on the battlefield; these were the men who deployed the troops and led them into the zone of danger. The outcome of the battles often hung on the skill, inspirational abilities, and raw courage of such midranking officers.

Winfield Scott Hancock was among the best of these men. In his report on the Battle of Williamsburg in May 1862, Gen. George B. McClellan described Hancock's performance as "superb," and the description became a standard one: In fact, he became known as "Hancock the superb." In presenting Hancock's story, historian Ethan Rafuse, of the United States Military Academy, West Point, New York, gives readers a glimpse of the role and importance of midlevel commanders in the Civil War. Professor Rafuse is the author of several articles on the Civil War as well as *A Single Grand Victory: The First Campaign and Battle of Manassas* (2002), and he is currently revising his dissertation on Hancock's army commander George McClellan for publication.

The actions of presidents and army commanders have traditionally dominated discussions of the military history of the Civil War. However, the course of military operations was frequently—and often decisively—shaped by decisions made at the corps, division, and brigade levels. The Civil War was the first conflict in which the American people fielded armies of fifty thousand men or more. These armies were too large and conditions in the field changed too rapidly for commanders to exercise close supervision over the entire range of an army's operations. To achieve success on the battlefield, it was therefore essential that leaders in the second echelon possess the character and ability to exercise independent judgment and make sound decisions. Fortunately for its cause, the Union found men equal to the task. This is the story of one of the best of them.

Although he never held a major independent command, few officers were held in higher regard by professional soldiers and the general public by the end of the Civil War than Winfield Scott Hancock. Ulysses S. Grant's postwar relations with Hancock were often strained, yet in his memoirs, Grant wrote: "[Hancock's] name was never mentioned as having committed in battle a blunder . . . his personal courage and his presence with his command in the thickest of the fight won for him the confidence of troops serving under him."[1] On Hancock's death, former New York governor Samuel J. Tilden spoke of "the dashing bravery and consummate abilities of the superb soldier whom the country has lost."[2]

Hancock was one of twin boys born on February 14, 1824, to Benjamin Franklin and Elizabeth Hoxworth Hancock in Montgomery Square, Pennsylvania. The family moved to Norristown, Pennsylvania, three years later, where, after passing the bar in 1828, Benjamin Hancock enjoyed a forty-year career in law and local Democratic politics. From his father, Winfield inherited a powerful respect for the law and for the states' rights and limited-government doctrines of the Democratic Party—qualities that would shape his behavior in war and peace.

Benjamin Hancock hoped his sons would follow in his footsteps and become lawyers. However, it did not take long for the child named after the great soldier of the War of 1812 to exhibit an uncommon fondness for the military. While attending the Norristown Academy, for example, Winfield organized a company of his classmates and led them in drill. In 1840, Benjamin yielded to his son's desire for a military education and secured for him an appointment to the United States Military Academy at West Point, New York. Although he did not devote himself as seriously as he could have to his studies, Hancock nonetheless impressed his fellow cadets; one of them later said Hancock was "as manly a fellow as the Academy ever produced."[3] He completed the program in 1844, graduating eighteenth in a class of twenty-five. When the Mexican War began two years later, Hancock was on recruiting duty and did not reach the theater of operations until midway through the final campaign against Mexico City. He did well in his first battles—at Churubusco on August 20, 1847, and at Chapultepec on September 7—winning a brevet promotion for gallantry.

The benefits of service in Mexico were not limited to the experience Hancock gained managing men in battle. Garrison duty after the fighting ended proved to be a thoroughly pleasant experience for the young officer, who shared a highly congenial mess with Virginians Henry Heth and Lewis Armistead. Together, they toured the magnificent Valley of Mexico, maintained a festive and bountiful table, and enjoyed the company of many attractive young señoritas. "Never," Heth would later recall, "was a mess happier than ours."[4]

Soon after the Treaty of Guadalupe Hidalgo was ratified in March 1848, Hancock and his unit returned to the United States. In June, he was appointed regimental quartermaster for the Sixth Infantry Regiment, a post he held until October 1849, when he was made regimental adjutant. While stationed in Saint Louis, Hancock met and won the hand of Almira Russell, the daughter of a prominent local merchant. They were married on January 24, 1850. The weather on their wedding day was stormy, but the same could never be said of the marriage. During their thirty-six-year union, which produced a son and a daughter, Winfield and Almira Hancock's devotion to one another was unshakable, in good times and bad.

Life in the antebellum army could be hard indeed, not least of all because of the limited opportunities for advancement available to junior officers. In fact, Hancock was not promoted to captain until November 5, 1855. Soon thereafter, he was ordered to Florida and assigned the task of managing the base of supplies for forces operating against the Seminoles. It was a miserable experience, but Hancock's performance impressed his superiors. When William S. Harney, commander of the campaign against the Seminoles, was assigned to duty at Fort Leavenworth, Kansas, in 1857, he secured Hancock's transfer to that post. During his nine months in Kansas, Hancock supported efforts to maintain a truce that had been forged between Free-Soilers and proslavery forces in that troubled territory. He also helped organize Albert Sidney Johnston's expedition to Utah to quell unrest among the Mormons, and he served as quartermaster for a force sent to support Johnston in May 1858.

One year later, Hancock was appointed chief quartermaster for the southern district of California. His duties were not particularly onerous, and he was able to engage in a number of business ventures, none of which were very successful. He also kept an eye on political developments back east. As a states' rights Democrat with many Southern friends, he viewed the prospect of Abraham Lincoln's election to the presidency in 1860 as, in his wife's words, "[a] situation pregnant with danger."[5] He cast his vote for John C. Breckinridge in the November election but did not hesitate to express his determination to stand by the Union when news of the fall of Fort Sumter reached California during the last week of April 1861.

Before Hancock and his Southern colleagues parted company, they gathered at his and Almira's home for one last "never-to-be-forgotten evening." They sang songs, shed tears, and vowed everlasting friendship. But civil war is the cruelest form of war. "Three of the six from whom we parted on that evening in Los Angeles," Almira Hancock would later note, "were killed in front of General Hancock's troops."[6]

On arriving in Washington in September 1861, Hancock received unpleasant news. The army grapevine had it that he was to be assigned to quartermaster duty in Kentucky. Fortunately, George McClellan, commander of the Army of the Potomac, reached Hancock before the War Department did. Horrified at the prospect of his fellow Pennsylvanian's talents being wasted in mundane quartermaster duties, McClellan directed Hancock to maintain a low profile until he could find a brigade for him to command. Hancock did so and was rewarded on September 23 with a commission as a brigadier general of volunteers and a brigade in William F. "Baldy" Smith's division of the Army of the Potomac. He and his wife were delighted, although her enthusiasm was dampened a bit when someone informed her that "if a cannon were fired down Pennsylvania Avenue it would strike a hundred or more newly created brigadiers."[7]

McClellan's regard for Hancock was so high that he probably could have gotten command of a division if he had arrived in Washington sooner, but it was likely for the best in the long run that he did not. Hancock, in the words of staff officer James H. Wilson, became "a warm admirer of McClellan," with whom he shared a keen appreciation of the need to carefully prepare and thoroughly train their volunteer army before operations began.[8] Hancock also shared McClellan's distaste for meddling by politicians in military affairs and those who wanted to make the abolition of slavery a Union war aim. But as the war progressed, officers of prominence in the Army of the Potomac who were loyal to "Little Mac" and his conservative principles came to be viewed with deep distrust by the meddlesome and powerful radical faction of the Republican Party. Starting out as a brigade commander enabled Hancock to steer clear of the open factionalism that distinguished the Army of the Potomac's high command during the first two years of the war; it also allowed him to establish an unimpeachable combat record that somewhat inoculated him from radical criticism when he rose to a level where loyalty to McClellan could be a liability.

Hancock brought an ideal combination of military professionalism and personal magnetism to the task of leading men. Over six feet tall and weighing 170 pounds, with a dark, imperial beard and deep blue eyes, he had a presence that inspired both awe and respect. "Hancock is," proclaimed one soldier, "the tallest, and most shapely, and in many respects

. . . the best looking officer of them all . . . dignified, gentlemanly and commanding. I think if he were in civilian clothes, and should give commands in the army to those who did not know him, he would be likely to be obeyed at once, and without any question."⁹ Hancock expected much from his men and could be ferocious when they failed to meet his high standards (the art and munificence of his profanity became legendary within the army). But he also recognized that Americans expected their leaders to be democratic as well as heroic, and he endeared himself to his men by sharing their hardships, learning as many of their names as possible, never failing to appear where the fighting was heaviest, and being as lavish in his praise when they did well as he was in his criticism when they did not.

Hancock also mastered the mundane but no less crucial aspects of generalship. During his years as a staff officer he had developed a command of regulations and learned the value of attention to detail, which enabled him to dispose of paperwork and negotiate red tape with alacrity and efficiency. Hancock also did not underestimate the importance of good public relations in what President Abraham Lincoln proclaimed to be "a people's contest."¹⁰ Unlike many of his fellow officers, he made a point of maintaining a good relationship with the reporters who followed the movements of the Army of the Potomac. Moreover, as one fellow officer recalled, "correspondents of the principal journals yielded, like every one else, to his captivating bearing and manners."¹¹

On March 23, 1862, after six months of arduous training, Hancock and his brigade boarded ships bound for the peninsula between the York and James Rivers, where McClellan planned to make his grand campaign on Richmond. "I am off at last," Hancock wrote his wife, "and it is a matter of great pain to me that I am unable to see you again before we part—God alone knows for how long."¹²

Unfortunately, the campaign immediately bogged down in front of Confederate works at Yorktown and the Warwick River. Not until after a month-long siege, during which Hancock and his command fought a number of minor skirmishes, did the rebels abandon the lower peninsula. To cover their retreat, they posted a rear guard east of Williamsburg, which the Federal army attacked on May 5. At 11 A.M., Hancock received orders to seize a redoubt at the northern end of the enemy line. The position was unoccupied, and he easily accomplished this task before pushing his men forward to capture a second redoubt and open artillery fire on the Confederate line. When the rebels counterattacked, Hancock pulled his command back slightly. Once the enemy was within thirty paces of the new line, he had his men unleash two volleys that broke the attackers' momentum. He then ordered a bayonet charge that swept the field and turned a stalemated battle into a complete Federal victory. Like a proud father, he beamed with delight over his men's performance. "My men behaved brilliantly, and captured the first color yet taken," he exulted to his wife, "showing hard and determined fighting."[13]

Hancock's superiors were similarly lavish in their praise for *his* performance. General Smith commended him for "the brilliancy of the plan of battle; the coolness of its execution; the seizing of the proper instant for changing from the defensive to the offensive . . . and the completeness of the victory."[14] McClellan's assessment of his performance was more succinct. "Hancock," he wrote his wife, "was superb."[15]

Despite his fine performance at Williamsburg, Hancock remained a relatively minor figure in the Army of the Potomac until the Battle of Antietam on September 17, 1862. During that horrible contest, Israel Richardson, commander of the First Division of the Second Corps, fell mortally wounded, and McClellan personally ordered Hancock to take his place. At the time, the shot-torn division held "Bloody Lane" in the center of the battlefield, which it had captured after a savage struggle. When Hancock reached his new command at 3:00 P.M., the bulk of the fighting in that sector was over. Under orders to hold his ground, he spent the rest of the day shoring up and consolidating his unit's position. The battle was not renewed the following day, and Lee withdrew his army back into Virginia.

McClellan's delay in recrossing the Potomac after Antietam exhausted President Lincoln's patience, and on November 7 the general was replaced as commander of the Army of the Potomac by Ambrose Burnside. Neither McClellan's removal nor Lincoln's Preliminary Emancipation Proclamation, issued on September 22, were popular with Hancock. He respected McClellan and feared that making emancipation a Northern war aim would be counterproductive because it would only induce the South to fight harder. But he refused to join those who spoke of taking the army to Washington to compel a reversal of policy. "We are," he sternly admonished them, "serving no one man; we are serving our country."[16]

Burnside immediately marched the army to Falmouth, Virginia, where he planned to cross the Rappahannock River at Fredericksburg and push on to Richmond. However, by the time he managed to get the troops across the river, the Confederate army was in an impregnable position south of Fredericksburg. Burnside decided to attack it head-on.

The decision was a foolish one, and Hancock knew it, but he was a soldier, and soldiers follow orders. So, on December 13, 1862, he led his three brigades forward. The first advanced to within twenty-five yards of the Confederate position but no further. The second brigade did no better, and neither did the third. The attack cost the division over 40 percent of its manpower. Hancock was unscathed, although a bullet had passed through his overcoat—"just escaping my abdomen," he informed his wife, "one-half inch more and I would have had a fatal wound."[17] The army recrossed the Rappahannock on December 16. On January 25, 1863, Burnside was removed from command, and Joseph "Fighting Joe" Hooker was chosen as his replacement, thanks in part to his ties to the radical Republicans in Congress.

Hooker did a magnificent job reinvigorating the army, and when the time came for operations, he devised a good strategy. But just as he was on the verge of success, Fighting Joe lost his nerve, giving Confederate general Robert E. Lee the opportunity to inflict yet another humiliating defeat on the Army of the Potomac at the Battle of Chancellorsville. For the Federal cause, one of the few bright spots in the battle was Hancock's stellar performance. He and his men fought brilliantly as they covered the army's retreat from the field on May 4. "When all others had left," a staff officer later said, "Hancock held his command in two lines of battle, back to back, one fronting towards Gordonsville, the other towards Fredericksburg, with his artillery firing down the line between; and so kept the enemy at bay until the roads leading to the rear had been cleared . . . and the way was open for his own slow and orderly retreat."[18]

The defeat at Chancellorsville infuriated Hancock. "I cannot stand any more inflictions of this kind," he wrote to his wife, "our last failure . . . should have been a brilliant victory. . . . But it seems that Providence for some wise purpose intended our defeat." If the Lord had, in fact, sided with the rebels at Chancellorsville, Hancock was not surprised. After all, he noted, "the day before the fight Hooker said to a general officer, 'God Almighty could not prevent me from winning a victory to-morrow.'" "Could we," he asked rhetorically, "expect a victory after that?" Hancock did, however, take pleasure in advising his wife that "Hooker's day is over." Like most officers in the Army of the Potomac who strongly identified with McClellan, he never liked Hooker, whom he viewed as a member of "that class of generals who the Republicans care to bolster up." As to whom he hoped would replace Hooker, Hancock did not say, but he knew with certainly it would not be him. "Under no conditions," he assured his wife, "would I accept the command."[19] He did, however, accept promotion to command of the Second Corps on June 10.

Hancock had barely familiarized himself with his new duties before the time came for action. On June 13 the army was once again on the march, this time heading north toward Pennsylvania in pursuit of Lee's army. Hancock pushed his men hard. On June 26, they crossed the Potomac; three days later, they marched thirty hot, dusty miles to Union-town, Maryland, where they rested before pushing on to Taneytown on the morning of July 1. During the march north, Hancock's wish for a change at the top was fulfilled, for on June 28, Washington gave command of the army to his good friend George Gordon Meade.

As his men were arriving at Taneytown, Hancock rode over to Meade's headquarters, where the two men briefly discussed the situation and Meade's contingency plan to pull the army back to a position several miles to the south, behind Pipe Creek. As they conversed, however, Federal troops were hotly engaged near a small Pennsylvania town called Gettysburg. When news of the battle and the death of John F. Reynolds, commander of the engaged units, reached headquarters, Meade immediately ordered Hancock to Gettysburg to take control of the situation.

Hancock arrived at Gettysburg around four that afternoon and was greeted with a truly depressing sight. Two corps had been overwhelmed north and west of the town, and thousands of Union soldiers could be seen scrambling through the streets and up Cemetery Hill without order or direction. Hancock's arrival turned the tide. The men, recalled one general on the scene, "knew him by fame, and his stalwart figure, his proud mien, and his superb soldierly bearing seemed to verify all the things that fame had told about him. His presence was a reinforcement, and everybody on the field felt stronger for his being there."[20] By nightfall, Hancock had rallied his forces and placed them in a formidable defensive position on the heights south of town. That night, Meade ordered the rest of the army to Gettysburg.

Hancock's heroics at Gettysburg did not end on July 1. The following day his forceful, untiring leadership prevented the folly of Third Corps commander Gen. Daniel Sickles from fatally compromising the Federal position on Cemetery Ridge. On July 3, Hancock and his corps bore the brunt of the famous Pickett-Pettigrew charge; during the preliminary bombardment, he boldly rode the lines through a horrifying rain of shot and shell, encouraging and inspiring his men. Although severely wounded in the groin during the charge, he refused to relinquish command until the enemy attack was repulsed. "I have never seen a more formidable attack," he informed Meade once the rebel tide had ebbed, "and if the Sixth and Fifth Corps have pressed up, the enemy will be destroyed."[21] Although

Meade did not "press up," a great victory had been won, and Hancock became a national hero. For his services at Gettysburg, he would receive the thanks of Congress in 1866.

Hancock's wound kept him away from duty for nearly six months. In December, he returned to the army, then in winter quarters near Culpeper, Virginia. His friend Secretary of War Edwin Stanton, however, recognized Hancock was in no condition for the field and ordered him to the less arduous task of raising recruits. (Hancock was one of the few men who maintained cordial relations with both McClellan and Stanton, who despised one another.) Although his recruiting efforts were not particularly successful, a comfortable billet in Harrisburg and the enthusiasm that greeted his public appearances made the assignment rewarding both physically and psychologically.

Hancock returned to Meade's headquarters on March 23, 1864, where he learned of plans to reorganize the army. Two corps, the First and the Third, were to be disbanded, with their units transferred to the Second, Fifth, and Sixth Corps. Hancock formally reassumed command of the Second Corps, now the largest in the army, on March 24, and he threw himself with characteristic energy into the task of organizing and drilling his troops. By the end of April the corps was ready for the campaign being planned by the new general in chief, Ulysses S. Grant.

Hancock's still-painful wound forced him to ride in an ambulance during much of the 1864 Overland campaign, which began on May 4, but when the fighting started, he was back in the saddle, leading and inspiring his men. "I suffer agony on these occasions," he confided to his wife, "but must go into action on horseback."[22] During the Battle of the Wilderness, his sledgehammer attack along Orange Plank Road on May 6 overwhelmed one Confederate corps before the arrival of another, but the failure of other Federal units to come up in support forced the Second Corps back to prepared positions along Brock Road. Hancock rallied his men there and fought off a series of desperate enemy attacks before nightfall put an end to the fighting. A staff officer who encountered him during the battle later remembered being "lost in a contemplation of the dramatic scene presented in the person of the knightly corps commander . . . his right arm was extended to its full length in pointing out certain positions as he gave his orders, and his commanding form towered still higher. . . . It was itself enough to inspire the troops to deeds of unmatched heroism."[23]

At Spotsylvania Hancock's massive assault on the morning of May 12 crushed the "Mule Shoe" salient at the center of Lee's line, and his unit took over twenty-eight hundred prisoners. Included among the prisoners was Gen. Edward Johnson, who, on being brought to Hancock, embraced his old friend from the antebellum army and proclaimed, "This is d---d bad fortune; yet I would rather have had this good fortune fall to you than to any other man living."[24]

Despite Hancock's great success on May 12, Lee was not beaten, and fighting continued without letup for several weeks. The low point for the Federals came on June 3 when Hancock and his command joined in an assault on Lee's position at Cold Harbor. The situation was every bit as hopeless as that at Fredericksburg. "The loss in commanders," Hancock wrote afterward, "was unusually severe . . . a blow to the corps from which it did not soon recover."[25]

On June 12, three corps, including Hancock's, were directed to cross the James River to seize Petersburg and the railroads that supplied Richmond. Three days later, when his men arrived in front of the lightly held Confederate works at Petersburg, Hancock deferred to the judgment of his old friend Baldy Smith and did not attack them as vigorously as he could have. A great opportunity was thereby lost, and Grant was forced to resort to siege operations.

On August 21, nine days after receiving word of his promotion to brigadier general in the regular army, Hancock was directed to take his command to Reams' Station to help tear up the railroad on which Lee depended for supplies. Hancock and his troops arrived there on August 24 and were savagely attacked the following day. After a hard fight, the Union troops were driven from the field, with a loss of twenty-seven hundred men and nine guns. In his report, Hancock attributed the defeat to the poor location of "the defensive position at Reams' . . . selected on another occasion by another corps," the fact that the Second Corps had lost twenty thousand men since May, and the poor quality of both the raw recruits and the substitutes Washington had sent to replace them.[26] Years later Hancock's adjutant wrote that, although the men redeemed themselves during an operation along Boydton Plank Road in October, "the agony of that day [at Reams' Station] never passed away from the proud soldier, who, for the first time . . . saw his lines broken and guns taken."[27]

On November 26, Hancock was ordered to Washington to direct the effort to recruit the First Veteran Corps. He remained on this duty until February 1865, when he was named commander of the Middle Military Division and the Department of West Virginia. He spent the rest of the war dealing with guerrillas and preparing for a push southward from Winchester that was never ordered. Then, in the aftermath of Lincoln's assassination, he was called to Washington to oversee the trial and execution of John Wilkes Booth's fellow conspirators.

In August 1866, one month after receiving a promotion to major general in the regular army, Hancock assumed command of the Military Department of the Missouri, where he directed an unsuccessful expedition into western Kansas "to intimidate, and, if necessary," in the words of one participant, "make war on the Indians" in the spring of 1867.[28] The expedition was a complete and utter failure. Hancock's heavy-handed treatment of the Indians with whom he came into contact, which culminated in the destruction of a village in April, provoked a war that would plague the Department of the Missouri for months. By the time a treaty ending the fighting was signed in October 1867, Hancock had left the Great Plains. Two months earlier, he had received orders directing him to replace Philip H. Sheridan as Reconstruction commander in Louisiana and Texas.

Hancock's appointment was part of President Andrew Johnson's effort to regain control over Reconstruction from the radicals in Congress and their allies in the military. Hancock proved to be everything Johnson hoped he would be. During his own tenure in command, Sheridan had repeatedly antagonized white Southerners by intruding into civil affairs in order to protect the interests of freedmen and the radical party in Louisiana. But Hancock's first action upon arriving in New Orleans in November 1867 was to issue General Orders No. 40, in which he made clear his determination to restrain the influence of the military over civil affairs. "When insurrectionary force has been overthrown . . . and the civil authorities are ready and willing to perform their duties," he declared, "the military power should cease to lead."[29] He had drafted the document while traveling from Saint Louis to New Orleans and first read it to his wife, who approved its sentiments but expressed concern that it might lead the "conscientious reconstructionists" to "use their power against you." Hancock had no doubt that it would. "They will crucify me," he predicted, "I warned the President of my intentions. . . . I shall have his sympathy, but he is powerless to help me."[30]

White Southerners and Northern conservatives cheered the order, its author, and his subsequent efforts to reverse policies put in place by Sheridan. And, as expected, Republicans fumed and pressured the commanding general, Grant, to rein in Hancock. A clash with Grant over the removal of officials appointed by Sheridan led Hancock to request relief from the command in February 1868. On March 16, he was directed to report to Washington; he was placed in charge of the Division of the Atlantic twelve days later.

Hancock's stand against radical rule in Louisiana attracted the attention of Democrats looking for a conservative war hero to nominate for the presidency in 1868. By the time the party's nominating convention met in July, Hancock had a large number of supporters, but they were poorly organized, and the nomination went to Horatio Seymour instead. Although disappointed, Hancock fully supported Seymour's candidacy. After the convention, he wrote to a friend that "the preservation of Constitutional Government eminently depends on the success of the Democratic party in the coming election. . . . Had I been the Presidential nominee I should have considered it a tribute . . . to principles which I had proclaimed and protected; but shall I cease to regard these principles, because by the judgment of mutual political friends another has been appointed to put them in execution? Never!"[31]

On March 5, 1869, Hancock was given command of the Department of Dakota, headquartered at Saint Paul, Minnesota. He remained there until November 1872, when he was put in charge of the Division of the Atlantic, the post he would hold for the rest of his life.

Hancock assumed his new position just before the panic of 1873. Several major railroads responded to the economic depression that followed by ruthlessly slashing wages in an effort to maintain profits, provoking the Great Railroad Strike of 1877. The companies first turned to state and local leaders for assistance in breaking up the strike, but governmental efforts were ineffectual, which compelled President Rutherford B. Hayes to commit Federal troops, under Hancock's direction, to the task. Hancock moved swiftly and surely, and in less than three weeks, the strike was broken. Laurels won in strikebreaking duty and a better-managed campaign enabled him finally to capture the Democratic nomination for president in 1880. Hancock's supporters primarily emphasized his war record in their appeal to the American people. But in the end, that record wasn't enough. In November, James A. Garfield, thanks, in part, to the end of the depression, was elected president by a margin of less than ten thousand votes out of approximately nine million cast.

After attending Garfield's inaugural in March 1881, Hancock returned to his duties as commander of the Division of the Atlantic, which he had performed during his run for the presidency. He spent the remainder of his days administering his command and attending public ceremonies. After a short bout with illness, the old soldier passed away at his home on Governor's Island in New York on February 9, 1886.

News of Hancock's death provoked an outpouring of grief across the nation. To the people of the North, even those with whom he had disagreed politically after the war, he was still and always would be Hancock the Superb, whose consistently magnificent leadership on the field of battle had been critical to the preservation of the Union. And white Southerners mourned the loss of a man whose effort to restore the ascendancy of civil authority in the South and sympathetic attitude toward restoring white Democrats to power had been rays of sunlight in an otherwise dark time.

Hancock's ability to appeal to Americans on both sides of the bloody chasm of war was, in part, due to his selective accommodation to the forces of change that divided the nation between 1850 and 1877. During his lifetime the United States was transformed from a loosely connected society of subsistence farmers and small workshops, where political, economic, and social life revolved around the local community, to an industrial, capitalist nation. Revolutions in transportation and communication and the rise of complex bureaucratic organizations and labor specialization encouraged Americans to view themselves as members of national, professional communities in which a man was defined by what he did rather than where he was born. At the same time, the politics of deference that prevailed early in the nineteenth century, in which government policy making was almost exclusively the concern of elites, was being replaced by mass democratic politics. Now, popular sentiment, even when misguided, had to be taken into account by those who would formulate and implement government agendas. These changes took place much more rapidly in the North than in the South; indeed, the sectional conflict over slavery that produced a civil war was a manifestation of the tension between Northerners who welcomed political, economic, and social modernization and Southerners who wanted to preserve their more traditional society.

As a soldier, Hancock had what it took to perform at a consistently high level in what many historians have labeled the first "modern" war. During his years of service in the antebellum army officer corps, he developed the managerial ability to function effectively in the complex bureaucratic institution that was the Civil War army. Although he practiced an old-fashioned style of battlefield leadership, which demanded conspicuous displays of personal courage from officers, Hancock also recognized that innovations in weapons technology had rendered obsolete the popular notion that war consisted of climactic battles decided by grand assaults on entrenched positions. He appreciated the virtues of well-prepared fortifications and fighting on the tactical defensive, virtues that too few in the Western world would be able or willing to recognize until World War I.

Hancock also understood that in a democracy, the influence of politics, with its petty intrigues and narrow-minded partisanship, could not be ignored in the conduct of military affairs. Politics was a constant concern for him, as it was for the entire Army of the Potomac high command. Yet his unwavering commitment to the modern concept of military professionalism, in which the duties of the soldier and the politician were strictly segregated, led him to focus his energies on the soldier's task of implementing national policy; he resisted the temptation to play the political game to promote his political views or personal interests. Unlike too many of his colleagues, Hancock let his fortunes rest on maneuvers on the battlefield rather than in Washington.

When it came to politics in general, however, Hancock was thoroughly traditional. Although he was a member of the national community of the army officer corps throughout his adult life, he nonetheless embraced the conservative political principles—limited government, states' rights, and a strict construction of the Constitution—that traditionalist segments of American society espoused in their efforts to resist economic, social, and political change. He was uncomfortable with the tendency toward centralizing political authority that was typical in the modern nation-state and the unprecedented expansion of the power of the Federal government during the Civil War. Furthermore, he was not enthusiastic about the transformation of the war from a struggle to preserve the Union and Constitution "as they were" to one that would alter the nation and provide it with a "new birth of freedom" through the destruction of slavery.

Hancock was able to accept these developments during the Civil War by rationalizing that it was his task to implement, not make, policy and that they were necessitated by wartime exigencies. But the postwar effort by the Radical Republicans to consolidate and build on these changes to ensure that the fruits of victory would not be lost and that justice would be done to the freedmen was too much for Hancock's sensibilities. When finally placed in a position where he had a hand in the formation of policy, his conservatism, lack of sympathy for the plight of the freedmen, and discomfort with the idea of using Federal power to remake the South in the image of the egalitarian, free-labor North pushed him into the often sordid world of Reconstruction and Gilded Age politics, a world for which he was ill suited.

In the end, although Hancock's political endeavors were distinguished primarily by frustration and failure, they did little to diminish the fame he had earned on the battlefields of America's bloodiest war. His consistently stellar service, from the peninsula to Petersburg and particularly at Gettysburg, was critical to the preservation of the Union. For these rather than for his inauspicious efforts in the political arena, Winfield Scott Hancock would be most remembered by the American people.

Notes

1. Ulysses S. Grant, *Personal Memoirs of Ulysses S. Grant,* 2 vols. (New York: Charles L. Webster, 1885), 2:585.

2. Almira R. Hancock, *Reminiscences of Winfield Scott Hancock* (New York: Charles L. Webster and Co., 1887), 259.

3. Ibid., 244.

4. Henry Heth, *The Memoirs of Henry Heth,* ed. James L. Morrison (Westport, CT: Greenwood Press, 1974), 56.

5. Hancock, *Reminiscences of Hancock,* 58.

6. Ibid., 69–70.

7. Ibid., 78.

8. Ibid., 255.

9. Frank L. Byrne and Andrew T. Weaver, eds., *Haskell of Gettysburg: His Life and Civil War Papers* (Madison: State Historical Society of Wisconsin, 1970), 133.

10. Roy P. Bassler, ed., *The Collected Works of Abraham Lincoln,* 9 vols. (New Brunswick, NJ: Rutgers University Press, 1953–1955), 4:438.

11. Phillipe Regis de Trobriand, *Four Years with the Army of the Potomac,* trans. George K. Dauchy (Boston: Ticknor and Co., 1889), 597.

12. Hancock, *Reminiscences of Hancock,* 91.

13. Ibid., 92.

14. U.S. War Department, *The War of the Rebellion: Official Records of the Union and Confederate Armies,* 128 vols. (Washington, DC: U.S. Government Printing Office, 1881–1901) (hereafter cited as *OR*), series 1, vol. 11, pt. 1, p. 528.

15. Stephen W. Sears, ed., *The Civil War Papers of George B. McClellan: Selected Correspondence, 1860–1865* (New York: Ticknor and Fields, 1989), 256.

16. Hancock, *Reminiscences of Hancock,* 92.

17. Ibid., 93.

18. Francis A. Walker, "Hancock in the War of the Rebellion," in *Personal Recollections of the War of the Rebellion: Addresses Delivered before the New York Commandery of the Loyal Legion of the United States,* ed. James Grant Wilson and Titus Munson Coan, 4 vols. (New York: Published by the Commandery, 1891), 1:357.

19. Hancock, *Reminiscences of Hancock,* 94–95.

20. Harry W. Pfanz, *Gettysburg: Culp's Hill and Cemetery Hill* (Chapel Hill: University of North Carolina Press, 1993), 103.

21. *OR,* series 1, vol. 27, pt. 1, p. 73.

22. Hancock, *Reminiscences of Hancock,* 101.

23. Horace Porter, *Campaigning with Grant* (New York: Century, 1897), 57–58.

24. Hancock, *Reminiscences of Hancock,* 104.

25. *OR,* series 1, vol. 36, pt. 1, p. 346.

26. *OR,* series 1, vol. 42, pt. 1, p. 227.

27. Walker, "Hancock in the War of the Rebellion," 363.

28. W. J. D. Kennedy, ed., *On the Plains with Custer and Hancock: The Journal of Isaac Coates, Army Surgeon* (Boulder, CO: Johnson Books, 1997), 58.

29. Hancock, *Reminiscences of Hancock,* 223.

30. Ibid., 124.

31. Ibid., 138–39.

17

LaSalle Corbell Pickett
"What Happened to Me"

Lesley J. Gordon

LaSalle Corbell Pickett simultaneously overstepped and affirmed the accepted role of a woman in mid-nineteenth-century America. The wife of the tragically famous but hapless Confederate general George Pickett, she used both her status as his widow and her own considerable literary talents during the decades after the Civil War to remake her own and her husband's past, forging an idealized version. In doing so, she was moving beyond the conventional role assigned to women in the mid-1800s. Yet at the same time, she validated the cultural forms of her society, for the idealized Sallie Pickett of her retouched memories was far more meek and retiring than the forceful woman who made her husband a hero after the fact and herself "the child-bride of the Confederacy."

Lesley J. Gordon, who presents LaSalle Pickett's story, is an associate professor of history at the University of Akron, author of *General George E. Pickett in Life and Legend* (1998), and coeditor, with Carol K. Bleser, of *Intimate Strategies of the Civil War: Military Commanders and Their Wives* (2001).

In her 1917 autobiography, *What Happened to Me,* LaSalle "Sallie" Corbell Pickett described a dream she had soon after the end of the Civil War when she and her infant son were traveling by train to Canada to rejoin her husband, ex-Confederate major general George Pickett. The sound of the train had kept her up much of the night, she wrote, reminding her "of the sound of the executioner's axe. All night long it rose and fell through seas of blood—the heart's blood of valiant men, of devoted women, of innocent little children." When LaSalle finally drifted off to sleep near morning, she dreamed that "it was I who had destroyed the world of people whose life blood surged around me with a maddening roar, and that I was destined to an eternity of remorse."[1]

Portions of this chapter have been taken from Lesley J. Gordon, *General George E. Pickett in Life and Legend* (Chapel Hill: University of North Carolina Press, 1998). © 1998 University of North Carolina Press. Reprinted by permission of the University of North Carolina Press.

In this passage and throughout her many published writings, LaSalle Corbell Pickett blended the personal story of her life with a public retelling of war and defeat. In this excerpt, she blamed herself for the suffering and death that all of America, not just her native South, endured in its bloody civil war. But Pickett was no unimpassioned chronicler of events that had occurred decades before, nor was she a helpless victim. As the widow of a famed Confederate general, she claimed a personal role in the dramatic saga of Southern defeat. Despite the passive title of her autobiography, Pickett wrote in a decidedly active and powerful voice. She outlived her husband by five decades, supporting herself and her son with a lucrative career—touring the United States, giving lectures, writing ten books and numerous articles, visiting veteran reunions, and bringing her "firsthand" account to a national audience.

Although Pickett insisted on the veracity of her recollections, scholarly research shows that she fabricated much of her published writings. She lied about her age, lied about her husband's defeats and failures, and lied about her contemporaries. She erroneously presented herself as a child in many of her writings, so that, it would seem, she could better hide the assertiveness and independence she attained as a successful writer and single mother. In writing of the past, she transformed herself into a "child wife," highlighting her husband's strength and masculinity and emphasizing her own delicacy and fragility. Pickett smoothed over embarrassing aspects of the past, using the shield of widowhood to protect her husband's memory and deflect any challenges to her own authority.[2]

Yet there is still "truth" in the emotionally charged words Pickett wrote. Her mix of fact and fiction provides important insights into the war's meaning for a white Southern woman. Underneath her Victorian romanticism and occasional morbidity was a strong-willed woman desperate to make order out of war's chaos. The voice telling these stories spoke of real anguish, true despair, and a steely determination to set things right again.

LaSalle Corbell was eighteen years old in 1861. The first of nine children, she had spent her childhood at her family home in Nansemond County, Virginia. Her parents, John David and Elizabeth Phillips Corbell, were wealthy slaveholders and owned a sizable plantation. War shattered her family's peaceful existence, and Sallie's life, like that of so many of her contemporaries, was never the same.[3]

War first touched LaSalle while she was a student at Lynchburg Female Seminary in Lynchburg, Virginia. She was not attending the elite academy to expand her intellectual capacities; as the eldest daughter of a large Tidewater planter, she was learning how to be a cultivated white Southern lady and preparing to assume the traditional role of devoted wife and mother.[4]

Pickett's published memoirs vividly recalled the early days of secession and crisis. Her autobiography recounted how she and her classmates clustered excitedly in their schoolrooms, believing "that we knew something of war." They cheered at the sight of the first Confederate national flag and felt confident that their brothers, fathers, uncles, and male friends soon would come home, safe and victorious, from the battlefront. They also held a springtime festival to raise money for knapsacks to equip a local rifle company. LaSalle admitted to her postwar readers that she, like so many other Southerners, believed the war would be relatively bloodless and quick. "We saw then," she remembered, "only the bonfires of joy and heard the paeans of victory."[5] Her impression changed when she met a man wounded in battle: "I began to feel that war meant something more than the thrill of martial music and shouts of victory." In retrospect, she stated that "not only soldiers in the field had obstacles to encounter; they loomed in the pathway of the school-girl."[6]

Historians have recently explored the ways in which white elite Southern women such as LaSalle Pickett tried to reinvent themselves during this time of great social crisis. Traditional gender roles no longer sufficed, and new ones were created, tried on, and tested by war.[7] Pickett's wartime recollections showed a young woman eager to play an active role in the conflict, but often frustrated by conventional attitudes and restrictive gender expectations.

In one story, Pickett told of visiting her uncle Col. J. J. Phillips in camp on the day of the famed naval battle between the *Virginia* and the *Monitor* in early March 1862. When her uncle readied a dinghy to join in the action, Pickett begged to accompany him. "'No, No!' he shouted. 'Go Back.'" Unshaken by his refusal, she took a seat in his small vessel when he turned his back. As her uncle realized that she had defied him, "a look of horrified amazement" came over his face. According to Pickett, he declared, "'You needn't think I am going to try to keep you out of danger, you disobedient, incorrigible little minx. . . . It would serve you right if you were shot.'" Pickett attested that she had given little thought to the danger she faced, wanting only to get a good view of the fight.[8]

LaSalle Pickett claimed that the Battle of Seven Pines "brought the war closer to me than any other had yet done."[9] In 1862, she went to Richmond to spend her summer vacation, unable to return to her Tidewater home because it was caught behind Federal lines. This time she did not have to go looking for action, for Northern troops came dangerously close to the Confederate capital. Her portrait of a city reeling from its first brush with enemy invasion is riveting. She wrote to readers of *Cosmopolitan*: "If I could lay before you the picture of the Richmond of those battle-days, you would say that I had written the most powerful peace argument ever penned." Emphasizing the terrible sights and sounds the Richmond citizenry witnessed during the two-day battle, she described the Confederate capital "shaking with the thunders of the battle while the death-sounds thrilled through our agonized souls." Carts loaded with the wounded and the dead crowded the streets, and most residences were open to the injured. Women and children found that the horror of war had come directly into their homes: "Women, girls, and children stood before the doors with wine and food for the wounded as they passed." Soldiers and civilians flooded into Capitol Square, anxiously awaiting news of loved ones, and black crepe was draped on doorways and windows. Remembering a mother who lost her son at Seven Pines, Pickett declared, "Sometimes the Richmond of those days comes back to me now, and I shudder anew with terror."10

Her writings mixed traditional gendered reactions to war, blending the stereotypical feminine repulsion to fighting with the equally stereotypical masculine fascination with battle. She often depicted herself at the forefront of the action, impervious to the danger surrounding her. It appeared that she could not pull herself from the violence. In one account, she told readers of accompanying George as he inspected the lines. As shells began to explode dangerously close, her husband pleaded with her to leave:

> "No indeed," I said. "I'm not a bit afraid, and if I were do you think I would let Pickett's men see me run?"
> "Come, dear, please! You are in danger, useless danger, and that is not bravery."

Despite his entreaties, she stayed at the front, snatching a pair of field glasses to gaze across the lines and allegedly catching a glimpse of General Grant and his wife.11

In another story, Pickett spoke of witnessing the decapitation of a young officer just after he, too, had warned her of the danger she faced in visiting the front. She watched him "riding in that graceful way which the Southerner has by inheritance from a long line of ancestors who have been accustomed to ride over wide reaches of land."12 Regretting her "obstinate resistance to his appeal" that she take shelter, she was mortified to see his death. "Impulsively I sprang from my horse," she wrote, "and ran and picked up the poor head, and I solemnly believe that the dying eyes looked their thanks as the last glimmering of life flickered out."[13] This was a strange portrait, indeed—an officer's wife standing defiant to the dangers of battle.

Most of LaSalle Pickett's books and articles had a decidedly martial tone to them. In *The Bugles of Gettysburg, Pickett and His Men,* and her serialized *Cosmopolitan* article, "The Wartime Story of General Pickett," she became an official military historian. Perhaps this explains why she unabashedly plagiarized large portions of a staff officer's book for her own writings. Realizing that veterans might question a woman's authority to speak of battle, she inserted a male author's voice for the purely military passages. Pickett insisted to readers that she had a right to publish battle narratives; after all, as a general's wife, she had loyally shared in his victories and his defeats. "My story has been so closely allied with that of Pickett and his division," she wrote in *Pickett and His Men,* "that it does not seem quite an intrusive interpolation for me to appear in the record of that warrior band." She asked, "How could I tell the story, and the way in which that story was written, and not be part of it?"[14]

She believed her wartime romance with George Pickett and their subsequent marriage justified her role as historian of this grand American saga. In her published recollections, she never failed to include details of her whirlwind courtship and the marriage to her "Soldier." It is unclear exactly when their courtship began. LaSalle always maintained that she fell in love with George in 1862 when she first met him on a beach in eastern Virginia. Certainly by the spring of 1863, there was supporting evidence from witnesses of a budding romance. It was apparently during the 1863 Suffolk campaign that things really began to heat up. LaSalle described to readers how George saw her nightly after she went to stay with her aunt some ten miles from his command. "Here when all was quiet along the lines," LaSalle attested, "my Soldier would ride in from his headquarters almost every night between the hours of sunset and sunrise to see me—a ride of about thirty miles."[15]

Two officers corroborated LaSalle's assertions. Col. William Dabney Stuart of the Fifty-sixth Virginia complained to his wife that his division commander was "continually riding off to pay court to his young love, leaving the division details to his staff."[16] And Maj. G. Moxley Sorrel criticized George's "frequent applications to be absent" to see his lover. These nightly rides were long, and the major general did not return to his command until early the next morning. Sorrel sensed that even George's close friend James Longstreet, the corps commander, was irritated with Pickett's constant requests to leave camp, and he recounted how Pickett once asked him (Sorrel) for permission instead. The staff officer declined. He felt he could not justifiably take responsibility for a major general's absence should the division move or be attacked. "Pickett went all the same," Sorrel wrote, "nothing could hold him back from that pursuit." He concluded, "I don't think his division benefited from such carpet-knight doings on the field."[17]

LaSalle Pickett also shared her wartime romance with postwar readers by publishing a collection of letters George allegedly sent her from the battlefront. As already mentioned, scholars have seriously questioned whether her husband actually penned these letters. Comparing them to LaSalle's other published writings and a staff officer's history of Pickett's division, they accuse her of fabricating the letters' contents because the published correspondence contains information George could not have known at the time the letters were purportedly written. Scholars have also pointed to the emotional and romantic tone of the published letters as betraying LaSalle's authorship. Some have wondered if LaSalle heavily edited original letters.[18]

It does seem likely that Pickett constructed the bulk of these missives herself, perhaps basing them loosely on some original love letters George sent her. Her other writings repeatedly stressed her husband's devotion to her, even in the thick of battle. This published collection of wartime letters made her "Soldier" speak for himself and thus bolster her claims. Even the title is telling: *The Heart of a Soldier: As Revealed in the Intimate Letters of Genl. George E. Pickett CSA.*

While Pickett yearned to be at the forefront of battle, these letters show her husband was growing weary of war. In one of the published letters, George declared: "Oh, my darling, war and its results did not seem so awful till the love for you. Now—now I want to love and bless and help everything, and there are no foes—no enemies—just love for you and longing for you."[19] Until the war ended, LaSalle attested that her husband frequently interrupted important military operations to write her. In another published letter, he pleaded to know why she had quipped "never mind" to him at their last meeting. "It troubled me all night," he declared. "I wanted to follow after you and ask you what you meant, but couldn't. I would have jumped on Lucy [his horse] and ridden in to Petersburg and found out if it had been possible for me to leave. I was so troubled about it that I was almost tempted to come in anyhow." He wondered if he had hurt her feelings by telling her she need not come to the front anymore, that he had enough men to do soldiers' work: "Were you aggrieved because your blundering old Soldier told you there was no necessity for your coming out to bring dispatches, any longer, that, thank heaven, the recruits and reinforcements were coming in now and that we could manage all right?"[20]

In the published Pickett letters, George appeared more impatient to marry than LaSalle. In one, he urged: "So, my Sally, don't let's wait; send me a line back by Jackerie saying you will come. Come at once, my darling, into this valley of the shadow of uncertainty, and make certain the comfort if I should fall I shall fall as your husband." According to LaSalle, he suggested that they "overlook old-time customs" and marry immediately in his camp. She hastily explained to her postwar audience that some might disapprove of the impropriety of his proposal, noting that for those who knew of the "rigid system of social training in which a girl of that period was reared," it would not be "strange that a maiden, even in war times, could not seriously contemplate the possibility of leaving home and being married by the wayside in that desultory and unstudied fashion." LaSalle felt bound by "social laws" even if George did not, and she convinced him to wait.[21] But her lover was a professional soldier and high-ranking general and had to go where orders sent him. "Cupid does not readily give way to Mars," she stated to her readers, "and in our Southern country a lull between bugle calls was likely to be filled with the music of wedding bells."[22]

Pickett naturally chose to include a description of her wedding day in her writings, and it was a dramatic one. She alleged that she and George had difficulties just getting to the Petersburg church. Unable to obtain a furlough, George instead received permission for "special duty" to leave the front, and LaSalle and her family had to sneak across enemy lines, traveling by ferry and train to reach Petersburg from Chuckatuck. LaSalle's father, two uncles, and a female chaperone accompanied her; her mother had to stay behind to care for her baby brother. At the church, she reunited with George, his brother Charles, and his faithful Uncle Andrew and Aunt Olivia. Finally, after a brief but dramatic delay in obtaining the marriage license, George and LaSalle married on September 15, 1863. She recalled: "I felt like child who had been given a bunch of grapes, a stick of candy. Oh I was happy."[23]

A honeymoon was out of the question, but the couple allegedly managed a festive reception in the Confederate capital. The Picketts's personal celebration became public: LaSalle claimed that several Confederate luminaries attended the party, including President and Mrs. Jefferson Davis, members of Davis's cabinet, and officers in Lee's army. There was also plenty of food, drink, and dancing. "If people could not dance in the crises of life," LaSalle explained to her postwar audience, "the tragedy of existence might be even darker than it is."[24]

In reality the man whom LaSalle Corbell married in 1863 was deep in a personal and professional crisis. A West Point graduate and brevetted Mexican War veteran, George found himself ill prepared for civil war. His former comrades and the nation he had pledged his life to defend became the hated enemy. As the violence escalated, he grew more disturbed. He complained repeatedly, showed flashes of quick anger, and failed when left with any sort of autonomy on the field. As a brigadier general, he was a zealous and aggressive fighter, but when promoted to division commander in October 1862, he seemed overwhelmed with his responsibilities. At Gettysburg, he watched in stunned disbelief as his division shattered itself in a desperate attempt to break the Union line. George never forgot Gettysburg: He brooded over the loss of his division, blaming everyone but himself. He increasingly felt a demise of control and began to perceive the North as uncivilized and demonic.[25]

Soon after his marriage to LaSalle Corbell, George showed further evidence of this loss of personal and professional restraint. When he failed to reclaim Union-held New Bern, North Carolina, in February 1864, he turned his rage on a group of Union prisoners, former members of the North Carolina home guard. Pickett ordered a hasty court-martial and execution of these men, mocking the pleas of Federal officials and ignoring the anguish of victims' family members. Later, this episode would nearly earn Pickett indictment for war crimes by the U.S. government.[26]

Readers of LaSalle Pickett's books and articles will find no mention of this troubled, angry man. Instead, her Soldier was loving and sensitive, courageous and chivalrous. Her literary George Pickett was not perfect, to be sure, but LaSalle used her morally superior female sex to monitor his weakness for drinking and swearing. But as destruction and chaos raged around them, she said, love and serenity thrived within their union. The wartime marriage Pickett described in her books and articles was, indeed, a haven in a heartless, senseless world.[27]

Pickett's memoirs contain several examples of her efforts to seek "rifts of sunshine to break the gloom."[28] In the bloody summer of 1864, while General Pickett and his men faced grueling siege warfare, LaSalle insisted that "there was no lack of social diversions. In a small way we had our dances, our conversaziones and musicales, quite like the gay world that had never known anything about war except from the pages of books and the columns of newspapers. True we did not feast."[29]

Pickett set the final chapter of her wartime story in Richmond in April 1865. Separated from her husband during the Confederacy's final days of existence, she waited in the Southern capital, anxious for news. On April 2, 1865, the Confederate government abandoned Richmond, and the next day, Union troops entered the city. Pickett described her terror and fear as she found herself alone with her baby son. Her slaves had long gone, and rumors circulated that her Soldier was dead. Fires set by Confederates spread, and frenzied crowds looted stores and warehouses. Broken furniture, shattered glass, and other wreckage filled the muddy streets. LaSalle likened the experience to a "reign of terror": "The yelling and howling and swearing and weeping and wailing beggar description. Families houseless and homeless under the open sky!"[30] The surreal, hellish picture was made complete by the presence of black Union soldiers. She recalled that "they were the first colored troops I had ever seen, and the weird effect produced by their black faces in that infernal environment was indelibly impressed upon my mind."[31]

An unexpected visitor supposedly came in the midst of the terror. One day after Richmond fell, Pickett answered a knock at her door and saw before her a "tall, gaunt, sad-faced man in ill-fitting clothes, who asked with the accent of the North: 'Is this George Pickett's Place?'" President Abraham Lincoln had presumably stopped by to pay her a personal visit during his tour of the fallen Confederate capital. As pure fantasy, the account illustrates the delusive pathos of Pickett's latter-day recollections, as well as her overinflated sense of self-importance. Nonetheless, she shrewdly played to her postwar audience's renewed feelings of reunion and Lincoln nostalgia. It made a great story.[32]

All of LaSalle Pickett's published memories of her war experience and marriage were carefully presented. Deliberately crafting her literary self and that of her husband for national consumption, she followed the Southern Plantation Tradition initiated by authors such as Thomas Nelson Page and Joel Chandler Harris. When she described the antebellum South, she celebrated "de good ole times 'fo' de wah," putting herself and her husband in a setting that featured paternalistic slaveowners and loyal, passive slaves. Her racist images were eagerly bought up by the white reading public, North and South, at the turn of the twentieth century.[33]

Besides sheer profit and celebrating the Lost Cause, LaSalle Pickett seemed to have had additional personal motives for publicly recounting her wartime experience. As a Confederate general's wife, she could only celebrate her husband; it would have been highly unacceptable for her to write anything negative about him or her marriage. So instead, she cloaked the suffering and difficulties she must have endured in the conventional role of loving wife and mourning widow. She sought to conform to acceptable gender roles by emphasizing her husband's courage and bravery and de-emphasizing her own autonomy and strength. The resulting picture was a contradictory one: Her husband often appeared in her writings as pacifistic and emotional, and she seemed reckless and bold, eager to be in the thick of battle yet sickened by war's destruction and chaos. Pickett struggled to make sense out of it all decades after the war ended. "Years away from that time of anguish and terror," she wrote, "I awaken suddenly with the crash of those guns still in my ears, their fearful sounds yet echoing in my heart, only to find myself safe in my soft, warm bed."[34] Haunted by these images, she wondered if she were "destined to an eternity of remorse."[35]

Few historians have taken LaSalle Pickett or her published works seriously, for she was overtly dishonest about her husband's failings and difficulties and about people she allegedly met and events she allegedly witnessed. Yet should historians question the sorrow she described? Should they doubt the disturbing nightmares that she told readers she continued to suffer years after the war ended? After all, men such as James Longstreet and George McClellan publicly exaggerated and stretched the "facts" of their wartime experiences. Clearly, LaSalle Pickett's recollections of the Civil War pose difficult questions for modern readers to consider. The line between fact and fiction in her writings is often so blurred that it is nearly impossible to separate myth from reality. But her reconstructed memory of her Civil War experience tells us a great deal about the war's lasting meaning to one of its singular participants. It tells us about powerful gender conventions during and after the war. And it tells us of a woman seeking desperately to stake a personal claim for a painfully uncivil past.

Notes

1. LaSalle Corbell Pickett, *What Happened to Me* (New York: Brentano's, 1917), 216. This chapter is drawn from the author's larger study of the Picketts, *General George E. Pickett in Life and Legend* (Chapel Hill: University of North Carolina Press, 1998).

2. Obituaries in the *Confederate Veteran* 39, no. 4 (April 1931): 151, and the *Washington Post*, March 23, 1931, refer to Pickett as the "Child Bride of the Confederacy." She called herself a "child wife" in her autobiography, Pickett, *What Happened to Me,* 189. The age discrepancy appears in U.S. Census Office, 7th Census of the United States, 1850: Population Schedules, Nansemond County, Virginia, and U.S. Census Office, 8th Census of the United States, 1860: Population Schedules, Nansemond County, Virginia. Both census records list Pickett's age as five years younger than she later claimed to be in her autobiographical writings.

3. U.S. Census Office, 7th Census of the United States, 1850: Population Schedules, Nansemond County, Virginia, and U.S. Census Office, 8th Census of the United States, 1860: Population Schedules, Nansemond County, Virginia; obituaries in *Confederate Veteran* 39, no. 4 (April 1931): 151, *New York Times*, March 23, 1931, and *Washington Post*, March 23, 1931.

4. Pickett, *What Happened to Me*, 83; Dorothy T. Potter and Clifton W. Potter, *Lynchburg: "The Most Interesting Spots"* (Lynchburg, VA: Progress Publishing Co., 1976), 1; Christie Anne Farnham, *The Education of the Southern Belle: Higher Education and Student Socialization in the Antebellum South* (New York: New York University Press, 1994), 72–73, 174; Anne Firor Scott, *The Southern Lady: From Pedestal to Politics, 1830–1930* (Chicago: University of Chicago Press, 1970), 71.

5. Pickett, *What Happened to Me*, 89–92; George Morris and Susan Foutz, *Lynchburg in the Civil War: The City, the People, the Battle* (Lynchburg, VA: H. E. Howard, 1984), 10.

6. Pickett, *What Happened to Me*, 89–90.

7. Drew Gilpin Faust, *Mothers of Invention: Women of the Slaveholding South in the American Civil War* (Chapel Hill: University of North Carolina Press, 1996); LeeAnn Whites, *The Civil War as a Crisis in Gender: Augusta Georgia, 1860–1890* (Athens: University of Georgia Press, 1995); Catherine Clinton and Nina Silber, eds., *Divided Houses: Gender and the Civil War* (New York: Oxford University Press, 1992).

8. Pickett, *What Happened to Me*, 99–100.

9. LaSalle Corbell Pickett, *Pickett and His Men* (Atlanta, GA: Foote and Davies, 1899), 170.

10. LaSalle Corbell Pickett, "The Wartime Story of General Pickett," *Cosmopolitan* 56 (January 1914): 178–80. Pickett repeated this same passage in her 1917 autobiography, *What Happened to Me*, 104–8; see also idem, *Pickett and His Men*, 170–74.

11. Pickett, *What Happened to Me*, 143.

12. Pickett, *Pickett and His Men*, 361.

13. Pickett, *What Happened to Me*, 144–45. An abbreviated form of this story is included in her *Pickett and His Men*, 360–61, but Pickett left out any mention of her retrieving the head.

14. LaSalle Pickett, *Pickett and His Men*, 7. For discussion of her plagiarism, see Gary Gallagher, "A Widow and Her Soldier: LaSalle Corbell Pickett as Author of the George E. Pickett Letters," *Virginia Magazine of History Biography* 94 (July 1986): 335–37.

15. Pickett, *What Happened to Me*, 121.

16. Quoted in William A. Young Jr. and Patricia C. Young, *56th Virginia Infantry* (Lynchburg, VA: H. E. Howard, 1990), 74.

17. G. Moxley Sorrel, *Recollections of a Confederate Staff Officer* (1905; reprint ed., Dayton, OH: Morningside, 1978), 153.

18. Gallagher, "A Widow and Her Soldier," 329–44; Glenn Tucker, *Lee and Longstreet at Gettysburg* (Indianapolis: Bobbs-Merrill Co., 1968), 44–45; George R. Stewart, *Pickett's Charge: A Microhistory of the Final Attack at Gettysburg, July 3, 1863* (Boston: Houghton Mifflin Co., 1959), 297–98; Douglas Southall Freeman, *R. E. Lee: A Biography*, 4 vols. (New York: Charles Scribner's Sons, 1935), 4:563.

19. LaSalle Corbell Pickett, ed., *The Heart of a Soldier: As Revealed in the Intimate Letters of Genl. George E. Pickett CSA* (New York: Seth Moyle, 1913), 65–66.

20. Ibid., 125.

21. Ibid., 75–76.

22. Pickett, *What Happened to Me,* 124.

23. Quoted in Arthur Crew Inman, *The Inman Diary: A Public and Private Confession,* ed. Daniel Aaron, 2 vols. (Cambridge, MA: Harvard University Press, 1985), 1:328; wedding details gathered from Pickett, "The Wartime Story of General Pickett," 764, and idem, *Pickett and His Men,* 320–21; also *Richmond (Virginia) Dispatch,* September 22, 1863.

24. Pickett, *Pickett and His Men,* 320–21; see also idem, *What Happened to Me,* 126–29.

25. Douglas Southall Freeman, *Lee's Lieutenants: A Study in Command,* 3 vols. (New York: Charles Scribner's Sons, 1942), 1:158–59, 192, 242–43; Ezra Warner, *Generals in Gray: Lives of the Confederate Commanders* (Baton Rouge: Louisiana State University Press, 1959), 239–40.

26. Freeman, *Lee's Lieutenants* 3:XXXVI; Warner, *Generals in Gray,* 239–40.

27. Pickett, *What Happened to Me,* 136; see also Pickett, *Pickett and His Men,* 326.

28. Pickett, *What Happened to Me,* 141.

29. Pickett, *Pickett and His Men,* 357; see also idem, *What Happened to Me,* 141.

30. LaSalle Corbell Pickett, "The First United States Flag Raised in Richmond after the War," in *The Fourth Massachusetts Cavalry in the Closing Scenes of the War for the Maintenance of the Union,* ed. William B. Arnold (Boston, n.p.: 19–), 19–22, quote from p. 21.

31. Pickett, *What Happened to Me,* 164–65. See also idem, LaSalle Corbell Pickett, "My Soldier," *McClure's Magazine* 30 (March 1908): 563–71. Richard N. Current, ed., *Encyclopedia of the Confederacy,* 4 vols. (New York: Simon and Schuster, 1993), 3:1331.

32. Pickett, *What Happened to Me,* 167–70.

33. LaSalle Corbell Pickett, *Jinny* (Washington, DC: The Neale Co., 1901), 59.

34. Pickett, *Pickett and His Men,* 343.

35. Pickett, *What Happened to Me,* 216.

18

Willis Augustus Hodges
"We Are Now Coming to New Things"

Richard Lowe

The black experience in the Civil War and Reconstruction era was as varied as the members of the African American population themselves. And that population showed as broad a variety of occupations and levels of education as white society did. Some Southern blacks were not even slaves, and the free blacks often were among the most highly educated of their race. As such, many of them, including Willis Augustus Hodges, were well prepared to assume leadership roles when the end of the Civil War brought many new things to what had been the Old South.

Richard Lowe, Regents Professor of History at the University of North Texas, Denton, Texas, first became interested in Hodges while writing *Republicans and Reconstruction in Virginia, 1856–1870* (1991). He is also the author of *The Texas Overland Expedition of 1863* (1996). In recounting the story of Hodges's life, Lowe explores the challenges faced by blacks during the period known as Reconstruction, as well as the ways in which many of them responded.

One of the most persistent myths about the era of the Civil War and Reconstruction is that the millions of African Americans freed from slavery were all or nearly all illiterate and ignorant field hands, totally unprepared for citizenship and leadership. Many Southern and even some Northern white observers estimated that black Americans would require a generation or two before they could be trusted with the rights to vote and hold public office. Stemming from that myth was a widespread assumption among many white Americans, North and South, that African Americans would have to be shown the way to literacy and good citizenship and that they had no ideas, leaders, or initiatives of their own. They were like clay to be molded, according to this view, not actors in the great drama of the Civil War and Reconstruction.

Historians who have studied this period understand that these attitudes were wrongheaded. Courageous and intelligent black men such as Robert Smalls of South Carolina were natural leaders who only needed an opportunity to develop their talents and political skills. While Smalls spent his early years as a slave in Charleston, another black American some 350 miles to the north—Willis Augustus Hodges—led a very different life as a freeborn and educated African American from a prosperous family in southeastern Virginia. Although they came from different backgrounds, Hodges and Smalls both demonstrated that black Americans were capable of thinking for themselves, developing their own leaders, and participating in their own elevation from slavery and second-class status.

Willis Augustus Hodges, the son of free mulatto parents and the grandson of a Revolutionary War veteran, was born a few weeks after the end of the War of 1812, on February 12, 1815. His birthplace, Princess Anne County in the southeastern corner of Virginia, was home to about three hundred free African Americans. The number of free blacks in the county was increasing at the time of his birth, doubtless because of the growing numbers of manumissions in the wake of the American Revolution. Flourishing in numbers, free black Virginians in Princess Anne County were also able to acquire land and become property-holding taxpayers. At the time of Willis's birth, his father, Charles Augustus Hodges, owned a fifty-acre farm, where Willis and his two older brothers and three older sisters played the usual children's games and romped around the family home. By the time Willis reached his midtwenties, his father had bought still more land, nearly two hundred acres in all, and the Hodges farm produced large crops of corn and other vegetables for sale in the nearby cities of Portsmouth and Norfolk. The hardworking and prosperous family also produced lumber, hogs, and other livestock for the markets of southeast Virginia.

During Willis's youth his family enjoyed cordial relations with their neighbors, both black and white. The family, eventually including twelve children, attended Sunday religious services along with whites in the neighborhood Baptist church, albeit sitting in a segregated corner. Willis and his older brother William played in the woods and fields with their cousins and with the sons of a nearby white family. The Hodges boys were unrestricted by the kinds of regulations that would later bedevil black Virginians.

Willis's father was not only prosperous; he was also ambitious for his children. He arranged for them to receive a proper education at a time when many white Virginia children had no schooling at all. He hired a white woman to tutor his children in the rudiments of reading, writing, and arithmetic. He later employed an Englishman to teach his sons and daughters in the home, and one of his white neighbors sent his own children to sit beside Willis and his siblings to learn the three Rs. Charles

Hodges was determined that his children would have as many of the benefits of freedom as the times permitted. He kept a gun in his house and used it on several occasions to scare off hostile, harassing whites. He also sued a white man who had attempted to intimidate him into paying a fraudulent bill. His wife, Julia, was equal to her husband in her determination to resist second-class status and the indignities that many African Americans, slave and free, faced in antebellum America.

Willis's older brother William inherited his parents' pride and hatred for slavery—and then some. He became a preacher and had the courage to speak out against slavery and racial discrimination even to the white people in Princess Anne County. Soon, rumors began creeping through southeastern Virginia that William was doing more than preaching, that he was, in fact, forging documents to show that particular slaves were free, thus enabling those fugitives to make their escape from bondage. His outspoken sermons and rumored involvement in antislavery activities eventually landed him in a Norfolk jail, along with one of his cousins. In April 1829, shortly after a trial and conviction, William, his cousin, and four other black men made a daring escape from the jail. Eluding the posses on their trail, Hodges and his cousin fled all the way to Canada.

The prominent and prosperous family now became the target of hostile white vigilantes, who blamed their troubles on "uppity" black preachers like William. On one occasion a white mob searching for the fugitive brother invaded the Hodges house and knocked Willis's mother to the floor, and one of the crowd held a pistol to young Willis's head, threatening to blow out his brains if he did not reveal his brother's whereabouts. "I saw him cock his pistol and place it at my head," he recalled. "I then shut my eyes expecting to open them in eternity. I heard the report [of the gun] and thought I was shot until I heard our dog that was by my side howl out. I looked and saw that he had received the contents of the would-be murderer's pistol instead of myself." Incidents like this outraged Willis, and he soon became, in the eyes of local whites, "a very proud and saucy young fellow."[1]

Before this series of assaults and threats completely subsided in Princess Anne County, white Virginians in general, terrified by the famous Nat Turner slave uprising in nearby Southampton County, turned on the entire class of free blacks in the Old Dominion. The state legislature passed laws to prohibit black men from acting as preachers, and old laws that no one had bothered to enforce before were now revived to suppress free African Americans such as the Hodges family. Slave patrols crisscrossed the county, searching for black people who could not show proper authorization to travel about the countryside. Free black men were now required to show "free papers," documents proving their free status. And white mobs forced their way into the Hodges' home, carrying off "books, papers, bibles, dresses and many small and useful articles."[2] They arrested the family's English tutor for consorting with black folk and generally terrorized the black neighborhoods in Princess Anne County.

These and similar events in the late 1820s and early 1830s convinced Charles Hodges that his family was no longer safe in the land of their birth. He moved his wife and children to New York City, where they joined William, who had become a resident of the city after leaving his refuge in Canada. Although most of the family returned to Virginia after the Nat Turner hysteria subsided, the path between Princess Anne County and New York would be worn smooth over the next few decades as one or another of them moved back and forth between Virginia and the great metropolis on the Hudson River. Willis stayed behind to care for the farm when the family first relocated, but by early 1836, disgusted with the treatment of black workers in the South, he, too, went north to join his brother and an older sister in New York.

When Willis left Virginia at age twenty-one, he was required to have his "free papers" with him to prove his status as a free man. This document described him as "a light complexion free negro man, with bushy hair, with scar over his right eye, five feet six inches and a half high."[3] For the next twenty-five years, Willis occasionally visited his Princess Anne home, but the important events of his life took place in the North. A completely new and exciting era opened for him when he relocated to New York. At his sister's insistence, he improved his reading and writing and changed his countrified way of dressing and speaking. He got a job in a city store, joined the Abyssinian Baptist Church, began reading antislavery newspapers, and blended into the crowds at abolitionist meetings. No longer an innocent young rustic, he was now merging into the exhilarating city life of Northern free African Americans.

Willis Hodges later described his years in antebellum New York City as "some of the happiest days of my life."[4] He worked at various jobs—clerk, stevedore, painter, grocer—to support himself, plunged headlong into the public life of the city, and soon established himself as one of the leaders of New York's black community. He mobilized the residents of his neighborhood to start a school for black children, organized a temperance society to fight against alcohol abuse, joined the movement for equal suffrage rights for African Americans in the state of New York, attended abolition meetings, and frequently spoke up to remind his Northern friends of the plight of Southern slaves and free blacks.

When Hodges was in his early thirties, he joined with another free African American in New York to establish a newspaper that would advance the antislavery cause. Hodges and his partner (a locally prominent restaurateur named Thomas Van Rensselaer), hoping to knock down the walls of slavery, called their weekly paper *The Ram's Horn*, recalling the biblical story of Joshua and his army using rams' horns to bring down the walls of an enemy city. In his role as editor and publisher of the newspaper, Hodges soon became friendly with a man he called "a good and noble-hearted Christian gentleman who has always been a friend to the poor and oppressed."[5] This man was John Brown, the white antislavery crusader who later became famous for his assault on Harpers Ferry, Virginia.

Willis Hodges and John Brown held some ideas in common, especially their conviction that mere words and long-winded prayers were not enough to bring down the institution of slavery. His attendance at countless abolition meetings had convinced Hodges that some of his Northern comrades were more interested in attracting attention to themselves with flowery speeches than in taking direct action on behalf of the South's persecuted blacks. They were, in his words, "more men of words than deeds."[6] Hodges had seen antiblack violence firsthand, and he and Brown reinforced each other's determination to do something more than talk. As the years passed, the two men cooperated on various projects, including the newspaper and an attempt to settle black families on farmland in upstate New York.

During the winter of 1848–1849, while he was still in his early thirties, Hodges wrote his autobiography. This document described his early years in Princess Anne County, the harassment of his family by local whites in the aftermath of his brother's escape from jail, his own move to New York, and his transformation from a country boy into an outspoken leader for black rights in New York City. His purpose in writing the autobiography, Hodges wrote, was to tell the world of "the wrongs and sufferings, the free people of color in the southern states have undergone, and are still undergoing." He did not intend to distract attention from the growing crusade against slavery. Rather, he said, he would "present them [slaves and free blacks] as one man of sorrow worthy of your aid and attention." Adhering closely to his belief that words alone could not end slavery, Hodges included in his autobiography a stirring declaration: "I further hold and truly believe that blood is the only thing that can wash the stain of slavery from this land."[7]

While Willis continued his antislavery activities in New York during the 1850s, his friend John Brown followed through on their shared belief that direct action was needed to erase the sin of slavery. In October 1859, he led eighteen followers into Harpers Ferry, Virginia, to arm the slaves and begin active resistance to the bondage of black men. It is very probable that Brown had discussed his idea for an invasion of Virginia with Hodges. If they did discuss the plan, Willis doubtless gave his whole-hearted support to the project. However, the raid failed almost immediately, and Brown and his men were captured and put on trial for treason, incitement of slave rebellion, and murder. On his way to the gallows after his conviction, John Brown echoed the earlier call to action made by his friend Hodges in eerily similar language: "I John Brown am now quite *certain* that the crimes of this *guilty land* will never be purged *away* but with Blood."[8]

Brown's raid on Harpers Ferry was one of the events that catapulted the United States into a civil war in 1861. Willis Hodges, forty-six when the first shots were fired, was too old to serve in the Union army once it began enlisting African Americans two years later. But early in the war, he seized the opportunity to take direct action against the Confederate regime in his home state. In May 1862, shortly after Confederate forces evacuated Norfolk near his family home in Princess Anne County, Hodges acted as a scout for Union army patrols in the old neighborhood. With his intimate knowledge of the woods and roads of southeastern Virginia, he was doubtless an invaluable resource for Federal units stationed around Norfolk. On frequent occasions from 1862 onward, the Federal army sent columns into the countryside to ferret out Confederate bands hiding in the forests and swamps of Princess Anne County. The services of local African American guides such as Willis Hodges made life miserable for some of the same men who had persecuted his family when he was a teenager.

Hodges did not confine his wartime activities to scouting for the Union army, however. In the summer of 1864, acting on behalf of charitable organizations in New York City, he investigated charges that the free blacks and recently freed slaves of southeastern Virginia were being cheated and mistreated by the Federal occupying forces around Norfolk. After traveling around the farms and fields of Princess Anne and other nearby counties, he discovered that "there were a lot of speculators" who were selling the food and clothing sent by relief agencies in New York.[9] Instead of providing relief for poor black families, these supplies were being sold to line the pockets of some army personnel. When Hodges brought these activities to light and arranged for a public meeting in Norfolk to protest the situation, military officers ordered him out of town. Willis demanded justice, not only from Southern whites but also from the U.S. Army.

Even before the Confederacy finally collapsed in the spring of 1865, Willis and three of his brothers moved back to Virginia from New York. Almost immediately, they began organizing and agitating among the black residents of southeastern Virginia. Now that slavery was breathing its last, many black Virginians expected to enjoy full rights as citizens, including the rights to vote and hold public office. On April 4, five days before Robert E. Lee's army surrendered at Appomattox, older brother William presided at a public meeting of black Norfolk residents. William and the other African Americans at that meeting demanded that they be allowed to participate in the election of a new government for Norfolk. He—and doubtless his brothers—also helped to organize a black club to demand full political rights in the new age of freedom.

William, the long-ago fugitive from a Norfolk jail, also organized a school for the black people of southeastern Virginia. His high visibility finally landed him back in jail when local whites dusted off the charges first filed against him nearly forty years earlier. In 1866, he was sentenced to five years in prison for his activities in 1829. Willis, well known in abolitionist circles, immediately came to the rescue of his brother. He quickly secured an appointment to see Gen. Oliver O. Howard, the chief of the national Freedmen's Bureau, at his Washington office. At Willis's urging, General Howard convinced the Unionist governor of Virginia, Francis H. Pierpont, to pardon William. Nevertheless, the conservative white press in southeastern Virginia began referring to the Hodges brothers as criminals, often confusing William and Willis in their denunciations.

Undeterred by these public defamations, the brothers continued to organize the black people around Norfolk. When Congress initiated a more radical plan of Reconstruction in 1867—a plan that included black voting and officeholding—they redoubled their efforts around Norfolk and Princess Anne County. They addressed large crowds of African Americans, urging them to participate in the political process for the first time. They also traveled throughout the region, organizing voter-registration drives and urging blacks to elect their own representatives to a new state constitutional convention scheduled for late 1867.

Their past political experience in New York and their widely recognized names in Princess Anne and Norfolk Counties made Willis and his brother natural candidates for seats in the constitutional convention, now scheduled to meet in Richmond in December 1867. On election day in October, William was defeated for the seat from Norfolk County, but Willis—with 807 black votes and not a single white vote—was elected over two white candidates in Princess Anne County. All his years of attending meetings, making speeches, writing newspaper columns, and agitating for black rights had paid off and put him at the center of political power in his home state. The frightened young boy who had been threatened with a pistol in 1829 was now a popular leader among his people and an important political figure in Virginia.

The constitutional convention that assembled in Richmond in December 1867 was unlike any public meeting ever seen in the long history of the Old Dominion. This meeting had not been initiated by local citizens or institutions; it was mandated by Congress's new plan of Reconstruction. And the membership of the new assembly was completely different from those of earlier constitutional conventions. Northern-born immigrants (the so-called carpetbaggers), native whites who had joined the Northern-dominated Republican Party (the so-called scalawags), and especially black delegates—some former slaves but mostly African Americans free before the war—outnumbered the native white element that had always governed and written constitutions in the past. A new era had obviously dawned in old Virginia, and Willis Hodges had helped to bring it about.

The white conservative newspapers of Virginia, especially those in Richmond, were disgusted to see former slaves and other black men sworn into high public office, and they blistered Hodges and his fellow African Americans with scornful editorials and reporting. The *Richmond Whig and Advertiser*, among the more moderate journals to report on the convention, ridiculed Hodges by describing him as a "bacon colored son of Ham." The *Whig*'s reporter, like most white observers, dismissed him as a man out of his depth: "He is a field hand, but appears in the convention clad in his Sunday clothes, wears enormous brass-rimmed spectacles, and boasts a suit of glossy, well greased hair." The newspaper made no mention of Hodges's experience as a newspaper publisher, his antebellum political activities in New York, or his background as a public speaker. The white press instead had enormous fun at his expense, referring to him as "Specs" or "Uncle Specs" or "the Hon. Spectacles Hodges," alluding to his large eyeglasses. At times, the Richmond newspapers reported the comments of Hodges and other African American delegates in slave dialect, all to demonstrate how unfit these men were for their lofty positions.[10]

Hodges was a favorite target of such derision primarily because he took a leading role in the convention's proceedings and voted a straight Radical Republican line. He voted for a white Radical Republican as the convention's chairman, against a proposal to exclude blacks from voting in state elections, for an amendment to exclude most former Confederate military officers from the franchise, for an amendment to disfranchise those whites who had voted for secessionist delegates to the secession convention of 1861, for a proposal to exclude from public office any white Virginians who had supported the Confederacy, and for a provision that required racial integration in Virginia's public schools. No delegate to the convention was more determined to root up the old Virginia and replace it with a new, racially integrated, and forward-looking society. Willis Hodges had seen the old Virginia, and he did everything in his power to change it. "I hope we will soon be able to re-organize Old Virginia, or New Virginia, as it will then be," he said. "The old one has passed away with a great noise, and we are now coming to new things."[11]

He demanded that the convention adopt policies that would protect "the poor but loyal laboring men" of Virginia "who have been distressed and intimidated on account of their voting and supporting the Union Republican ticket." These men "were not only thrown out of employment, but were at once thrust forth from their homes" by former Confederate employers and landlords. Hodges also took a swipe at the editors and reporters who ridiculed the African American delegates in Richmond: "These are the men who are found in every community and may be likened unto the unclean bird which is found all over our State, and which has two z's in its name, that turns from everything clean, wholesome and healthy to feast upon filth and corruption."[12]

Hodges found it particularly ironic that white conservatives should be so scornful of the more modest educational levels of former slaves and free blacks. "They have made it unlawful for us to read, to preach, or in any way to elevate ourselves. They have kept us down with a brutal and a cruel hand. The degradation, the ignorance which they presume to despise in us, is all the work of their own hands."[13] In this and many other matters before the convention, he demonstrated that a supposedly dull-witted and ignorant "field hand" was quite capable of detecting inconsistency and deceit among his political foes.

He objected to every attempt by other delegates—black or white—to inject racial categories into the new constitution. There should be no racial references at all in the new Virginia, according to Hodges. The state should be totally color blind in all its business, including the education of its children. On this matter, he proved to be more radical even than some of his black colleagues, for the measure requiring racially integrated schools was defeated by a vote of 67 to 21, with 10 black delegates opposing the measure and 12 favoring it. He was more successful in another attempt to equalize the burdens and benefits of citizenship. Hodges proposed that the state's tax system be restructured by dropping the regressive taxes on individuals and replacing them with taxes on real and personal property. The final version of the new constitution incorporated these ideas, to the great benefit of the lower and middle classes in Virginia.

After months of debate and voting, the convention finally completed its work in April 1868. The constitution written by Hodges and his fellow Republicans provided Virginians with their first system of public education, distributed the tax burden more equally among the various classes, enacted suffrage and office-holding for African American males for the first time, prohibited racial discrimination in jury selection, made more public offices elective, and gave debtors additional opportunities to escape bankruptcy and ruin. For a convention dominated by men described in the newspapers as ignorant field hands and greedy carpetbaggers and scalawags, it had managed to produce one of the best constitutions in the state's history, and Willis Augustus Hodges had been one of the leading figures in the proceedings.

Hodges's role in the constitutional convention of 1867–1868 was the peak of his public career. He failed to win a seat in the state senate in 1869, but he continued to be active in Republican party politics and local government after the constitutional convention. He served in various county and local posts in Princess Anne County, and three of his brothers held state and county offices in the early 1870s. Within a few years, however, the Hodges brothers were, one by one, removed from office and relegated to the political sidelines, either by more moderate white Republicans or by old conservative enemies.

Out of office and out of public life, Willis eventually returned to New York City in 1881, but the old soil called him back to Princess Anne County a few years later. Now in his seventies, he spent his last years working as a plasterer and serving as a minister to black Virginians around Norfolk. On September 24, 1890, at age seventy-five, Willis Hodges died at his home near Norfolk, not far from the scenes of his boyhood romps with his brothers and sisters, his scouts for the Union army during the Civil War, and his speeches demanding justice and equality for all Virginians. It had been a good life.

The private and public careers of Willis Hodges contradicted the popular perception, then and later, that the African Americans who emerged from the Civil War had few if any intelligent and experienced leaders. Raised in a free, tight-knit, and prosperous family, he learned to read and write while still a child. Later, he took part in various reform movements in New York and published an abolitionist newspaper. He formed a friendship with John Brown and guided Union army columns through the back-country of southeast Virginia. And after the Civil War, he served his people as a local and county official. He organized former slaves for their new roles as voters and officeholders and took a leading part in drafting a new constitution for Virginia. His life was marked by courage, intelligence, persistence, and a vision—far ahead of its time—of a new America based on equality for all its citizens.

Notes

1. Willis Augustus Hodges, *Free Man of Color: The Autobiography of Willis Augustus Hodges*, ed. Willard B. Gatewood (Knoxville: University of Tennessee Press, 1982), 17, 29.

2. Ibid., xxvii.

3. Ibid., 43.

4. Ibid., 53.

5. Ibid., 78.

6. Ibid., 1–11.

7. Ibid., 4, 56.

8. Quoted in James M. McPherson, *Ordeal by Fire: The Civil War and Reconstruction*, 2d ed. (New York: McGraw-Hill, 1992), 120.

9. *The Debates and Proceedings of the Constitutional Convention of the State of Virginia, Assembled at the City of Richmond, Tuesday, December 3, 1867* (Richmond, VA: Office of the New Nation, 1868), 163.

10. *Richmond Whig and Advertiser,* December 10, 1867, and January 7, March 2, March 28, April 8, and April 17, 1868.

11. *The Debates and Proceedings,* 164.

12. Ibid., 60, 61, 62.

13. Ibid., 62.

Index